WITHDRAWN

3 3013 00078 9812

W9-BWM-651

WITHDRAWN

BY ALFRED STEINBERG

THE FIRST TEN: THE FOUNDING PRESIDENTS AND THEIR
ADMINISTRATIONS

THE MAN FROM MISSOURI: THE LIFE AND TIMES OF
HARRY S. TRUMAN

MRS. R.: THE LIFE OF ELEANOR ROOSEVELT

MY NAME IS TOM CONNALLY
(*with Senator Tom Connally*)

SAM JOHNSON'S BOY: A CLOSE-UP OF THE PRESIDENT FROM
TEXAS

THE BOSSES

"Lives to Remember" Series

RICHARD BYRD	JOHN MARSHALL
DWIGHT EISENHOWER	ELEANOR ROOSEVELT
HERBERT HOOVER	HARRY TRUMAN
DOUGLAS MACARTHUR	DANIEL WEBSTER
JAMES MADISON	WOODROW WILSON
JOHN ADAMS	THE KENNEDY BROTHERS

THE BOSSES

Alfred Steinberg

THE
BOSSES

The Macmillan Company, New York, New York
Collier-Macmillan Limited, London

E
747
.S76

Copyright © 1972 by Alfred Steinberg

All rights reserved. No part of this book may be reproduced or transmitted in any form or by any means, electronic or mechanical, including photocopying, recording or by any information storage and retrieval system, without permission in writing from the Publisher.

The Macmillan Company
866 Third Avenue, New York, N.Y. 10022
Collier-Macmillan Canada Ltd., Toronto, Ontario

Library of Congress Catalog Card Number: 73–190158

FIRST PRINTING

Printed in the United States of America

For Peter Ritner
Whose Idea This Was

Contents

Any people to govern themselves must get experience in the art of self-government. . . . We cannot expect a great democracy to rest upon a foundation of local dictatorships.

—*In inaugural address of New Jersey Governor Charles Edison, as president of the National Municipal League.*

THE BOSSES

INTRODUCTION
Some They Beat; Some They Bought; All They Swindled

THROUGHOUT its long existence, the United States has suffered grievously from the ravages of political bossism. Yet at no time in American History have local bosses been collectively more powerful and more debilitating to democratic principles than during the 1920s and 1930s. Why was this so? Why this period? And with what results?

The blunt truth was that most political-social observers foresaw a balmy era of brotherly political democracy at the local level following World War I. Typically, one Yale professor called it inconceivable that a people so united and inspired toward public good during the war emergency would ever "permit the return of the boss system." But it was this very unity plus a spirit of sacrifice when robbed of attained goals that helped create the disillusionment of the postwar period and produce a widespread revulsion against participation in government. "Heatless" Mondays, "wheatless" Tuesdays, "meatless" Thursdays, "gasless" Sundays, and sugar rationing were willingly entered into during wartime by the American people to beat the wicked Germans and make the world safe for democracy. But such privations brought on cynicism and public apathy afterward with the failure of the Woodrow Wilson postwar mission.

Into this void stepped the bosses and their machines to broaden their power and profits, and they found a public increasingly dulled to politics by further events. The Teapot Dome scandal, involving the bribing of Cabinet members and other government officials by oil-company executives was "proof" to millions that *all* government was bad. Then when Calvin Coolidge succeeded Warren G. Harding as President in 1923, his antipathy to government action had an additional dampening effect on citizen participation in politics.

There were also strong economic and social changes that distracted Americans from their civic duties. Across the nation a people dreamed of becoming millionaires through stock-market gains. Competing with the stock fever was the desire for national lawlessness to thwart the prohibition amendment. There was the rise of a new class of people known as gangsters and a new institution called Hollywood to whet the public's appetite and delight in murder and scandal. "Drink, dope, vice, wild parties—the public prints are filled periodically with such stories from Hollywood," moralized *Liberty* magazine, itself seeking such stories to boost circulation.

Besides the disillusionment with government as a force for good and the growing looseness in social mores, bosses gained from the class fears of the twenties. Norman Thomas, perennial Socialist candidate for President, aptly observed during the time, that bosses were forever "collecting money from the rich and votes from the poor, on the theory that they were protecting the one from the other."

In addition, the prevalent mood of the middle class against civil liberties and equal rights for minorities, as exemplified by the enormous backing of the Ku Klux Klan in almost every state, made the antidemocratic activities of bosses seem reasonable. That full exercise of civil rights was dangerous radicalism was even maintained in the official *U.S. Army Training Manual* No. 2000–25 of the Coolidge Administration. The manual told officers and enlisted men: "Democracy is a government of the masses. . . . Results in mobocracy . . . demagogism, license, agitation, discontent, anarchy."

Despite the notion in some quarters that bossism faded with the advent of Franklin Roosevelt's New Deal, this was not so. Certainly the widespread practice of the bosses of distributing food baskets and shoddy clothes to the poor on the holidays as a means of buying their votes was antiquated by the billions of dollars in Federal welfare funds. Yet most bosses grew even stronger with the latter because they became the distributors of these monies and determined who would get them.

In his book, *The Shame of the Cities,* Lincoln Steffens, muck-raking journalist, declared, "The boss is not a politician, he is an American institution, the product of a free people that have not the spirit to be free."

Bossism came early to America, as early as colonial days, when bosses had their henchmen occupy most of the benches at New England town meetings and elect town officers who would do their bidding on taxation and spending.

In the cities, the initial and most long-lived political machine was Tammany Hall. Established by William Mooney, an upholsterer, in New York City in 1789, the year George Washington became President of the United States, it was at the outset just a benevolent masonic society. But a decade later Tammany moved into politics to promote Thomas Jefferson for President, and the honors of being its first machine boss went to Aaron Burr.

After that, Tammany organized in army fashion throughout the city wards, and its fights for its candidates in elections followed by its thirst for spoils of office and graft set the pattern for other sordid bossdoms that developed up and down the eastern seaboard and copied its methods. Tammany's practice of illegal repeat voting to thwart honest elections resulted in tragedy in Baltimore in October, 1849, when Whig ward ruffians drugged or intoxicated Edgar Allan Poe and dragged him from polling place to polling place, leaving him dying afterward in the gutter.

Although every grand sachem and his lieutenants measured politics in terms of what they could steal, it fell to Tammany's William Marcy Tweed to go down in history as the synonym for the crooked boss—because he was caught. Publicized both in words and in telling editorial cartoons by Thomas Nast, this affable 320-pound behemoth died in prison after he and his "ring" stole more than $20 million in New York City funds.

Following Tweed, the more cautious Tammany thieves resorted to what they called "honest graft" to make their fortunes and stay out of jail. One exponent was George Plunkitt, Tammany boss of the fifteenth district in New York City, who explained:

> There's honest graft, and I'm an example of how it works. I might sum up the whole thing by sayin': "I seen my opportunities and I took 'em." Suppose it's a new bridge they're goin' to build. I get tipped off and I buy as much property as I can that has to be taken for approaches. I sell at my price later and drop some more money

in the bank. . . . It's honest graft, and I'm lookin' for it every day in
the year.

As rotten as the Boss Tweed gang was in New York, Philadelphia's notorious Republican Gas Ring did an equally effective job
for decades on end, controlling elections and milking the city. A
student of the ring's activities and the millions stolen by its eventual
Republican successors properly dubbed Philadelphia "The City of
Brotherly Loot."

Inland and across the country, the situation was no better. In
Minneapolis, for example, Dr. Albert Ames, from a Puritan family
background, was four times elected mayor, twice as a Republican
and twice as a Democrat, in the final quarter of the nineteenth century. Ames and his ring amassed their boodle take selling police
protection to out-of-town gamblers, thugs, and thieves and turned
Minneapolis into a crime center. Lincoln Steffens called the genial
doctor-mayor a boss "never equalled for deliberateness, invention
and avarice."[1] In San Francisco, Abe "Curly" Ruef, heir of a wealthy
French-Jewish family and with a brilliant law school record, became
Republican boss around the turn of the century. Ruef's chief use of
his bossdom status was to exact large bribes from private companies
in exchange for special municipal favors from Ruef's puppet mayor.

Harold Zink, in a study of bosses of the pre-World War I period, drew various conclusions pertaining to the boodle kings.[2] Contrary to public belief, only a minority were of Irish ancestry. Even
Boss Tweed, stamped on the public's mind as the stereotyped Irish
boss of Tammany, turned out to be Scotch. Martin Behrman, mayor
and boss of New Orleans, was of German-Jewish extraction, and
George "Old Boy" Cox of Cincinnati was English. The parents of
most of the bosses studied by Professor Zink were foreign-born,
poor, and had large families. Several bosses were fatherless at a
young age and had to go to work early. In education, they ranged
from Abe Ruef, the college man, to "Colonel" Edward Butler, the
Republican and Democratic boss of St. Louis, who did not spend a
single day in a classroom, yet was so far ahead of educated political
reformers that he could openly brag, "I've been stealing elections for
thirty years."

[1] Lincoln Steffens *The Shame of the Cities* (New York: McClure, Phil-
lips, 1904), p. 69.
[2] Harold Zink, *City Bosses in the U.S.* (Durham, N.C., Duke University
Press, 1930).

Other characteristics of bosses were further revealing. Most were big men and quite heavy, yet in sharp contrast to this image was "Duke" Ed Vare, powerful Philadelphia Republican boss, who was small and thin and handicapped by a leg that was shorter than its mate. With few exceptions, bosses tended to be calm individuals, rather stubborn and talkative, whose code demanded loyalty to friends and the carrying out of promises. In their private lives, they were devoted family men, and many did not smoke or drink. One asset characteristic of all of them was their excellent mental equipment.

In general, the bosses of the post-World War I era fitted the profile of their predecessors. Like their earlier brethren, most were poverty-stricken youths who clawed their way to wealth through political power. Czech-born Anton "Tony" Cermak, mayor and boss of Chicago, until he was struck down by an assassin's bullet in February, 1933, while conversing in Florida with President-elect Franklin Roosevelt, rose from mule driver in a coal mine to happy possessor of a $7 million fortune. Tall, thin, silent Pat Nash of the Kelly-Nash machine, which succeeded Cermak, was born in the Patch, an Irish ghetto close to Lake Michigan. Nash thoroughly enjoyed owning several palatial vacation homes across the country and a Kentucky stable of prize thoroughbred steeds. Frank Hague of Jersey City, collecting coal from railroad cars and tracks as a boy to heat the family tenement, earned enough from politics to have millions of dollars worth of property, maintain a year-round suite at the Waldorf, and travel abroad like an Arab potentate.

There were some major differences between the earlier and later bosses. The postwar bosses frequently were not satisfied with merely acquiring plunder but were intent on telling their citizens what they could or could not do. Mayor "Big Ed" Kelly, for example, barred Chicagoans from seeing the play "Tobacco Road" and abolished junior high schools. There were also more Irishmen among the postwar bosses, and Democrats predominated more and more, though some of the largest machines were in the hands of non-Irish bosses.

Another important difference was that among the postwar bosses were some of the leading demagogues who ever shouted from political stands. Few speakers in American history have packed the emotional wallop of Huey Long of Louisiana, Jim Curley of Boston, and Gene Talmadge of Georgia. In contrast, boss Ed Crump of Memphis, dictator of manners and morals in his city, was tongue-

tied in public, while rough Mayor Kelly of Chicago was a civic embarrassment with his fractured English.

Dominating the world of the bosses during the twenties and
thirties were about a dozen political machines. This book is a study
in depth of six of the bosses of these machines. That all six were
Democrats and that half were of Irish descent, two were lawyers,
four were office-holding bosses, and five came from poor families
were not reasons for choosing them. Rather, the six held power in
both decades and were considered the leading representatives of
their profession.

First and foremost in the municipal league was Mayor Frank
Hague of Jersey City, for thirty years the mean-tempered embodi-
ment of an American dictator. "I am the law," he once said, and in
truth he was. Out in Kansas City, Tom Pendergast, the only boss
during this time to have a member of his machine become President,
was more like the early-day bosses in his insatiable appetite for
boodle. By his use of gangsters as lieutenants and his unswerving
insistence on running a wide-open town, he sped the decline in
morality. Ed Crump, his long, bushy red hair, which gradually
turned white in his seemingly endless dictatorship over Memphis,
decided from his real estate and insurance company office what laws
the city council and state legislature would pass and who would be
the next mayor, governor, and United States Senator. "We don't
need politics in Memphis," he chortled. James Michael Curley, four
times the mayor of Boston and percentage taker on government contracts, added to the acceptance of immorality in his area by creating
a long political career despite a jail stay.

On the state scene, brilliant Huey Long, running Louisiana like
a South American banana republic, could say in honesty, "I'm the
constitution around here." Gene Talmadge, relying on props such as
snapping his red suspenders and acting the demagogue with sweat
moistening the trained shock of unruly hair on his forehead and
pouring past his Harold Lloyd glasses and down his ham-brown
face, did much to increase anti-Negro feeling in Georgia. In office
as governor, he stomped on the state constitution by decreeing laws
without going through the legislative route, firing elected officials,
and running the state's spending as he wished, not bothering to get
a required legislative budget. As an antilabor man, he gave Hitler
competition by throwing workers into concentration camps when
they went out on strike.

Besides these six, there were a host of bosses from coast to coast who looted public treasuries, made a mockery of the First Amendment's guarantees, beat some opponents, bought off others, ruined the careers of protesters, filled jails with enemies, laughed at the helplessness of do-gooder political amateurs, and narrowed the lives of those who lived within their reach.

In the broiling mesquite and cactus country of Duval County in South Texas, Archie Parr and his son George, bosses and self-made political millionaires, ran a tight, wretched dukedom populated by illiterate, cringing Mexicans living in appalling squalor and fear. Expressionless pistoleros guarded the Parrs in their treeless empire of cattle herds and oil derricks lest some of their peons got out of line. Occasionally the Parrs permitted their Mexicans to queue up on the dusty street of San Diego and enter the bosses' office one at a time to plead for a crust of justice.

In eastern Tennessee, Sheriff Burch C. Biggs of Polk County used vote-altering and fake counts to control three counties and used shootings, beatings, curfews, home invasions, and threats to keep citizens cowed. In Albany, New York, the four O'Connell brothers—Ed, Pat, Dan, and John—installed their own mayor in 1921 and then maintained control in the following decades through wholesale registration, falsification, and ballot-box stuffing. Despite the presence in their domain of such strong governors as Al Smith, Franklin Roosevelt, Herbert Lehman, and Tom Dewey, the O'Connells enforced a monopoly on beer sales and operated a tax-extortion racket and an illegal national lottery. Republican homeowners by the thousands registered as Democrats to avoid stiff property assessments.

At an eastern tip of the continent, in Atlantic City, New Jersey, where deeply tanned college-boy lifeguards lolled on high white stands and the nearby steel pier stalked into the ocean, Enoch "Nucky" Johnson, Republican dictator, held sway during the twenties and thirties. Nucky Johnson inherited the machine from his father, and from his post as treasurer of Atlantic County, he fixed elections and controlled the police, judges, grand juries, brothels, bookie parlors, numbers banks, and the amount of kickbacks from road-building contracts. Nucky's police met the slightest expression of opposition to their boss from local citizens with third-degree interrogation, whippings, and kidnappings.

In Chicago, "Big Bill" Thompson, three-term Republican mayor and a top-notch demagogue, gained office with a threat to punch

England's King George "in the snoot," demeaned the city with endless shenanigans, and made its name synonymous with gangland
killings by turning it over to Al Capone and his syndicate. Thompson's view of his main constituency revealed itself in his campaign
oratory. "They call you lowbrows and hoodlums," he told audiences.
"They call me that, too. We lowbrows have to stick together. Look
who's against us!"

The Democratic machine of Tony Cermak finally ousted
Thompson in 1931; and Cermak's successor in 1933, the Kelly-Nash
machine, was an improvement only in degree. With 30,000 local
jobs to dispense and an open New Deal bankroll offered by an administration that quashed an income-tax fraud charge against
Mayor Kelly, Big Ed, the mayor, could accurately boast to a reporter,
"I tell a million people what to think, and they listen to me because
they vote for me."

Ironically, New York City's Tammany Hall failed to prosper
during the heyday of the bosses. "Judge" George W. Olvaney, who
succeeded to Tammany's leadership with the death of "Commissioner" Charles F. Murphy in 1924, almost tore the organization
apart the following year by putting Tammany behind his protégé,
State Senator James J. "Jimmy" Walker, for mayor over the strong
objections of several of his colleagues.

In his prime, dashing, debonair Jimmy Walker, with his ever-
ready wisecracks and sophisticated man-about-town manner, made
himself a basic symbol of the fast-action Jazz Age. Behind the
mayor, Tammany could preen with success, for it owned sixty-four
of the sixty-five aldermen, all five district attorneys, and most of the
judges, while it collected its take from the more than 40,000 speakeasies and the thousands of gamblers, and swelled the public payroll with Tammany hacks whose sole function was to pick up their
weekly checks.

But in 1932, Tammany's stranglehold over Manhattan began
coming apart. At the instigation of Governor Franklin D. Roosevelt,
the Seabury investigation's exposure of Mayor Walker's dubious
acquisition of wealth brought his quick resignation and flight to
Europe. Then that same summer when Tammany, in control of the
New York delegation at the Democratic National Convention, stub-
bornly refused to support Governor Roosevelt for President, its doom
was sealed. Roosevelt, in retribution, favored Fiorello LaGuardia, a

nominal Republican, who served as New York City's mayor from 1934 to 1945.

The significance of the bosses of the twenties and thirties was that they collectively made the profession of democratic government and civil rights a hollow phrase in their time.

Their broader meaning to future generations is that under given circumstances, such as disillusionment with national policies, the efficacy and justice of government, and the importance of the individual vote, local citizens may again by default abdicate their rights and responsibilities to the bosses with more permanent results next time.

Chapter One

FRANK HAGUE
I Am the Law

I F ever a large city belonged to one man in the decades between World Wars I and II, it was Jersey City. Mayor Frank Hague, dictator over the lives of 300,000 subjects, objectively described his authority as "I decide. I do. Me."

The strangest feature of this autocracy in the midst of the great American democracy was that most people in Jersey City did not object to his rule. In fact, they showed their strong faith and loyalty on numerous social occasions during the year, and especially on each January 1, when Hague held a New Year's Day reception for "my people" at city hall. At his side in the receiving line stood his chosen United States Senator, Teddy Edwards; his governor, Harry Moore; his congressional selections, Mary Norton and Oscar Auf Der Heide; his Federal and state judges, Hudson County freeholders, and Jersey City commissioners. Thousands upon thousands of local citizens braved the cold each year just to walk past him for a handshake and a few words. "I made the city," he liked to say. "Nobody cared a damn about it before I came along." To children, his normally sour expression would subside somewhat as he told them, "If you will keep clean and work hard like your mayor, you can grow up like him and be respected as the first citizen of your city."

Those who walked past him saw a tall, straight, lean, gloomy-looking, but well-dressed man who was proud of his physical appearance. He wore an expensive, dark, doublebreasted tailor-made suit; a black Sulka tie with a pearl stickpin always placed at the same point; an old-fashioned, high, stiff Berry Wall collar, and Vici kid-leather shoes that he bought at half price for $25 a pair. He did not smoke or drink liquor, despite the mounting advertising campaign of the Lorillard tobacco empire centered in Jersey City and the wild development of speakeasies and the bootleg whisky business during the twenties. In fact, he did not even drink tea or coffee. Despite a height of six feet, Hague maintained a weight of 175 pounds by his mania for walking.

As a rule, he restricted his walking in Jersey City to night hours, for he claimed that the smoky, industrial atmosphere of the city's daytime period irritated his sinus condition. But there were many who said he did not walk during the day because of fear, as witnessed by his retinue of bodyguards and armored car. Yet he always strutted at the head of the parade march of the Holy Name Society and patriotic organizations, for these had an enormous vote-getting influence in town.

So did the image he created of the efficiency of the city's services. In his nighttime walks, which covered miles of the city, he had an opportunity to test the speedy response of his police and fire departments and ambulance service in emergencies. Firehouse crews were so concerned he might drop in unannounced that they were forever polishing their trucks, pots and pans, and the pole slide from the upper floor. Occasionally during his brisk hike, he would halt to place a feigned hysterical call for aid to the police or pull a false alarm. If the police and fire fighters did not respond in a minute or two, he would meet them with a string of foul words when they finally drove up, and sometimes even strike them. One time he came upon a fire in which a man had been hurt, and he phoned for an ambulance. "It was 45 minutes before the ambulance got there," Hague told a reporter for the Newark *Evening News*. "I asked the doctor why it had taken him so long. He mumbled something like, 'Don't you know I had to put on my clothes?' I knew he was mad at being called out at that time of night. I hauled off and punched him in the face."

When Hague's New Year's Day reception ended and he was alone with his machine subordinates, his normal personality asserted itself. He was a natural, earthy sort—loud, profane, talkative, with a thick trace of an Irish brogue. His heavily lidded blue eyes and thin lips mirrored the irritation and suspicion that enveloped him. He jabbed listeners in the chest with a stiff index finger to emphasize his point, used four-letter words for adjectives, and re-

ferred to himself as "Hague," not as "I." Not even his closest associates called him Frank in his presence. His grammar was atrocious,
and he commonly said, "He have went" and "He don't."

He also possessed a considerable vocabulary in describing
opponents. Anti-Hagueites were "scurrilous," "sinister," "irresponsible," or "Reds." He called one man "a common scold and nothing
but a bum sport." But in the tensions connected with holding power,
his subordinates realized that if he did not call his enemies names,
he would turn his tongue on them.

Over the years, Hague's control of the city was so thorough that
he made a mockery of the Bill of Rights. He banned free speech and
assembly, frightened newspaper publishers, dominated private organizations by having his henchmen invade them and take them
over, and had his police beat and jail protesting opponents. This
control permitted him to dip his hands into the city's business and
emerge a multimillionaire. It also made him an important state and
national figure. Hague was so powerful that he ordered a United
States Senator to resign and return home to run for governor, saw
to it that his business partner and lawyer became a Senator, and
had his young son, Frank, Jr., appointed to the highest state court
even though the lad had not graduated from law school.

It was little wonder then that other local bosses looked upon
Frank Hague as a master boss.

Frank Hague rose to his immense power from the most meager
of backgrounds. Born in 1876 to immigrant parents in the squalid
slum area of Jersey City known as the Horseshoe, he was expelled,
at age thirteen, from the sixth grade. "I was what folks call a bad
boy," Hague enjoyed admitting years later.

For three years after his expulsion, Frank led a street life,
hanging out with young hoodlums whose sport was street fights and
gang warfare in the mile-square Horseshoe. This small area had
forty saloons and reeked from New York City's garbage, which was
hauled across the Hudson River and dumped in the Horseshoe's tidal
flats. Then when Hague was sixteen, at his mother's pleading, he
took the only private industry job he would ever hold—as a black-
smith's helper at the Erie Railroad yards.

When he quit, two years later, he became manager of a light-
weight boxer, and he found this elevated him to the rough Horseshoe's envied society of worthy citizens.

While he earned little money on his fighter, his new status changed his entire existence. Saloon and racetrack proprietor Denny McLaughlin, the Horseshoe and second ward's Democratic boss, came to the fights, and his attention was drawn to the talkative Frank Hague, whose lithe frame was attired in the lastest style four-button suit.

A boss needed assistants to keep an eye on things in the ward between elections and to bring out the vote on election day. He also needed someone who would help keep order in the social club for young Democrats he had opened in the Horseshoe. This was what Denny had in mind for Frank. Frank's answer was a quick yes.

For a year, Frank was an enthusiastic aide to McLaughlin, but when the pinchpenny boss of the Horseshoe offered him no money rewards, he developed a seething hatred for him. His first opportunity to strike at McLaughlin came in 1897 when Edward "Nat" Kenny, known as the "Mayor of Cork Row," because of his popular Greenwood Social Club saloon, broke with the boss. Kenny agreed to back twenty-one-year-old Hague for ward constable against McLaughlin's man, and Frank jumped at the chance to run for office.

This was Frank Hague's first political victory. With the help of the remnants of his old, tough, street gang, he made a strong campaigner on the streets and on door-to-door tenement calls. But it was Kenny's stealing of an important precinct box and altering the ballots that made Frank the winner.

It took Frank only a short time, however, to discover that his victory was hollow: Nat Kenny did not make him his second-in-line as he had promised; nor did the constable receive a salary. Frank's earnings came entirely from fees and depended chiefly on how many of his friends he arrested.

Nevertheless, despite his impossible situation he held on to his constable's badge while he set to work to damage both Kenny and McLaughlin. First he organized his Horseshoe pals into a tight Hague faction. Then he bypassed the two Horseshoe machines to offer his support directly to McLaughlin's boss, Robert "Little Bob" Davis, top man in the Hudson County Democratic machine that covered all of Jersey City, plus Hoboken, Bayonne, Union City, and Weehawken. Besides his political control of the county, Davis had substantial holdings in insurance companies, utilities, and railroads.

Davis was not anxious to stir up more trouble in the Horseshoe, and at first he ignored the upstart's offer to do anything he requested. But in 1899, when Hudson County Sheriff Bill Heller appeared to be in re-election trouble against his Republican opponent and Denny McLaughlin was not working hard, Davis gave Hague and his boys their first assignment, to bring out the vote for Heller in the second ward. When Heller won, Davis' reward to Hague was to name him and Skidder Madigan, his boyhood pal, deputy sheriffs with a salary of $25 a week, or almost three times the wage earned by Erie shop-men.

With his new status and regular salary, Frank became seriously interested in a girl for the first time in his life and he now began courting Jenny Warner, a pretty girl of the Horseshoe. But it was not until four years later, when Frank had passed his twenty-seventh birthday, that they were married.

Marriage hastened Frank's large ambition to rise to second place in the Davis machine, and he strove constantly to show Davis how useful he could be. Unfortunately, his strong-arm methods at the polls and his sympathy for criminals while serving as a deputy sheriff won him few friends in the organization. Frank received press notoriety when a Republican county prosecutor charged him with arresting some Negroes for vote registration frauds as part of his "scheme to intimidate colored Republican voters." At the same time, the papers wondered why he was so solicitous of those found guilty of felonies. When assigned to take a prisoner to the state prison at Trenton, he invariably treated each man to an excellent meal, drinks, and a smoke at county expense before depositing him at the dismal, block-square, red stone-walled penitentiary on Federal Street in the capital.

Nor was he above perjury. In 1904, Red Dugan, a Horseshoe friend, who was out on parole after serving time for shooting a minister's wife in the head during a burglary, had gone to Boston where he deposited a forged check for $1,000 in a bank and withdrew $500 in cash. Red's mother came to Hague and begged him to testify at her son's trial in Boston by providing Red with an alibi. Hague agreed to lie, and he and Skidder Madigan took the train to Boston where they swore in court they had seen Red in a Jersey City park the day he was alleged to have defrauded the bank. Unfortunately, after Frank and Skidder returned home, Dugan confessed to the crime, and the Massachusetts authorities demanded that the two deputy sheriffs be extradited back to Boston to stand criminal trial for perjury.

Nor was this all of Hague's troubles. On the day he went to Boston he was supposed to appear as a witness in a Hudson County court case. For being absent without leave, he was hailed before a judge for contempt of court and threatened with jail, following his indictment by the grand jury.

But in both instances "Little Bob" Davis intervened. In the local case, Hague got off with a fine of $100, a tongue-lashing, and a warning not to be seen inside the courthouse again. In the extradition matter, despite the continuing clamor from Boston, the request was never honored.

Davis' reason for being kind to Hague was that he desperately needed help from all quarters to regain the control of Jersey City, which he had lost in 1901 to a thirty-two-year-old Republican, Mark Fagan, a leader for social and economic reforms. Fagan's record had also gained him re-election with ease over Bob Davis' candidates in 1903 and 1905. Among his achievements were the construction of thirty-one public schools and a new high school where 2,000 adults attended evening classes; free dispensaries and a public bath house; a free milk program for children; and the development of several new parks where summer bands provided free concerts.

It was not until 1906 that the long-suffering Bob Davis began to see the light on the far side of the tunnel. First, he stole Fagan's reform program and had the Hudson County Democratic organization adopt it as its own. Then he chose able Democratic progressives as his candidates for the state assembly elections that year. Among this group was a young lawyer named Joseph P. Tumulty, who would one day serve as President Woodrow Wilson's secretary.

In addition, Davis modernized his creaking Hudson County machine by dropping several aging lieutenants and replacing them with young, ambitious Democrats. Even so, Little Bob surprised the organization by choosing Frank Hague, still smelling of the Red Dugan affair, as the new boss of the second ward. Davis also named Hague to the select Democratic executive committee of Hudson County, and when the state assembly went Democratic in 1906 for the first time since 1893, he named Hague its sergeant-at-arms as one of his patronage rewards. A statewide editorial flood of abuse poured out against the choice of "Red Dugan's Friend." However, the assemblymen registered no complaints against him, and Sergeant-at-Arms Hague was seen at the Trenton statehouse only at check-collecting time, for Bob Davis needed him at home to help oust Mayor Mark Fagan in the coming city election of 1907.

Davis already had his candidate for mayor: H. Otto "Dutch-man" Wittpenn, an energetic, high-minded man of the German eighth ward and Hudson County supervisor, a post similar in some respects to a city mayor. Wittpenn had infuriated many in the Davis machine by ignoring their suggestions for patronage jobs and by attacking graft in the county courthouse, but he had won election as supervisor so overwhelmingly that Little Bob thought his appeal could be transferred to the mayoralty contest. Also, in his desire to become mayor, Wittpenn had agreed to forsake his political moral-ity and promised Davis control of city patronage, a job as city col-lector in charge of its fiscal affairs, and a contract to his newly formed Jersey City Supply Company to furnish the city's water.

Mark Fagan was in serious trouble from the outset of his con-test against Dutchman Wittpenn because he had organized a state-wide "New Idea" Republican faction to install the liberal ideas of President Theodore Roosevelt in New Jersey. Fagan's New Idea faction infuriated the Republican old guard who determined to ruin him in Jersey City.

When the Republican old guard's man lost the local primary to Fagan, it shifted its support to Wittpenn, the Democratic nomi-nee. Fagan appealed for backing to President Theodore Roosevelt, but Roosevelt, in a show of weakness, said he would not interfere in New Jersey politics, and Fagan was doomed. Yet even with Wittpenn's mouthing of Fagan's New Idea program, the Republican old guard's support of the Democrats, and a fired-up Davis organiza-tion in the field, Fagan lost to Wittpenn by only 9,500 votes.

Second-ward leader Hague had worked hard for Dutchman Wittpenn, and he was determined to get his due reward. Early in the campaign he had organized the "Tammannee Club" in the Horseshoe, a rowdy, quick-to-fight organization of young rooters personally devoted to himself. Members proved highly useful in hustling up support for Wittpenn and frightening Fagan voters from the waiting lines at polling places. Nor did these hoodlums restrict their threats to Horseshoe voters, for Hague generously lent some of his Tammanneeites to other ward leaders for election-day rough work.

During the campaign, Bob Davis had grown increasingly sus-picious of Frank Hague's allegiance to him for a variety of reasons. First of all, his Tammannee Club would take orders only from young

Hague. Second, Hague was discussing campaign tactics directly with other ward leaders instead of working solely through Davis headquarters. Third, Hague did not show the proper subservience to him in conversations. However, Davis did nothing to straighten Hague out because the important job was to elect Wittpenn over Fagan.

Shortly after Wittpenn was sworn into office early in 1908, Hague dropped into Davis' headquarters on Mercer Street to discuss his reward. Davis flashed a lightning temper when Hague said he wanted to be appointed city hall custodian as his patronage dessert. The job paid $2,000 a year, and on the surface the custodian was in charge of emptying the trash baskets, dusting the offices, oiling the floors, washing windows, and polishing the two hundred brass spittoons. But the custodian left these tasks to underlings—a hundred persons—whose selection would be his own. As for the pay, custodians traditionally picked up several times their salary each year for doing favors for outsiders at city hall.

With characteristic bluntness, Davis rejected Hague's demand as soon as it was made. But after his meeting with Davis, Hague rushed to Wittpenn's office and made the same request to the new mayor. He came at an opportune time, for Wittpenn was brooding about his campaign pledge to name Davis as city collector and let him supply water to the city. Moreover, Davis had reminded him recently that he considered all city patronage jobs to fall under his control. As he listened to Hague, Wittpenn suddenly saw an opportunity to show his independence from the Hudson County boss. On the spot, he told Hague he was the new city hall custodian.

When Little Bob learned of this he was furious. First he announced that Frank Hague was no longer his second ward leader and that John Sheehy of the Horseshoe was his replacement. He also removed Hague from the county Democratic executive committee, ordered the Tammannee Club to disband, and sent word to the Jersey City board of aldermen to pass an ordinance giving them custodial control of city hall instead of Hague.

Frank was not concerned about any of Davis' ukases except the last order, for the aldermen were almost all machine puppets. But he prevented such action by having his Tammannee boys administer beatings to Sheehy's chief aides and by sending word about the beatings to various aldermen.

The *Jersey Journal,* the local daily newspaper, in reporting

Hague's tactics against the Davis ordinance, revealed how successful the fear of physical violence could be: "The bill to cut off the
head of City Hall Custodian Hague has not made its appearance,"
noted the *Journal.* "It is said that the aldermen have concluded that
it would be better not to molest Hague at this time. Hague is a
fighter, and some of the aldermen do not care to run up against the
Hague following, it is said."

So Hague gave the Davis machine a minor jolt by besting the
top boss.

In 1909, when Wittpenn ran for re-election against Mark Fagan, Bob Davis had no alternative except to put his machine behind
the Dutchman once more. In a rerun of 1907, old guard Republicans
again opposed Fagan, and Wittpenn was returned to office for a
second term.

Shortly after the Dutchman's re-election, Hague urged him to
become a candidate for governor the next year on a platform denouncing Davis and the other bosses. Wittpenn refused to attack
Davis but he put himself on a collision course with the boss by permitting his city hall custodian to organize Wittpenn-for-Governor
Clubs in all the wards of the city. What doubts Wittpenn had regarding the wisdom of this course were swept aside by A. Harry
Moore, his secretary and close friend of Hague.

In March, 1910, the Wittpenn-Davis competition was made
public because Hague told the mayor to ask Davis for his open
support for governor. When Wittpenn did this, Davis blandly countered with a comment that he preferred to wait a while before making his choice. This led Hague to egg the mayor on to make immediate public announcement of his candidacy and to denounce the
Davis machine for "its persistent endeavors to block the administration in carrying out plans in the interests of people of Jersey
City."

Davis was so concerned with the possibility that Wittpenn
might become governor and make Frank Hague the power behind
his throne that he took a desperate step to prevent this. When "Big
Jim" Smith, his rival and enemy and Democratic boss of Essex
County, suggested that they unite in supporting the horse-faced,
long-toothed Woodrow Wilson, president of Princeton University,
for governor, Little Bob was amenable. Smith, a wealthy bank president, publisher, and businessman, as well as a former U.S. Senator,
had spent a decade trying to undermine the Davis machine in Hudson County.

Following the surprise Smith-Davis announcement of support for Wilson, Mayor Wittpenn met with Hague and Harry Moore, his secretary, and the hotheaded Dutchman raced off to Princeton for a talk with Wilson. In their confrontation, Wittpenn told Wilson that while he was running for governor as the enemy of the bosses, Wilson was their tool. But Wilson refused to accept the Dutchman's browbeating attempt to force him to withdraw from the campaign or denounce his Smith-Davis backing.

In the face of such major opposition, Wittpenn's chief hope for the nomination was to elect a Hudson County delegation of his own to the September, 1910, state convention in Trenton that would choose the party's gubernatorial nominee. Hague now became his key man to whip up enthusiasm through the Wittpenn Clubs and his own Tammannee Club boys, with the reminder to his charges that if a large pro-Wittpenn delegation whooped and hollered at the state convention, other delegations would swing behind Wittpenn and there would be rich patronage plums afterward for the loyal lot.

But Big Jim Smith was also aware of the importance of the Hudson County delegation, and with Bob Davis' approval he poured money and election workers into Jersey City in Wilson's behalf. Election day was one of the wildest in Jersey City's history, with thugs on both sides influencing the vote. In Hague's own ward, the *Jersey Journal* reported: "Cops on duty were using clubs and blackjacks in their efforts to assist Mayor Wittpenn and Frank Hague to defeat the Davis men. Sheehy men appeared in court with open wounds on their foreheads and arms in slings. Even John Sheehy, the Davis leader, appeared before the court charging that a drunken policeman on orders from Hague battered him with a nightstick." But when the fighting was over, Wittpenn had only a third of the delegates, and Wilson had the rest. Wilson's nomination for governor was now assured.

The crushing defeat rankled Hague far more than it did Wittpenn. When Wilson asked the mayor to campaign for him in the general election, Wittpenn readily agreed despite Hague's arguments that this was a mistake. Wilson also asked Wittpenn not to run candidates against the Davis choices for local offices in the fall election, on the grounds that this would damage the state ticket; and though the Dutchman complied, Hague proceeded to muddy the Democratic picture by creating his own slate of "independent" candidates.

In addition, Hague became a speaking campaigner for the first time, lashing out at Bob Davis with claims that he pocketed most of the campaign contributions he collected and overcharged Jersey City a million dollars a year for the water he sold it. The Davis machine made no public effort to combat Hague, but before election day all Hague candidates except those in the second ward dropped out of the running. And on that day, while Wilson was achieving a spectacular victory throughout the state, Davis plug-uglies flooded the second ward, and Hague's candidates there for city alderman and county freeholder ran far behind Davis' candidates.

With Wilson's success, Frank Hague was written off locally as a young, thorny rose killed in the first frost. But events soon occurred to prove this assessment entirely wrong. Boss Jim Smith had publicly promised Wilson not to enter his name in the senatorial preference primary, nor make any effort afterward to return to the U.S. Senate. But following the election, Smith announced he was "yielding to the wishes of his friends to have the state legislature appoint me to the United States Senate." Wilson realized he would be accused of trickery with a boss if he now consented. In a face-to-face meeting, Smith refused to take Wilson seriously, and Wilson decided to carry his fight against Smith to the people.

In this controversy, Hague spied a path for reviving his and Mayor Wittpenn's low fortune. Echoing Wilson, the two came out as enemies of bossism. Progressives throughout the state cheered the Jersey City political unknown named Hague whose speech supporting Wilson gained widespread newspaper coverage.

When Big Jim Smith finally withdrew his candidacy before the legislature voted, Wilson could claim he had smashed a powerful political machine, and Hague and Wittpenn could say they had helped him.

Still another event that revived Wittpenn and Hague was the death of Bob Davis from intestinal cancer in January, 1911. Wittpenn had assumed he was a sure loser if he ran for a third term in the Democratic primary that fall against a Davis candidate. However, with the Davis lieutenants soon involved in an intramachine battle for supremacy, Wittpenn's fears evaporated.

Wittpenn's new lease on the mayoralty meant continued political existence for Hague. But this was no longer enough for him. To move out of Wittpenn's control, Hague announced himself as a candidate for a place on the five-man street and water commission

in the coming September, 1911, primary. He also soft-soaped Wittpenn into lifting Harry Moore (who was now Hague's alter ego)
from his clerical spot as the mayor's secretary to the late Bob Davis'
powerful position as city collector. The mayor agreed further that
the Wittpenn Clubs should be expanded and strengthened so that
Wittpenn candidates could erase the old Davis runners in the primary.

The Davisites failed in their last-ditch effort against the Hague-
Wittpenn machine in the primary contests throughout the city, both
in the vote count and in the physical warfare with Hague's roving
Tammannee boys. By now, Hague's personal antics on election day
were a standardized roughhouse routine that received almost repetitive coverage by the press. One reporter noted that the winning
street and water commission nominee "used police to unduly influence the action of the election officers. It was claimed that Hague
had taken possession of the registration books."

After the 1911 primaries were over, Hague hoped, as did the
other Democratic nominees throughout the state, that popular Governor Woodrow Wilson would work personally for his election in
November. Before the election was over, he was grateful for Wilson's silence.

Only five months in office, Wilson began his 1912 presidential
quest in May, 1911, with a nationwide speaking tour. Then to safeguard his home base, on his return he announced after the New
Jersey primaries that he would make a tour around the state for all
Democratic nominees except those sponsored by the Smith machine
in Essex County.

Hardly had Wilson begun his statewide tour when the name
Frank Hague threatened to endanger the entire fortune of the Democratic ticket. In Atlantic County, Wilson drew a great deal of attention castigating the local Republican boss, Louis Kuehnle, who was
under indictment for using gangsters and bribes in the last election. This led George Record, one of the governor's aides, to suggest
to Wilson that to reveal his true statesmanlike character he take a
nonpartisan approach toward all unsavory politicians. Record, who
had been a Mark Fagan associate in Jersey City, had dredged up
copies of a news story on the old Red Dugan affair, and he showed
them to Wilson and reporters. It was Record's plan that Wilson
would make an attack on the Democratic Hague after newspapers
reprinted the 1904 perjury incident.

Hague awakened one day to find the Red Dugan story of 1904

on the front pages in 1911. "Wholly unfit for the important office of street and water commissioner," read one newspaper editorial. "All his life he has been a political roustabout." In self-defense, Hague scheduled a series of talks, explaining at each that he had gone to Boston to lie for Red Dugan solely because his little Irish mother had come pleading in tears to him. The Wittpenn Clubs cheered him resoundingly, but Hague realized that his fate lay in the hands of Woodrow Wilson, who was scheduled to speak at Jersey City's St. Peter's Hall on November 3, the Friday before the 1911 general election.

Tension rose to fever pitch in Jersey City over the Hague story long before Wilson cut through the enormous crowd at the hall and stepped to the stage for his speech. Wittpenn was present to introduce the governor, and Hague was conspicuous by his absence.

In a shouting, angry tone, Wilson denounced bossism, and the crowd waited expectantly for the mention of Hague's name. He spoke of "plunderers" existing in both parties, and the audience was on edge when he yelled: "Would you vote for such men because they call themselves Democrats when you know they are rogues?"

But he was on to other topics without speaking Hague's name; and Hague's career was saved.

Hague on the rise was never daunted by the position or power of his opposition. Even Governor Woodrow Wilson, now a swift-growing national figure, was not untouchable. Once election day passed, with Hague elected street and water commissioner by 7,300 votes and Wittpenn elected to a third term by his largest majority, Wilson asked the mayor to visit him in Trenton. Hague thought this was a good opportunity to give Wilson a face-to-face explanation of the Red Dugan affair, and he joined Wittpenn on the trip to the state capital. However, Wilson was furious when he learned that Hague, though uninvited, was inside the governor's mansion, and he told his staff that under no circumstances would he talk to him. A newsman who was present reported, "Hague had to cool his heels in his outer office," and when Wittpenn emerged from his conference, Hague was told to leave with him.

The handling of the Red Dugan business and now this show of contempt by the governor turned Hague into a raging Wilson-hater. Within a month he was in touch with sulking Big Jim Smith to plan a program for thwarting Wilson's presidential ambitions. Word was that J. P. Morgan, the biggest financier, had given Big Jim Smith a quarter of a million dollars to fight Wilson in New Jersey and that Big Jim gave part of this money to Hague to develop anti-Wilson feeling in Hudson County.

When Mayor Wittpenn called a routine meeting of the twenty-two-man county's Democratic executive committee to endorse Wilson as a means to influence voters in the coming primary, Hague had already handed out Big Jim Smith's money to a majority of the committee members. The result was that the executive committee voted to pass the question along to the 305-member Democratic general committee.

There were just too many persons to bribe now. So Hague was forced to play an open role at the general committee session, in a yelling and threatening effort in futility to prevent the Wilson endorsement. Unable to swallow his defeat, he issued a public statement, saying: "I am in this anti-Wilson fight and will stick to it because I do not think the governor is treating the Democrats of Hudson County squarely." He then threw a political brick at Wilson, calling him dishonest and disloyal.

The Morgan money paid off only in Big Jim Smith's Essex County on primary day, for the twenty other counties, including Hague's Hudson County, voted overwhelmingly to send Wilson delegates to the national convention. Although he was not a delegate, Hague went to the Baltimore convention where he worked on the twenty-four Wilson delegates to switch to Big Jim Smith's four-man support crew for House Speaker Champ Clark. But after Wilson won the nomination for President on the forty-sixth ballot, Hague told reporters: "I have never bolted a Democratic ticket. I am for Wilson, heart and soul."

On Hague's return home, he found Wittpenn at war with him. Not only was the Dutchman still furious with the street and water commissioner for attempting to befoul the Hudson County committee's endorsement of Wilson, but he was wrathful over Hague's new campaign to destroy him as Wilson's successor as governor. Printed interviews with Hague revealed that he told reporters Wittpenn had secretly conspired with Big Jim Smith against the Wilson candidacy, and as Wittpenn's lieutenant, he—Hague—had been impelled to give his word to Smith that he would participate in their foul plan against the governor. Wittpenn, said Hague, had then deserted them when Wilson appointed a friend of the mayor to a state job, and Hague had been left stuck with his pledge.

Instead of attacking Hague by name for this preposterous talk, the Dutchman took action against him within his administration. Hague could not be fired from his elected post as street and water commissioner, but dozens of his boys worked on city jobs; and on the pretext of eliminating waste, Wittpenn went on a firing rampage against them. When Hague publicly questioned this activity, Wittpenn declared it was necessary because these "city leeches" were responsible for whatever corruption existed in his administration. In turn, Hague charged Wittpenn with being in league with the water-supply monopolists. "So long as I am on the board," Hague told reporters, "I am going to do my best to serve the interests of the people of Jersey City as against that of the corporations." By now, Wittpenn was sick of these dirty back-and-forth exchanges, and he publicly brought to an end his long association with Frank Hague with a short statement: "I don't believe traitors will gain anything in the long run. It was a mistake on my part to support Frank Hague."

While Hague had been fighting with Wilson and Wittpenn, he was also busily creating an image of himself as a progressive public servant. Hardly had he joined the four other commissioners on the street and water board when he exerted his strong personality and made the decisions for the board with only weak cries of "aye, aye" coming from the other members.

His first campaign for attention as a reformer was an attack on Jersey City's foul streets. Before his time, a handful of street sweepers appeared occasionally in good weather on the streets. Hague ordered street cleaning to be done every night chiefly by attaching hoses to fire hydrants and flushing the streets. He claimed to be the first to clean streets in this fashion, and won publicity for his enterprise and community spirit from out-of-state newspapers.

Hague also gained considerable publicity mileage by demanding that Jersey City's street-littering ordinances be enforced. The street and water commissioner sent a letter to Police Chief Benjamin Murphy demanding that his men arrest any person dropping even a speck of paper on the sidewalks or streets. Murphy snarled and tossed this letter out the window. But Hague continued to demand arrest action against litterers in talks to reporters, who wrote him up as a zealous reformer, and Mayor Wittpenn soon realized that Hague was painting his administration as the champion of a dirty city. Murphy found himself meekly ordering his men to arrest anyone caught dropping a candy bar wrapper outdoors, and for a month the police force continued this detail before Murphy called a halt. This time Hague did not resume his attack because he knew he already was viewed as the relentless antilitter watchdog of Jersey City.

Hague also sought the image of an economizer. With loud public announcements, he told local citizens that the street and water board planned a cut in the number of employees from 218 to 116, along with a severe slash in its spending. When both were done, newspapers applauded Hague as the model skinflint administrator. But only months later he quietly acquired supplemental appropriations and embarked on a large spending program, raising the personnel count far higher than the original figure and rewarding his Tammannee boys with easy jobs.

Ironically, it was Governor Wilson who gave the Jersey City street and water commissioner the means to best Mayor Wittpenn in their growing warfare. One of Wilson's successful reform measures in the 1911 legislative session was the Walsh Act, which permitted cities to drop the unwieldy mayor-council type of government and adopt a simple and responsible commission form of local control.

While Wittpenn was slow to take a stand, Hague seized leadership of the local do-gooder Commission Government League. He led the petition drive sponsored by the Catholic Church, women's clubs, businessmen's associations, AFL unions, and professional organizations to call a special election to vote on the proposed change; and he found himself applauded when he spoke of the need to get rid of the current, corrupt city government. To prove his idealism, Hague never failed to point out that if the commission government won approval, he would be giving up two years of remaining service as a street and water commissioner.

After Jersey City citizens approved the commission government, Wittpenn, concentrating on becoming Wilson's successor as governor in 1913, did not choose to run for any of the commission posts and instead sponsored a five-man ticket for commissioners. Hague ran his own slate that included himself.

The results were disastrous to the mayor, for when the votes were tallied, only Harry Moore of the Wittpenn ticket was elected, and in truth Moore was a secret Hague lieutenant, as he had been since he first became Wittpenn's secretary. Wittpenn's disaster was further revealed by the election of Hague and two Hague lieutenants. The fifth member was Mark Fagan, who received more votes than any other candidate.

After the debacle of the Wittpenn slate in the contest for commissioners, Wilson, who was now President, asked Wittpenn to drop out of the race for his successor as governor and support James Fielder, who was serving as interim governor until the election in November, 1913. Wittpenn did as ordered, accepting as a balm the small position of collector of customs for New York. So the Hague battle with Wittpenn appeared at an end.

With the local five-man commission government making decisions by majority vote, Hague with his four votes was in control of its policies and activities from the outset, though Mark Fagan became mayor as an acknowledgment that he had received the most votes in the recent election. As for the county's Democrats, Hague was already well on his way to one-man domination with his elevation to Bob Davis' old post as chairman of the Hudson County Democratic executive committee, which gave him final say on all county patronage jobs.

According to the new law, each of the five Jersey City commissioners was to administer his own segment of public business, upon the approval of the other commissioners. Hague astutely chose the department of public safety for himself. Control of the police was not only important for the power it gave him over Jersey City citizens but for the publicity an aggressive director could attract. Hague was fully aware that Mark Fagan was still beloved locally and remained a threat to elect his own slate of commissioners in the next election. By clever use of his new assignment, Hague hoped to cut Fagan down to size and destroy him as the Jersey City statesman.

With steady complaints to the press that his job was made difficult by the leniency of his predecessors, Fagan and Wittpenn, toward crime and criminals, Hague was soon off to a running start as the champion of honest citizens. He also attacked the police department as a band of crooks in order to show the enormity of the task facing him to bring crime under control. Certainly the Jersey City police department was no stronghold of angels, but it was no worse than in other cities where the pay was low and appointments were political.

What infuriated Hague most about the police department were two factors. Jersey City police belonged to unions, and he was concerned that they might react to his blackening of the force by going out on strike. Even more important, his authority under the commission government charter did not permit him to act as judge and fire members of the department; and if he could not do this, he was unable to replace the lot with his own crew.

Hague carried his attack on the police into the state legislature, demanding authority to fire policemen at will. Jersey City policemen, he blackened his force to a committee, were "a lot of drunken bullies swaggering around with a pistol in their pockets and a nightstick in their hand."

On the question of the affiliation of Jersey City firemen as well as policemen in AFL unions, Hague one day bluntly ordered them to quit. Frightened by his manner and unsure of their own strength, the police and firemen surprised him by voting to quit their unions. But they retained membership in their state benevolent societies, which had influential friends in the state legislature. And when Hague had a Hudson County assemblyman introduce a bill in the legislature to permit him to fire police and firemen for violating any rule of the departments, members of the Patrolmen's Benevolent Association lobbied legislators, and the bill failed.

But while the benevolent groups congratulated themselves, Hague won the war by trickery. A proposed amendment to the city commission government statute would permit voters to approve or disapprove salary changes for commissioners. By law, the original statute and the proposed change had to be included in the printed measure to be voted upon by the state legislature. Hague had the word "judicial" slipped into the original statute's restriction of commissioner powers to "executive, administrative and legislative."

Not until the amendment cleared the legislature and was signed by Governor Fielder did the benevolent societies awaken to the treachery. They immediately instituted court action, but the decision went against them, and now Hague was prosecuting attorney, jury, and judge over the lot of them.

His reign of terror was swift and deep. In a single day he put 125 policemen on trial for various charges. Hundreds of others were summarily ordered to turn in their badges, and a continual shifting of high officers to outlying beats was another Hague maneuver. On occasion, after staging a trial, he let the cop stay on the force, but fined him several months' pay. Then he would shrewdly turn over most of the fine to the man's wife, who was expected to act as a sort of bail bondsman to guarantee his future loyalty to Hague. Still another technique Hague applied was the establishment of a force of one hundred undercover agents to spy on fellow policemen and report their conversations and activities directly to him.

By 1916, the Wilson reformers and Mark Fagan followers considered Hague a sinister politician who must be stopped without delay. Singlehandedly, he had punctured the hopes of commission-government enthusiasts and had induced widespread fear in many quarters. He had also worked relentlessly to create a new bossism, undermining the authority of progressive ward chairmen by giving city jobs to their top lieutenants. In addition, he was spreading his authority beyond the county line through his friendship with Governor James Fielder.

Despite his involvement in his own re-election campaign, President Wilson listened to the recital of the woes of Jersey City and took what he considered to be the best step to stem Hague's tide. Otto Wittpenn was brought back from the Customs Bureau, and with the publicity of a Presidential recommendation, he became a candidate that year for the Democratic nomination for governor.

With Wittpenn as governor and head of the New Jersey Democratic Party, Wilson believed Hague would be contained and then weakened. This hope was surprisingly the same as Big Jim Smith's, for the Essex County boss came out strongly for the Dutchman because of Hague's growing influence in Essex County. Hague realized how formidable his opposition was when he announced his support of Governor Fielder for a second term, but he had fought all these opponents in previous contests and, as he put it, he was still alive.

Wittpenn was an easy winner over Fielder in the Democratic primary, and New Jersey newspapers predicted that he would have no trouble defeating Walter Edge, the Republican nominee for governor. However, the editors and political predictors had failed to consider Hague, the strategist. On election day, his machine was under orders to keep the Hudson County Democratic vote at home and away from the ballot boxes. Wittpenn looked like a sure winner until the Jersey City count; and when the votes were tallied here, Edge was governor.

The year 1917 saw the last challenge to Hague, with the city undergoing its second election of commissioners in May. Three chief slates were offered again: a five-man Republican ticket headed by Mark Fagan; a Wittpenn-blessed ticket; and the Hague-fivesome, whom Hague labeled "The Unbossed."

The campaign had hardly started before the Fagan and Wittpenn candidates became aware of the large amount of money the Unbossed leader was spending. Even though he was a Republican, Mark Fagan appealed directly to the White House for help in combatting Hague. So did Big Jim Smith. Wilson did not underwrite Fagan, but he did decide to interpose in the municipal election.

World War I had begun that spring, and the White House was a scene of frenzied action. Yet Wilson sent his indispensable secretary, Joe Tumulty, to Jersey City to help in the campaign against Hague. In speeches in his home town, Tumulty begged voters to defeat Hague and his "double-dealing" political dictatorship.

Nevertheless, on election day, in May, 1917, all five on the Unbossed slate won. Harry Moore, who had switched from a Wittpennite to an Unbossed, had received the most votes, with Hague running second; and though the accepted rule in commission governments was that the high man became mayor, Moore stepped aside and Hague took the mayor's office.

Jersey City was to know no other mayor for thirty years.

Wilson was not amused after the Jersey City election when Joe Tumulty handed him an editorial from the Newark *Evening News* of May 15, 1917, that warned: "Jersey Democrats had better get acquainted with Frank Hague, who has just emerged on top in one of those political fights which make Jersey City famous."

Word about the mayoralty victory of Frank Hague, his name-calling enemy, reminded the President he had recently established Hoboken, New Jersey, as the key troop embarkation point for Brest and the European fighting. Hoboken abutted Jersey City to the north and lay snugly in Frank Hague's Hudson County dominion. If Hague wanted to interfere with the war, the door was indeed open to him.

With the excuse that Hoboken was the most un-American town in the nation, Wilson sent the Secret Service to imprison hundreds of German immigrants and Americans of German ancestry and to seize the Hamburg American and North German Lloyd offices and docks. Then he placed the city under military control for the duration.

While the Battles of the Somme, the Marne, St. Mihiel, and Meuse-Argonne were bloodying France in 1918 and killing hundreds of thousands of young men, a major political war was shaping up in New Jersey. Frank Hague, mayor only a single year, had begun a do-or-die competition for control of the state against the Wilson-Tumulty reform Democrats and the Big Jim Smith–Jim Nugent Democratic machine of Newark and surrounding Essex County. Jim Nugent was Smith's nephew and political partner.

Hague wanted to humiliate the President; but even more important at the moment was his need to gain state power so he could get his hands on a large amount of public funds in order to increase his own wealth, pay off the expenses of his growing local machine, and protect himself from domination by the state government.

Up and down every street in the burgeoning industrial section of Jersey City he had watched companies growing rich on war orders. The railroad "tubes" built under the Hudson in 1914 had made Jersey City a strategic center by connecting New York City and New England directly to the South and West through Mayor Hague's domain. Not even the Black Tom powder depot explosion on the city's waterfront, that destroyed docks and ships in July, 1916, had slowed down the industrial pace.

With a mind as scheming as his Hague sat only a short time in his second floor office in the old, green-domed city hall and pondered means for getting his cut of the millions. He thought he found a way to put his hands on city funds by raising property valuation for taxes. Railroads were assessed at only $3,000 an acre compared with $17,000 an acre for other commercial real estate. Assessments on Standard Oil and the monopolistic Public Service Corporation's properties were also far below the commercial rate. So Hague abruptly raised the railroad property assessment 240 percent, or from $67 million to $160 million; he raised Standard Oil from $1.5 million to $14 million, and the PSC from $3 million to $30 million.

Since none of the companies could pick up and leave, Hague considered his handiwork with great satisfaction. However, his joy collapsed when the companies appealed to the state board of tax assessments, and the Hague boosts were rescinded.

It was at this point that Hague decided on broad political action as the immediate solution to his problem. He would elect his own governor, who in turn would replace the tax-assessments board with Hague men.

World War I ended in November, 1918, and two months later Wilson, who had kept an eye on New Jersey politics, went to Paris to write the peace treaty. That same January, Joe Tumulty called a meeting of New Jersey Democratic leaders to promote his own candidacy for governor, in the September 23, 1919, primary. However, he had little chance to talk, for Hague took up most of the meeting in an exchange of insults with Essex County boss Jim Nugent, aging Big Jim Smith's nephew.

Afterward, Tumulty learned that Hague had good reason to keep him from discussing his own candidacy and developing a groundswell of support among those present. For Hague wanted a disorganized opposition while he ran Edward Irving "Teddy" Edwards, his henchman in the state senate and president of the First National Bank in Jersey City, for the state's chief executive. Edwards was a man despised by Wilson, for as the miserable little state comptroller when Wilson was governor, he had withheld his $880 monthly salary during the periods Wilson campaigned for the presidency.

When Joe Tumulty heard that Hague was promoting Teddy Edwards, his first reaction was one of contempt. But he soon learned that Edwards planned to spend a good deal of his own large fortune to campaign. In addition, the "Beer Barrel," as the ample political fund of the liquor lobby was called, was to be made available to Hague for the effort. Since Tumulty could not command a similar campaign war chest, he quickly decided to hold on to his White House job.

As for Essex County boss Jim Nugent, when he heard the news about Edwards, he offered to put his Newark and Essex County machine behind any of a half dozen men he favored. When each rejected his offer, he had no alternative except to run himself.

This was a particularly bitter contest because the winner would gain statewide control of the Democratic Party. When the primary battle was over in September, 1919, Edwards had the nomination and Hague, the power.

Hague did not rest once Edwards had the nomination, for he was aware that the national tide was anti-Democratic, as witnessed by the Republican takeover of Congress in the 1918 elections. With his control of Hudson County's election machinery, Hague was not concerned about the outcome there. But the rest of the state might go overwhelmingly Republican, and he sought an issue that could slash the vote of Republican nominee, Newton A. K. Bugbee, outside his county. He found it in the controversial Eighteenth Amendment, which was scheduled to go into effect in January, 1920; and though neither Hague nor Edwards drank, Hague had Edwards proclaim in every speech his intention to "make New Jersey wetter than the Atlantic Ocean." Hague also had Edwards attack the highly unpopular Public Service Corporation, the monopolistic utilities combine; and despite Edwards' heavy ownership of PSC stock, he shouted to audiences: "The Republican Party is owned body, boots and breeches by the Public Service Corporation!" Then for a touch of lightness to the campaign, Hague sent a male chorus with Edwards to render patriotic and Victor Herbert airs.

Republican leaders were convinced that Bugbee would carry the state outside of Hague's Hudson County by a moderate majority over Edwards, and if the Hudson vote could be kept fairly honest, Bugbee would be the next governor. But their worst fears were confirmed on election day in November, 1919, when Hague's police barred Republican observers from the vote count at several polling places in Jersey City. That evening the returns gave Bugbee a state-wide lead of 21,008 coming into late vote-counting Hudson County. But Hague announced that Edwards was so popular there he had overcome Bugbee's lead by capturing a 35,518 plurality and winning the governorship by 14,510 votes. The outraged Republicans did not demand an investigation, choosing instead to be satisfied with winning both houses of the state legislature.

There was little doubt how Edwards would reward his benefactor, once he moved to Trenton, rented a house for his residence as governor, and rendered his inaugural address at the outset of his three-year term. The commissioners on the state board of tax assessments were quickly ordered out, and the newly constituted board approved the Hague property assessments. Edwards also fired the entire state highway commission and replaced it with Hague men. The state's attorney general and the Hudson County prosecutor were other Hague choices, and Hague's men also filtered into a variety of openings on the state bench.

As soon as he put Edwards into the governor's chair in 1919, Hague started thinking of a national role for himself. With President Wilson a victim of a paralytic stroke, the contest for the Democratic presidential nomination in 1920 loomed as a wide-open affair to Hague. Visions of vaulting into national bossdom led him to file petitions for Edwards to run in several state presidential primaries, and he sent the governor on a speaking tour with a stock speech attacking the Eighteenth Amendment.

That summer Hague went to San Francisco as chairman of

the New Jersey delegation to the Democratic National Convention, and of the twenty-three nominees receiving votes on the first ballot, Edwards ran in fifth place, or one position higher than Warren Harding's level on the first ballot in the recent Republican convention. But Hague dropped Ted Edwards and swung his support to Governor James M. Cox of Ohio because he wanted to be with the touted winner, and Cox carried the big prize on the forty-fourth ballot.

Cox let Hague know he was counting on him to swing Wilson's state into the Democratic column in November. But nothing could be done in the wake of a national demand for a "return to normalcy" and a weariness, distrust, and disillusionment with Wilsonian ideals. The Republican team of Harding and Coolidge swept to victory not only in the state but in Hague's Hudson County as well. The Democratic debacle would have been far worse, a state senate committee charged, if Hague had not seen to it that "the election law was violated with impunity."

In 1921, when Hague and his subordinate fellow commissioners ran for another four-year term, Jersey City reformers sensed this might be their last chance to dislodge Hague before he was established too solidly, and they fought him almost hysterically with a five-man slate of their own. Besides a heavy schedule of speeches, they relied on a mass distribution of the state senate committee's report denouncing Hague's vote-stealing machine as "a saturnalia of crime."

But the voters did not understand the long word and Hague continued to be the cautious electioneer. With the inevitable Hague vote-counters on hand, he made certain his victory would be one-sided. For instance, in his home second ward only his act of generosity permitted his opponent to get 120 of the 4,620 votes cast. Afterward, newspapers described Hague's victory celebration at city hall as a noisy and crowded affair, with the host explaining that the election had proved that "the decent and liberty-loving people of Jersey City are not to be fooled."

Hague also celebrated his victory by helping to stage the biggest sporting event in American history to that time. This was the heavyweight championship fight between champion Jack Dempsey and French challenger Georges Carpentier, which attracted 91,000 spectators. The fight was promoted by John F. Boyle, Hague's friend and secret business associate, who staged it on a piece of his Jersey City property known as "Boyle's Thirty Acres."

Because the New Jersey constitution barred a governor from serving successive terms, Hague was forced to extend his power into the U.S. Senate in 1922. Teddy Edwards' three-year term ended that year, and in an effort to keep him politically happy and active, Hague backed him for the Senate seat held by Republican Theodore Frelinghuysen.

With Edwards about to leave state office, Hague chose Circuit Judge George S. Silzer of New Brunswick as his replacement as governor. He succeeded in electing both men, though with the Republican trend as strong as a gale, he was forced to extreme measures to insure their victory. Silzer was 34,000 votes behind his Republican opponent when all the state's votes except those from Hudson County were tallied. But Silzer emerged 46,000 votes ahead of Mr. Runyon when Hague submitted his county's totals.

Besides owning a U.S. Senator, Hague decided he should also have female representation in the House of Representatives. The Nineteenth Amendment, granting women the vote, had gone into effect in August, 1920, and the likelihood that a woman would win election to Congress in the near future seemed preposterous at that time. But Hague saw a way to ingratiate himself with the ladies, and he chose Mary Teresa Norton, a forty-nine-year-old widow, to be his ambassador in the House.

Hague had started Mary Norton in politics by naming her representative of Hudson County women on the state Democratic committee in 1920. Next, he elevated her to vice-chairman of the state committee in 1921; and in 1923 she was his successful candidate as the first woman elected to the board of chosen freeholders for Hudson County, as the county commissioners were called. Finally after exposing her to national politics by naming her to the delegation to the Democratic National Convention in mid-1924, he ran her for a seat in Congress that November, and she became the first woman elected to the national legislature.

In time, seniority elevated her to chairman of the House District of Columbia Committee, making her in effect the mayor of Washington, and of the House Labor Committee through which the New Deal's labor bills had to pass. However, her principal use to Hague in Washington was to run errands and acquire Federal funds and patronage for him.

If Hague's Mrs. Norton was the boss' complete puppet, his governor, George Silzer, revealed a black-Irish streak on occasion when he felt hemmed in by Hague. One time he fired the Hague state highway board and stunned the mayor by charging that "for years there had been graft in the paving of New Jersey highways and everybody knew it." Hague quickly recovered when he saw that Silzer was not determined to end his pork barrel, and he went so far as to endorse the governor for the Democratic presidential nomination in 1924 and cast New Jersey's thirty-eight votes for him on the first ballot before discarding him.

Hague had a more substantial candidate for President that year, and his name was Al Smith. At the 1920 Democratic National Convention, Hague had met the brown-derbyed, cigar-smoking Irishman from "the sidewalks of New York," and the two men and their families became close friends in the years that followed. The Hague and Smith families often took vacations together, and Frank and Al enjoyed talking politics and attending sporting events in the New York area. Smith had served a term as New York governor from 1918 to 1920 and a second term beginning in 1922, emerging in 1924 as the national leader of the anti-Eighteenth Amendment "wets."

But the front-runner that year was William McAdoo, son-in-law of Woodrow Wilson and the "dry" darling of the Ku Klux Klan. So it was little wonder that after the first ballot Hague dropped Silzer and put his votes on Smith. Then with neither McAdoo nor Smith willing to concede to the other, the convention wearily plowed through 103 ballots before compromising on John W. Davis, the corporation lawyer for the J. P. Morgan interests. Although Al Smith was saddened by the results, Hague came out a winner for he was elevated to vice-chairman of the Democratic National Committee.

When Silzer's three-year term as governor expired in 1925, Hague was glad to be rid of him. For his next gubernatorial candidate, he chose his long-time political lieutenant, smiling Harry Moore, who had worked his way up from secretary to Mayor Otto Wittpenn to Jersey City's commissioner of parks and then commissioner of revenue and finance. The *New York Times* accurately portrayed Moore editorially in May, 1925, as a candidate who "can talk circles around any other politician in New Jersey. He has joined every social organization that is helpful to a candidate. . . . There is nothing of interest to the average citizen that he can't 'orate' about with the facility of a river flowing over a dam. He has a speaking acquaintance with everybody whom he ever met in New Jersey and expects to take every voter by the hand before election day. Mr. Moore will have a dripping wet platform. No wonder the Republicans are worried."

Moore's opponent was wealthy Arthur Whitney, a state senator, who traveled from one end of the state to the other charging that the chief issue at stake was "Hagueism as opposed to Coolidgeism." Throughout the rest of the state this had significance, for Whitney held a 65,000-vote lead without counting Hudson County. But Hague country gave Moore a 103,000 edge over his Republican opponent, and Hague had his third governor in a row.

The Republicans later presented the Hudson County prosecutor with conclusive evidence that Hague had voted dead people and repeaters. In one district, the number of voters was larger than the number registered to vote; and in a polling place where some Republicans were known to have voted, the Democrats were recorded with 100 percent of the votes. Unfortunately for the Republican complainers, the county prosecutor was John Milton, Hague's attorney, friend, and business associate; and the evidence never reached the grand jury.

As Hague's bossism began lengthening in years, it grew commonly apparent that the boy from the Horseshoe had become a wealthy man who lived better than some in the proverbial Four Hundred despite a salary of only $8,000 a year. This gave Republicans the impetus to demand an investigation; and in 1929, State Senator Clarence Case's committee probed into Hague's public and private activities, with 335 witnesses contributing 8,200 pages of testimony.

Case's investigators found that Hague, his wife Jenny, and their son, Frank, Jr., lived in a fourteen-room duplex apartment in the sumptuous Duncan Apartments on Hudson Boulevard in the Bergen Hills district of Jersey City. Hague paid no rent, though others with similar quarters at the Duncan paid $7,000 a year; and the reason Hague lived rent free was that he had paid $75,000 for the land on which the apartment house was built and was suspected of being its owner. To care for his apartment, Hague employed a cook and two maids plus a handyman-chauffeur to drive his wife about in her Cadillac.

In May of each year, the Hagues moved to their palatial estate near the ocean at the fashionable resort town of Deal, New Jersey, for which Hague made cash payments through John Milton of $18,000, $65,000, and $59,520.50. The Deal place had two gardeners to roll the lawns and tend the sunken garden, as well as several house servants to handle the big parties Hague gave there.

Generally after two months at Deal with daily commuting to Jersey City, Hague took his family abroad to Europe on the society-class liners. Then it was back again to the Duncan Apartments until winter when they went to Florida's Biscayne Bay where he owned an ocean-front villa. Hague also held annual leases on suites either at the Waldorf-Astoria or the Plaza Hotel in Manhattan; and when he was in Jersey City, he crossed almost daily to New York City for lunch at the Plaza or Ritz.

Hague was known as a lavish tipper, and he dispensed his rewards from the large bankroll bound by a stretched wide rubber band that he carried in a pants pocket. As a man who found pleasure in sporting events, he could be seen in the front row seats at championship prizefights, in the most coveted box at world series baseball games, and in the owner's box at Saratoga, Hialeah, and Churchill Downs racetracks. He enjoyed betting heavily on the horses, though he was not a compulsive gambler.

The Case Committee, in its efforts to determine the source of his money, found he had substantial deposits in the National City Bank in New York, plus large quantities of stock in Teddy Edwards' First National Bank and in the Trust Company of New Jersey. In its search, the committee came across a pocket diary owned by the late John Ferris, a Hague pal who was awarded a Jersey City construction contract of $1,409,392.76 to improve Journal Square. One notation in the Ferris diary read: "Hague and Freeholders . . . 200,000."

The committee also probed the maneuverings of a Mr. H. S. Kerbaugh of New York, an obvious front for Hague, whose whereabouts could not be determined. Mr. Kerbaugh bought a parcel of property in Hudson County for $60,000, which the county then condemned and bought from Kerbaugh for $386,215. Another Kerbaugh deal involved buying a natural lake and surrounding acreage for $125,000, and then selling it to Jersey City through condemnation proceedings for $325,000. John Milton, Hague's attorney and county prosecutor, handled the purchase for the city. In a third known transaction, the mysterious Kerbaugh paid $218,000 for a

tract of land at Journal Square in Jersey City. The inevitable condemnation of the property came not long afterward with the county
paying Kerbaugh $320,000 for only one-twelfth of the property.

Many other financial plums were traced to Hague. Millions
came to him over the years through a 3 percent assessment on the
salaries of public employees, supposedly to meet campaign expenses. Additional money came from the large Christmas charity
fund collected annually by the fire department. No records were
kept of the way the campaign assessments and Christmas fund were
spent.

The committee found that some of his money-raising schemes
were of an offbeat nature, while others followed the customary
graft route. For example, city bus operations reported gross receipts
on individual street runs hundreds of thousands of dollars below
their true figures. Investigators learned that in the first eight months
of 1928, the Bergen Avenue line's gross receipts were in excess of
$330,000, yet only $155,000 was reported; and the Central Avenue
line's $233,000 take was reported as $123,000. Another source of
Hague revenue resulted from a Sunday blue law barring the showing of motion pictures. However, for an annual payment of $50,000
the Jersey City government was willing to ignore the law. In a more
typical money-raising plan, Hague awarded a firm a Jersey City
contract for $910,000 to construct a sewage disposal plant and sewer
line. This eventually evolved into payments totaling $2,887,607.77
for an incomplete and shoddy job, with the ubiquitous John Milton
on record as attorney and registered agent for the contractor.

Constantly on the lookout for trustworthy underlings, Hague
had discovered Bernard McFeely of adjoining Hoboken to be cast in
his own image. Over time, he had seen to it that McFeely became a
city commissioner and then boss of Hoboken. It was to be expected
that McFeely would learn from the master. The Case committee
found that for the five-year period before 1923 Hoboken had contracted to pay $179,940 for the collection of its garbage and ashes.
Then McFeely personally took over the contract, awarding a
$470,000 deal to a dummy company "owned" by his brother James
and two sisters, one of whom was Bernard's housekeeper.

There seemed little doubt that the Case committee's findings
would ruin Hague politically and serve as the springboard for legal
action to put him behind bars. But Hague was left untouched by
events. John Milton was expected to be a vital witness against his

friend and associate. Called before the committee to testify, he smilingly told the members he had destroyed his checkbooks and records. "I have gotten rid of an office force, and I have gotten rid of the law business," he insisted.

Other key witnesses, such as the elusive Mr. Kerbaugh, could not be found before Hague was hauled before the committee to testify. He was the calmest person present as he listened, relaxed, to each question about his financial operations and then replied every time, "I decline to answer."

Finally, at the committee's request, he was ordered to appear before the entire legislature. This was expected to be an ordeal for Hague because there were only two Democrats in the twenty-one member state senate and twelve in the sixty-member assembly. But Hague was again at ease as members screamed at his repetitious refusal to answer questions on the grounds that his personal affairs were his own business and that the legislature lacked jurisdiction. One member, Alexander Simpson, who was Hague's man in the state senate from Hudson County, added to the snarling scene by his numerous interruptions and challenges to those who would besmirch his leader's reputation.

Finally, with the attack getting nowhere, the overwhelming Republican majority ordered Hague arrested for contempt. But before he could be carted off to jail, Vice-Chancellor John J. Fallon, formerly a Hague assemblyman and now a member of the Chancery Court, issued a writ of *habeas corpus* for Hague's release. Fallon gave as his reason an alleged unconstitutional use of judicial power by the legislative branch. This led the state to appeal Fallon's action to the Court of Errors and Appeals, New Jersey's highest court, and here the vote was a six to six tie, with four abstentions. A tie was a victory for Hague and a defeat for the state legislature. "I am very much pleased and satisfied by this decision," Hague told reporters. "It is exactly what I expected."

Frank Hague never forgot that all of his financial and political empires rested on his Jersey City base, and this he controlled in harsh dictatorial fashion. At bottom, the key to his entire political operation centered on a single word—ballots.

A Jersey City philosopher once observed: "It ain't how the ballots go into the box that counts. It's how they come out." Certainly, skulduggery in the voting had been an essential Hague tool ever

since 1897 when Nat Kenny had put him up for constable against
Denny McLaughlin's man, Jack Harnett. Young Frank had been
there when Kenny seized the ballot box from one precinct polling
place, carried it to the back room of his saloon, and with a smile announced the results as Hague, 300; Harnett, 1. The lesson was not
lost on Frank Hague.

But though Hague used every time-honored trick of the ballot-
box stuffers, this was not his sole method for winning elections. He
knew that unless he maintained a solid core of free-controlled
voters, in time the outrage of a vocal and antagonistic majority
would doom him. So he sought to control the 600,000 residents of
Hudson County, including the 300,000 in Jersey City, by constant
pressure from his aggressive political machine.

Hague kept a huge chart hanging on his office wall that served
as his personal computer in determining the political health of his
organization. Jersey City had 12 wards and 306 districts, and each
of the latter was subdivided into precincts that were saturated with
Hague workers. On Hague's chart were outlined not only the election districts of the city, but also the names of the male and female
leaders in each and the vote there in recent elections hour upon hour
on election day.

Hague insisted his machine was far superior to Tammany Hall
across the Hudson because it did not miss any citizen in the community. His thousands upon thousands of election workers acted
like an army of occupation over a conquered enemy. Every house in
each precinct fell under the watch and care of precinct workers
operating under precinct captains. The precinct captain, in turn,
answered to a ward lieutenant; the ward lieutenant to the ward
boss; and the ward boss to Hague.

This crew ran ward clubs, social clubs, parades, excursions,
outings; passed out the food, clothing, and coal to the poor and
found jobs for them; served as go-betweens with the police over
nonfelony troubles; and handled specific complaints such as garbage
pickups like Scandinavian ombudsmen.

For these activities, the machine expected votes in return. But
rather than leave this to chance, citizens were rated by Hague machine workers to determine what course to take in working on them
politically. Ratings found in the files at city hall listed citizens with
the following after their names: "Friendly"; "Okay"; "Republican,
but friendly"; "Republican, no good"; "Received favors but proved
ingrate."

Two days before an election, Hague met with the election district leaders, their lieutenants, and workers in Jersey City's Grotto auditorium where he exhorted them to do their utmost. "Three hundred and sixty-four days you want favors from me," he made his pitch. "Now, one day in the year I come to you." Loud applause always greeted his remark, as the machine members fanned out to their wards to do their duty.

Then on election day when Hague sat before his chart, hourly voting figures were put up for comparison with the past. If he didn't like what he saw, he would place telephone calls and demand an explanation. Perhaps the requisitioned number of cars to take voters to the polls had not shown up, or Republican poll watchers were too nosy.

In the 1921 Jersey City election, 245 Princeton University lads, imbued with a post-World War I desire to take a relevant part in the struggle for democracy, served as poll watchers for the New Jersey Honest Ballot Association. Only an hour after the polls opened, five were so critically beaten as to require hospitalization; and others, still ambulatory, went to city hall to complain in person to the mayor. A state legislative investigation revealed that Hague told the boys, "Well, you fellows can go back there if you wish. But if you get knocked cold it will be your own hard luck." To a reporter who asked about the beatings, Hague chuckled and replied, "Animal spirits, that's all. I told my boys to lay off, but it was a pretty dull election, and they couldn't resist the temptation to have a little fun."

Sometimes election watcher deputies were offered bribes, and sometimes they were walloped. One woman deputy told an investigating committee, a Hague man said to her, "If you won't mind stepping outside I am going to give you the price of a brand-new hat." In one election, a state-appointed election superintendent in charge of the watcher brigade detailed a long list of brutal Hague actions against his workers. He said: "Where were my deputies? Some of them were locked up in the police stations; some were stuck on corners, with a threat that if they moved from there, a nightstick would be wound around their necks." One of the deputies, he said, "when endeavoring to arrest an illegal voter was arrested himself by the police, held in $3,500 bail, and I did not succeed in getting him out of jail until ten o'clock that night, with the coat torn off his back."

"Always deliver when a man delivers for you," Hague once explained the general contentment of his machine to a young re-

porter. And there were many to reward for the 100,000-vote plurality Hague possessed in Hudson County. With approximately
375,000 eligible voters in the county, the Hague machine could brag
that 345,000, or 92 percent, were registered. Even more astounding, about 300,000, or over 85 percent of those registered, were
listed as having voted in elections!

Hague's reward to his machine was to saddle Jersey City and
Hudson County with the largest per capita payroll of any city or
county in the United States with a population exceeding 100,000.
Many of his lieutenants were given titles and salaries without any
required job duties. John Coppinger, for instance, was the vote-getting fourth-ward boss whose reward was the county sheriff's office.
Hailed before the Case committee, Coppinger admitted he did not
know the duties or salaries of his thirty deputies. Another rewarded
machine aide was Alfred Mansfield, who drew a salary as a county
health inspector. Mansfield, charged the Case committee, was "unable to give the name and address of any place he had ever inspected." One public servant claimed he was paid to keep "two
blocks of the highway clear. If boxes would fall off a truck and block
the road, it would be my job to keep the road clear." Seventy men
were listed as "county mechanics" to repair county buildings. But,
reported the committee, "no record of their work is kept. There is
no timekeeper, no time cards and no individual records." Several
persons were on the city payroll "for keeping ballot boxes in repair";
others were tree-trimmers on an annual salary; dozens upon dozens
of "park employees" would have almost filled the thirty-seven acres
in the fourteen city parks; one big vote collector collected his county
check as "foreman of vacuum cleaners"; and four others who formed
the Hague singing quartet were paid as policemen. One ward district
leader was willing to be listed as "laborer at the bathhouse" in order
to pick up $2,200.

In several instances, Hague lieutenants received two paychecks. One man, John Saturniewicz, was on the city's roll as the
mayor's "senior clerk-stenographer" at the same time that he sat as
judge of the Second Criminal Court. Theodore Smith, another
Hagueite, was chairman of the state civil service commission while
he was collecting an extra $10,000 a year as a condemnation commissioner in Jersey City. The 1908 law required city and county employees to be hired from a civil-service register, but Smith ignored
this in his home county. Even the chief clerk of the state civil service

commission's office in Jersey City had not taken a civil-service examination. This man also collected a second salary from the police and fire departments.

Besides rewarding himself and his henchmen lavishly, Hague punished his opposition with whatever tools he considered necessary. Some he beat, some he bought, and others he deported from Jersey City. He successfully infiltrated and controlled most local private organizations and neutralized leaders of others by threats, poor service, and high taxes. The Bill of Rights in the Constitution did not exist, so far as he was concerned.

Hague's police were under orders to use their clubs and fists freely on the boss' enemies. The *New York Times* of July 18, 1928, reported a city hall meeting where James Burkitt, a Hague foe who would not give up, asked for a police permit to speak at various street corners. According to the *Times*, the talk went like this:

> "What's the matter with your face?" asked the mayor [Hague].
> "Some of your mugs beat me up," Burkitt replied.
> The mayor laughed heartily.
> "Don't laugh, Mr. Mayor," Burkitt said, irritated.
> "I'm not laughing at you, but your face looks so funny," cried Hague.

In 1920, Hague tried to end free speech and assembly in Jersey City by pushing through his commission a city ordinance that made it necessary for Burkitt and others to obtain a police permit to hold a public meeting in the city. Permits were to be denied persons "advocating the abolition, overthrow, or change" in the Federal or state governments by unlawful means, proposing "the use of force or violence," or speaking "upon the subject of obstructing the Government of the United States or any state thereof." It was left to the chief of police to determine the "Americanism" of the permit seeker, a judicial decision that boiled down to the simple question of the individual or organization's pro-Hague or anti-Hague status.

James Burkitt seldom could get a meeting permit, but even when he did, Hague prevented the meeting from taking place. One time the rent on the hall was raised to $750 for the evening, and this forced Burkitt to cancel his meeting. More often Burkitt suffered mishaps that forced a cancellation. On one occasion he caught a bus to his meeting place, but when he climbed down to the street, police met him and took him by police car to the city courthouse. There they dragged poor Burkitt into the basement where they took turns punching him. Then the next morning, almost unconscious, he was propped up before Judge Leo Sullivan, a Hague magistrate, who sentenced him to ninety days in jail for using abusive language on the police officers.

Nor could Burkitt distribute handbills opposing the Hague administration. Here again, a city ordinance passed in 1924 barred the distribution of leaflets without the signed approval of the chief of police. Violators were beaten, fined, and imprisoned.

Another of Hague's most persistent foes to suffer the mayor's special wrath was John R. Longo, who had the audacity at the age of twenty-four to form an anti-Hague Democratic slate and enter it in the Hudson County primary. This infuriated Hague, who prided himself on having no opposition in the primaries; and rather than forget Longo or buy him off with a nonwork job, he ordered his police to arrest him.

What followed was incredible. A Hague-named grand jury was impaneled, and Longo found himself indicted on the cooked-up charge of having filed fraudulent primary petitions. Then a Hague-selected jury convicted Longo after a farcical trial, and a judge who was a member of the Hague machine sentenced him to prison for nine months.

Besides strong-arm and railroading methods, Hague was a master at more subtle techniques. The New York *Post* noted that those who expressed opposition to the mayor might not get their mail, or if they did, it would come opened. Telephones were known to be tapped because policemen would show up at private meetings discussed and arranged only over the phone. Magazines containing unfavorable pictures and articles about the mayor and Jersey City were seized by police from newsstands.

In other instances, opponents would be picked up as vagrants. If they had businesses requiring licenses, they would not get renewals; and if they owned theaters or apartment houses, these would be condemned as fire and health hazards. The *New York Times* reported on one occasion that a Jersey City resident, "belonging to one of the oldest families in the city, who recently has been outspoken against the mayor was sued on a nine-year-old note he had forgotten about. The assessment on his brother's property was raised from $2,500 to $25,000.

There were several instances when Hague ordered local citizens "deported." In a legal action, Ashley Carrick, a local attorney, said that two police officers held his arms while one of them clubbed his knees and a plain-clothes officer punched him in the face. Afterward, he was forced onto a ferry bound across the Hudson to New York. "Do you think deportation is within the power of the police and the right of the police?" Hague was asked. Hague replied: "Well, I think it is discretionary in a great many cases. The police as a rule are very considerate and very faithful in their duty."

For a time Hague tolerated the *Jersey Journal,* an outspoken local paper that called him "Czar Hague" and exposed his personal financial dealings. When Hague finally decided to "reform" the *Journal,* he started by issuing an order to city and county employees that anyone caught reading that paper would be summarily fired. Then he proceeded to lay a heavy tax boost on its property and made a public charge that the Dear family, owners of the *Journal,* had tried to "rob" the city by demanding $250,000 more than the valuation placed on a piece of their property condemned for a civic improvement.

Now his tactics broadened against the *Journal.* Firemen and police were assigned to distribute a Hague leaflet door-to-door that denounced the paper as "vicious" and having "selfish and dishonest motives." Next, the city commissioners ordered the name of the principal plaza in town changed from Journal Square to Veterans' Square. Deliveries were made difficult with newsboys arrested for violating child labor laws. Then came a serious economic squeeze, when Hague told theater owners to quit advertising in the *Journal.* One theater owner who at first refused finally agreed to withdraw his ads upon being handed summonses for two dozen alleged violations of fire, health, building, and police regulations. The dessert of the Hague menu was his order to police and firemen to go door-to-door again, this time soliciting subscriptions for the *Journal's* rival. Each of his solicitors was told not to return without four new subscribers, not counting his own.

While the *Journal's* owners pondered their course, a Hague state assemblyman in Trenton introduced a resolution in the state assembly to impeach Judge Joseph Dear, the principal publisher of the paper and one of the six lay members of the sixteen-man Court of Errors and Appeals, New Jersey's top court. At this point the *Journal* decided that Hague was not a bad sort after all. Favorable stories about the mayor appeared, and on one occasion when a machine henchman was sentenced to jail for embezzlement, the *Journal* did not run a story on the trial. As a result of the newspaper's change of direction, Governor Harry Moore gave Judge Dear another six-year term when his judgeship expired; Veterans' Square once more became Journal Square; movie theater operators advertised again in the paper; and Jersey City police and firemen were permitted to read the *Journal*.

Hague was surprised at the ease with which he could buy individuals and organizations. Jersey City was 75 percent Catholic, and Hague knew it was vital that he have the unwavering support of the church's hierarchy. He gained this by an umbrella of activities. St. Aedan's Roman Catholic Church in Jersey City boasted an altar costing $50,000 paid for by Hague; and the Mount Carmel Guild, the mother charitable organization of the city's twenty-eight Catholic churches, had an honorary chairman named Frank Hague, who personally raised hundreds of thousands of dollars for it. Along with Catholic members of the Hague machine, Jewish and Protestant members were also required to sign contribution pledges for Catholic charities, and those who fell behind in their payments received unfriendly letters from the mayor.

To placate the church's animosity toward nonparochial schools, Hague appointed a Catholic to head the school board, an action ensuring that no public schools would be built. At the behest of the Catholic Church's local spiritual leaders, his police raided bookstores in search of books on the church's proscribed list. These were seized and destroyed. In one raid, police not only carted off all copies of *The Memoirs of Cardinal Dubois* but the store's files, typewriters, and stationery as well. Hague also took action against his opponents after labeling them as "Reds," a name bound to win him the backing of the church, which considered communism its worst foe. Monsignor John J. Murphy in an address to citizens of Jersey City told them they should get down on their knees and thank the Almighty that they had a wonderful mayor who let his enemies know, "whether they are parlor pinks from Montclair or social scum from Brooklyn, that Jersey City does not want them."

Continuing in the religious field, Hague quieted potential opposition from individual priests, ministers, and rabbis by naming them as paid chaplains to the hospitals, the prison, and the police and fire departments. One minister who made a nuisance of himself preaching about the dirty sidewalks and streets in Hague's Jersey City concentrated on spiritual sermons after Hague appointed him a chaplain. When the payroll finally wallowed in chaplains, Hague put men of the cloth on the public paycheck lists under such titles as clerks and plumber's helpers. Others lowered their voices when members of their families were given county and city jobs.

In only a single instance did Hague eschew his policy of buying the clergy. This occurred when Rabbi Benjamin Plotkin testified as a defense witness in the fraudulent trial of John Longo. Plotkin found himself labeled a "Red," and his congregation lost the lease on its building.

Hague's scheme for controlling professional and business organizations followed the Communist tactic of infiltrating an organization and of putting their own men into positions of power. Typical was Hague's procedure in taking over the Hudson County Bar Association. James A. Tumulty (not related to Joe Tumulty), a Jersey City attorney and a son of a Hague opponent, was the second vice-president of the Bar Association. Past precedent meant that he would automatically be raised to vice-president at the next election and then president the following year. But Hague intervened with tradition because of young Tumulty's desire for the bar to investigate the Hudson County courts.

On the night of the bar election, Mayor Hague ordered every police court in the county closed, and judges and lawyers left by special buses for the Bar Association's meeting hall. Other buses picked up the rest of the Hague machine attorneys and whisked them to the meeting, where they were under instructions to vote for Edward O'Mara of the city counsel's office, whom Hague had put up to oppose Tumulty for the vice-presidency. O'Mara had not attended a Bar Association meeting in years and was long delinquent in his dues, as were most of the Hague lawyers. But they paid their dues that night, and with a Hague man standing alongside the ballot box to check off their names, they gave O'Mara a one-sided victory over Tumulty.

Hague's control of the State Federation of Labor, the Medical Association, the Chamber of Commerce, the American Legion, and various lodges took a generally similar path of infiltration. In some instances, public jobs for the old leaders eased the transition to Hague domination. Veterans' organizations were so thoroughly under Hague's thumb that he could call on them at will to assemble and use force against his proclaimed enemies. A writer reported that on one occasion when two out-of-state members of the House of Representatives were scheduled to speak in Journal Square against Hague policies, full-page ads told World War I vets to keep them from talking. In giving instructions, said the writer, an officer "of the Catholic World War Veterans told a meeting of 800 men to come armed each with two feet of rubber hose."

In several instances, Hague gained his consensus by catering to specific segments of the population. Most conspicuous was the special attention he paid women. Besides giving the ladies Mary Norton as their congresswoman, Hague barred taxi dance halls, speakeasies, burlesque shows, and night clubs from Jersey City; and his police were under orders to fight a relentless war against prostitution. "Jersey City is the most moralest [sic] city in America," Hague enjoyed telling his women voters, though the men knew they had only to go outside the city to other parts of the county to enjoy the old diversions.

Hague's crowning point when talking to the women as well as to the poor was the Jersey City Medical Center, a grouping of seven skyscrapers built at a cost of $30 million with the money coming from county, state, and federal treasuries. The mayor's brochure called the 2,000-bed, fireproof complex "ninety-nine floors of hospitalization," and his flyer went on to say that the first of the structures "was born in the mind of Mayor Hague in 1921."

Certainly, the Medical Center was the equal of any in the United States. Its top administrators were enticed from other leading hospitals, and it had an excellent staff of 200 doctors, 70 interns, and 500 nurses. The surgical building, rising twenty-three stories high, was able to care for 1,000 patients at a time; and a nearby sixteen-story building served as the modern quarters for the staff. The most widely advertised building was the Margaret Hague Maternity Hospital, which Hague explained was "in memory of the humble mother of a distinguished son." In talks to women's groups, he could move many to tears with the maudlin tale of a poor mother carrying puny Frank to the city's free clinic a half-century earlier and waiting all day for a doctor to give a moment of his time to the sick baby. "Have your baby or your operation on Mayor Hague" was the call word in the city. Each year doctors delivered 5,000 babies with only fifteen deaths, and few families paid for the service. In fact, the Center gave free service to 100,000 persons annually, with the result that a large portion of county revenues was needed to pay expenses. Accountants at one time determined that the cost of running the Medical Center equalled the cost of running an entire city the size of Jersey City.

Hague fully realized the political value of the Medical Center. He had an expensively furnished office in the dowdy city hall, a second office above a police station, and a third at a firehouse close to his apartment. But his fourth office where he spent most of his time when he was not at his Waldorf suite, Deal summer estate, or villa at Biscayne Bay was the one in the Medical Center. There he assumed a proprietary air, spoke formally with the doctors, proudly showed visitors through the buildings, and picked up gum wrappers he found on the floor. Yet his relationship to the Medical Center went beyond pride in its facilities and the knowledge of its political value. Doctors and other employees had to give his machine 3 percent of their salaries; the homes of many of his lieutenants had the same odd brick exterior as the hospital buildings; and most of the construction companies doing the building and making repairs were connected in some way with John Milton, Hague's lawyer and business associate.

By 1928, Frank Hague was leading a fairy-tale existence for a former Horseshoe boy. In New Jersey, the city, county, and state recognized him as the Democratic Party's supreme commander; and when he went down to Washington for meetings of the Democratic national committee, Senators and governors listened to him carefully. For he was not only vice-chairman of the committee but also spokesman for presidential front-runner, genial Al Smith.

That June a boisterous Hague led a handpicked state delegation to the Democratic National Convention at Houston, and he had his lads and Mary Norton scream their voices away to hoarseness as they cheered Al Smith's nomination on the first ballot. But this was a year of continuing national prosperity, and Herbert Hoover, the high-collared Republican nominee, rode its crest to an overwhelming victory.

It was also the year the Case committee dug into the mayor's complex financial and political affairs. In state politics, the committee uncovered Hague's role in Republican as well as Democratic kingmaking. Harry Moore's three-year term as governor was closing out, and Hague hoped to replace him with Judge William Dill. However, Robert Carey, who was Hague's sharpest Republican foe in Jersey City, and the party's strongman in the state, planned to run for his party's nomination. If Carey became governor, he could be expected to remove Hague's protective layers in the courts, in the prosecutors' offices, and throughout the election machinery, thus dooming Hague's untouchability.

But forewarned of what Carey would do, Hague jumped into the Republican Party's primary. State Senator Morgan Larson was the weakest Republican seeking the gubernatorial nomination, and Hague passed word along to his machine aides to cross party lines and vote for Larson. And Larson it was who won the Republican nomination, thanks to Hague. The Case committee hauled several of Hague's switch voters before it for questioning, but all witnesses, said the committee's report, "were evasive and vague." Typically, Arthur Foley, a police lieutenant and member of the Hudson County Democratic Committee, was asked whether he was a Democrat or Republican. "Well, I don't know," he told the Case committee. "At night I changed my mind, at 12 o'clock."

Hague's cross-party strategy backfired, for Republican Morgan Larson was swept into office over Judge Dill, the Democrat, in the November general election on the tide of the Hoover victory margin. Nor were Smith and Dill the only victims of the Republican presidential triumph. Teddy Edwards, whom Hague had made governor and United States Senator, had desperately wanted a second six-year sojourn in Washington. But he was also wiped out. The resulting shock so embittered him that he blamed Hague personally for his loss, and he joined those who sought to end the "Hague Plague." In a public statement that by association also condemned himself, Edwards insisted, "For years the Democratic officeholders of Hudson County and Jersey City have been subjected to an illegal and cruel system of political peonage. By threats, good Democrats have been forced to pay heavy tribute to Mayor Hague. . . . Millions have been purloined from needy families and never a solitary cent has been accounted for."

The first year of the Hoover Administration was a trying one for Hague. The Case Committee had him arrested for noncooperation, and only the mayor's allies on the state's highest court saved him from jail. To celebrate his close-call victory, Al Smith came to boatside to throw an arm of friendship around his lean but muscular shoulder just before Hague and his wife embarked on a European vacation.

However, his troubles were not yet over. James Burkitt, the much-punched and jailed Hague enemy, wrote President Hoover that the Case Committee had uncovered the mayor's $400,000 cash payments for property, acquired despite a salary of only $8,000 a year. Burkitt further charged that a thorough investigation would show that Hague was worth $40 million. With a corroborative statement by Teddy Edwards, Hoover ordered the Treasury Department to determine whether Hague had cheated on his income taxes.

In an attempt to make Hague shiver with fear, the Treasury Department's Internal Revenue Commission leaked word to reporters that Hague was going to be required to pay $1.8 million in taxes and penalties. But this leak came as a relief to John Milton and Hague, his client, for it revealed that Internal Revenue was planning civil and not criminal action. Emboldened by this, Hague let out a fighting blast from his Florida villa, "I don't know where they get their figures from. They flatter me."

The timing of the Government's investigation was poor, because the Treasury investigators were concentrating that year on putting Scarface Al Capone behind bars for income-tax fraud in an effort to break up his criminal syndicate in Chicago. The result was that Hague held the advantage in the settlement bargaining, and the Government's lawyers finally agreed to close his past files for a measly $60,000.

When the Great Depression settled like poison gas across the nation, following the stock market crash in October, 1929, Hague's political fortunes revived vigorously. The political trend so handsomely Republican at the start of the Hoover Presidency turned Democratic once more, and Hague's 100,000 plurality in Hudson County was sufficient to install Harry Moore in a second term as governor in 1931.

Once sworn in, Moore re-established his first-term routine, which was to spend half the work week in Trenton and the other half in a Jersey City office where he could be quickly available to Hague. He also installed a private telephone line between his Trenton office and Hague's city hall quarters. However, frequently in the months ahead, Hague had to turn Moore over to his subordinates because the 1932 nomination fight was warming up between Al Smith and New York Governor Franklin Roosevelt. At Smith's request, Hague was working closely with Democratic National Committee Chairman John J. Raskob, the former General Motors board chairman, to help him win this honor a second time.

Hague came roaring into Chicago as Al Smith's floor manager

a week before the Democratic National Convention began, in order to mount a "Stop Roosevelt" movement. Meeting with other Democratic bosses gave him hope for success.

A few days before the convention convened, his effort reached its climax when he issued a vicious statement condemning Governor Roosevelt, who he pointed out was opposed by his own home-state delegation. "Governor Franklin D. Roosevelt, if nominated, has no chance of winning the election in November," said Hague. "He cannot carry a single state east of the Mississippi and very few in the Far West. . . . Why consider the one man who is weakest in the eyes of the rank and file?"

Having gone to Chicago with the expectation of being a kingmaker, Hague returned a beaten man to Jersey City once Roosevelt won the nomination. Not even the tearful thanks of Al Smith, who called to praise him for sticking loyally to him to the unhappy end at the convention, eased his worry that he had done himself irreparable harm.

But hardly had Al Smith completed his encomium before Hague determined to throw their close twelve-year friendship overboard in order to develop a new relationship with Roosevelt. For Hague knew that if he failed, he would be ousted as vice-chairman of the national committee and would be denied even a Federal dime if Roosevelt defeated Hoover in November.

So Jim Farley, the nominee's campaign manager, and the nominee himself soon received enthusiastic phone calls from Jersey City's mayor inviting them to kick off the presidential campaign in New Jersey. Despite Roosevelt's animosity toward Hague, in the end he reluctantly agreed to make a speech at Governor Harry Moore's summer executive mansion at Sea Girt on August 27, 1932, after Hague promised to assemble a crowd even larger than the 50,000 listeners he had provided nominee Al Smith at the same place in 1928.

Farley and Roosevelt were flabbergasted at the mob they saw before them when they stood on the platform at Moore's summer place. Hague had arranged for special train after special train to carry his machine members down the Atlantic Coast to Sea Girt, and Farley's observation was that "the crowd seemed endless. If it wasn't the biggest rally in history up to that time, it must have been very close to it." Far more than 100,000 made up the crowd.

This noisy Hague show included free lunches, fireworks, barber shop quartets, bands, vaudeville acts—and finally Franklin Roosevelt. "There is no general who could have assembled such a host but my old friend, the mayor of Jersey City," said FDR, offering a full measure of public forgiveness of Hague for his comments and acts at the late national convention.

When he defeated Hoover in November, 1932, it was not lost on Roosevelt that Hague had contributed more money to his campaign than he earned in a year as mayor, or that Hague had provided him with a catchy slogan for a country mired in a depression —"Hoover fed the Belgians and starved the Americans." Most of all, the new President was aware that New Jersey's sixteen electoral votes were a gift to him from the Jersey City mayor. Although the Democrats had carried the state by 31,000 votes, the victor would have been Hoover had not Hague's Hudson County produced a plurality of 118,000 ballots for him over unhappy Mr. Hoover.

During Roosevelt's first term, Hague was often a White House guest, a frequent adviser at party strategy meetings, and the dispenser of millions of New Deal relief program dollars. And though he considered himself a big businessman, Hague was careful to mouth New Deal sympathy for the underprivileged when he was with New Dealers or on the speaker's platform.

The man who sailed to Europe in the royal suite, went to lush Hot Springs, Arkansas, merely to shoot a round of golf, toured Africa like a potentate, and carried a thick bankroll of big bills, told crowds: "My life has been spent with the poor, humble Christian people. In standing by the poor, I propose to die for them, and live for them, and fight for them." This pretense of favoring welfare legislation paid off handsomely for him, for it brought his county and city more than $100 million in Federal largesse and gave him personal control over thousands of Federal patronage jobs in New Jersey that otherwise would not have been his.

Long before Roosevelt moved into the White House, Hague's profession of unity with the poor had been put to the acid test, and he revealed himself to be fanatically antilabor. However, confusion on this point had existed during the twenties because of his close association with Theodore "Ted" Brandle, an iron worker who had become president of his local union, of the state building trades council, and of the state Federation of Labor.

"Hagueism" and "Brandleism" became the rallying charge of

the Republicans as the twenties faded and the thirties began. Hagueism, of course, meant ruthless boss rule; Brandleism, harsh labor
racketeering. Contractors knew they could not get construction jobs
unless they made payments to Ted Brandle and also sent part of
their take to the Hague machine's campaign chest. In addition,
Brandle seemed to be coming at them from several directions simultaneously, for he had his own construction companies, a bank, a
loan company, and a bonding firm; and he headed the truck owners
association. Millionaire Brandle had only to threaten a strike, or
tight money, or the nondelivery of supplies to get his way.

By 1932 the Depression had grown deep-seated, and many companies that had survived the shock of dwindling business laid plans
to leave the county and avoid further high tributes to Brandle. In
alarm, Hague met with these employers and promised them freedom
from Brandle's exactions and strike threats if they remained.

Soon afterward, Hague showed his sincerity by letting a nonunion company get a contract to build part of the $21 million Pu-
laski Skyway. When Brandle got wind of the contract, he called a
strike of his iron workers against this firm.

Hague ordered Brandle to call off his strike, and when Brandle
refused, the mayor publicly labeled him "a gorilla labor leader." Violence came in the soggy marshlands with a clash between Brandle's
pickets and the nonunion workers. When one worker died, Hague
had his police arrest more than twenty pickets on a charge of murder. The crushing blow to Brandle descended after Hague's infiltra-
tors packed the union hall and voted to oust their president. With
the strike smashed and Brandle ruined, Hague bragged, "We simply
cleaned the place out. We didn't allow pickets; we didn't allow anything then."

With Brandle destroyed, Hague proceeded to turn Jersey City
into an open-shop town at the very time that President Roosevelt
was strengthening labor union rights to collective bargaining
through Federal legislation. Hague got rid of the most troublesome
local unions by having his judges declare them bankrupt, even
though they had healthy assets. Then the judges appointed Hague
machine lawyers to serve as receivers, and these attorneys milked
the union assets dry through mammoth receivership expenses that
were readily approved by the judges.

To nip any labor squabbles, Hague judges on the Chancery
Court were under the boss' orders to issue swiftly injunctions that

barred strikes, union meetings of the squabblers, union ads in newspapers, and the distribution of leaflets. If the Chancery Court judges were slow, Hague prevented picketing by having his police department rule that no strike existed: without a strike, there could be no picketing. Still another major weapon was the New Jersey Disorderly Persons Act of 1936 that Hague pushed through the legislature. This law gave police the power to arrest anyone "on foot or in any vehicle who cannot give a good account of himself." The American Bar Association found that under this law Hague's police dragged to jail persons brave enough to picket, and their bail was set so high that they were forced to stay in their cells until the strike was crushed.

The creative boss found many other ways to keep highly industrialized Jersey City from becoming an organized union town. On the pretense that their union heads were criminals, he broke up many locals. In his ungrammatical way, he described his action in one instance: "I found that four gangsters was the head of that union. I drove them out of the city and disorganized the union." His principal method to "disorganize," he said, was "to apply nightsticks on an element of that character; and we will apply it again tomorrow if they make their appearance." Hague closed other unions by denying them meeting halls, driving their leaders out of town, and ordering printers not to publish their literature.

The supreme test of Mayor Hague's antilabor program came in 1937 when the Congress of Industrial Organizations (the CIO) undertook a drive to organize workers on an industry-wide basis in Jersey City. All of Hague's tried and tested techniques were put into play. The first CIO action was to call a Hudson waterfront strike of seamen when shipowners refused to recognize the union as a bargaining agent. But Hague declared that no strike existed, making picketing illegal and grounds for imprisonment.

The next CIO drive came late that year when union personnel attempted to pass out folders explaining the rights of workers under the National Labor Relations Act of 1937. The American Bar Association reported the results: "Police officers stationed at the Hudson Tube stations stopped and attempted to turn back all persons identified as CIO." Inside Jersey City, "police seized and searched without warrants persons and automobiles, confiscated on the spot all CIO literature found." Those caught distributing literature "were forced to proceed on ferries going to New York, forcibly placed on such ferries and transported to New York, despite protests that they were Jersey City or New Jersey residents." The police also "forced many persons into automobiles and caused them to be transported outside the limits of Jersey City."[3]

Despite all this physical handling of CIO people, Hague managed to avoid the national spotlight until he ordered seven of the leaflet distributors jailed without a jury trial. " 'I am the law,' Hague," the liberal press labeled him, using Hague's own words.

Just before the outbreak of the CIO troubles in November, 1937, Hague had used these words in an entirely different context. In a speech on juvenile delinquency at a local Methodist Church, Hague had attempted to prove he had a heart overbrimming with compassion for the young. For his clinching example, Hague cited the case of two boys arrested as repeated truants who were brought to a police station while Hague happened to be there. The boys told him they wanted to quit school and work even though they were underage. But the head of the bureau of special services said that the law did not permit this, ordering jail instead for such truants.

"Who the hell are those guys to say a boy ought to be sent to a reform school?" Hague claimed he yelled at his bureau chief. "Frank Hague was a problem child. Suppose those guys sent him to an institution? They'd have made him sore. He'd have learned how to be real bad, and he might have come out 'Frank Hague, the public enemy,' instead of 'Frank Hague, the first citizen of his city and leading citizen of New Jersey.' "

When the bureau chief repeated that he could not issue work papers to the boys, Hague said he pounded on the table and told him, "Listen here! I am the law! Those boys go to work!"

So the mayor became " 'I am the law,' Hague" to the reporters on hand to describe the struggle between him and the CIO.

Hague believed that by a show of total resistance he could throttle the CIO indefinitely. Unable to picket or pass out leaflets, the CIO tried to rent halls for mass meetings in Jersey City. But Hague called the owners of the buildings, and as he later bragged, "A mere expression from me is sufficient for the owners to know they are not working within the proper scope."

Frustrated again, the labor organizers declared they would hold an outdoor meeting in Jersey City shortly before Christmas in

[3] Report of the Committee on Civil Rights of the Junior Bar Conference of the American Bar Association (1938), pp. 18–19.

1937. Once more Hague proved the spoilsport by denying a permit for this fresh-air gathering on the ground that it violated a 1930 ordinance prohibiting permits for public assembly when the police chief believed such action necessary to "prevent riots, disturbances, or disorderly assemblages."

A great outcry greeted Hague's decision to bar an open-air meeting place to the CIO, and several organizations and individuals requested permits for outdoor meetings in order to shame the mayor. An organization numbering New York racket buster Tom Dewey and Mayor Fiorello LaGuardia in its membership asked for a permit and was haughtily denied one. Two members of the U.S. House of Representatives, John Bernard of Minnesota and Jerry O'Connell of Montana, made an attempt to hold a permitless meeting. The meeting was held, but Hague prevented the congressmen from speaking by assembling a group of veterans in Journal Square. The din was so great there and the brandishing of weapons so commonplace on the meeting day that the two men were forced to cancel their speeches. Later, the American Bar Association reported that O'Connell was taken into "protective custody" by the police.

Hague's technique in dealing with the CIO and its friends was not entirely negative. Over radio and in public speeches, he called himself the champion of Americanism and asked his listeners to join him in a holy crusade "to keep out the Communist agitators of the CIO."

He drummed up programs for patriotic recitals in the schools, sought endorsements from church and civic leaders, and established Americanization Day parades and meetings. The man who attended 10:30 Mass every Sunday at St. Aedans had no trouble getting Catholic clergy to praise him as "America's public enemy number one of communism." Nor with his control over the city and county payrolls did he experience any difficulty in drawing enormous throngs at his Americanization Day celebrations.

Despite all of Hague's clever footwork and strongarm manners, the issue between him and the CIO passed from the streets to the courts in January, 1938. Joined by the American Civil Liberties Union, the CIO asked the Federal District Court in Newark, which Hague did not control, for an injunction forcing Hague to issue a permit for a meeting place. The trial finally took place the following June, and Hague treated the court to a loud three-day attack on the CIO.

In October, Judge William Clark issued a 15,000-word decision that ordered Jersey City to abstain from interfering with the right of the plaintiffs to pass out leaflets, "move freely in Jersey City ... and to address public meetings in the parks."

While the CIO and ACLU rejoiced at the decision, Hague told reporters that Judge Clark had not found unconstitutional the Jersey City ordinance that required permits for public meetings. Hague added that he planned to continue keeping "radicals and Reds" from the city. He also appealed to the United States Circuit Court to overturn Clark's decision, and when he lost here he went to the United States Supreme Court, only to suffer defeat again. In this final court, the permit-requirement ordinance was declared unconstitutional.

However, Hague was not a trounced, dispirited boss even on learning the Supreme Court's opinion. Instead, he invited CIO representatives to a meeting at city hall, and afterward he undertook his practiced campaign to tie the CIO to his organization. Four years later the CIO endorsed him for mayor.

Despite his troubles with the CIO and Roosevelt's mounting distaste for him, Hague's political power did not diminish during the thirties. There were several social historians who predicted that the day of bosses like Hague and others about the country was on the wane because their bushels of coal and baskets of food to voters who were poor could not begin to compete with the billions of dollars of Federal welfare handouts. Yet locally, Frank Hague's continued domination of his fiefdom's election machinery and the various citizens' groups remained so complete that he was able to boast with accuracy after the 1937 municipal election, "Recently I was re-elected by an almost unanimous vote."

Mayor Hague's authority over state legislation also remained strong, thanks to his agent, Alexander Crawford, who served as clerk to the assembly's Democratic leader, and Jersey City Criminal Court Judge Louis Paladeau, who was Hague's lobbyist with the state legislature and told Hague's legislative puppets how to vote.

Hague had started the Roosevelt era with his lieutenant, Harry Moore, in his second term as governor. Then when smiling Harry's term expired in 1934, he rewarded him by sending him to the Senate to team with Congresswoman "Aunt Mary" Norton as his patronage agents. While Hague and Moore were loud backers of FDR for a second term in the White House in 1936, Moore turned out to be a conservative Senator. He mystified New Dealers by some of the stands he took, such as his position against Social Security legislation on the ground that "it would take the romance out of old age."

The mayor's effort to have another Hague governor as Moore's successor in 1934 came to naught when he ran Judge Dill again. Observers believed that he cost Dill much support outside of Hudson County by his intemperate, rough, ungrammatical speeches throughout the state in the judge's behalf.

Nevertheless, Hague was not a loser when Republican Harold G. Hoffman beat Dill. For the new governor was willing to give Hague about half the state's patronage, plus contracts and judges for his support of a sales tax bill that Hoffman had campaigned against the previous fall. "That little fellow, he's a million," Hague praised Hoffman sincerely. Years later there were those who concluded that Hoffman had permitted Hague to boss him because the mayor had come upon his secret. Before he died in 1954, Hoffman left a sealed envelope containing his confession to stealing $300,000 of public funds while serving as commissioner of motor vehicles and governor.

Republican leaders, angry at Hoffman's handling of the Lindberg baby kidnapping case and furious at his business association with Hague, sought to humiliate him in 1936. Hoffman was running that year for a delegate-at-large seat in the New Jersey delegation to the Republican National Convention, and he suddenly found himself faced with a highly popular Republican as an opponent. However, Hague decided the outcome by ordering his crowd to vote in the Republican primary. Hoffman's five to one lead in Hudson County was the result. "What's wrong with it?" Hague asked with a shrug when questioned about his role in sending Hoffman to the Republican convention. "My boys have just as much right to be independent as George Norris or La Follette, haven't they?" "If most politics is queer, New Jersey politics is queerer," the *New York Times* editorialized.

In 1937 Hague ordered Harry Moore to resign from the Senate and come home to run for a third term as governor. Even though he wanted badly to stay in Washington, Moore did as Hague wished because Hague was concerned that no other friendly Democrat could defeat the Republican nominee, the Rev. Dr. Lester H. Clee, head of the party's Clean Government faction. And despite Moore's personal vote pull, he would still have been drubbed had

Hague not pulled off perhaps the biggest vote swindle of his career.

Stung by this suspicious Moore victory, Clee did a little potshot checking. The vote in one district of the first ward in Jersey City was 443 for Moore and only one for Clee; yet in the earlier Republican primary there had been 103 Republican votes. Also a swift spot-check of a few pages of the Hudson County registration roll books led to a conclusion that the total rolls contained at least 50,000 fraudulent registrations.

When Clee deposited the $10,000 required for a recount, Hague moved swiftly to thwart him. First, he refused to let Clee examine any of the election materials without a court order. Second, he made full use of his legal associates in public office to prevent him from getting this. When Clee petitioned Chief Justice Thomas Brogan, a former Hague corporation counsel and personal attorney, for permission to compare signatures in registration rolls with those at polling booths on election day, Brogan summarily denied the request. Clee next tried a different approach by having friends on a state assembly committee ask for Jersey City's poll books. But Attorney General David Wilentz, who blessed Hague as "my political benefactor," ruled that a legislative committee could not examine registration books without the invitation of a city administration or a governor. Another Hague judge then ruled that the committee was an unconstitutional body because it was illegally attempting to take on duties of a court.

With the Clee move squashed, Hague expected a personal bonus from jovial, talkative Harry Moore for installing him in the governor's chair for a third time, and he got it. Hague associates spoke of an order from the boss whereby Moore would hold his Senate seat until he was sworn in as governor in order to prevent outgoing Governor Hoffman from appointing his successor in the Senate; then once Moore was governor he would appoint Hague to take his seat in the upper chamber.

However, while Hague was known to covet a Senate seat, his growing controversy with the CIO organizers at that time and rumors of a Justice Department investigation of his earnings gave him pause. In addition, there was talk that the Senate Committee on Privileges and Elections had begun to collect data on Hague's connection with Jersey City's "Horse Bourse" for interrogation purposes should Moore name him as his replacement.

Over radio, Frank Hague had boasted that Jersey City was the "most moralest [sic] city in America": Prostitution and burlesque shows were banned, and women could not patronize bars. Yet he failed to mention that Jersey City functioned as the stock exchange for the American horse-racing, bookmaking world. Westbrook Pegler, the leading investigative reporter of his time, called Jersey City "the Wall Street of the horse-gambling business." Pegler also noted that as "a protected racket handling millions of dollars it would not exist an hour if the local administration were not interested in its preservation." The plausible inference was that the mayor collected a share of the "take" and told his police not to interfere with its activities. For the bookmakers operated openly, using elaborate communications systems set up by the New Jersey Bell Telephone Company and Western Union Telegraph to connect their Jersey City centers to race tracks, pool halls, and other betting places throughout the country.

Whatever his final reason, Hague decided not to become a United States Senator. Nevertheless, he carried the drama through to the end. On January 16, 1938, reported the Newark *Evening News*, reporters were called to Hague's office to hear important news. This was Hague's sixty-second birthday, and Governor Moore who was present told him: "This morning it occurred to me that this is your birthday, and that the best birthday gift I could bestow would be an appointment to the United States Senate. . . . I know what you could do for the country in the broader field of the Senate. All your life, you have been battling for the people."

Mayor Hague, said the reporter for the *News*, rose from his desk and put a hand on Moore's shoulder. Then he thanked him and expressed his appreciation, calling attention to the "numerous requests from Democratic leaders and the people" that he accept. "But, Governor, I will have to decline," said Hague. "You know of my activities against the Red group. . . . The people would think that Hague had deserted them, that he was selfish. Sooner than have them misunderstand, I must decline."

So Harry Moore did not appoint Hague to the Senate but instead named John Milton, the mayor's private attorney and business associate. However, Moore bestowed another high honor upon his benefactor, this time on the mayor's son, Frank Hague, Jr.

The junior Hague had led the pampered existence of a son of a wealthy, doting father. Sent to the best private schools, he failed miserably at academic studies, dropping out of Princeton and two law schools. Yet Frank, Jr., mysteriously passed the New Jersey bar exam, though two-thirds of law school graduates failed. It was after Junior had spent a year as an apprentice clerk to a judge that Governor Moore announced his appointment as a member of the state's highest court, the Court of Errors and Appeals. Said Moore, "I know this will make his dad happy."

So Hague in the heyday of his power had many reasons for feeling blessed; and the citizens of Jersey City, Hudson County, and the rest of New Jersey had many reasons for feeling cursed.

As Frank Hague's rule extended well into the thirties, there were many who wondered why President Roosevelt did not prosecute him instead of giving him control of New Jersey's Federal patronage and millions of dollars in Federal work relief projects. In fact, Roosevelt was once asked for an explanation, and he replied, "Suppose Hague were removed from office today and there was an election tomorrow. What do you think would happen?"

The questioner answered, "He would be re-elected."

"Exactly," said Roosevelt. "Don't you think this is a problem for the people of New Jersey?"

The truth was that Roosevelt played along with Hague through most of his first two presidential terms because the boss controlled the state's delegation to the national convention and the presidential electoral vote. If Roosevelt were ever in doubt about Hague's value, the boss provided visible evidence by the enormous crowds he collected whenever the President visited New Jersey. In 1936, for instance, when Roosevelt came to dedicate a $5 million federally financed building in the Jersey City Medical Center complex, Hague had 250,000 cheering onlookers present.

However, in 1939, Roosevelt's basic dislike of Hague came to the fore, and he ordered Attorney General Frank Murphy to go after Hague. But action against Hague evaporated because of the boss' understanding of the Attorney General's character. The redheaded, beetle-browed Murphy came to Jersey City, and Governor Moore was on hand to greet him and serve as his host. Murphy had once been mayor of Detroit and governor of Michigan, and Moore soon had him exchanging tales of their experiences. Jersey City, Moore repeated, had "no vice, no crime, no racketeering"—a favorite slogan of Frank Hague. Murphy should have known better because J. Edgar Hoover, his FBI director, for years had been calling

Jersey City's low crime figures falsified statistics. But he ate some excellent meals and Moore took him to the John Marshall College of Law, where he was awarded an honorary LL.D. degree after hearing from the dean about the heartwarming lecture Governor Moore had recently delivered there on "Ethics."

When he returned to Washington, Murphy did no further work on preparing a case on Hague. And when he left the department in January, 1940, to become an Associate Justice on the Supreme Court, the Hague file was labeled "unfinished business." No future Attorney General was to finish that business.

In 1940, when the Nazis overran France, President Roosevelt named two Republicans to his cabinet in order to gain bipartisan support for his defense effort. One of these Republicans displaced Charles Edison, the almost deaf son of Thomas Alva Edison, the great inventor. But in displacing him, Roosevelt felt he owed a debt to dedicated and honest Charles Edison, who had been the prime mover in the navy's intensive warship-building program; and when Edison said he would like to be governor of New Jersey, the President assured him he would talk to Frank Hague.

This was an "iffy" promise, as Roosevelt well knew, because Hague was at an all-time high in arrogance. Recently he had been quoted in a description of his own power in New Jersey as declaring, "I decide. I do. Me."

It was Postmaster General Jim Farley, the chairman of the Democratic National Committee, who called Vice-Chairman Hague about Edison. Hague had permitted Edison to hold various New Deal posts in New Jersey in the early Roosevelt years, and having found him an easily managed person, he gave Farley his consent. Years later, Farley claimed he had called Roosevelt after his talk with Hague and had expressed concern. "Hague is a hard taskmaster, and he might want Charley to keep certain obligations that Charley wouldn't want to fulfill," Farley had told Roosevelt. "I don't think it would be fair to Charley to get him involved. He's an honorable man."

However, Farley's misgivings about an Edison-Hague alliance proved to be without foundation. In August, 1940, Hague collected almost 200,000 Democrats and delivered them by chartered trains and buses to Sea Girt to hear Edison's first campaign speech. Hague was reported to have fumed when the mild candidate with the big hearing aid declared: "If you elect me, you will have elected a gov-

ernor who has made no promises to any man. You can be sure that
I'll never be a yes-man except to my conscience." But Hague gave
this outburst little thought afterward, for he considered it campaign
fluff.

In that fall's politicking, Republican presidential nominee
Wendell Willkie vowed to put Hague behind bars if he won the
election. This may not have frightened the mayor, yet he personally
saw to it that both Roosevelt and Edison carried the state. Roosevelt
came into Hudson County 101,500 votes behind Willkie; but with
Hague's plurality of 173,000 votes, he carried New Jersey by 71,500.
Edison fared half as well, though he won. He was 64,000 behind
with Hudson County uncounted; and by the end of the evening with
a plurality there of 108,000 over Republican Robert Hendrickson,
his winning margin was 44,000.

From his first day in office, Governor Edison showed he meant
what he had said at Sea Girt. Governor Moore had installed a special
telephone connecting his office directly with a phone in Mayor
Hague's city hall room; and when this was pointed out to Edison, he
angrily ripped the wire out of the wall.

Hague shrugged off this action as a childish display, but only
a week later he was ready to do some ripping himself. The cause
was the filling of a vacancy on the State Supreme Court, the second
highest court in New Jersey. Hague sent word to Edison that he
should appoint one of his machine men, "whose vote you can depend
on in a pinch." Edison's retort was that he was going to end "Jersey
justice" of the Hague variety. He followed up on his threat days
later by nominating Frederic R. Colie, a Republican attorney from
Newark, who had spearheaded the opposition to the appointment of
Frank Hague, Jr., to the state's highest court.

This was the end. Hague was vacationing in the splendor of his
Florida holdings when he learned about the Colie appointment. In a
blasphemous mood he put through a call to Edison's office in Trenton. "I'm going to break you, Charley, if it's the last thing I do," he
warned the governor in a conversation replete with obscenities.
"You're a damned ingrate . . . a Benedict Arnold!"

Edison succeeded in winning confirmation for Colie in the state
senate despite the effort of Judge Paladeau, Hague's too dapper and
perfumed legislative lobbyist. But Paladeau was better prepared for
Edison's next move, which was to rid the patronage-heavy state
highway department of its commissioner who was a Hague friend.

It took Edison a year before he could get the state senate to vote on the new man he nominated, and he won confirmation by threatening to investigate the activities of the highway commission.

The governor's momentum carried him through the next confrontation with Hague, which was a public brawl over radio and in full-page newspaper ads on the issue of railroad taxation. Hague wanted to soak the railroads despite their poor earnings while Edison proposed a lower assessment. Before Edison won legislative approval of his plan, his ads told newspaper readers that "Mayor Hague is trying with calculated abuse to pay me off for the appointment of Justice Frederic Colie."

Thanks to President Roosevelt, Edison's impressive victories over Hague came to an abrupt end in 1942 when a vacancy appeared on the Federal bench for the northern district of New Jersey. Roosevelt sent the request to name the next judge to Hague instead of to Governor Edison.

When Hague chose Thomas F. Meaney, an insignificant Hudson County judge, Governor Edison went to Washington to fight the nomination in hearings before the United States Senate Judiciary Committee. There Edison disclosed that Meaney had performed in a highly questionable manner as a court-appointed counsel in the liquidation of a large Jersey City bank. Edison had fired him because he had accepted a large fee from a special group to work against the interests of the general depositors. "The people," testified Edison, "will always be dubious of the quality of justice obtainable from a judge who all his life has been a part of, and obligated to, a sordid political machine."

But Hague had no intention of taking another shellacking from Edison, and he put his team to work to get Meaney confirmed as a Federal district judge. Harry Moore, at his genial best, strolled through the Senate office building and put in several good words for Meaney with his former colleagues. And Congresswoman "Aunt Mary" Norton, chairman of the House Labor Committee, testified before the Senate Judiciary Committee that Governor Edison was "the most arrant hypocrite that ever walked in New Jersey." Then at Hague's insistence, she went to see President Roosevelt and insisted that Meaney was a fine person with an outstanding legal ability despite Edison's charges and the sour report by the Justice Department on Meaney's background and lack of qualifications.

The result was that overworked Roosevelt revealed an annoyance with Edison for fomenting trouble and asked his assistants on Capitol Hill to push for Meaney's confirmation. Even so, the former county judge barely made it to the Federal bench in a close Senate vote.

Hague's victory on the Meaney issue was not an omen of peace or compromise between him and Edison. The governor stormed back by firing the entire five-man Hudson County tax board for assessing property strictly on the basis of the owner's standing with the Hague machine. But not long after Edison named a new tax board, a Hague-selected grand jury indicted its president on the false charge that he was a draft dodger. A second official found himself the defendant in a fraudulent suit involving $150,000.

Still another revengeful action by Hague came when Mayor James J. Donovan of Bayonne in Hudson County said some kind things about Edison. County papers soon carried headlines that Donovan and other Bayonne officials had been indicted for permitting vice to flourish. Then there was poor John Longo, earlier railroaded to jail by Hague because of his public opposition to the mayor. Edison appointed Longo as deputy clerk of Hudson County in February, 1943, and Hague now railroaded him to prison again with the trumped-up charge that Longo had altered his own voter registration record to change his party designation from Republican to Democrat. A Hague-controlled jury found Longo guilty and a Hague judge gave him eighteen months to three years.

Hague felt more relaxed about his political future when Edison entered the last year of his three-year term in 1943. At his New Year's Day reception, Hague told his boys that Harry Moore was going to run in the September primary. Although Moore kept his smile on during Hague's pitch, he told his boss afterward that he did not want a fourth term. Hague did not consider this seriously, but throughout that spring and into the summer Moore continued his refusal.

Finally, after a meeting to settle the issue, Hague broke with Moore in vindictive rage. Organizations that customarily invited Moore as a speaker were told to drop him. "More important, perhaps," wrote Professor Dayton McKean, a deep student of Hagueism as it occurred, "word went out from city hall that Moore was to be kicked around by Hague judges and prosecutors when he appeared in court."

Because of the time Hague spent trying to force Moore to run, he was without a candidate when the deadline for filing came in the summer of 1943. The Edison forces hee-hawed at the mayor, for the governor had a candidate to succeed himself: Newark's Mayor Vincent J. Murphy, a plumber who had risen to the post of secretary-treasurer of the State Federation of Labor before entering politics. This left Hague with two alternatives once Murphy won the September primary. He could make a deal with the Republican nominee to throw the machine's votes to him in the general election, or he could take Murphy over and make him his candidate instead of Edison's. The Republican candidate was seventy-three-year-old Walter Edge, whom Hague had put into office back in 1916 rather than permit his enemy, Otto "The Dutchman" Wittpenn, to become governor.

However, in 1943, Hague chose to woo Murphy instead of throwing the election to Edge again. Murphy proved so amenable to Hague that Edison woke up close to election day with the realization that his handpicked candidate was campaigning in opposition to his own position on major issues. Besides being physically almost deaf, the double-crossed Edison turned voiceless by choice on the subject of Murphy during the rest of the campaign. The result was that anti-Hague Democrats outside of Hudson County made a poor turnout on election day; and despite Hague's heavy plurality for Murphy in his county, Walter Edge emerged the winner.

Although Hague's war with Charles Edison seemed at the time to be a passing episode in the mayor's long career, it proved to be the beginning of the end for one of the most dictatorial bosses in American history. The image of the invincible man who could take on national and state authorities with impunity was now eroded.

So was his actual power. No longer did he own a governor who would appoint a Hague attorney general, a county prosecutor, or a highway board that would give him control of half the state's budget. Nor could he any longer order the four judges of the county common pleas courts to punish his enemies in criminal and civil suits, for the occupants of this bench, who were so important to him, were also appointed by the governor.

Besides having successive governors who were unfriendly to him, Hague now discovered he had lost his touch for putting his sponsored candidates into office. In 1944, he failed to put his man into the Senate; and when he tried again in 1946, his candidate lost by a whopping 250,000 votes. In 1946, Hague was further chagrined when his machine vote in Hudson County was not sufficient to prevent victory for the Republican gubernatorial candidate, Alfred E. Driscoll. As for his own candidacy, Hague won his eighth four-year term as mayor in the spring of 1945, but his margin was not so one-sided as it had been in the past—as in 1937, for instance, when his total was 110,743 to 6,798 for his opponent.

With the end of World War II, Hague was beset with several severe problems. Returning servicemen, filled with hope for a better world, blamed Hague personally for what they saw in Jersey City. Hague's boasts about the Medical Center failed to balance the endless blocks of sordid slums that Federal officials labeled "unfit for human habitation," or the choking tax rate and the rough police.

Within the machine there was also trouble. Young ward heelers could not rise because Hague would not enforce a retirement program for old but loyal lieutenants. As one young grumbler put it, "All we can look forward to is funerals." Then there were the Italians, Germans, and Poles, who believed that Hague's rewards went only to Irishmen.

In neighboring Hoboken, where the identical conditions were mirrored, Mayor Bernard "Barney" McFeely faced re-election on May 13, 1947. Twenty-one years earlier, Hague had installed him in office, and Barney had acted as a smaller edition ever since that time. Barney had fared almost as well, managing to save about $3 million on his $5,000 annual salary as mayor, and his ability to cow opponents would have received a high grade from Hague.

But 1947 brought McFeely a new experience. Young citizens were noisy for a change that promised civic improvement, and they helped form a "Fusion" ticket of dissident Democrats and reform elements. McFeely was shocked on election day when the Fusion slate of five commissioners ran far ahead of his ticket and forced him out of public office.

Hague was also stunned by the Hoboken happening. A quick check of his own organization revealed his situation was hardly better, for he found that a large-scale rebellion was about to explode. And the greatest piece of irony was that the leader for trouble within the machine was John V. Kenny, son of Nat Kenny, the Horseshoe saloonkeeper who had sponsored Hague in his first election for constable back in 1897!

Hague had made a protégé of young John Kenny, weaned him

on machine maneuvers, given him the second ward to operate on his own, and considered his rise to millionaire's status with pride. Now little dark Kenny was plotting Frank Hague's undoing with other lieutenants of the machine.

Hague had lost his sure touch, for instead of mollifying Kenny by promoting him, he expelled him. This produced increasing fights with the Kenny faction which expanded its numbers under the excitement. There were still two years of Hague's term as mayor remaining, but these were certain to be two years of public brawling with the warring Kenny crew. So Hague developed what he believed was a foolproof plan for avoiding a public war with Kenny while retaining political control. He would name a puppet mayor immediately and continue to run the city and county from offstage.

"Hague retires," the *New York Times* announced on June 5, 1947. Hague told reporters that after thirty years of running Jersey City, he was turning over the mayor's office to his nephew, forty-six-year-old Frank Hague Eggers, the commissioner of parks. "The time has come," said seventy-one-year-old Hague, "to pass the heavy burden of administrative duties to younger men."

On that day 4,000 insecure local government employees who had known no other master filed past his room at city hall to shake his hand. Outdoors, when word spread throughout the county, there was great rejoicing among his enemies. John Longo, twice framed by Hague, spent the day riding through the streets in a jeep covered with messages that read: "Good Riddance." A beaming former Governor Edison was quoted as saying, "Hague evidently thinks it is better to desert the ship before being thrown overboard."

But all of Hague's opponents proved too hasty in their joy, for Mayor Eggers showed himself to be only a figurehead who did nothing without first consulting his uncle. In addition, Hague continued to go to Washington on national party matters as New Jersey's Democratic national committeeman and vice-chairman of the national committee. Furthermore, President Harry S. Truman, who had succeeded to the Presidency on the death of Franklin Roosevelt in April, 1945, funneled all Federal patronage in New Jersey through Hague.

The aging boss' goal was to weaken John Kenny's forces and elect Eggers to a four-year term in May, 1949. But Hague committed another error in 1948 that damaged his cause. His was one of the loudest voices promoting General Dwight D. Eisenhower for the

Democratic presidential nomination and hooting at Truman as a man who "didn't have a chance" against the Republicans in November, even if he won the nomination in July. When Truman embarrassed the professional polltakers by defeating Thomas E. Dewey in November, 1948, he remembered Hague's activities and began channeling patronage in Kenny's direction.

On quitting public office, Hague had no idea how rapidly the old fear of him would vanish. At opening-day ceremonies at the Jersey City Giants baseball season in the spring of 1949, the International League honored the former mayor by declaring "Frank Hague Day" at the ballpark and presenting him with a plaque. But the booing was so loud and sustained that Hague's speech could not be heard. Then during the campaign between the five-man commissioner slate headed by Eggers and the Fusion "Freedom for All" slate led by Kenny, Hague did not prove to be a drawing card at most rallies. His worst experience was on May 3 when he went to the Horseshoe to speak and was pelted with overripe vegetables and drowned out by jeers. When Kenny's ticket swamped the Eggers slate on May 10, the Hague era was over.

"It's a funny thing," said Kenny. "If Hague hadn't thrown me out, I probably would still be a member of his machine."

In the 1950s, the man who had won his first political race more than a half century earlier still dreamed of regaining his old power. "I stay in politics. It's in the blood," he said. Disillusion soon set in about the Kenny regime, for the new mayor had learned his lessons at the feet of his old mentor, and his methods were imitative of Hague's. At the beginning of 1953, discontent with Kenny seemed so widespread that Hague once more backed an Eggers slate against the Kenny gang in that spring's commission election. The results were close, but not good enough, for Kenny and two others in his organization won, giving Kenny a majority over Eggers and another Hague man.

Afterward, Hague resigned from the national committee, and he spent his time betting on the horses, sitting at ringside at championship fights, and in a highpriced box at world series games. He led the life of a retired millionaire, though occasional lawsuits broke the peaceful pattern. He had called an opponent a "tax racketeer" in the 1940s, bringing on a libel suit that dragged along for eleven years before Hague settled the case out of court. In another suit that was never completed, the city attempted to recover an alleged $15 million that Hague was charged with taking from city and county employees as wage assessments for campaign purposes.

"In the Horseshoe I was born, and in the Horseshoe I will die," Hague was fond of telling crowds in his days of power. But when he died on January 1, 1956, two weeks before his eightieth birthday, he was living in a posh Park Avenue apartment in New York City.

Oddly, some of the old-timers who had spent their lives under Hague's iron rule, when told of his passing, remembered not the " 'I am the law,' Hague" but the man who always held a friendly New Year's Day reception throughout his reign. As for Kenny, he had learned too well from the master boss, and in time he would be another Hague, oppressing Jersey City and the county, and enriching himself in the process.

Chapter Two

ED CRUMP
Plan Your Work and
Work Your Plan

W HEN a tall, skinny, redheaded boy of eighteen with a few years of schooling and a Mississippi drawl boarded the Illinois Central's dingy coach train for Memphis, Tennessee, one morning in 1893, he would have been labeled mad had he boasted that within a decade he would be on his way to becoming the total master of that city. Yet through native craftiness, ambition, brains, and an immense understanding of the weaknesses of his fellow men, Edward Hull Crump, Jr., from Holly Springs, Mississippi, managed to do just this. Even more, he came to rule surrounding Shelby County just as thoroughly and extended his bossdom to make and break governors as well.

Crump was only two years older than Frank Hague, but he gained power long before the Jersey City dictator. "Plan your work and work your plan" was Crump's byword. In the flush of his power, Crump enjoyed telling underlings that his success resulted from following that aphorism and others he scribbled on note pads. "Observe, remember and compare" was another thought to live by. So were "Read, listen and ask"; "Nothing worthwhile is easy and easy things are not worthwhile"; "Everybody must work"; and "Never put a sponge on the end of a hammer if you expect to drive a nail."

This explanation was too simple and pat for those who tried to discover how a single person could paralyze more than 200,000 citizens of Memphis day in and day out, year after year after year. Similarly unconvincing was Crump's further belief that his red hair made him a child of destiny. A newspaper clipping preserved from early youth noted that "the greatest men of this world were red-headed, from bold adventurers to kings." Redheads, said the clipping, were able to "keep their brains alert and active under conditions which make men of other complexions dull and despondent."

The wiry, blazing hair came from his mother's side, the plantation-owning, slaveholding Nelms clan from Anson County, North Carolina, on the South Carolina border. Mollie Nelms married Edward Hull Crump of Mississippi on his return home from service as a lieutenant with the vaunted Confederate Morgan's Raiders. Edward Hull Crump, Jr., born on October 2, 1874, was their third child.

Little Ed was four when his father died of yellow fever, and for five years the Crump family was in want. Then an uncle died, leaving Mrs. Crump farmland and a share of a plantation to lease for a regular annual income. In addition, she inherited a house in Holly Springs that had high ceilings and eight tall pillars in front.

In his early years, Ed showed no promise for anything except mischief-making. Enrolled by his mother in the public school, he spent much of his time bedeviling the poor teacher, a wounded Confederate veteran. Finally, at fourteen, Ed quit school and went to work as a typesetter for John Mickle, his cousin, who owned the local newspaper.

After a year with Mickle, he picked cotton one season at the rate of 50 cents a hundred pounds, took a quick course in book-keeping, and went to work as a bill clerk at the general store in Lula, Mississippi. Here he developed chronic indigestion and came home in the spring of 1893 to recover and earn money as the lanky first-baseman for the Holly Springs team.

But young Crump yearned for big-city life, and six months later, with only 25 cents in his pocket he rode the train to Memphis, Tennessee, 60 miles away. He worked first for a cotton house on dirty, smelly Front Street, spent two years at clerical jobs, and in 1896 became a bookkeeper at the Woods Company, an old carriage and saddlery firm. Two years later he was rewarded with a promotion to cashier in charge of the money cage, and in 1900 Crump became secretary-treasurer.

Crump now moved heavily into Memphis' social and business

organizations, and he became interested in local Democratic politics. There was curiosity at the blue-nose Tennessee Club when a member mentioned that Ed Crump was doing some ward heeling in the roughneck fourth ward. But a man had to start somewhere. Then only a few months later, Crump ran in 1901 for delegate to the Shelby County Democratic Convention and won. The following year he won election as a delegate to the state convention and began eyeing paid political offices in the city government. The year 1902 was a vital one for him in other respects. That summer he married Bessie Byrd McLean, whose socially prominent parents provided them with $50,000 to gain control of his company. He was now a man of substance in business and a rising politician.

By the spring of 1903, twenty-eight-year-old Ed Crump had many blessings to count. He had a wife who called him "Rudy" (and would throughout life) because to her he was a modern-day reincarnation of Rudolph Rassyndale, the romantic character of the novel *A Prisoner of Zenda*. He also had his own profitable business, a proper social standing, and friends among the city's top politicians.

"Plan your work and work your plan" became a motto of urgency to him now, for he was eager to promote his chief interest, which was to move from political machine worker to public officeholder. As he analyzed things, there was little likelihood of this if he stayed with Mayor Joe Williams' machine, for the mayor's top and middle-level officeholders seemed set for life in their jobs.

But before he could throw his big hands up in despair, a political highway suddenly opened in 1903 thanks to his cousin, Walker Wellford. Walker, in the wake of the startling revelations of the muckraker writers, led the demand for municipal reforms in Memphis with a public outcry against the blasé attitude of Mayor Williams toward the major ills of the city. Cousin Walker Wellford made his pitch strictly along nonpartisan lines, and he was soon joined by businessmen and ministers, and a demand rose for reforms.

The businessmen were particularly concerned with onerous tax rates, rutted streets, inadequate fire protection, and a foul-up of local mail service. The churchmen and the average citizen found a different focus: The streets were not safe at night; parks were especially dangerous places after dark; 600 saloons made too many citizens tipsy, and drunks were everywhere, lying in stupors on the pavement; prostitutes numbered in the thousands; some alleys were clogged with dice players around the clock; gambling joints were more numerous than grocery stores; and anyone could buy dope in tiny 10 cent boxes at the drugstore.

Worst of all, Memphis was the "murder capital of the country," with a rate far in excess of any other city keeping statistics. Killings were so commonplace along Beale Street, the main thoroughfare of the black ghetto, that the police made no effort to apprehend slayers. The Memphis *Commercial Appeal* editorialized one day that "killing is now the most thriving industry in this part of the country." With thousands of persons carrying guns for protection, it was small wonder that the pistols were used at the slightest pretext.

Cousin Wellford soon gave way to younger "reformers" intent on riding the reform wave into political office. The one who took charge was Kenneth Douglas McKellar, a beetle-browed young lawyer with a bulbous nose, a normal expression of deep indignation, and a foghorn voice. "Kay Dee," as he was called, began by bringing suit to force Mayor Williams to open the city's books. McKellar also organized the Jackson Club, whose goal was to modernize the city's charter and end "political bossism." In 1905, when Williams and his crew came up for re-election, Kay Dee put up his own reform ticket and pushed the old pro back into civilian life.

Kay Dee had his sights set on going to Congress, so he was no candidate for local office. But Ed Crump, whose political ambitions were then strictly local, got on McKellar's ticket in 1905 as a candidate for the board of public works. The board not only handled street construction, lights, and public buildings but also served as the lower house of the mayor's city council, with the board of fire and police commissioners acting as the upper chamber.

This was Crump's big test, and if he failed, he knew he was politically dead. Unfortunately, he confirmed early in the campaign what he had long feared—he was unable to address a large audience. But this ineptness was not fatal, for he was a sincere handshaker and made an excellent impression in person-to-person small talk. Then there was his red hair, which made a lasting imprint on voters who tried to recall the various candidates. Crump's tension on November 9, 1905, gave way to joy when the returns showed he led all fourteen candidates for the board.

Crump assumed he was now on a swift road to power, but after he was in office a few months, he found he was on a footpath. First, as a member of the public works board, he was relegated to supervising the setting of telephone and arc light poles around town. This was hardly a suitable way to get his name in the papers. Second, he noted the pattern of total rejection of all ordinances he introduced. What rankled Crump most was that James Malone, the reform mayor, John Walsh, the vice-mayor, and members of the fire and police commission ignored the presence of the public works board at legislative council sessions. But Crump shrewdly used his unsatisfactory state of affairs to advance himself.

In the summer of 1907, a vacancy appeared on the fire and police commission. If Crump had announced himself as a candidate, he knew the papers would have put him down as just another petty opportunist. So he took the long route by resigning from the inconsequential public works board and blasting the city administration for failing to carry out its campaign pledges. Newspapers now joined in praising him as a true reformer and expressing regret that a man of his caliber was no longer in politics.

After this buildup, Crump declared, as he had planned all along, that he had been talked into running for the fire and police commission. His timing was excellent, and on November 5, 1907, he won the election.

On the very day Ed Crump was sworn in as a police commissioner in January, 1908, he began his drive to become mayor the following year. The work he planned and the plan he worked started with that day's assault on Mayor Malone and Police Chief George O'Haver, with the charge that they were closing their eyes for unknown reasons to after-hours saloon business and gambling joint operations.

While Malone and O'Haver were still stunned by his surprise attack, Crump hastily swore in eighteen friends as deputies; and with a *News Scimitar* reporter in tow, he led the group on a night of dashing raids into several gambling parlors. It was a one-shot affair that had no lasting results, but it landed him the widespread publicity he wanted as "Mr. Crump, the Crusader." What many townfolk remembered after his stunt was his carefully planned explanation: "If Police Chief O'Haver and his men can't suppress gambling in town, I can."

Another part of Crump's plan for winning the mayor's office in 1909 was to paint Malone and the local Democratic organization as an undemocratic lot. Before the beginning of a well-publicized meeting of the Shelby County Democratic executive committee, Crump and his friends discussed ways in which he could disrupt the meeting and appear to be in the right. Then at one point in the proceedings, when the opposition would not recognize him, he shocked everyone as he leaped upon a table "directly in front of the chairman and demanded a roll call," reported the *News Scimitar*. "I say you will never get it," returned the chairman. Also at this same meeting, Crump rendered a plea he had rehearsed to let the citizens of the suburbs vote in the city's Democratic primary. When this was quickly voted down, "Mr. Democracy" was now added to "Mr. Crusader."

Still another vital link in his drive for mayor was his work in taking over the leadership of the civic do-gooders who were wallowing in their inability to bring the commission form of government to Memphis. Many of the most respected local families were involved in this effort, and there was much for Crump to gain by carrying their flag.

Crump gave them a slogan: "The People Shall Rule"; put up a slate of the most influential commission-government supporters to run against the Democratic organization choices for the state legislature; and watched his entire slate win. Then when the next state legislature met in January, 1909, Crump and his lieutenants showed up in Nashville to lobby for a bill to establish a commission government in Memphis. A month later, when the governor signed the measure establishing a mayor-commission set-up for the Bluff City, Crump went home assured of the votes of the reformers.

Crump was now racing toward the climax of his political drive. Months before his August, 1909, announcement that he was running for mayor in the November contest, his friends, his enemies (who were listed in his red notebook), and the newspapers considered him a candidate. But there would be no walk-away win because former Mayor Joe Williams also declared himself a candidate for his old perch in city hall. Crump knew he was in for a hard fight, for Williams owned a large share of the bought Negro vote with his drawer full of poll-tax receipts and had ample funds to entice the blacks to the polls. Three other candidates announced, but none of these three had a chance.

Joe Williams was an excellent speaker, and Crump's spies noted the enthusiasm of his audiences. They also estimated that

Williams' backers had paid 2,000 Negroes to register and had poll-tax receipts for the lot, and with about 6,000 votes needed to win the election, this alone put Williams one-third along the road to victory.

Because he could not deliver a speech, Crump employed substitute speakers to talk in his behalf at large rallies. He smoothed over this strange technique by shaking the hand of everyone present and uttering friendly small talk. "His handshake is so hearty that no one can doubt his sincerity," said the admiring *News Scimitar*. That paper also described the Crump on the 1909 hustings as "all bone and muscle . . . red hair . . . tall and spare . . . and when he stands the calves of his legs bow out backwards like a barrel stave."

Crump also employed two other campaign techniques. The first was the extensive use of newspaper ads extolling himself as the commission government's pilot and attacking the low tax rate set on railroads and utilities. His second technique was a remarkable crowd raiser at street-corner rallies.

This was his use of a band and a theme song, both coming from William C. Handy, who played the trumpet, led the band, and gave birth to wailing songs called the "blues." Handy took a lead from Crump's political platform to write his "E. H. Crump Blues," which went as follows:

> *Mr. Crump won't 'low no easy-riders here,*
> *Mr. Crump won't 'low no easy-riders here.*
> *I don't care what Mr. Crump won't 'low,*
> *I'm gonna barrel house anyhow.*
> *Mr. Crump can go and catch hisself some air.*

What Handy was slyly saying was that the good-time folks on Beale Street did not believe Crump would carry out his campaign promises. But Crump and his helpers offered no objection to the words of the "E. H. Crump Blues" because when Handy and his band played it at street corners, crowds came alive with whistles and cheers, and Crump gained a great deal of good will. (Later Handy changed the words and renamed the song the "Memphis Blues," and it became an American classic. Still later Crump, who did not like the way Handy was gaining national attention, insisted the song had been written a year after the 1909 campaign.)

The November, 1909, election day finally came. Certain that Joe Williams' boys would be working hard to get their quota of illegal black votes, Crump had his own men keep an eye on the polling places in the black fifth ward. During the day Crump made a personal inspection of one polling place in that ward and confronted a Negro with a marked ballot waiting to vote. Crump barred his path, and in the argument that followed, said a reporter, the candidate struck the Negro in the face. Williams did not take Crump's election-day activities without fuming anger and publicly charged that in some precincts favorable to Crump, the redhead's men were throwing out votes for Williams on the flimsiest grounds.

All the boxes were carried at the end of the day to the old courthouse, where they were opened and counted in a second-floor room. The vote between Crump and Williams was so close that the outcome depended on the ballot box that had been brought from a tent set up at Peabody and McLean.

When the contents of this box were added to the previous totals, Crump emerged ahead with 5,894 votes to 5,815 for Williams. By a paltry 79-vote margin, Ed Crump had the beginning of his four decades of control over Memphis.

The fruits of Crump's victory in 1909, however, were not to be immediately enjoyed. Joe Williams proved a spoilsport by suing him for vote fraud. Then the utility companies, fearful that the new mayor would carry out his campaign promises, ordered their lawyers to start court action to have the new commission form of government declared unconstitutional.

But the "Red Snapper," as Crump's friends nicknamed him, weathered both attacks; and after favorable court rulings, he started to consolidate his power. With his two top trusted lieutenants, Frank Rice and Will Hale, he devised the basic machine for his self-perpetuation of authority. Frank Rice, his organizational, election, and legislative aide, had masterminded the Red Snapper's first campaign for director of the Business Men's Club in 1905 and later handled the details that brought Crump into the city council and mayor's highback chair.

Rice was a heavy drinker and given to outbursts of profanity, but his ability and loyalty to Crump were unquestioned. Some called him the "Mr. Hyde" to Crump's "Dr. Jekyll" because he did the necessary dirty work while Crump could appear above the mean tactics he ordered Rice to apply. Besides establishing the Crump organization ward by ward, Frank Rice was a fixture at every session of the state legislature, where he was Crump's personal lobbyist.

Will Hale, pallid in contrast with the boozing, profane Rice, had charge of Crump's county politics. When Crump became mayor, Shelby County was an administrative monstrosity, run like a circus by fifty-two justices of the peace who also had administrative duties. With no central direction or standards, anarchy prevailed. Moreover, the individual justices, dependent on fines for most of their income, had money-sharing arrangements with constables to haul persons into their courtrooms for "trifling infractions of the law, or no infractions of the law."

On Crump's order, Rice and Will Hale combined to bring a revolution to Shelby County's administration in 1911 and give control to their boss. This was done by getting the state legislature to end the administrative duties of the justices of the peace by establishing a three-man county commission. In addition, the number of justices was cut to twenty-two, and fear of further cuts brought on by Crump made the remaining justices friendly and subservient to the Memphis mayor.

Aside from the county and state framework the machine was building for itself, its big job was to bring out a winning number of votes in elections in Memphis. After careful assessment of local conditions, Crump, Rice, and Hale concluded that the basic components of the Red Snapper's voting bloc should be the city's large Negro population and its public employees.

Crump's opinion of the black race was entirely negative, as should have been expected of anyone with his Mississippi-Confederate background. To Crump, Negroes were childish, useful for hard, physical labor under strict guidance, and easily given to thuggery and murder. Yet despite his personal feelings, Crump, like Mayor Joe Williams before him and unlike politicians in other southern states, recognized that a black vote equalled a white vote on election day. He assigned Frank Rice to register blacks in ever larger numbers and buy a sufficient number of poll-tax receipts for them.

Rice made use of policemen in the black wards to shepherd Negroes in wagons and on foot to registration places, many of which were in saloons. In addition, the saloonkeepers cooperated, with the expectancy of special favors from the Crump regime. The *Commercial Appeal*, in a sarcastic jibe at these goings-on, reported that "all the dive keepers are now enthusiastic and registering bums, black and white, that make business for their beer pumps." That newspaper also noted that the August, 1911, registration for the November mayor-commissioners election was the highest in history.

City employees, the other bloc of voters Crump nailed down for himself, were afraid of losing their jobs and therefore easy to control through veiled threats. Crump tarred the entire lot when he first took office by declaring that they must henceforth refrain from accepting gifts, railroad passes, and free meals from those who dealt with the city. He also said that there was too much use of city-owned horses and carriages after work hours, and he ordered all the buggies painted butter-yellow so that any citizen could spot a wrongdoer.

The first test of the ability and industry of the Crump machine came in 1911 when the Red Snapper had to stand for re-election to his second term. As in 1909, Joe Williams was Crump's opponent. But this time Williams knew he had no chance, despite the hard-hitting support of the *Commercial Appeal*. Crump had betrayed his reformer backers, charged C. P. J. Mooney, the paper's railing editor, and "made his commission a one-man organization" that "grasped not only the political machinery of the city, but that of the county." Mooney also took note of the rising murder rate and said that "within gunshot of Court Square or the police station are dives that would not be tolerated in the tenderloin of a mining town."

A week before the November, 1911, election, 1,400 city employees paraded through the streets carrying pro-Crump signs, and Crump rode in front in his new Premier automobile, acknowledged to be the biggest and most expensive car in town. On election day, thousands of Negroes collected their liquor and money for voting for the mayor. Frank Rice did his job too well, importing one hundred Negroes from an island in the Mississippi to vote for Crump. The extra push was unnecessary, for the election results showed Crump with 11,432 votes to 3,536 for Williams.

What was especially sweet about winning in 1911 was the dividend from the state legislature, which increased the terms of the Memphis mayor and commissioners from two years to four. This meant that Crump would be in power at least until the beginning of 1916 and would have ample time to consolidate his authority with the thoroughness of an absolute ruler. However, the Red Snapper was too impatient, too ambitious, and too greedy to take a leisurely approach, and his self-made troubles almost ruined him before his term expired.

Cocksure Crump had hardly taken the oath of office for a second term when he cast his eyes on the county sheriff, a man who did little work but collected over $30,000 a year in fees. This was several times Crump's own salary, and the idea struck him that he should combine the sheriff's office with that of the mayor. But the office did not become available by election until 1914, and for two years Crump suffered until it was time to announce himself a candidate for sheriff. The reason he wanted to be mayor-sheriff, he told skeptical reporters was "to break up some of the crooked work going on and to meet the assaults upon me personally by the blood-thirsty outs."

It was editor Mooney who spoiled Crump's plan by declaring that state law barred the holding of two offices by one official. Crump asked Frank Rice to get an opinion from the state's attorney general, and when Rice reported that Mooney was right, Crump withdrew from the race. But before Mooney could gloat over his success as a giant killer, Crump announced that his good friend, John Riechman, owner of a successful mill supply company, would be his candidate for sheriff.

This time Mooney appeared to have the last word because Riechman's announced candidacy came too late to put his name on the ballot. But Crump's anger matched his hair, and he was determined that Riechman get the job, even though the only way he could do so was through a write-in vote on the election-day ballots. This brought a loud laugh from Mooney because Riechman needed a substantial Negro vote to win the election, and only a tiny fraction of Memphis blacks could read or write.

But Mooney stopped laughing when Crump sent dozens of white "teachers" along Beale Street to teach the Negro population how to write "Riechman." They came a week before the election with blackboards and chalk and patiently taught Negroes to print the name. In addition, Crump's men hung huge street signs with only "Riechman" written on them, and trucks with the candidate's name on their sides toured the ghetto. In fury, Mooney charged Crump with "seeking to teach a gin-drinking nigger enough to make a mark and write a name."

The test came on August 6 when Crump's Negroes were led to the polls. Admonitions were loud that the "*i* comes before the *e*," for if the name was not spelled correctly the anti-Crump election judges would toss out the ballot. By the end of that day Mooney admitted defeat, for Riechman won by a majority of 8,996 votes over Galen Tate, a former Crump aide whose name was correctly spelled in Crump's Red Book of enemies.

Besides almost overplaying his hand on the sheriff affair, Crump foolishly believed himself so strong that he next took on the utility companies and Tennessee governors on the emotional issue of prohibition. In this instance, he was left on the ropes.

Prohibition had come to Tennessee in 1909 when the state legislature overrode the veto of Governor Malcolm Patterson and voted the state dry. The law was highly unpopular in Memphis where the Anti-Saloon League had never been able to amass a following outside of the city's churches. Crump did not drink or smoke, but he took the legislative action as an infringement on the rights of saloonkeepers, and his expressed position was that the times called for a modern-day repetition of the Jefferson-Madison Virginia and Kentucky Resolutions of 1798, which said that the local community could declare a Federal law unconstitutional. On this basis, Mayor Crump issued a signed statement pledging himself not to enforce the state prohibition law in Memphis.

Although the state made no effort to enforce the law in wide-open Memphis, in 1912 Crump attempted to formalize the wet island of Memphis with Republican Governor Ben Hooper, who was a Prohibitionist. In a meeting with Hooper, Crump offered a deal: He would use his influence with the state legislature to help the governor get his bill approved to end the "back tax collection racket" in exchange for Hooper's promise not to enforce the dry law.

When Hooper refused, Crump declared war on him by calling his own Democratic state convention in Nashville, where Benton McMillen, who was Crump's man, was nominated to oppose Hooper. But despite Crump's hard drive in McMillen's behalf, Hooper won re-election and he sought revenge on Crump. This took the form of a "nuisance act" under which any ten citizens could apply to a state court for an injunction to close a saloon or any other illegal business on the grounds that it constituted a nuisance. Memphis saloonkeepers recognized what this meant, and almost 600 wanted to relinquish their licenses. But with the backing of the city administration they all stayed in business by turning their saloons into "clubs" or "back-door knock-twice" speakeasies.

So things continued in this fashion throughout the rest of Hooper's term. In 1914, Democrat Tom Rye succeeded him as governor, thanks to the help of President Woodrow Wilson's Secretary of State, William Jennings Bryan. Bryan took time off to come from Washington to speak for Rye, despite the outbreak of the European war that summer. With Rye in office, Crump looked forward to the dissolution of the prohibition squabble. But the new governor was in office only a month when he pushed through the legislature a bill to oust any public official who did not carry out the laws of the state. It dawned on Crump then that Bryan, the rabid dry, had campaigned for Tom Rye in exchange for his pledge to do something about Crump and Memphis.

Despite this ouster law, Crump had come to believe he was untouchable. His plan for dominating Memphis had worked so well that in the April, 1915, mayoralty election the Republicans and other Democratic factions had failed to put up a slate to oppose him and his handpicked city commissioners; and with only the tiny Socialist party opposing him, he won election almost unanimously.

But in the course of this campaign among his promises was one pledging to take over the Merchants Power Company of Memphis when its franchise expired in January, 1916. This had frightened the company, and the weight of this opposition spelled great trouble for him.

Shortly after Crump's re-election in 1915, Charles Patrick Joseph Mooney flipflopped the *Commercial Appeal*'s crusading stand against prohibition to a demand for the mayor's ouster for not enforcing the 1909 dry law. It was generally known that Mooney's paper was controlled by the utilities. This ominous editorial change was followed by a visit to Crump's office by Luke Wright, the electric company's lawyer. Wright told Mayor Crump that if he renewed the franchise the electric company would not use its friends to bring an ouster suit against the mayor. "I didn't fall for his taffy," Crump commented on Wright's offer. Wright was a fine one to act so righteously, he added, for "when Luke Wright was attorney general of Shelby County handling cases on a fee basis, women from the red light district were hauled up and fined at intervals."

Intrigue and danger followed Wright's visit, Crump claimed. He said that the private utilities had "the old master, William Pinkerton himself [head of the famed Pinkerton Detective Agency] dogging my tracks day and night. A pistol shot was fired on two different occasions from my side porch, when I was entering my house at midnight."

In October, 1915, Guston Fitzhugh, another utilities lawyer, brought an ouster petition against Crump to the state's attorney general, who then entered a bill against the mayor and his city administration in the Shelby County chancery court for not enforcing prohibition in Memphis. "Put a crimp in Crump," the earlier reformer friends of the mayor now played with words. Crump pleaded innocent, declared the 1909 prohibition law unconstitutional, and requested a jury trial. When the judge ruled against a jury, Crump knew what the verdict would be.

The verdict of the chancery court was that Crump could not continue to serve as mayor; and when the State Supreme Court upheld the ouster bill, the Red Snapper's career appeared at an end. But Crump's lawyers posed an interesting legal question: The ouster applied only to his present term, not to the new term to begin on January 1, 1916; for an official could not be ousted from an office he did not hold.

Fitzhugh also thought of this, however, and obtained a stay order from the supreme court to delay the swearing-in ceremony. Then on February 12, the court ruled that Crump could take office, but another ouster bill could be granted based on his acts during the previous term.

Crump put on a brave show because he had a different plan. Mooney ran a story of the organization's jamboree after the court's ruling:

> Up jumps Mr. Crump, off flies the lid. The suds flowed and the dice rolled as of old amid the glad hosannas of the spear toters. Down on Gayoso Street, blacks milled around flashing half-pints. Stanley Trezevant and other Boys steered Mr. Crump around the happy streets. So much jubilation that Mr. Crump almost made the only public speech of his life: "I feel very grateful to all my friends for their extreme loyalty." By nightfall a big parade started when it began raining. The banners proclaimed, "Down with the Muckrakers! Hurrah for Crump! One for All and All for One!"

Crump had ten days after the February 12 ruling to take the oath of office or resign. Day after day passed with Gus Fitzhugh waiting impatiently for this event to take place so he could begin his second ouster suit. Late on the night of February 21, a few hours before George Washington's birthday, a national holiday, Crump and his fellow commissioners went to the house of John McLemore, the city clerk and a Crump appointee, and took their oaths. Then early the next morning the group met again in the home of a commissioner. Here Crump resigned as mayor and was handed a check for $678.31 for back pay. Then his vice-mayor, Aleck Utley, took the oath as mayor, resigned, and got a check for $439.65 in back pay. Then Thomas C. Ashcroft, a commissioner who had been designated by Crump to serve his four-year term, was sworn in as mayor after the other commissioners went through the formality of electing him to that office.

After word got out that Mayor Ed Crump had resigned from office, the *Commercial Appeal* gloated that a dictator had fallen. But many of Crump's enemies had the uncomfortable feeling that he would be back again one day, while his friends knew he was still in charge of Memphis through his puppet, Tom Ashcroft.

When he packed his belongings and quit his quarters in the new Shelby County courthouse, Crump had cheery waves for his followers who were jammed below the marble columns outside the white stone building. Yet for the first time in his adult life he was worried because he was in a financial bind, and he had a wife and three sons to feed.

Certainly he could have gone into any of dozens of successful firms in town as a welcomed addition, but he knew he had to retain an aura of complete independence if he wanted to continue projecting an image of the lone political leader who ran the city from behind the scenes. Therefore, he had been eyeing the comfortable existence of Harry Litty, who held the elected office of county trustee. This was a profitable sinecure that combined the jobs of county tax collector and treasurer, and what Litty chiefly had to do was to collect his legal fee from every money transaction between Shelby County residents and the county.

Little wonder that Litty howled in pain when he learned that Crump, the Red Snapper, planned to challenge him in the August, 1916, election, for Litty's fees as county trustee ran between $30,000 and $50,000 a year. And little wonder, too, that Crump-hating Charles Patrick Joseph Mooney, the hard-hitting editor of the Memphis *Commercial Appeal*, was enraged when he heard the news, because Mooney believed he had stomped Crump's political career to death by helping to drive him from the mayor's office.

The bitterness of the contest between Litty and Crump was occasioned by the money involved. Litty put it bluntly in his numerous trips around the county when he scoffed at Crump who, he said, had only a single campaign issue, and that was: "I need the money!" Litty was suddenly the statesman, proposing that the fee system for the county trustee be abolished, and he demanded that money-hungry Crump debate him on this issue. Litty's demand was a safe sortie because he knew that despite his immense ego, the former mayor possessed a tongue that lay in his mouth like a heavy anchor whenever he was called upon to speak in public.

Crump may have been silent in public, but in private he spoke in his rapid drawl to those who could help him most. Enterprising editor C. P. J. Mooney knew who these mangy creatures were, and he emphasized to his readers the news that Crump's principal backers were the illegally operating saloonkeepers; and of these, Johnny Margerum was "Crump's friend and loudest shouter."

Mooney was right, for Crump had turned to Margerum and his pouring clan for aid. The friendly saloonkeepers, as helpful as in Crump's better days, bought bushel baskets of poll-tax receipts and busily registered every derelict and vagabond they could haul into their saloons. Then on election day, they carried these pathetic souls, plus Negroes by the wagonload, to the polling precincts, handed them poll-tax receipts, told them to scratch an "X" alongside Crump's name, and slipped them a drink afterward. When the county's returns were tabulated, Crump was the new county trustee, a post he held for eight years while collecting a profitable half million dollars.

From the ignominious position of having been expelled from office and possessing no income, Crump seemed to have made a remarkable recovery in only a few months. Not only did he have an assured income but Tom Ashcroft, the city commissioner whom he had elevated to be his successor, was the complete puppet. In fact, Ashcroft was an embarrassment, telling several persons he considered Crump to be the actual mayor, and he pleaded so fervently for an autographed picture for his office wall that when Crump gave him one he said it would remind him that Crump was everpresent. He did not object when city officials phoned and wrote Crump for advice regarding their work. Nor did he show concern when they explained their actions at meetings by insisting that Crump had told them to do so.

But the burden of walking in a deep crouch eventually proved too much even for a mild man like Tom Ashcroft. The first explosion came when he fired Marvin Pope, his male secretary and Crump's spy in his office. Pope had been Crump's secretary and confidant. While Crump angrily waited for an explanation, Ashcroft instigated legal action to oust his vice-mayor, a man named Tyler McLain, who was a Crump messenger, and Sheriff John Riechman, Crump's old pal. The charge against both was that they were abetting saloons and saloonkeepers.

Crump's reaction to Ashcroft's show of independence was to stamp into the mayor's office one day and pull his autographed photograph from the wall. But he did not reach full rage until he heard that Ashcroft was promoting a bill before the state legislature that would bar any person from holding public office who had been ousted from one within the past ten years. The bill had successfully cleared the house and had gone to the senate before Crump worriedly caught the train for Nashville. Here only hard effort kept it from passing the upper house.

On returning home, Crump declared war against Ashcroft by having lawyers in his organization start legal action to oust the mayor. When Ashcroft was reminded that the local bench was staffed with Crump judges, the mayor considered the situation and his old fears surfaced. Rather than fight for his honor, he announced his resignation shortly before the case reached the calendar's call.

But Crump did not benefit. After Ashcroft's departure, Crump agreed with his machine lieutenants that Harry Litty, his recent foe, should have the support of the Crump friends on the city council to serve out the rest of the mayor's term. However, although Litty enjoyed being mayor, he would not cooperate with Crump. Then when the next mayoralty election came late in 1917, Crump supported Frank Monteverde under the supposition that this nonmachine candidate would be amenable to the county trustee's suggestions. This proved a sad mistake also, for Monteverde reacted to Crump's order to retain the low property tax rate by boosting it 40 percent.

But even with the depressing experience of having three opposing mayors in a row, Crump would not give up. In sly form, he organized a "Committee of 100" to promote a city-manager type of government that would eliminate the office of mayor, and he led a local contingent of reformers to Nashville to lobby Monteverde out of his post.

Both house and senate committees quickly approved the Crump "reform," but it ran aground on the Woodrow Wilson administration's post-World War I repression of civil rights. With a Red scare enveloping Tennessee, the bill was doomed when one of Monteverde's friends fought back after the bill reached the house floor by telling his fellow legislators in a quivering voice that the city-manager plan would lead to a victory for "the dread Bolsheviks."

When the Jazz Age hit Memphis after World War I, Ed Crump was the county trustee and a fading political leader. He suffered still further ignominy in the 1919 mayoralty race when his name was a useful punching bag for Rowlett Paine, an aristocratic-looking young man, who had the blessings of the newly enfranchised women and the do-gooder Citizen's League, and who swept into office along with his entire slate of anti-Crump city commissioners.

At this point, Crump was so far removed from power that all except his closest friends spoke of him in the past tense. In addition, the Red Snapper, now in his mid-forties, was turning gray, and his health appeared in serious decline. He had malaria, a low blood count, and a gallbladder requiring immediate removal.

Crump on the sidelines could only mutter the sour but safe complaints of a politician out of power, and he seemed to be slipping further away from reclaiming authority in 1923 when his candidate for mayor against Paine withdrew on the henpecked grounds that his wife objected. Instead of a Crump ticket, Paine was opposed by a slate put up by the Ku Klux Klan whose ranks were burgeoning with returned veterans.

As the local campaign grew heated, Crump paled even more when he expressed his neutrality in the contest and announced further that he would not seek another term as county trustee in 1924. But coming down to the wire, when political observers rated the Paine-Klan fight an even affair, Crump suddenly bounded onto the scene. With great fanfare, on the day before the election, he sent Frank Rice, Will Hale, Joe Boyle, and others in his organization to Paine's headquarters. Here they rolled up their sleeves, helped on the phones, and worked on last-minute strategy with the surprised Paine crew. Crump also issued a statement that he expected all his friends to support Paine.

The mayor won by just under 4,000 votes as a result of written promises to Negro leaders of aid to the squalid black ghettos where almost 40 percent of Memphis' population lived. But it was Crump who claimed afterward that his final day's support had given victory to Paine. Many believed him because the Negro leaders who had corralled the black vote for Paine now heard themselves denounced by the mayor who no longer needed them.

With his bombastic claim that he had made Paine mayor in 1923 gaining local credence, Crump now began to plan for a return to power in the 1927 local election. He, Frank Rice, and Will Hale tightened and then expanded their organization built on his county trustee following, and Crump began to voice opinions regarding candidates for governor as though he were already a political power. When the man he backed for governor in 1926 lost by a narrow margin, Crump claimed the same credit as he had for Paine's victory in 1923.

As the 1927 mayoralty campaign approached, Crump decided not to run on his own, and he carefully shopped about for his candidate. His choice for stooge mayor finally narrowed down to Watkins Overton, a member of Memphis' "best family." Crump felt that Overton's family tree, plus his credentials as a Harvard man and World War I veteran, would bedazzle those voters the Crump organization could not buy or control directly. Also, for insurance, Crump chose Clifford Davis, a city judge and only Ku Kluxer to win in 1923, to run with Wat Overton for vice-mayor and police and fire commissioner. Davis, a rather homespun character, was judged by Crump as an important asset because of his past Klan connections, his remarkable mimicry of Paine, and his "ham" story, a humorous tale involving some "niggers" that always brought down the house.

By the time the 1927 campaign was under way, Paine recognized who his real opponent was, and he pitched his entire effort against Crump. Crump was "the political boss," the "nigger-lover," and the crook who "was ousted from the office of mayor." In contrast, cried Paine, if he were given his third consecutive term, "there will be no Negro policemen, no Negro firemen, and no admittance of Negroes to the white parks of the city."

While the Crump boys who wrote Overton's speeches emphasized his war record (in the ambulance corps) and Cliff Davis recited his ham story, Crump chose to go after Paine through full-page ads in the newspapers. He charged the mayor with acquiring a "secret salary raise to $12,000," and he demanded that he end his slanderous lies about the reason Crump was "ousted twelve years ago."

In desperation, Paine asked the city's black Republican leaders to a meeting. If they would put up a Republican ticket in the city and siphon votes away from Overton, he would assure them of fair treatment when he was re-elected. But there was no reason for the Negroes to believe Paine had changed; and when they refused, they doomed Paine, for an estimated 10,000 votes were against him in the black ghetto.

When Crump's boy Overton defeated Paine by almost 13,000 votes on November 7, 1927, Mistah Ed Crump was back in power after an absence of eleven-and-a-half-years, and he was to hand-pick every mayor after that until his death in 1954.

In the years Crump was out of power, he had gone to great length to secure a financial base that went far beyond his high earnings as county trustee. Given some Federal patronage early in Woodrow Wilson's first term, he had boosted his friend Stanley Trezevant for United States marshal for western Tennessee. Then when Trezevant retired in 1920, County Trustee Crump quietly formed an insurance agency with Trezevant as the active partner.

Now with Overton as mayor and Crump as boss, Crump & Trezevant prospered to such an extent that the *New York Times* described the firm as "the South's largest insurance writing company." Citizens found it wise to buy their insurance from the boss, let his company buy and sell their houses, and get their mortgages from him, even though his interest charge might be higher than elsewhere. As a starter, the Metropolitan Insurance Company had given Crump & Trezevant the local agency, and then followed with branch agencies in Pittsburgh, Little Rock, and St. Louis. Metropolitan also supplied Crump with the financial backing necessary to engage in making mortgage loans in those cities and to acquire a network of mortgage correspondents in a dozen other cities.

As Crump moved into the millionaire class, he expanded into other businesses. Reporters uncovered the fact that he owned two large Mississippi cotton plantations and was a major stockholder in several banks, though he avoided publicity by not becoming a director of any of them. Still another immensely profitable venture was his acquisition of the Coca-Cola franchise for upstate New York and ownership of several bottling plants there.

By the time he returned to local power in 1927, Crump had learned his political lessons well. The troubles that had brought on his ouster as mayor had resulted from an unfriendly state legislature and governor. The significance of controlling the legislature had still another facet: The legislature could change a city charter at will, a power that was not ended until 1953. Therefore, to maintain a permanent dictatorial control over Memphis, Crump had to dominate the state government.

This project seemed a bit presumptuous in 1927, for the grip of Colonel Luke Lea on the Tennessee Democratic organization was firm. Lea, a war hero, former United States Senator, publisher of the Nashville *Tennessean*, the Memphis *Commercial Appeal,* and the Knoxville *Journal,* and millionaire businessman, controlled the choice of governor and the activities of the state legislature. Lea was so powerful that he had the state legislature pass a law declaring his son a legal adult even though he was under twenty-one. That many of Lea's financial activities were dishonest and others too speculative even for that wild inflationary era did not disturb the state's biggest wheeler-dealer since Andrew Jackson.

Besides his publishing and politicking, Colonel Lea was tied in with the sprawling, speculative trust known as Caldwell & Co., which controlled ten insurance firms; eighteen banks; the Nashville Baseball Club; hotels; laundries; hosiery, cotton, and silk mills; an oil company; paving concerns; department stores; and a coal mine.

Fresh from his success in placing Watkins Overton, his own puppet, into the mayor's office in Memphis, Crump readied himself to take on Luke Lea in the contest for governor in 1928. Lea was running Governor Henry Horton for another term, and Crump came out for Hill McAlister.

By the time the campaign got under way, the Nashville *Banner* had uncovered the story that Horton had ordered state roadbuilders to use Kyrock, a rock asphalt produced by Lea's business associate, Rogers Caldwell, and its editorials and cartoons provided Crump with his campaign material. In newspaper ads and through his machine's speakers, he labeled Governor Horton as "the Kyrock Kid" and "Governor-in-Name"; Luke Lea, "Governor-in-Fact" and "Musso-Lea-Ni"; and Caldwell as "Kid Kyrock with the money bags." Collectively, he called the trio "the three Rock-Asphalteers."

As the campaign proceeded, the strategy of the Lea group was

diffuse. Ministers and businessmen issued statements calling Caldwell a man of great character and business integrity and "the Moses
that will lead us out of bondage and make possible a new freedom
such as the old South has struggled for since the days of the Confederacy." In Knoxville, Lea used his *Journal* to urge Republican
readers to vote in the Democratic primary for Horton; and in Nashville, his paper charged the rival *Banner* with being a Republican
paper sticking its nose into a Democratic primary. As for his Memphis outlet, the *Commercial Appeal* claimed truthfully that Crump
was trying to control the election with his fraudulent voting of the
Negro population. The paper demanded that the Shelby County primary board act like those in other Southern states and bar black
votes because "the Democratic Party is the white man's party in the
South."

Lea also found an ally in Memphis who had visions of replacing Crump as the Great White Chief in his hometown. This was
Clarence Saunders, a merchandising genius who had started the
first self-serving food supermarket in 1916 with his Piggly-Wiggly
stores. Saunders had lost his fortune in the early twenties when he
tried to corner Piggly-Wiggly stock, and the New York Stock Exchange prevented this by suspending its rules. But Saunders had
picked himself up from bankruptcy and court suits to make a second
quick fortune through his "Clarence Saunders, Sole-Owner-of-My-
Name, Stores."

Two years earlier, Saunders had joined Crump in opposing a
third term for Governor Austin Peay; but now he was working alongside Luke Lea to defeat Hill McAlister, Crump's candidate for governor. So concerned was Crump that the eccentric Piggly-Wiggly
Saunders planned to hire plug-uglies and stage a pitched battle
when McAlister came to Memphis to campaign that he ordered
McAlister to stay away from his town. Instead Crump decided to
hold McAlister's "real old-fashioned welcome" at Covington, 40 miles
north, in adjoining Tipton County.

For this rally for McAlister, Crump ordered all city and county
offices closed, and the thousands of employees and their families
were told to report to Covington on the day of the gala affair. There
was real excitement among the government workers at Covington
when two Saunders-hired airplanes buzzed the crowd during Mc-
Alister's dull mumbling and dropped thousands of handbills announcing: "Horton Is The Man."

Following the rally and Saunders' ploy, the supergrocer and Crump warred through full-page newspaper ads. Said Saunders in one:

> Mr. Ed Crump Gets Mad—and the Buzz of a Little Airplane Did It. . . . Mr. Crump, in utter disregard of the Public's business, issued orders for these men to quit their jobs—leave the business of the taxpayers of Shelby County and strut their stuff like martial peacocks 40 miles to Covington so Mr. Hill McAlister might before such a worshipful audience pay tribute to the uncrowned redheaded King of Shelby County.

In his reply, Crump declared that Saunders was not even a registered voter. Even worse, he said, a Federal court had found him guilty of "fraud, embezzlement, misappropriation and defalcation." Saunders, he went on, was in league with the "three Rock-Asphalteers, Lea, Caldwell and Horton," who were the "chain newspaper owners, seekers and procurers of noncompetitive road contracts." Still another Crump attack charged Saunders with spreading "dirt and filth," and called him "a little squirt."

Shortly before the August 2 primary, Luke Lea grew worried about the extent of voting fakery that could be expected in Crump's Shelby County. So several Caldwell firms set up a large slush fund to buy off local politicians who were also willing to play the game of vote fraud. Even so, the race came down to the wire as an unknown quantity.

On election day, Lea sent reporters and photographers throughout Memphis to write stories and take pictures of the busloads of Negroes brought to the polling places by the Crump machine. However, Crump had been alerted and Lea's newsmen were arrested and beaten before being thrown into jail by a Crump judge, who charged that "they threaten a breach of the peace by taking pictures."

When the votes were counted, McAlister carried Shelby County over Horton by a total of 23,939 to 3,649, and he surprisingly carried Lea's Davidson County (Nashville) by 11,388 to Horton's 4,455. Yet despite this big county vote for McAlister, the rural counties were so overwhelmingly for Horton that the governor was returned to office with 95,278 votes to McAlister's 90,014. Crump's fury afterward was directed not so much against Horton and Lea as it was against Lewis Pope, the third candidate, whose 23,985 votes would have gone almost entirely to McAlister had he dropped out of the race.

The Crump-Lea rivalry did not end with this election. In the presidential contest that November Crump came out strong for New York Governor Al Smith, the Democratic nominee, while handsome Luke Lea in his high, stiff Hoover collar lent his boyish enthusiasm to the cause of Republican nominee Herbert Hoover. Crump lost again. In a state estimated to be 98 percent Protestant, it was remarkable that Crump could show a margin of 6,367 for Al Smith in Shelby County. But the Crump machine had limited authority, and Hoover carried Tennessee by 35,100 votes.

The bitterness between Crump and Lea continued during Horton's 1928–1930 term. The colonel's choices for speaker of the senate and secretary of state failed to win confirmation because of the opposition of the Shelby County delegation in the state legislature and the astute lobbying efforts of Frank Rice, Crump's legislative lobbyist. Governor Horton's sales tax proposal also failed as did his redistricting bill to cut a state senator and two representatives from the Shelby County total. But Lea's political failure was offset to a great degree by the economic gains bestowed on him by Governor Horton.

Citizens of Tennessee were baffled in mid-1930 when the Crump war with Lea-Horton-Caldwell mysteriously changed to a lovefest. Now suddenly Crump lowered his voice and spoke of "going to the bridge" with his old enemies, adding, "I'll take them across the river and I won't let them drown." He also declared he planned to vote that year for another term for Horton "with the greatest pleasure," and asked the people of Shelby County to show their "appreciation for the assistance Horton has rendered by rolling up a tremendous majority for him in the August primary."

If Tennessee citizens were shocked to discover that the warfare was just a fight for power and not a philosophic encounter, this was confirmed by the effusive praise showered on Crump by the Lea papers. The Memphis *Commercial Appeal,* for example, wrote on July 11, 1930, of the "evidence of the esteem in which Mr. Crump is held by the people of Shelby County."

This new mutual admiration society was occasioned by Crump's decision to go to the U.S. House of Representatives for the Tenth Congressional District, or Shelby County.

The trade of aid between Crump and Lea was of far greater benefit to Governor Horton than to Crump, for the Red Snapper did not need Lea's help to win the Democratic primary, which was tantamount to election. In sharp contrast, Horton would have lost without Crump's support. Two years earlier, Crump had given him only 3,649 votes to 23,939 for Hill McAlister. In 1930, Crump reversed this, giving Horton 27,634 votes and L. E. Gwinn, his opponent in the primary, only 2,267. Without this Shelby County plurality, Horton would have been defeated.

It was the amazing change in the Horton vote from one election to the next that brought U.S. Senator Gerald P. Nye of North Dakota and his investigating subcommittee to Memphis after the primary. Nye said he had come to look into charges that soon-to-be-Congressman Crump had brought this about by "herding carloads of Negroes from one Democratic primary polling place to another, expulsion of designated watchers, and wholesale distribution of [poll] tax receipts." However, witnesses who had submitted advance affidavits were tongue-tied on the stand, and Nye was forced to quit Memphis without any confirming verbal testimony.

And even while Nye was being laughed out of town by the Crump machine, the boss' honeymoon with Lea, Horton, and Caldwell was about to explode. In October, 1929, when the stock market crashed, "Morgan of the South," as Caldwell & Co. was generally called, did not collapse. That it survived, however, was not based on the nature of the company or its methods but on its frantic efforts to delay insolvency. Caldwell & Co. was in essence a gigantic holding company overseeing intermeshed firms; and in its vast labors to expand by taking over additional concerns, it had recklessly borrowed margin money to buy the controlling stock to those companies at wildly inflated prices.

When the bottom fell out of the stock market, Caldwell & Co. began dipping illegally into the state road bond money deposited in its banks. Because its liabilities failed to decrease appreciably, this borrowing went on at an increasing pace throughout 1930. All this continued until November 6, two days after Governor Horton's reelection when Caldwell & Co.'s Bank of Tennessee in Nashville was forced to close its doors with a loss of $3,418,400 of state money. Also its Holston Union National Bank of Knoxville failed with a state loss of $2,630,000 in road bond deposits. Examination revealed that on the day of its demise, the Bank of Tennessee had only $32.55 in cash on hand.

While the repercussions of Caldwell & Co.'s collapse were like a massive financial earthquake throughout the South, newly elected Congressman Ed Crump immediately recognized his opportunity to gain political control of Tennessee. However, he did not join others in holding mass meetings and forming citizens' investigating committees to look into the company's failure. Instead he quietly spent two months preparing a plan to demolish Horton.

Early in January, 1931, he called for a "thorough and sweeping investigation of state affairs," and he left for Nashville to direct the attack on the administration. First order of business was to prevent Horton from organizing the state legislature. In the house, Crump and Frank Rice settled for Walter Haynes, an anti-Horton man but not a Crumpite, for speaker. But in the senate, where its speaker stood first in line to succeed the governor, they insisted on Scott Fitzhugh of the Memphis machine for this post. Following Fitzhugh's victory, the Memphis *Press-Scimitar,* formerly called the *News Scimitar,* understood Crump's motive, and wailed that there was "no advantage in exchanging a puppet of Lea and Caldwell for a puppet of E. H. Crump."

The expected came next. After he possessed the senate speaker, Crump demanded the impeachment of Horton, whom he labeled "an easy prey for designing selfish interests, gougers in the taxpayers' money," and a man guilty of "mismanagement of commonwealth affairs." Then in late May when the state senate reconvened after a recess, he led a large crew to Nashville to take charge of the impeachment fight.

The air was rent with the charges and name-calling of the two combatants. Crump let the press know that "temporary Governor Horton" was "the square root of zero." Crump also offered further words about "a mangy, egg-sucking dog" and "a distempered, windbroken horse."

Horton, who resembled a tired and disheveled Warren Harding with his white hair parted in the middle and rimming his forehead and his hooded, bone-shielded eyes, would not succumb without a struggle. In the name-calling department, he described the Memphis boss as "a man who struts like a peacock with his cane on his arm and crows like a bantam rooster. I heard Mr. Crump is starting out tomorrow with a brass band," he said boldly. "He has already rented one hundred rooms at a hotel. They are going to storm the legislature with the cry, 'Oust Horton.' What has Crump done in Memphis that would justify turning the state over to him?"

Almost all the articles of impeachment involved Horton's relationship with Luke Lea and Rogers Caldwell, and the use the two
made of the governor to enrich themselves. Crump was confident
of success, for a legislative investigating committee had uncovered
much of the illegal operations of the Lea-Caldwell-Horton ring.
However, many anti-Horton legislators had second thoughts about
rendering themselves unto the Memphis Caesar; others felt sorry
for Horton, calling him a weak pawn of Lea and Caldwell. Still others lost their enthusiasm for impeaching the governor when he
passed out jobs, pardons, and new road projects at a wholesale rate.
The vote finally came on June 5, 1931, and the Crump forces were
stunned when the totals showed 58 against impeachment and 41 in
favor. The Memphis *Press-Scimitar* angrily concluded, "It is a sad
commentary that a political outfit as dumb or as crooked as the one
that has controlled the state of Tennessee can remain unconvicted
by the judge and jury which is the legislature." Yet even in victory,
Governor Horton was so shell-shocked that control of the state's affairs went to Crump by default.

There still remained the opportunity for redress in the courts
against Lea and Caldwell. But fortunately for the two, the attorney
general for Davidson County (Nashville) was their man; and only
after a great deal of legal bickering among judges, grand juries,
and lawyers did Caldwell finally come to trial under a different prosecutor. The jury found Caldwell guilty of fraud, but when the Tennessee Supreme Court ordered a retrial, this was never held and
Caldwell escaped imprisonment.

Tennessee justice failed to take action against Luke Lea. Nevertheless, he suffered a far different fate from Caldwell. Lea and his
son, Luke Lea, Jr., were indicted in North Carolina and charged with
defrauding their Central Bank & Trust Co. of Asheville in Buncombe
County of $1,000,000. This bank had suffered a $17,000,000 failure
thanks to Caldwell & Co. Lea was sentenced to six-to-ten years and
his son to two-to-six years. As long as Horton was governor, he
would not permit their extradition, but the next governor, a Crump
man, did this.

So Crump's enemy was no more, and the Memphis boss was
now the boss of Tennessee.

Crump's attack on Horton had not cut into his congressional
work, for in that sleepy Hoover era, a man elected to Congress on

November 4, 1930, had to wait until December 7, 1931, for the beginning of the next legislative session. By the time Crump went to Washington, Governor Horton was a broken man despite his escape from impeachment; and the Congressman from Shelby County could go about his national business with the smug assurance that he was his state's leading power.

Crump served two terms in the House; and as a member low on the seniority totem pole, he was without influence there. Since he could not speak in public and was silent during floor debate, he gained no authority in this direction either.

Nevertheless, he looked like a Congressman, and reporters who had not known him in Memphis considered him a fresh maxim tosser. "Bland, perfectly self-possessed," one newsman wrote; "he ambles as quietly about the Capitol as a tiger stalks its prey on a Persian rug." Crump, he went on, was a man of "smooth words and gentle hints, polish and suavity and custom-made clothes." In the maxim department, reporters quoted him as saying that a freshman Congressman should "observe, remember, compare, read, confer, listen and ask questions," as well as "plan his work and work his plan."

Crump's real authority in Washington was with the Tennessee congressional delegation, which recognized him as the boss of Tennessee, now that the Lea machine had collapsed. Aloof and wary of Crump was Senator Cordell Hull from Overton County in the middle of the state, who would later serve as Secretary of State for twelve years under Franklin Roosevelt. Crump had opposed Hull in his first race for the Senate in 1930 after eleven terms in the House. But two days before the primary, Crump without explanation had ordered his machine to drop that opposition, and Hull had won. One link Hull had with Crump was that during the Spanish-American War he had served in the same army company with Frank Rice, Crump's lobbyist in Nashville.

Much closer to Crump was the other Senator, Kenneth Douglas "Kay Dee" McKellar, a chunky man who had been in the Senate since 1916. In 1928, with Crump the undisputed boss of Shelby County and Memphis, Kay Dee McKellar realized it was the Crump machine vote that was essential to his own third-term victory in the face of an expected Hoover win for President in Tennessee. Afterward, he fought for his independence from Crump yet gave him what was essential to hold his support.

Freshman Representative Crump was an early supporter of New York Governor Franklin D. Roosevelt for the Democratic presidential nomination in 1932, and he took the Tennessee delegation to the national convention in Chicago that June to work for his man. Senator Cordell Hull had to be catered to, both as a former chairman of the Democratic National Committee and as a politician who wanted to show pro-Roosevelt convention floor efforts in order to win a cabinet post. But Representative Crump was the real boss of the delegation.

That same summer, with Lea gone from power and Governor Horton, although still in office, "as dead as Barnum and Bailey," as Crump put it, the Memphis boss had to show the state he was its master. Another Democratic primary for governor was coming up and Representative Crump could not afford to lose this first crucial test. Playing things safely, he resurrected clerical-looking, dull Hill McAlister, the state treasurer, whom he had supported in 1926 and 1928. McAlister was like mashed potatoes in his plate, though he exasperated Crump by referring to him publicly as "Edwin," instead of Edward Crump.

Arrayed against McAlister were Lewis Pope, a Governor Peay administrator who had run for governor in 1928, and old Malcolm Patterson, reformed alcoholic and many-time governor, who had first held that post in 1906. Pope was by far the more dangerous opponent, but Crump concentrated on an abusive newspaper-ad attack on Patterson, then serving as judge, for this let him use the raw language that gave rural Tennesseans deep emotional pleasure.

"Drunk or sober," Crump charged in ads, "he is the same Patterson today as of old . . . the same local and long-distance liar that he has been for years." When Patterson came to Memphis to speak, Crump notified newspaper readers that "his unfair and unjustified remarks about me to a *small* crowd emphasizes one thing above all else—that a leopard cannot change its spots nor can a hog remove the swallow-fork brand from its ear."

To newspaper charges that he planned to install McAlister through "phantom voters" and other "election irregularities," Crump's giant-size ad type replied: "Thieves Don't Work for Something They Intend to Steal." If he were a crook, Crump declared, why would he spend "large sums of money for paid advertisements [the only newspaper publicity available to McAlister] and for banners, cards, stickers, bands, hurdy-gurdys, picture show slides?"

The August 4, 1932, primary showed Crump he could control the state from his bastion in Shelby County. Lewis Pope came roaring into Shelby County that night with a vote lead of 20,000 ahead of McAlister. But Mistah Crump had voted and revoted the city's Negroes all day long, and he still had registration cards and poll-tax receipts to be recorded in the after-hours vote tally. When his boys finally submitted their vote tally, it gave McAlister 31,439; Pope, a tiny 2,318; and Patterson, a generous 6,661.

Pope, an unwilling loser, railed at Crump for using "Cossack methods" in "rounding up voters by the truckload" and "delivering them to the polls like so many dumb, driven cattle." "Liars, Blackguards and Thieves," Crump struck back in a paid ad at Pope and his backers. Pope went beyond words to file a charge of fraud with the Democratic state committee, but since this body was Crump-controlled, his charge was hurriedly dismissed.

With McAlister elected governor and a Democratic administration in Washington, Crump now took direction of state affairs with one eye on the Federal government for financial help. By the end of 1933, the rampant Depression had forced a third of the state's industrial plants to shut their doors. In Memphis, for instance, when Fisher Body closed, 1,200 workers were thrown on the nonexistent job market.

As a noneconomist, Crump's view of the Depression's cause was a catchy "We're overbuilt and oversold." In his first set of orders to Governor McAlister, he demanded that he retrench vigorously and cut spending to a minimum. At the same time, Crump reminded him he was expecting a large share of remaining state jobs.

Crump's belief in retrenchment as the proper course to beat the Depression by the state did not apply to the Federal government. For aid to the paralyzed economy of Tennessee, he used his status as a Congressman plus the help of patronage-hungry Senator Kay Dee McKellar and House Majority Leader Joe Byrns of Nashville (soon to be Speaker) to acquire millions upon millions of New Deal project dollars. Kay Dee, from his perch on the Senate Appropriations Committee, saw to it that seventy-two post offices were built in Tennessee. He also boasted about the numerous Tennessee Valley Authority dams he won for his state—"Many of them built over the protest and opposition of the board of directors of the TVA," he said proudly.

As for the effect of the Depression on the attitudes of the population, Crump believed that no matter how great the suffering and desperation, citizens had to be kept docile. Anyone caught reading the liberal *New Republic* was bound to be arrested, questioned, and threatened with serious trouble if he were caught again. When hundreds of unemployed veterans came to Memphis and clustered there, Will Lee, a Crump chief of police, announced that unless they rode freight cars out of town, he planned to lock them up in "a large building at the fairgrounds." They were gone before he could carry out his threat.

Crump was especially alert when it came to picking up strangers in town who looked as though they might want to discuss politics with the unemployed or minority groups. According to Will Lee, anyone who wanted to meet with Memphis blacks had to be a "Communist-son-of-a-bitch." From his third-floor business office, Crump sent orders to Police Chief Lee to arrest and beat up agitators; and as Lee explained his action to a *Press-Scimitar* reporter, "We intend to stamp out the seed of communism in Memphis" and prevent the "dictatorship of the pro-lat-erate [sic]." The response of the paper to Lee's activity was an angry insistence that "he has no more right to arrest a man suspected of being a Communist than he has to arrest a man suspected of being a Methodist."

Crump's ideal officeholder was a man like Mayor Watkins Overton, who, in his first two terms, acceded to whatever demands Crump made on him. He had sized up his man, Hill McAlister, as cut from the same bolt of cotton cloth, and it soon infuriated him that McAlister as governor was not the same as McAlister the servile campaigner.

Rumors reached Crump that McAlister was speaking apologetically about his relationship to the Memphis boss. Also, the governor moved cautiously in spending Federal road-building funds, after Crump and McKellar had gone to such great lengths to acquire money to pave Tennessee roads willy-nilly. Even Secretary of the Interior Harold Ickes, noted for his slowness in doling out public works money after it had been appropriated by Congress, wrote McAlister he was going to reclaim much of the funds because of the governor's crawling pace. In addition, Crump found that his barrage of letters of "advice" to McAlister was being answered at an average interval of a week's delay per letter, and the tone lacked the expected subservience.

As a result, when the next gubernatorial primary neared in 1934, Representative Crump searched for a replacement for McAlister; but finding no one satisfactory, he reluctantly announced in his favor for a second term. McAlister's reaction enraged Crump, for on announcing his candidacy he spoke of his intention to retain prohibition in the state, despite the repeal of the Eighteenth Amendment and Crump's clamor for special legislation permitting the sale of liquor in Memphis. Then throughout the campaign, McAlister refused to pay any attention to Crump's letters and telegrams on how to deal with Lewis Pope, who was his opponent again.

A break between the governor and the boss was inevitable in McAlister's second term. To raise revenue for Tennessee's collapsing school system, McAlister proposed a sales tax measure to the state legislature without consulting Crump. The initial head count revealed the governor had the votes to insure passage. But he did not take advantage of his surprise move, and Crump was soon racing to Nashville to join Frank Rice in fighting the proposal.

The tide turned, and after Crump defeated the sales tax, he promised reporters that McAlister was finished in Tennessee politics. "Our sorriest governor," he labeled him, blasting him as a miserable creature "who kept the sales tax hidden in his stony heart and tried in a sneaking way to put it over on us."

Crump was right about killing McAlister's political career. The governor was more or less isolated throughout the rest of his term, and when it ended Crump was pleased that he left the state. But this pleasure changed to fury, for McAlister polished his Phi Beta Kappa key and went to Washington, where President Roosevelt named him chairman of the Bituminous Coal Commission.

By 1936, Crump was reaching the zenith of his immense power in Tennessee. This authority, both local and statewide, was in truth a crunching example of dictatorship in action. Most shocking of all, the man who created and wielded this power was in no way responsible to the voters. His last elected job had ended in January, 1935, when he left Congress to concentrate on Tennessee politics.

Stateside, Senator McKellar mistakenly believed in 1936 that he had earned the right to have his own governor that year. The man he chose was Burgin Dossett, head of a state teacher's college, and at the expense of American taxpayers Kay Dee franked statements back to Tennessee that Dossett would be the next governor. Kay Dee's smile changed to a beam when Crump offered no objections, and Crump lieutenants wore large Dossett buttons.

But on July 18, only nineteen days before the primary, a reporter found old Kay Dee in his Mayflower Hotel room in Washington "in many-wrinkled collapse in his chair." His dirty "crow's wing of hair was ruffled from distraught finger-combing" that sprinkled his lapels with dandruff. He had just received word from Crump that Dossett was not the man for the job and that Representative Gordon Browning, a Luke Lea friend and military subofficer in World War I, would most certainly be the next governor.

An editor for the Nashville *Tennessean* wrote of the Crump message: "The election for governor among the 3,000,000 people of Tennessee was over three weeks before election day. Dossett was finished, Browning was in." Another newsman said, "With Shelby County for Browning, there is no actual race." Back in Campbell County in eastern Tennessee, Dossett cried out in hopeless bravery: "The gentleman on the banks of the Mississippi in his effort to bulldoze me as so often he has bulldozed others has gone so far as to threaten to annihilate me politically if I dare to question his right to dictate to the people of Tennessee. I accept the threat and challenge it."

An outsider asked how it was possible for one man to name the next governor even before the people voted. "What about the 'popular' decision?" he wanted to know. The answer was simple: There was no political democracy in Tennessee. The citizens of the state did not collectively determine who would rule them.

What had happened was that Crump had taken advantage of an 1890 law that established a poll tax as the price to be paid by citizens for the privilege of voting. Two years before the poll-tax measure was enacted, 71 percent of eligible adults voted; by 1936, only 29 percent did. Of 1,200,000 persons eligible that latter year, a mere 350,000 went to the polls.

When the Lea-Horton combine failed in 1930, Crump was well aware of what he needed to take over the state. Six years later he owned a plurality of 60,000 to 70,000 votes in Shelby County; plus 30,000 to 40,000 more votes from other county bosses to the east who expected state favors in return; and an additional 10,000 from Republicans at the northern end of the Tennessee Valley who crossed party lines in exchange for political support in their own counties and some state patronage afterward.

Had there been no poll tax, no doubt the ingenious Crump would have found an alternate technique to maintain state control. Also, had a sufficient number of eligible voters who opposed him paid their poll taxes, his 100,000 votes might not have been decisive. However, the poll-tax payment of $2 was a financial burden during the Depression.

Memphis with its quarter million population and the rest of Shelby County with 100,000 more would have been poll-tax delinquent like most of the state had it not been for the aggressive Crump organization. In election years, city and county employees were assessed 10 percent of their salaries by Crump's machine, and much of this money went to buy poll-tax receipts. In addition, government employees were assessed for books of poll-tax receipts, and they were put to overtime duty selling them to their friends or door-to-door. If they failed to meet their quotas, they were forced to pay $2 apiece for those unsold. Would-be police and firemen first had to sell large blocs of poll-tax payments before getting on the force. One Crump aide justified this practice on the grounds that since a voter had to pay the poll tax to vote, these recruits were merely "helping them" obey the law.

Nor were bloc sales of poll-tax receipts restricted to civil servants. Several banks took consignments of receipts, divided them among employees, and deducted the money from their salaries. Other business firms engaged in the same practice so that despite the general decline in the number voting in Tennessee, Shelby County showed a steady growth. Even the houses of prostitution in Memphis' red light district bought and sold poll-tax receipts for the Crump machine. In 1940, when Crump decided to close the city's bawdy houses, the madams complained bitterly that they had done yeoman work on the poll-tax score besides voting "faithfully for Shelby County candidates."

Early in his political career, Crump had discovered the importance of the Negro vote in Memphis, and now that he wanted to stabilize his control of the state he used poll-tax receipts by the thousands to vote the blacks his way.

The Crump machine task of voting Memphis blacks required thorough planning and almost precision herding, since blacks constituted 40 percent of the city's population. The poll-tax receipts and the buses to haul them to the polls had to be at the right time and place. If there were extra poll-tax receipts, the "voters" had to be taken en masse from polling place to polling place for multiple voting. On occasion, truckloads of blacks were brought from Mississippi and Arkansas to Memphis, given poll-tax receipts and registration names, and carted through polling places to cast their votes.

Free food and drinks were a must to entice the black votes, but this was a worthwhile expenditure. After the Negroes left the voting places and brought back their registration slips and attached poll-tax receipts, which Crump's polling center employees had purposely failed to collect, they were given a silver dollar, a barbecue sandwich, a Coke or bottle of red eye whisky and were taken to the watermelon piles for a free choice before climbing back on the bus or truck. The story passed around Memphis at the time of the 1940 draft registration for military service that a Negro who registered was disgusted and angry afterward. "Whuh's m' barbecue and Coke?" he cried.

As for the 60 percent segment of the population that was white, Crump maintained a close watch on each voter through an up-to-date card-file system kept in a basement room of the courthouse. Each card showed the name, address, age, voting record election by election, and the registration certification number. Since registration came at a time of the year when there was no political interest, the machine was silent when it came to informing the hard-core opposition about the registration period.

In each precinct, a Crump captain had a gray book containing an alphabetical listing of all previous voters and a black book showing the names of voters by street numbers. He had access to the card file at the courthouse plus red books there revealing all political jobholders by precincts, men and women available to him for field-work.

Still another important tool was the tray of duplicate cards for qualified voters at each polling center that a Crump man brought there on election day. When a voter gave his name to the polling clerk, the Crump man pulled his card from his tray. At regular intervals, he gave the remaining names to Crump precinct workers who phoned the machine laggards and badgered them to make an appearance.

By such control, a totally unknown candidate backed by Crump was assured of election. At the same time, voters who did not want to support Crump's candidates knew that their records would be in his files, and it might prove economically foolhardy to vote their convictions. For instance, a Memphis reporter watched Crump stop his chauffeur-driven limousine one morning alongside a house owned by his firm. A call to a painter on a ladder brought the worker to his car for a short conversation. The painter then pulled his ladder down and shut his paint can. When Crump drove off, the reporter asked the painter what had happened. "Mr. Crump says I can't work here," the painter told him. "He remembered that I voted against his candidates in the last election."

> *Oh, the river's up and the cotton's down,*
> *Mistah Ed Crump, he runs this town!*

Roustabouts on the Mississippi waterfront below the high bluffs of Memphis chanted these lines as they worked during the thirties. People in Memphis came to know Mistah Crump as a colorful dresser, good family man, stager of free picnics, fairs, and boat rides, a prolific newspaper political ad writer, and as courtly as a planter out of the Confederacy. Few saw the shrewd, despotic politician who ran the city from his business office at Main and Adams. To those involved in politics, he was "the man on the corner," because of the proximity of his office to the courthouse and the force of his watchful eye, even though he never was seen there.

The Crump facade carefully obliterated any public show of the dictatorial boss that he really was. Reportorial stories about him noted the rich man who wore silk pajamas and slept in a four-poster bed in his big house at 1962 Peabody. On the night table next to the bed, he kept several pads of paper, and he woke frequently to jot down ideas. By the time he rose at 5:30 A.M. to start his day, there would be a pile of scribbled chits beside the bed.

Crump was a showman who dressed to catch the public's eye. His favorite attire consisted of striped pants, plaid jacket, two-tone shoes, a large hat, a flower as big as a saucer in his lapel, and one of his forty canes twirling in his hand. Crump's natural attributes added much to his clothing, for he was tall, straight, and graceful, and was immediately recognizable by the white puffy cloud of hair that had replaced his red thatch, the thick beetle brows, the blue eyes set wide apart and covered by amber tortoise-shell glasses and his pink, full cheeks the color of salmon. Crump was so vain about his appearance that he refused to pose for formal photos, believing that such stiff pictures hid his dynamic personality.

Once he finished breakfast, he climbed into the back seat of his Lincoln for the ride downtown. He generally walked the last few blocks, offering paternalistic hellos to those he passed. A magazine writer said that spectators gawked at him "as if they had spied the

Mad Mullah of Tud, nose ring and all, cracking pecans on the Hope Diamond."

In 1936, Crump bought out Stanley Trezevant and changed the name of their prosperous insurance, real estate, and mortgage firm to E. H. Crump Co., bringing in his three sons as executives. Crump's office was in an unmarked room on the third floor of his building, directly above the hardworking employees. As a rule, his desk was covered with papers, and there were neat piles on the floor, with a key to the city serving as a paperweight on one pile. Crump's pockets were filled with business notes, political plans, bright sayings, and lists of obscure, long words to use in his newspaper ads. He also carried his little red notebook with the names of those on his hate list. He had a fetish about cleanliness and polish, with the result that all metal in his office gleamed and the walls were frequently painted. He had a gold-lacquered phone through which he barked orders to his political lieutenants and city and county administrators.

Crump might call his closest associates by their first names, but he would not tolerate being called Ed in return, and no one did. He also insisted that his office employees address each other as Mister or Miss. Reporters who visited him in his office found little indication that he was a politician other than for the signed photographs of elected officials on his wall. He would shrug off mention of these persons and point instead to a wall sign that read: "Oh Lord, keep me alive while I'm living." A man of enormous ego, he would feign great modesty to reporters to throw them off the track. He liked to claim he was just a small-town boy, declaring one time, "I was born on a farm so far from town that the sun rose and set between the house and the post office."

He took walks during the business day, sometimes making several trips around the courthouse square, tipping his hat to each lady and slowing up for a greeting to male friends. He boasted that he had a better memory for names than Jim Farley, President Franklin Roosevelt's Postmaster General and glad-hander, and he enjoyed astounding reporters by reciting the lineups of major league baseball teams of the 1890s. If he were stopped in the street for an exchange of a few friendly words with one of his people, he was always popeyed, unlike in his office where he listened with closed eyes.

Other times, Crump's recognizable walk—a strut on the balls of his feet with slightly flexed knees—carried him down cotton-oil-

smelly Front Street to the Mississippi; or past the Poplar Avenue station, the starting point for Casey Jones' ill-fated trip in Cannon Ball
Engine No. 382 in April, 1900; or onto Gayoso Street, known as the
"street of shame" because of its twenty to thirty bawdy houses. The
walk might take him through the lobby of the Hotel Peabody ("The
South's Finest") where, said an observer, he approached "friends
with pastoral dignity and like an elder statesman." If he chanced
on Juvenile Court Judge Camille Kelley, whom he retained despite
her lack of any legal training, he invariably admired her red rose
corsage.

Crump's family life gained friendly newspaper attention, unlike his political existence. His three sons always greeted him with
kisses, and even after they married they frequently joined him for
lunch at home with their mother. Crump's greatest heartbreak
came in 1939, when his favorite son, John, died in a plane crash.

Rain or shine, Crump visited his mother every Sunday. In good
weather he'd ride the 46 miles in the center of the rear seat of his
open touring car back to his childhood in Holly Springs, Mississippi.
The best part of the visit with the tall, white-haired nonagenarian
was listening to her reminisce about the Civil War, all the while he
rocked on the column-laden front porch. He also spent a week with
her each year during the Holly Springs racing season where he
enjoyed remarkable success as a better. One of Crump's friends
said that his love for his mother made him "the finest bygod pecker-
wood in these parts."

Mistah Crump the family man had little in common with
Crump the political boss. The veneer of the Southern charmer would
give way to a hard, mean man whenever anyone tried to interfere
with his dictatorship. The designation "boss" infuriated him and
wiped the Southern warmth from his face. "Boss? Who said boss?
I'm no boss," he remonstrated to a reporter. "I'm just an unassum-
ing, good citizen working with and for the people." Another time,
he shrugged off the label of boss by describing himself as "a large
taxpayer interested in the welfare of the city." As Crump explained
his machine's role, most people didn't know how to vote, and he was
there to assist them. "Why if you put Judas Iscariot on the ballot," he
said with a fatherly sigh, "he'd get a thousand votes in Shelby
County."

Crump's assistance to voters was obviously highly successful,
for in 1931 the opponent to his mayoralty candidate collected only

869 votes, and in the next three elections the Crump choice ran un-opposed. Crump's argument was that the people of Memphis must have been pleased with his assistance because "even Louis XVI couldn't keep down a rebellion."

It was true, as nonofficeholder Crump put it, that he gave his Memphis "good, clean and cheap government." His interest in pro-viding an efficient city administration free from graft as well as his interest in an everexpanding street paving program, school and hospital construction, public park extension, harbor development, and noise abatement activities was genuine.

Memphis won the National Traffic Award for traffic safety and the city's compulsory automobile inspection system, the National Fire Prevention Award for its efficient fire department, the Ameri-can Public Health Association's award for its health program, and several other national honors for municipal activities. There was only one requirement private citizen Crump insisted on: All the im-provements had to be his alone, to decide upon and create.

The Chattanooga *Times* once judged his iron rule of Memphis in this way: "Memphis seems to have a good government if one overlooks the fact that the very essence of good government is missing there—the right of the citizen to vote freely and without fear for any man he chooses, and the right of the citizens to choose their candidates."

Probably a majority of Memphis citizens did not care that they had to become his complete wards, putting themselves in bondage to a man who did not stand for election and whose sole formal po-litical title was as Tennessee's national committeeman to the Democratic National Committee. Still another segment considered opposition hopeless, for he owned the 20,000 city and county em-ployees plus the votes of their families and the en masse Negro vote; and he had the backing of the American Legion, the Chamber of Commerce, the AFL, the church leaders of all faiths, and even the PTA. A major form of homage to Crump was the general view of each of these groups that it was wise to buy insurance from his com-pany.

The tiny part of the local population that opposed or offended him soon learned the error of its ways. When a woman leader of a school PTA asked aloud whether Memphis was best served by a one-man government, a county-wide PTA assembly was quickly called to oust her. A high school principal who did not want to attach stickers for Crump's candidate for governor to his car was transferred to an outlying school as a classroom teacher. A local editor whose writings displeased Crump was punished with a city council resolution attacking his character. Then there was the undertaker who expressed anti-Crump views and received around-the-clock harassment from motorcycle cops who followed, stopped, ticketed, and hauled away his hearses and ambulances on false charges. The Negro owner of a drug chain who wanted to end the corralled black vote fared no better. He was almost driven from business by the police search of all his customers for narcotics.

Crump's pettiness could be monumental. Scott Fitzhugh, who Crump put in as speaker of the state senate, introduced a minor bill to permit Sunday movies in Memphis. Crump was not opposed to Sunday movies, but he was outraged by Fitzhugh's audacity in acting independently. He ordered Fitzhugh and House Speaker Pete Hazen to come to Memphis to discuss the matter, and when the two came he barred Fitzhugh from entering his office while he harangued Hazen privately about his fellow speaker. Word was relayed to Fitzhugh to resign his post after a public apology to the senate, and he did as he was ordered.

In another instance, Crump had ordered his Shelby organization to an outing at Moon Lake, Mississippi. Here Charles Brown, a young lawyer and member of Crump's delegation to the state legislature, was playing gin rummy in the shade when the request came that the leader wanted him to join one of the softball games. Brown rose reluctantly and said, "When the boss says you gotta go, you gotta go." Crump's reaction was devastating. Even though Brown apologized, Crump ordered him stricken from the re-election list. Then Brown's law practice dried up, and he moved to Nashville to start anew.

The pettiness could be both animate and inanimate. The St. Louis *Post-Dispatch* in 1938 called attention to a woman on the Federal government's WPA work relief program in Memphis who lost her job when she admitted listening to an anti-Crump speech on the radio. Crump shrugged off such incidents with the comment: "We don't claim to be as pure as light or as stainless as a star."

His desire to be a total winner also produced strange results. In one election, the local ballot box at the Fisherville polling place gave his man only eighteen votes to the opposition's 25; in another election, the Donaldson store box rang up 79 votes against his man

and 38 pro votes. Another politician would have ignored the insignificant events, but in both cases Crump ordered the polling precincts abolished.

Through Crump's nonbenevolence, free speech dried up in
Memphis. With his belief that he knew what was best for the city,
he dictated what could be read and seen; and in doing so he created
an intellectual desert. Joe Boyle, a grocery clerk whom he had raised
to city commissioner, was the man Crump chose as censor. Boyle
was considered an illiterate joke by reporters because of his poor
grammar and his inability to speak coherently. Yet he was the man
Crump relied on to save Memphians from most current American
fiction. This pervasive censorship also applied to the theater. One
hit Crump ordered banned from Memphis was "Annie Get Your
Gun." In the musical, a Negro portrayed a railroad conductor, and
Crump's blunt explanation for keeping it out of town was that "we
don't have any Negro conductors in the South."

Freedom of speech was also absent in other important areas.
In non-civil service Shelby County, it was not possible to get a public
job without swearing fealty to the sovereign. As Crump said, "No
business institution wants a disloyal man any more than one is
wanted in the city hall or the courthouse." But even those who were
privately employed were careful not to show anti-Crump colors. For
Crump had fashioned a volunteer spy system that extended into
most businesses, and word came to him within minutes of adverse
private conversations. "We have friends everywhere," he cautioned
the public. "The man who talks against the administration is liable
to get into trouble." One newspaper called this "a form of social terrorism."

Opposition politicians found it difficult to be heard in Memphis.
Most often, they could not rent a hall for a speech. On occasion,
Crump let one rent a hall, and then he would send one of his plug-
uglies to pick a fight with the speaker. Alerted police would immediately close in and hustle both off to jail. A former governor managed to rent the fair grounds, and just as he started his speech, "the
Frisco railroad cars began switching and bumping in the yards
nearby, and blowing their whistles so you couldn't hear a word."

Opponents also recognized the dangers involved in being tried
before Crump judges. For that matter, judges understood the danger
in acting as independent jurists. Crump was fond of recalling that
the judge who ordered his removal as mayor in 1915 "fared ill from

then on." Once when a city judge acted as his own man instead of taking orders, Crump had the state legislature restrict his tenure to a specified short term; and when he was gone and a new judge sat in his place, Crump had the old law restored. Still another time, after a Crump judge on the criminal court died, an anti-Crump governor appointed a like-minded man in his place. The power of the judge included naming members of the grand jury, and this could spell danger to the boss' machine. So Crump had the state legislature change the law and provide that a child pick the names of jurymen from a hat.

Crump's control of the city's political thoughts was both impressive and ludicrous. The Civitan Club was debating the poll tax at a meeting, and the discussion continued until one member gained the floor and said, "Let's wait until we hear from the city administration." The officers then obtained Crump's position, and at the next meeting the Civitans voted unanimously for it. In another instance, a justice of the peace was told that the machine planned to push for a court of common pleas to replace the j.p.'s. His comment was, "If Mr. Crump wants it, I'm for it. Whatever Mr. Crump wants, I'm for."

Like Frank Hague, Crump extolled Franklin Roosevelt and denounced the CIO, one of the President's principal supporters. Crump had infiltrated and made the local AFL organization part of his machine chiefly so that he could offer industry freedom from labor trouble in Memphis. For such AFL docility, he always kept one of its officials on his Shelby delegation to the state legislature, and he put Oscar P. Williams, the reactionary head of the local AFL Carpenters' Union, on the city council as commissioner of public works.

All other genuine unions were poison to Crump. As the proprietor of cotton plantations in Mississippi, he was strongly opposed to the organizing efforts of the Southern Tenant Farmers Union. He made no effort to oust it from its Memphis headquarters during its successful strike against Arkansas cotton planters in 1935, but his police manned bridges and docks in an attempt to prevent its staff from crossing the Mississippi into Arkansas to run their strike.

When the CIO sent organizers into Memphis to unionize Ford and Fisher Body, an enraged Crump declared war. He had Mayor Overton call the CIO "un-American" and Police Commissioner Cliff

Davis declare that he would not "tolerate them." Crump chose more than verbal opposition, for police brutality against the CIO organizers was the order of the day with the worst beating being administered to Norman Smith, the head CIO organizer.

However, Crump could not stem the tide, and eventually the CIO came to Memphis. This did not end his hatred. When the harmless Memphis League of Women Voters undertook ladylike study of local politics, he called it a group "hatched by the CIO sympathizers."

As a white native of Mississippi, a large share of Crump's efforts in Memphis was devoted to retaining segregation and a bottom status for Negroes there. Crump, of course, found good use for Memphis' large black population on election day, but other than for this purpose he believed they should be kept down to the level of menials. True, he built schools and parks for them and acquired Federal public housing funds to erect the 600-unit Dixie Homes and 900-unit Will Foote project. He also employed Negroes as mailmen, but they could not become post office clerks or store salespeople, nor could they drive buses or walk into white parks. Judges were quick to prescribe the electric chair for blacks for attempted rape, and the police were casual about denying constitutional rights to black suspects who were unable to buy protection.

Crump always insisted he had done yeoman service for Negro health by creating twelve free hospital wards and some neighborhood clinics. Yet of the 13,000 black maids, cooks, nurses, and janitors who left the black ghetto daily for white employers, it was estimated that by World War II 75 percent were afflicted with venereal disease.

Despite his political bossism, Crump's rule over Memphis was not entirely grim. By reputation, the city was known as "one of the friendliest, most open-handed towns in the world." This genial atmosphere, compounded of a naive sentimentality and the excitement of a "sporting town," remained throughout most of Crump's rule.

After the season ended, cotton planters and shippers traveled to Memphis for their fun. William Faulkner called these trips the "private sabbaticals among the fleshpots of Memphis." There was awe with the Federal Compress, the world's largest warehouse that covered 250 acres and handled ten bales of cotton a minute. But the fun came on Gayoso Street at the bawdy houses and gambling joints, at the Palace theater shows on Beale Street, and at the numerous shady night spots. All the way down the Mississippi Valley, dry Memphis' reputation for cheap and plentiful liquor was well known; and even when local option finally came to Shelby County in the late thirties with bars outlawed and sales limited to stores, the bootleg trade was enormous. Judge Harry Kelly, a local Crump judge trying a Mississippi farmer on a drunkenness charge, remarked from the bench: "Remember, when you come to Memphis, there is plenty of liquor here, and it's useless for you to drink it all up on one visit. Case dismissed."

It was not until the end of the thirties, after the city's churchmen begged him repeatedly for action, that Crump finally cracked down on vice. He ordered the tenderloin red light district closed and told Sheriff Joyner to chase the gamblers across the Hanrahan Bridge to West Memphis, Arkansas, and south to adjoining DeSoto County, Mississippi. A mile from the Mississippi line, Crump had a large sign planted in the ground, and it read:

> Down the Road in Miss. are gambling dens and dives run by Thieves. They cheat you. They rob you. They slug you. They get your money. Sheriff Baxter of DeSoto County, Miss., knows these thieving joints are running wide open. He can stop them but won't. Why? Guy E. Joyner, Sheriff of Shelby Co.

Crump believed that personal showmanship was an important ingredient in maintaining control, and he worked hard to create exciting events that the public would relate directly to him. In 1932, he founded the cotton carnival, and every spring for a week this lavish carnival was held on the levee. Many who came compared it favorably to New Orleans' Mardi Gras, with its royal atmosphere of crowns, sceptors, and robes. In 1938, Crump showed his national connections when President Roosevelt opened the cotton carnival by turning a key in the White House that exploded a bomb in Memphis, releasing a thousand balloons.

In September, Memphis held the Mid South Fair, and for its setting Crump had ordered the purchase of the old Montgomery Park Race Track. To be expected, he was honored with an E. H. Crump Day celebration at the fair. On this day, he would strut in front of the band up the midway, applaud each of the many speakers who lauded him, and admire the free lapel streamers everyone wore, which read, "Thank You, Mister Crump." The machine picked up the tab that day, normally giving away 30,000 hot dogs, 35,000 Cokes, and 40 barrels of lemonade.

The fall was also the time for a different sort of Crump Day. This day in Crump's honor, city and county employees delivered 1,500 shut-ins, cripples, and orphans for a three-hour afternoon excursion on the Mississippi steamboat *Island Queen*. Crump led the band aboard ship each year and saw to it that everyone was stuffed with peanuts, popcorn, and hot dogs, before being carried back to their miserable existences for another year.

Then there were the autumn Saturdays when he went to the E. H. Crump Municipal Stadium to watch local football games. The crowd was expected to applaud his arrival, and the cheers were loud when the white mop and tortoise-shell glasses came into view as he strutted toward his seat. There was always a Crump Charity Game at the end of the season, and an overflow crowd was invariably on hand.

It was in 1936 that by his publicly pushing aside of the gubernatorial choice of Senator McKellar, Crump showed the rest of Tennessee it had fallen under his control just as Memphis and Shelby County had almost a decade earlier. Poor Kay Dee had been feted in mid-1936 with a banquet staged at the Gayoso Hotel by 2,000 Federal employees who owed their jobs to him. Yet he collected only three votes in his own polling precinct for his choice, Burgin Dossett, running in the Democratic primary against Crump's boy, six-term Congressman Gordon Browning. Everyone who glanced at the Shelby County vote understood where Browning's lopsided statewide victory was fashioned. For in the boss' home county, Mistah Ed Crump had given him 60,218 votes while dragging hapless Dossett in the mud with only 861. When the primary was over, Browning gave every indication he would become a stooge governor by wiring the Memphis boss: "More than 60,000 reasons why I love Shelby County."

When the next session of the state legislature began, Crump installed his own choices as speakers in the house and senate and gave Browning orders on legislation. But Crump soon learned that Luke Lea, freed from prison and granted a pardon, was a frequent visitor of Browning, his former military subofficer, in the statehouse. In addition, Crump was growing increasingly disturbed by Browning's popularity, for the bull-chested, thick-necked, almond-eyed governor drew large crowds wherever he spoke.

Nevertheless, Crump did not quarrel with his boy because the governor did not interfere with his control of state matters. But a lightning flash of trouble came when Nate Bachman, Tennessee's junior U.S. Senator died in April, 1937. Crump expected Browning to telephone him with the plea that he accept Bachman's Senate seat, and he was furious when Browning acted independently, appointing George Berry, head of the AFL's International Pressmen and Assistants' Union, and also a rich banker and TVA foe, to the upper chamber of Congress.

While Crump was still fuming, Browning named Lewis Pope, Crump's old enemy, as a $50,000 a year special investigator to collect back taxes. In a state of shock, Crump called Pope a "dead" man, and as for the Senate appointment, he said harshly: "The governor told me he would not appoint George Berry. Luke Lea dictated the appointment. Lea is back at the wedding feast in Nashville."

Crump finally called Browning to a summit conference, and the governor went to Memphis on September 13. Here a blistering argument took place, and a complete break occurred—the third successive break Crump had had with governors he had backed as candidates. Crump labeled him a "sneak" for his appointments, and Browning said in return: "He dealt with me about like a young man who would court a girl, make love to her and finally ask her to marry him and share his life; and when she declines his offer he goes off and talks about her and says she is a bad girl and ought to be run out of town." Crump's public rejoinder was to hoot at Browning as a "one-termer," to which the governor spat back, "I'd rather be a one-termer than a two-timer like Boss Crump."

After their blistering encounter, Browning was determined to hack Crump down to city-county size and remove him from state power. With his own belated success in putting tax bills through the state legislature despite Crump's disapproval, Browning believed he had wrested control of that body away from the Memphis boss. So he called a special session in October, 1937, with the specific purpose to end Crump's control of Democratic primaries.

Friend and foe alike were convinced Browning would ask for the end of the poll-tax payment voting requirement that had served as Crump's chief tool to dictate statewide Democratic nominees. However, the governor was not that democratic. Instead of seeking to widen the electorate, he favored continuing the poll tax but reducing the weight of the Shelby County vote. What Browning proposed was a county-unit system, a copy of the Georgia plan that was a sort of electoral vote. Each county would be assigned a number based to some extent on the popular vote in the last gubernatorial election, but with a maximum permissable number, or unit votes, for large counties regardless of the number of ballots cast there. A statewide candidate winning the popular vote in a county would be given the unit vote, and he would win election if he gained a majority of the number of county units. In the case of Shelby County, the county-unit system would cut its voting power from 25 percent of the state's total vote to only 13 percent.

A rancid fight developed in the state legislature when the bill came up for debate and vote. Crump ordered Kay Dee to hurry from Washington. Old McKellar addressed the Tennessee house like a champion of democracy; Crump added to the fight with a series of broadsides, declaring that "Huey Long in his desperation had not conceived so diabolical a bill"; and the Crump lobbyists roamed the floors and halls of the legislature. But Browning had the right wailing shade in his voice—and he had the votes.

After Browning signed the bill into law, Crump appeared to be finished even though he let out a condescending remark that the governor's action showed he "would milk his neighbor's cow through à crack in the fence." But Crump had a reason for keeping his buoyancy. He had brought legal suit against the act, and the State Supreme Court, which included a number of his friends, soon declared the county-unit law unconstitutional.

So Browning's opportunity to cut Crump down was gone, and despite his popularity in the state he faced an almost impossible task to win re-election in 1938. But he intended to win even with the setback. After firing all Shelby County employees from the state payroll and replacing them with his own loyal selections, Browning also gained control of the state elections board by doubling its membership from three to six persons. He then ordered the board to purge Shelby County's registration list of fraudulent names, a total he estimated at 40,000 of the 117,000 registered. When the board came to Memphis, Crump scoffed at the 40,000 figure and remarked, "I hope he won't give me that number familiar to him— 29,408—which was borne by his close Tennessee political adviser [Luke Lea] in the North Carolina penitentiary." Browning's people were harassed throughout their mission: For a long time, Crump's men would not turn over the list; and when they did, they had crossed through 5,000 names so that they could not be read. The board eliminated 14,000 other registrants, though members realized that when they left Crump would return those names to the list.

Browning also made the fight personal when he cancelled the Crump Company's insurance of a state teachers' college, and he tried to make the boss out to be an ally of gangsters by sending a crime commission to Shelby County to prove that crime control there was lax. But when it showed up, Crump lieutenants made public statements declaring that the commission members either had criminal records themselves or deserved to be prison inmates. In a letter to President Roosevelt in January, 1938, Crump informed the President that Browning "hasn't a sincere bone in his body and is surrounded by a coterie of bad men."

As the 1938 primary approached, McKellar again attempted to pick his own candidate for governor, this time choosing Walter Chandler, a member of the U.S. House of Representatives and a Crump aide. However, he quickly dropped Chandler when Crump chose harmless, obedient little Prentice Cooper, a state senator who had spoken out against the county-unit bill. Crump gave boyish Cooper nine political commandments as his platform: the first commandment read, "I propose to tear up Browning's Hot Taxes."

The 1938 gubernatorial primary was the state's bitterest political contest of the century. While Crump's boy, Prentice Cooper, who was a poor speaker, toured the state in his mumbling, faint manner, Crump and Browning traded libels and slanders and employed primitive electioneering techniques against each other. Browning said Crump was so senile he was almost beyond being institutionalized; and Crump retorted in an ad: "In a certain art gallery in France there are twenty-six pictures of Judas Iscariot. None of them is alike, but they all resemble Gordon Browning." Browning sent a sound truck into Memphis that blared out, "I Want to Meet the Bully of the Town"; Crump in return called him, "A bigoted boor [whose] heart had beat over two billion times without a single sincere beat."

Browning's supporters in Memphis lost their jobs, and some suffered beatings as the campaign went into its final weeks. Ben Kohn, a Memphis lawyer and Browning man, was blackjacked on the sidewalk in full view of a crowd. His assailant was charged with assault and was permitted to forfeit his $25 bond. Meanwhile Kohn was arrested for "carrying a gun," even though he was not armed, and when he was carried to a hospital Crump police guarded his room door as though he were a dangerous criminal who might escape.

Certain that Crump would run a dirty election, Browning announced he had ordered 1,200 national guardsmen to man Shelby County polling places. But this did not cause Crump to wince. Instead he asked his cousin, Federal District Court Judge John Martin, to issue a Federal injunction against Browning's move. Martin obliged, though he went far beyond the issuance of the injunction with a nonjudicial denunciation of a proposed "unjustified, tyrannical, unconstitutional, despotic invasion by a swashbuckling governor."

Crump's fun in that campaign came a day before the August 4 vote. That morning Memphians passing a busy downtown corner found a coffin on the corner containing a dummy of the governor and a sign reading, "Here lies Gordon Browning in State." In the dummy's suit pocket was a whisky bottle with a note: "Please handle carefully. He died so hard." To harangue the passing crowds, soap box orators at ten corners shouted their anti-Browning pitch, and replacements for the speakers took over at eight-minute intervals. Other crews walked through trolley cars and buses to campaign against Browning, and pretty girls in costumes sang their way through downtown Memphis and passed out literature. On Beale Street and through the Negro ghetto, Crump sent trucks with clanging church bells to remind the blacks that tomorrow was the day to be carried to the polls and collect their barbecues and watermelons.

The election results clearly proved Crump's one-man control of Shelby County. Two years earlier, he had given Browning 60,000 votes; now he totally reversed that vote, giving Prentice Cooper 60,000. In his revengeful zeal, however, Crump had ordered a microscopic vote total for Browning. But while the returns were pouring in, he realized he had gone too far in his hatred of Browning. So he sent word to his headquarters to raise Browning's total in order that the results would "look good and democratic." This decision increased Browning's vote to 9,000 in Shelby County's final tally, yet still permitted Cooper to win the governorship by a wide margin.

At the high-water mark of his power in 1938, tall, squeaky-voiced, popeyed, bespectacled, long-haired Boss Crump of Memphis did not appear to be suffering from the seeds of instability. His lieutenants were a strutting lot, what with their leader's ability to eliminate a popular governor. Even President Roosevelt had not ordered action when Crump admitted taking WPA money to build a heated dog kennel. "It will mean a lot of votes for you," non-office-holding Crump told the President over fried chicken and beer at a seven-state Democratic rally held in the Great Smokies.

But if Crump's dictatorship over Tennessee was real, it was never quite as stable as he would have desired it. The primary reason was that the least likely persons would suddenly erupt. The year 1938 was docile Mayor Watkins Overton's time to follow Gordon Browning's lead and stop responding properly to Crump's orders to "shut up" and "sign this."

First indication of Overton's change came when he ignored Crump's opposition and pushed through a city ordinance limiting the hours grocery stores could operate. Crump reacted by having the city commissioners repeal the ordinance. But Wat Overton went on to take independent action for the city on TVA electricity. This was unpardonable.

Back in 1934, while he was in the last of his four years in Congress, Crump had come home to spark a 17 to 1 approval of a local bond issue whose money was earmarked to bring cheap TVA electricity into Memphis. To celebrate the event, Crump had ordered Overton to rename a downtown road "November Sixth Street," in honor of the day the bond issue passed. Once he had the money from the sale of the bonds, Crump's first thought was to spend it on local power stations to receive the incoming TVA power and on a distribution system to carry it to consumers. But since the existing, privately owned Memphis Power and Light Co. had all such facilities, he changed his mind and determined to buy the "lightning trust, the interlocking, criss-crossing, circling, double-backing interests," as he referred to Memphis Power and Light.

Negotiations started in 1938, and at all the meetings Crump sat alongside Overton and the city commissioners at the table facing the head of the National Power Co., the large utility-holding company that owned the local service. Overton said exactly what he was told, frowned and smiled on cue, and kept in close touch with the boss between meetings. His subservience so pleased the Red Snapper that Crump graciously praised him to reporters as a good mayor who "has probably been in my office a thousand times and telephoned me at least that many times."

Crump was attending a football game on September 30, when

Mayor Overton acted on his own. With a scratch of his pen at 9:30 P.M., he signed an agreement in which the city would pay $13,500,-000 for the power company's steam generating plant and distribution facilities.

Crump was wild when he heard the news, for he had intended to complete the deal personally and take full credit. Orders went to the four other members of the city council not to approve Overton's handiwork; and though one councilman stood with Overton, the three who constituted a majority mouthed vicious anti-Overton statements supplied to them by Crump. Finally on December 12, Crump told reporters Overton was finished in Memphis and would be replaced in 1939. As for his opinion of his twelve-year stooge, Crump remarked: "The mayor's mind is as warped and out of shape with his peevishness and insincerity as a bale of cotton with three hoops off." Overton shocked Crump by having the audacity to reply. "I will never bow my knee to any tyrant, and I will never raise my hand in a Nazi salute to any dictator," he spat back at his long-time master.

Afterward, Crump reopened negotiations with the Wall Street holding company, and on February 15, 1939, he approved a $17,360,000 deal to buy the local company's electricity-distributing facilities and gas properties but not its generating plant. "All's well that ends well," he told a newsman. But his rancor against Overton held even on petty matters. That year on Armistice Day, the mayor was told not to participate in the march, despite his service in World War I and membership in the American Legion.

After Crump told Wat Overton he would not have his backing in the 1939 mayoralty election, Crump went on to devise a scheme to reduce two others in his camp whose popularity he believed was a threat to him. His Congressman, Walter Chandler, who had represented the Shelby County Congressional District since 1935, was getting national attention for his Chandler Bankruptcy Bill, and the boss could not abide a spreading spotlight. To cut him down a notch, Crump told Chandler, for instance, that in the Memphis Labor Day parade he could not march in the contingent labeled "Distinguished Citizens" but was to parade with the Typographical Union members. Another time, with his office filled with visitors, Crump called Chandler a thousand miles away in Washington and ordered him to sing "Old Black Joe" over the phone. Chandler complied.

In 1939, Chandler was basking in the Congressional limelight when he received another call from Crump, this time informing him that he was to be Memphis' next mayor. Chandler found this demeaning, but as a Crump-made man he did not argue.

At the same time that Crump had cast his wary eye on Chandler's growing national reputation, he was also aware that City Commissioner Cliff Davis of KKK renown and hero of the recent fight to keep the CIO from Memphis had become the most popular local official. Davis soon learned he was to be exiled to Washington to succeed Chandler in the House of Representatives.

Crump had still another part in his neat plan, and this was the role he had reserved for himself. First he would run for mayor so that the rest of the state could measure his solid strength in Memphis; then he would show his disdain for so small a job by handing it over to Chandler. This strange proposal was made public on September 22 when he announced himself as a candidate for the November 9 mayoralty election and stated that immediately after he took the oath of office on January 1, 1940, he would resign so that the city council could choose Chandler as his successor.

In a patriotic pitch, Crump declared that Chandler could not be an active candidate for mayor because he was needed in Congress to vote on the repeal of the American neutrality acts that were hamstringing England and France in their war against Germany, under way since the start of the month. In other words, said Crump, "I am announcing my candidacy as a pinchhitter for Congressman Walter Chandler, whom we want as our permanent mayor." He would be acting as "an elector" for Chandler, in a manner similar to national electors choosing a President, he explained.

No other candidate contested Crump in the mayoralty election, and he won a unanimous victory with 32,000 votes. True to his word, he was sworn in at 12:15 A.M. at Memphis Central Railroad Station and resigned a minute later. Then he denounced the reporters on hand as "CIO writers" and caught the train for New Orleans to see a New Year's Day football game.

In the World War II years that soon came to the United States, Crump had a fairly peaceful time with Chandler, his mayor, and Prentice Cooper, his governor. Each took Crump's interference and humiliating treatment with no show of public resentment.

In Chandler's case, Crump was being interviewed in his business office on one occasion and to show who was boss he phoned Chandler at city hall. "Walter," he drawled, "I bet you don't know the words to 'America.' . . . Oh, you do, huh? Well, let's hear you sing it." The reporter listened to a stirring rendition of "America" from the city's chief executive.

On another occasion, Crump phoned the mayor with the sad news that he had not seen a single bluebird that spring. Furthermore, while there were still some cardinals in Memphis, their numbers were few and he feared they would go the way of the bluebirds unless the mayor took swift action. Chandler did; he called a meeting of civic organization leaders, explained Mister Crump's concern and asked for suggestions. Juvenile Court Judge Camille Kelley, moved by the boss' worry, made a motion to establish the Crump Audubon Society, and her motion carried.

Chandler stayed on as mayor until 1946, when he grew angry with Crump's refusal to support him for the U. S. Senate, and he resigned.

Crump had few major problems with Prentice Cooper, whom he retained as governor for three terms before dropping him. "The little man with a big nose and a blue chin," as a reporter described the forty-three-year-old bachelor, came to office a mother-ridden, secretive, suspicious, and arrogant man. But he wanted further terms as governor and let Crump name 1,600 of the state's 10,000 employees to be fired as well as their replacements. He also showed political subservience by permitting Crump to name legislative officers and determine the legislative program.

Crump's biggest problem with Cooper was to emerge in the governor's final term, and it involved Crump's sacred poll tax. In 1938, while running for the first time, Cooper had campaigned in favor of repealing the poll-tax law of 1890 as a means of slashing Browning's support in middle and east Tennessee, where sentiment for repeal was strong. But once in office, Cooper made no effort to carry out his pledge, and Crump's legislative lobbyists saw to it that no repealer reached a vote.

Again in 1940, Cooper had the plank in his platform, but once more he did nothing to promote such legislation. Then in 1942, with Crump praising him as "a good little governor," Cooper's ran for a third term and once again used the poll-tax repeal in his platform. This time when the legislature met in January, 1943, newspapers favoring repeal scoffed at Cooper as a liar and a servant to poll-tax-loving Crump. The Memphis boss seemed on the defensive when he now said he would support the repeal if the legislature first passed a statewide permanent registration measure. Cooper suddenly came alive, introducing both bills, and when Crump's boys carried on a filibuster in the house against the registration bill, Cooper joined the fray personally, killing the filibuster and gaining a favorable vote on the registration legislation. Then before the house could relax, his men pushed hard for the anti-poll-tax bill and it also passed. Now the fight shifted to the senate, where Cooper again met success on the poll-tax bill.

But while Tennessee newspapers and League of Women Voters' clubs rejoiced, Crump was to have the last laugh. In March, 1943, he had Boss Burch Biggs, his ally at the eastern end of the state, initiate a legal suit to declare the repeal law unconstitutional. Biggs was a burly, rowdy dictator over three counties. When the case reached the five-man State Supreme Court, reporters discovered that three judges favored the repeal law and the other two opposed it. But before the case was heard, one of the three suddenly died and an exultant Crump ordered Cooper to name Frank Gailor, his most fawning Memphis aide, to the court.

Cooper regressed from his first show of independence and did as he was told. It was Gailor's deciding vote that invalidated the anti-poll-tax law. Gailor's argument was that the legislature lacked authority to repeal its own act of 1890! "The People Be Crumped!" was the reaction of the Nashville *Tennessean* to the court's decision. Afterward, the mood throughout the state was one of grim pessimism, that Mistah Crump could not be defeated on any issue.

During the war years the population of Memphis shot upward from 250,000 to almost 400,000 persons. These newcomers had no background in Memphis' history, and many were puzzled by the attention given a man who did not hold any public office, but with arrogant insistence ran the city, county, and state.

One thing that struck many as strange was the way old-timers howled in glee until the tears came on reading Crump's letters to editors and his paid political ads. C. P. J. Mooney, longtime Crump-fighting editor of the Memphis *Commercial Appeal*, was dead, but the boss had a new foe in Edward J. Meeman, who had come from the Knoxville *News Sentinel* to run the Memphis *Press-Scimitar*. For unearthing a variety of Crump's political activities, Meeman received several Crump letters calling him a host of names ranging from "stupid" to "a venal and licentious scribbler writing lying, misleading and colored stuff in your sheet." On one occasion, when Meeman wondered why the city grew eastward but not to the north or south, Crump read innuendoes of graft and corruption in the story. In drawling rage, he ordered a grand jury to investigate the story and subpoena Meeman to testify.

Crump's letters to Meeman (which the *Press-Scimitar* published) were mild compared with the campaign he conducted against pudgy Silliman Evans, who had bought Luke Lea's bankrupt Nashville *Tennessean*. Evans declared war on the poll tax and its chief defender, and his attacks evoked a stream of fierce replies from the boss.

The most famous of these was one Crump sent on January 29, 1945, and which became known as his "Slimy, Mangy, Bubonic Rats" letter. Evans printed it on his front page, and at Crump's request old Kay Dee in Washington inserted it into the *Congressional Record*. In this letter, Crump labeled Evans as a man possessing "a foul mind and wicked heart" and given to "ventosity." In addition to "Rat Evans," Crump went after *Tennessean* editor Jennings Perry and columnist Joe Hatcher. He called Perry an "insipid ass, moron, unworthy, despicable, low filthy scoundrel, pervert, degenerate . . . with the brains of a quagga" (African wild donkey) . . . who wrote unintelligently "just as one would expect of a wanderoo" (purple-faced ape). "Now we come to slimy rat, Joe Hatcher," Crump scribbled, charging that Hatcher had written that Crump sent his people "through the department stores of Memphis, asking them to send me [Crump] congratulatory birthday telegrams. That was a low, contemptible, lying statement," coming from "a low, filthy, diseased mind full of ululation."

Crump had replaced Governor Cooper in 1944 with Congressman Jim McCord, a former judge, mayor, and publisher; and he re-elected McCord in 1946 at the same time that he returned old Kay Dee McKellar to the U.S. Senate. Three weeks before President Roosevelt died in April, 1945, he had asked Crump to come to the White House and requested him not to support Kay Dee for another Senate term because he was growing infirm and senile. But Crump refused, and now McKellar was in for another six years as chairman of the powerful Appropriations Committee and as president *pro tempore* of the Senate with a limousine and chauffeur provided.

But despite such successes, all was not well with the Crump machine. Memphis had run down during the war: The schools were old and crowded; the streets were pockmarked and too narrow; and a shortage of housing induced short tempers. In addition, Crump was in his seventies and starting to ail, loyal lobbyist Frank Rice and secretary Marvin Pope were dead; others were slowing up, and some of the newer lieutenants were flaunting too much independence, arrogance, and ruthlessness.

Crump also would not change the values and "truths" he had brought to Memphis from Mississippi a half century earlier. Despite the large number of Negroes drafted into the Armed Forces during World War II, he refused to relax his policy of strict segregation. Moreover, he considered those who favored civil rights sinister and un-American. A. Philip Randolph, head of the Sleeping Car Porters Brotherhood, found his scheduled talk at the Memphis Mt. Nebo Baptist Church had been cancelled. Several months later, after Randolph sneaked into town and spoke, Crump's sheriff told reporters, "Had I known the Negro Randolph and those he brought with him were to make blackguarding speeches, I would have pulled them out of the pulpit." For the restless younger blacks, Crump was fond of reissuing the statement of an old Uncle Ned named Jesse Shankel: "If it hadn't been for the generosity of Mister Crump and Frank Rice on election day, many thousands of our people would not have been able to pay their poll taxes; and if they hadn't furnished us their fine cars to ride in, many of us wouldn't have voted."

Returning white servicemen, too, fresh from the fighting in Africa, Europe, and Asia, chafed under the Crump rules that told them what they could read, the movies they could watch, and how they must vote. There was even resentment from cat lovers, for Crump ordered a war on cats because of their enmity toward the birds he loved.

Then there was labor. Crump's fight to keep the CIO out of Memphis had collapsed with the development of Memphis' war industries, and by 1942 he went so far as to permit a CIO convention to be held in town. But by the end of the war, Crump denounced the CIO's Political Action Committee and worked through Governor McCord to bring about the enactment of an open-shop law.

First indication of coming trouble for the Crump machine came in 1946 when the East Tennessee Republicans in the Great Smokies Upper Tennessee Valley ended their long-standing pact with Crump. Under their agreement, they had promised to support his candidates for governor and Senator in exchange for his support of their Repub-

lican county candidates and his grant of state patronage. But now
the East Tennessee Republicans believed that a Republican trend
was coming to the state.

A far stronger indication of trouble came from the three eastern counties that Crump's Democratic ally, despotic Sheriff Burch
Biggs, ran. Returning veterans forced Biggs to retire after holding
a gun battle with his ballot-box thieves. Crump attempted to settle
the restlessness of his own Shelby County veterans by ordering five
county officers to retire and replacing them with five GI's. But this
was tokenism and did not stop the growing antiboss sentiment.

The gaining trend toward antibossism, as revealed in the Biggs
county, finally reached the Crump machine in 1948. Crump had
fought hard to re-elect old Kay Dee to the Senate two years earlier
over Ned Carmack, son of the assassinated former U.S. Senator and
editor Edward Carmack. But by 1948 news stories out of Washington noted that the Senate's longest-serving member presided over
that body in a senile fashion. On two occasions, after the Senate
had been in session for hours, McKellar called attention to his condition by rapping his gavel and asking for the chaplain's prayer, as
though the daily session had not yet begun. Another time dizziness
caused him to faint and tumble out of the Vice-President's presiding
perch.

It was difficult for Crump now to talk of McKellar as a dynamic
Senator from Tennessee, and he found that this image of decrepi-
tude was being transferred in the public's mind to himself. One rumor going around Memphis was that "Old Man Crump is reading
the Bible on street corners."

Crump further lost his firm grip on Memphis blacks in 1948
when he came out against President Harry Truman's civil rights
program. Moreover, he hastened the development of a substantial
black opposition when he announced his intention of deserting the
Democratic party in November and voting for the white supremacy
States' Rights party ticket headed by Strom Thurmond.

This was a crucial year for the Crump machine in Tennessee
because it had to put its prestige on the line in contests for governor
and U.S. Senator. In the gubernatorial contest, Crump backed Gov-
ennor McCord for a third term. The test would be made against Gordon Browning, whom Crump had installed as governor in 1936 and
then crushed in 1938. Browning had run unsuccessfully against

McCord in 1946 while serving in the American army in Europe. This time Crump sensed serious trouble, and he ran a libelous lot of anti-Browning newspaper ads that noted his desperation. In one silly ad he told the state: "Browning, as governor for one term, converted the proud capital of Tennessee into a regular Sodom and Gomorrah, a wicked capital, reeking with sordid, vicious infamy."

It was that year's Senate contest which oddly proved far more damaging to Crump's prestige than the gubernatorial race. Twice before Ed Crump had made Tom Stewart, the state prosecutor in the Scopes Monkey Trial, a U.S. Senator; and, in fact, in 1942 Stewart won re-election to the Senate even though he carried only Crump's Shelby County and the three under Sheriff Biggs, out of the total of Tennessee's ninety-five counties. But in 1948 Crump decided that Stewart was too weak a candidate because he was not a war veteran or an enthusiastic TVA backer. When Crump gave his support to Circuit Judge John Mitchell of Cookville, a colorless personality, the guess of the experts was that former G. I. Mitchell would nevertheless win over Stewart.

But this was not good enough, for a third candidate was in the field. Representative Estes Kefauver, a long man with a long nose and long ears and so slow talking and moving that his friends called him "a bundle of calm," had also entered the contest for Stewart's seat. Kefauver, whose father had been mayor of Madisonville in the Burch Biggs-controlled Monroe County for twenty years, had started out in Crump's favor as Governor Prentice Cooper's finance and tax commissioner. However, Crump's opinion of him had dropped sharply when Kefauver went to Congress and joined the liberal faction.

Kefauver's campaign for the Senate in the summer of 1948 was a bumbling and unenthusiastic effort until Crump decided to rip him to shreds with newspaper ads. Out went copy calling Kefauver the "darling of the Communists," and then came one ad that proved Crump's undoing.

In this spread inserted in papers across the state, Crump said: "Kefauver reminds me of the pet coon that puts its foot in an open drawer in your room, but invariably turns its head while its foot is feeling around in the drawer. The coon hopes, through its cunning," said Crump, "by turning its head, he will deceive any onlookers as to where his foot is and what it is into." Tennessee readers quickly got the point that what Crump was really saying was that Kefauver was pretending to be a loyal American when he was in truth a Red agent.

Yet the ad was just what Kefauver needed to bring his campaign alive. From that time on, the focus of his effort centered on the coon. "The coon is an easy animal to domesticate but a mighty hard little critter to put a collar on," he brought audiences to thumping cheers. "And I may be a coon, but I'm not Mister Crump's pet coon."

Once Kefauver had his Crump-given theme, a friend gave him a coonskin cap and in his eight-speeches-a-day campaigning tour, the cap gained more attention than what he said. Sometimes he would purposely enter a hall without wearing the cap, and the chant would turn into a roar—"Put it on! Put it on!"

As the campaign moved into its final weeks, observers were aware that something new was happening in Memphis. For the first time in decades, businessmen spoke out against a Crump candidate, and forty men dared hold a meeting in the Hotel Peabody to organize a Committee for Kefauver.

When the primary's results were in, Kefauver was the statewide victor, collecting 150,000 votes to 118,000 for Senator Stewart and 79,000 for Crump's man Mitchell. In addition, the hated Browning had defeated McCord for governor, 215,000 to 160,000. There was no doubt that the boss' machine had pulled all of its known stunts to give Shelby County to Crump's choices for the Senate and governorship, but the winning margins in the county were only a fraction of the old 50,000 to 60,000 Crump margins for his candidates, not enough to overcome the vote from the rest of the state.

The most significant change was in the Negro vote, for the barbecues, Cokes, watermelons, and free rides were no longer a sufficient inducement for them to vote like sheep for Crump. An estimated two-thirds of the black vote went to Kefauver, and one Negro explained his own change in these words: "For fifteen years I made up my mind that I would go to the polls and vote my convictions against the machine. But each time I went to the polling booth, and looking at all those machine watchers, I broke out in a sweat and voted the machine ticket, just like the sample ballot they put in my hands. This time I pulled my hat down on my head and voted for Kefauver."

Repercussions from the 1948 election were shocking to the

Red Snapper. The Kefauver-Browning victories removed Crump from the dominating position he had held over the state government for almost twenty years, and they shook his dictatorial control of Memphis, though no local force developed to contest his machine in the city. As one Memphis opponent put it, "The Browning and Kefauver victories didn't break the back of the Crump machine here, but it did give people courage to speak."

Crump had served as chairman of the committee to build a new bridge across the Mississippi; and when the work was finished in 1949, he expected that the bridge would be named for him. However, Governor Browning refused and called it the Memphis and Arkansas Bridge. The disappointed boss gained minimum comfort when the county government named the road leading to the bridge the "E. H. Crump Boulevard." But if Crump expected Browning to declare general war on him, he was mistaken, for the governor focused his efforts on school and rural road construction.

On the local scene, when Mayor Walter Chandler had quit singing telephone songs on request from Crump and resigned his office in 1946 because the boss refused to back him for the U.S. Senate, Crump engaged in a game of musical chairs to fill the top position at city hall. He first ordered the city council to name Commissioner and censor Joe Boyle as temporary mayor, then had him succeeded shortly afterward with Sylvanus Polk, and then with James Pleasants.

In the next year's municipal election, Crump ran Pleasants for the four-year term, and no opposition candidate appeared. But Pleasants, the unanimous winner, took to bitter public condemnation of the pay-increase demands of the police department; and late in 1948 after the Kefauver-Browning debacle, Crump fired Pleasants and had the city council appoint Watkins Overton, the ghost of yesteryear, in his place. Overton had once more pledged total subservience.

All seemed the picture of geniality between Crump and his former twelve-year stooge mayor. But after Crump went to the trouble of winning a four-year term for Overton in the 1951 election, Joe Boyle and other Crump aides came to the boss with stories of an ungrateful mayor quietly creating his own political machine. Charges and countercharges flew between "the man on the corner" and the mayor until a second break occurred between the two; and in March, 1953, Crump told Overton to clear his belongings from his office and Commissioner Frank Tobey was then appointed to succeed him. One of Crump's warnings to the new mayor was to avoid speaking to Negro organizations.

Meanwhile, Governor Browning, the winner of another term in 1950, managed to eliminate the basic political tools of the Crump machine. The poll tax was repealed, permanent statewide registration finally went into practice, and voting machines were ordered into the cities to replace the paper ballots.

But despite the elimination of some of his chief props, Crump still hoped to stage a comeback on the state scene in 1952. At the Democratic National Convention that year, Governor Browning had voted to seat the anti-civil rights Virginia delegation. Yet the Crump machine's advice to young Frank Clement, whom it was supporting against Browning, was that he claim Browning had opposed the seating. Clement was also advised to declare that the governor was known in the North as "Hubert Humphrey's boy." Other advice to Clement was that he charge Browning with being guilty of fraud and mismanagement in buying the Memorial Apartment Hotel in Nashville for the state's use.

Crump bought no newspaper ads in that election, nor did he hold his usual slanderous interviews with favored reporters. But his brightest sayings of the past were collected for use by Clement and his supporters. These included: "He lies by nature and tells the truth by accident"; "He has more avoirdupois and voice than intelligence"; and "A rogue might be reformed but there is no hope for a fool."

Aging Crump, who had been getting his political knocks in recent years, found himself described by editors as being "back in the saddle" when Clement beat Browning by 47,000 votes. But Crump's pleasure was marred by the defeat of eighty-three-year-old McKellar by Representative Albert Gore in Kay Dee's quest for his seventh six-year term as a U.S. Senator. Crump gave old Kay Dee Shelby County, but this was not enough to offset the Gore margin in other parts of the state.

Later that year Crump was wooed by the Democratic National Committee to aid Illinois Governor Adlai E. Stevenson in his campaign against General Dwight D. Eisenhower for the Presidency. But Crump had lost his old feeling for the Democrats and would do no more than give Stevenson the faintest support: "I really feel like a lost ball in high grass," he said. "Never voted for a Republican ticket and have opposed Truman. Between the two, I expect to cast my vote for Stevenson." Eisenhower carried Tennessee, the third Republican to do so since 1872.

By 1954, Crump was sick and exhausted. The world seemed to him to be crowded with elections. Browning was running again against Clement, and Representative Pat Sutton, a champion of Joseph McCarthy, was beseeching Crump for support against Senator Kefauver, whose six-year term was ending that year. But the old boss was approaching his eightieth birthday, and he was more interested in bringing black squirrels from Battle Creek, Michigan, to Memphis.

A malfunctioning heart and diabetes finally put him to bed, and he died on October 16, 1954, with a plea that his wife be brought to his bedside to hold his hand. At his passing, wrote the *New York Times,* flags in Memphis were flown at half-mast, and liquor stores were closed.

But even with the boss gone, his Memphis machine continued in power another five years until political reformers won the mayor's office and the four other commissioner seats in 1959.

Chapter Three

JAMES MICHAEL CURLEY
The Joyous Plague of Boston

"**I** CHOSE politics because prospects of ever getting anywhere elsewhere seemed remote," said James Michael Curley, for half a century a tempestuous Boston politician. Loved by thousands and hated bitterly by an equal number, Curley rushed through his long political career with more noise, excitement, and skulduggery than most of his peers.

His parents were potato-blight escapees, migrating from Ireland to the miserable tenement existence of the slum section of Roxbury in South Boston. Up from newsboy and soda fountain dispenser, James Michael was fifteen in 1889 when he finished grammar school and took an adult's job in the sweatshop run by the New England Piano Company. Fired nine months later, he put in eight years driving a horse and wagon as a grocer's delivery man for $7.50 a week, and one might have guessed at that point that James Michael Curley would lead a small, unrecorded life and pass on unnoticed by his fellow men.

But while he drove for C. S. Johnson, Grocers, young James Michael, husky at 5 feet 11 inches, began spending several evenings each week during the mid-1890s at "One-Arm" Peter Whalen's cigar store. This was where politicians gathered to fill the air with tobacco haze and political gossip. Curley, the wide-open-eared listener, was impressed with their good clothes and stylish gigs, and he was even more fascinated by their talk of politics.

In a self-assessment, Curley knew he was deficient on several scores that were considered basic to a successful political career.

134

First of all, he despised Pat "Pea-Jacket" Maguire and his lieutenant, John F. Dever, who bossed the seventeenth ward, where he lived. After Curley rang some doorbells for an opponent of the boss, Dever vowed to give him his "come-uppance" if he ever tried for a political career. In addition, Curley was a nondrinker at a time when hitting the bottle was equated with good fellowship. Still another serious drawback was his personality. Far from being a backslapper, he did not seem to possess a spontaneous fun-making nature. Some knew him as the strange young man who lived with his widowed mother, frequently shepherding her to morning mass, and taught Sunday School at Saint James Church. Also he had never been known to date a girl or to dance with one. Furthermore, when the young people of the neighborhood held a party, a church supper, a picnic, or a minstrel show, Curley was not a participant. Instead, he was always the person assigned to the drudge jobs. He arranged the affairs: handled ticket sales, bought the food, hired the band, arranged transportation; and at the parties he stood in the background waiting to supervise the clean-up.

Despite the drawbacks, James Michael Curley began working toward his goal of a political career. First, he joined the Ancient Order of Hibernians, the fraternal order of thousands of rich and poor Irishmen. With all his experience as the manager of youthful outings, he now took on the housekeeping chores of the A.O.H., which others avoided. Members were impressed with the new clockwork smoothness of the usually chaotic St. Patrick's Day parade and with the fact that all books of raffle tickets were sold. The goodwill he earned from doing such chores efficiently was like money in the bank for the future. Second, Curley used the Hibernians to spread word throughout the ward about his kind deeds.

Although James Michael was determined to enter politics, he suffered the timidity of the would-be beginner until one night in mid-1898 when "One-Arm" Peter Whalen told him to plunge into the race for the Boston common council. This was the lower house of the city's legislature, and it contained three members from each of Boston's twenty-five wards. The pay was only $300 a year, and the common council was limited to debating issues and sending recommendations, or orders, to the board of aldermen. The board of aldermen, nine men who formed the upper house, examined the recommendations and passed them on to the mayor for final decision.

Curley tried to back away from Whalen's suggestion by insisting he lacked campaign funds. But the cigar-store owner tossed him a $10 bill, and two others present gave him $15. With this $25, Curley was prodded into beginning his half-century career in politics.

In a secondhand suit once worn by a Harvard student, Curley undertook a vigorous campaign against enormous odds. Pea-Jacket Maguire was now dead and new ward boss John Dever saw to it that Curley was unable to rent a hall or even a store for a meeting. This forced him to rely on doorbell-ringing and street-corner rallies, but even at his outdoor meetings, the hand of Dever was present. Curley was an untrained speaker with an excellent voice, but he almost caved in at every stop when one of the boss' henchmen would demand to know why he was not with Teddy Roosevelt's Rough Riders, who were involved that summer in fighting the Spanish in Cuba.

Despite such campaign hardships, the worst was yet to come. On election day, observers estimated that Curley was a winner by several hundred votes. But this was before the count began. Dever and his lieutenant, Charlie Quirk, were in charge of computing totals in the back room of the ward's single polling place, and they barred Curley's friends from watching them. A short time after they disappeared with the box into the rear room, they came out and announced Curley a loser by 500 votes.

Rather than quit politics because of such frustration, Curley was even more determined to beat Dever and Quirk at their own game at the next annual election for the common council. His animosity toward them was heightened by the fact that the ward boss had reached his employer, C. S. Johnson, Grocers, and Curley was told one day to look for another job. Undaunted, he became a traveling salesman for a baking supply company with a route that took him through northern Massachusetts and southern New Hampshire; and as he handled the reins of his wagon, he developed plans for victory in 1899.

His inability to arouse audiences was one shortcoming he planned to correct. While on the road, he carried library books containing the orations of Disraeli, Gladstone, Burke, Lincoln, Daniel Webster, and other famous speakers. He studied them carefully, recited them frequently, and took note of melodic-sounding words. He also started a study of breath control and arm gestures, though it would be several years before he would be recognized as one of the best rabble-rousers of his era.

In his second campaign for the Boston common council, Curley's strategy was to gain public sympathy rather than disport himself as a strong man. He accomplished this by reciting at every stop the tale of Dever's crookedness in nullifying the vote of the ward at the last election. Curley also asked people he had helped through the Hibernian Order's welfare program to come to his meetings; and when he recognized one he would call out, "Where would Pat Kelly —that big fellow in the second row—be if I hadn't helped him?"

Curley employed other techniques to combat Dever and Quirk. At that time, candidates' names were placed on the ballot by the order in which they filed candidacy papers on filing day. Because so many voters were illiterate, the first name on the ballot was a large bonus for that candidate, for it was simple to tell such voters to put an "X" after the first name. In addition, voters who did not know the candidates generally voted for the first name.

Curley made certain he would have this priority by arriving at city hall the night before filing day with a large crew of muscular friends. Dever sent rowdies to oust them several times during the night; but the Curley crew withstood each attack by a better use of their own clubs and brass knuckles, and in the morning James Michael was first to stand before the filing clerk.

He also acted to prevent a second stealing of the ballots on election night. Using one of the few telephones in the seventeenth ward, he called the election department in city hall and was successful in getting the commissioners to take charge of the box at closing time. The ballots were taken to Faneuil Hall, and when the counting was completed, Curley was elected by a majority of 1,000 votes to a seat in the common council. So began the career of Boston's longest-serving officeholder.

Common-council member Curley knew instinctively how to build a quick record for himself. Maguire and then Dever had placed a large number of their henchmen in city jobs, and rather than enter into a protracted fight to fire them, Curley took a line calculated to win their affection. His first recommendation, or order, was to grant Saturday afternoons off for city employees, and the mayor was forced to accept it or face a total loss of support from local government workers. Curley followed this by introducing other orders to provide indoor toilets in the public schools, a gymnasium for the seventeenth ward, an eight-hour day for workers within Boston, and city action to end the backup of sewage in his ward.

Hardly had he taken his seat in the common council when Tom Curley, who was not related to James Michael Curley, offered him a proposition involving both their futures. Tom Curley, another rising seventeenth ward Democrat, had believed himself next in line, instead of Dever, to succeed Pea-Jacket as ward boss, and he now proposed supporting James Michael in that year's election for chairman of the Democratic ward committee—or ward boss—if James Michael would, in turn, let him run for his seat on the common council in the next election.

James Michael yearned to be a ward boss, but the thought of trying for it only a few months after his first election seemed presumptious. Yet with Tom Curley in his corner, success might be possible, so they shook hands over this deal.

Even though Dever considered the bakery route boy and new member of the lowly common council a joke of sorts, he took no chances once James Michael announced he intended to get the boss' job. During the campaign for Democratic ward chairman, his boys met Curley's street-corner rallies with "sticks, stones, bricks and brass spittoons." Curley claimed that if his crowds weren't sent running by such attacks, the Dever-Quirk rowdies then tried to drown him out while he spoke and threatened him afterward to his face.

But Curley was quick to learn from example. He organized his own bully boys who enjoyed mixing with Dever's men, and he had his own leather-lunged crew whose cheers at street-corner rallies drowned out opposing jeers. And sometimes James Michael used his fists to personal advantage to thwart Dever's strategy.

For example, Dever had hired a much-feared alley brawler to appear at every Curley rally and split the air after every Curley paragraph with "Curley, you're a lousy liar!" Despite his continuing interruptions, Curley's bullies were afraid to tangle with him.

After this had gone on at several meetings, Curley shouted back at him one time, "Tomorrow night I have a rally scheduled at the Vine Street Church. If the gentleman out there cares to show up, I'll answer any questions he has."

The brawler showed up at the church, and Curley pointed to him. "Make a path for the gentleman," he told his audience. "Let him come up to the platform." The brawler reached the top of the stairs, and with a smile on his face Curley reared back and hit him on the chin with a powerful roundhouse. Dever's man did a backflip and was removed unconscious from the church. "I think that answers the gentleman's questions," Curley announced to the delight of the crowd.

After weeks of the street-fight campaign, voting day finally came, and Curley made certain his own men stood behind the tellers when they tallied the count. The miracle had happened. Curley was elected boss of the seventeenth ward by the tiny margin of 7 votes.

Being ward boss was an immense step forward for a political newcomer, and Curley intended to use it to become a rich and powerful man. His first move in this direction was to quit his job as a bakery route salesman and enter the insurance business in partnership with his brother John. When dozens of merchants in his ward took out policies from him in the next few months, Curley acquired a secure financial base on which to plan a headful of money schemes.

Then Curley established the Roxbury Tammany Club as his private political organization. At first housed in a decrepit two-story building, the Roxbury Tammany Club later acquired a fancy spread complete with a reading room, pool hall, dance floor large enough for 200 couples, and a dining room. Members were assessed small dues, and local merchants were asked to contribute money for charitable outings and the Thanksgiving and Christmas baskets. Curley wanted no future contenders and successors developing under his auspices, so he named himself president of his Tammany Club and ruled that all other members would be considered privates.

As ward boss, Curley kept his eye on maintaining and enlarging his vote strength. Because of the large influx of immigrants into the seventeenth ward, he set up naturalization classes to help get them through the citizenship exams. He also devoted two days a week to counseling ward residents directly on their personal problems. On these days, Curley was in his office at the Tammany Club by 8:00 A.M. to meet with those who had legal problems. A good part of these mornings was spent accompanying these persons to police stations and the courts to straighten out their troubles. Curley's unflagging rule was that he would not help drunks or woman beaters. Then in the afternoon, he met with unemployed persons in a room at city hall and found jobs for about 500 each year and also stayed dozens of eviction and furniture repossession orders. In the evenings, he met with the needy. After each conversation, he arranged for the necessary solution—food, clothing, fuel, or medical care. A Tammany file card noted every ounce of aid.

Besides these charitable ways of increasing his support, Curley boasted that he expanded his voting registration base in an illegal manner. "Men who were in jail, in hospitals, out of town, or peacefully reposing in a cemetery often swung elections," he said cryptically.

When Curley became a ward boss, this automatically put him into the select club of Boston ward bosses who met at intervals to talk over problems; test each other through threats, flattery, and strategy; and discuss candidates for local offices, the state legislature, governor, and Congress. The very top bosses formed what was known as the "board of strategy," and they met regularly in Room 8 at the Quincy House behind city hall. Curley was not a member of this choice board until he underwent some years of seasoning, and even then he stood apart from the others.

At the time of Curley's rise, the strongest ward boss was Martin Lomasney, better known as the "Mahatma," who ran the West End's eighth ward, which extended from the back of Boston Common down to the Charles River. The Mahatma was a self-made man and always on the lookout for safe real estate ventures based on the inside information from political quarters.

All the other bosses, Republicans as well as Democrats, studied the Mahatma's techniques to determine the secret of his success. He met every boatload of immigrants and helped them find their way to relatives. Every night he passed out fifty tickets for a free night's lodging at flophouses to men down on their luck. At the polls, he used dozens of tricks to win elections. "Ballot boxes are never stuffed, unless it's absolutely necessary," was one of his rules to live by.

As part of his bargain for accepting Tom Curley's aid in his fight to replace John Dever as ward leader in 1900, James Michael Curley had agreed to relinquish his seat in the common council to Tom the following year. But having enjoyed the taste of office, James Michael did not relish the idea of becoming just a backstage politician, which was a common role of a ward boss. So he ran in 1901 for the lower house of the state legislature, and he and Tom easily won their seats.

By now, James Michael had money in the bank, good clothes, a comfortable home for his mother, political power, and a happy future. His first recognition from the other ward bosses came in 1902

when they elected him chairman of the Democratic ward committee. This in turn prompted James Michael to look for a political office with more prestige, and in 1903 he announced his candidacy for
a place on Boston's nine-man board of aldermen.

But just as Curley's star was twinkling brightly, the ugly dawn
came. Bartholomew Fahey and James Hughes were semi-illiterates
who had helped round up seventeenth-ward votes for the two Curleys
with the promise that they would be given jobs afterward. Unfortunately, the Curley patronage handouts were nonexistent when
Fahey and Hughes came to the Tammany Club for their rewards.
But for the sake of his political code, which required a man to keep
his word, James Michael felt obliged to get jobs for them.

Trouble descended swiftly. As James Michael explained his
own stupid solution: "Down in my ward we had a couple of fellows
who wanted to be mail carriers, and they were a little short on some
of the information required by Uncle Sam. So Tom Curley joined
me in taking the examination for their benefit. We looked up the
matter beforehand and could not find anything to show this was a
breach of the law, although we knew it was a breach of the rules.
We passed the examination, and some of our opponents got us into
trouble."

The truth was that someone present in the examining room
recognized the two Curleys and told the U.S. District Attorney. The
case came to the Federal District Court, and when their lawyer demanded a fee of $3,500, James Michael had his Roxbury Tammany
Club stage a minstrel show to pay him. In court, the lawyer tried to
argue that nothing in the law barred a proxy from taking a Federal
exam. But the judge ruled otherwise and sentenced the defendants
to spend sixty days in the Charles Street Jail. Twenty-nine-year-old
James Michael Curley appeared ruined as a politician as he was led
away manacled to a court officer.

But he led a charmed life. He quickly made a friend of the
warden and soon had the run of the jail. Most of his time in prison
was devoted to self-education and he passed his days reading history books, biographies, plays, essays, and poems. Much of what he
would quote in his later political career stemmed from his reading
during these two months.

Besides this wholesale reading, James Michael brazenly campaigned from his cell for the Boston board of aldermen while Tom
Curley ran for the state senate. The two wrote speeches that James

Michael passed on to henchmen for recitation to campaign audiences. James Michael recognized the folly of admitting guilt and begging forgiveness. Instead, he campaigned aggressively from jail by insisting he had been right. "I felt I had done a charitable thing for a man who needed a job so he could support his wife and four children," he said by way of explanation.

Public sympathy in the seventeenth ward was on the side of the two Curleys, and they won easily. But in Tom Curley's case, the state senate, which was securely in Republican hands, refused to seat him. James Michael Curley was made of tougher fiber, and when he stepped outside jail on January 6, 1904, he jumped into a carriage and ordered the driver to speed to city hall. He had heard that Daniel Whelton, the president of the board of aldermen, was to make a motion to bar him. With five of the nine members on Whelton's side, his ouster seemed certain.

When Curley came on the run into the second-floor board room, he immediately asked Whelton if he planned to make the motion, and when Whelton said yes, Curley pointed to the window and remarked, "If you do, you will go through that window." Whelton gasped, and when he did not offer his motion, Curley took his seat and remained an alderman for five years.

Shortly after Curley was released from jail and had assumed his seat as an alderman, he met Mary Herlihy, a pretty, dark-haired girl, at a minstrel show put on at St. Phillip's church. Curley courted Mary for two years, even taking her along to political meetings in order that his basic life's work would not suffer because of romance. Finally the boy who had been afraid of girls married the Irish lass on June 27, 1906, when he was thirty-one, and took her on a honeymoon to Canada and through New York State. But even on this trip, Curley could not refrain from stopping at every town hall and city hall along the way for long talks on political methods with local officials.

Irrepressible Curley's five years on the city's nine-man board of aldermen were stormy. The conservative members were thrown off balance by continual assertions from him that they were subhuman reactionaries. As a result of this taunting, several of his recommended orders in council were approved by the majority of aldermen in a face-saving effort to show they were not as he had characterized them. This jibing produced approval of orders such as the establishment of a business course high school, pensions for firemen, visiting hours in the city hospital, liberalization of the truancy law to keep youngsters out of prison for skipping school, and the need for union labels on all city horseshoes.

The Curley bag of legislative tricks included other delights besides name-calling. It was common practice, for instance, not to pay street laborers on rainy days when they could not work. Curley wanted them paid by the week, but he knew this would not win approval because all cities operated in this stingy fashion. So he used the technique known as "pinching other toes" and introduced an order barring wage payments to foremen and clerks in the street department on bad weather days. This outraged the aldermen and they rejected it, but most saw the meanness of the existing law and approved another Curley order to put day laborers on regular wages.

Curley used a different technique when he wanted a playground built in the seventeenth ward. Most aldermen opposed such frivolous spending on Irish slum children. Therefore, Curley had a friendly aldermen introduce the order, and when Curley stood up to denounce it in strong language, the board of aldermen quickly approved it afterward to show their opposition to him.

These five years as alderman were also turbulent political years for James Michael Curley, who was still the ward boss. Once he lost his seat in the state senate, Tom Curley had grown angry at James Michael's unwillingness to give him either the presidency of the Tammany Club or the chairmanship of the ward committee, and in 1907 he announced he would run against James Michael in the contests for the two positions.

James Michael won both elections handily and immediately threw Tom and his lieutenants out of the organization. This brought on open warfare between the Curleys that lasted decades. Once when James Michael was scheduled to speak at an indoor rally, Tom bribed the janitor to lock the doors and windows a few hours before the event and go home. Another time when Tom ran for office, James Michael had 200 of his boys boo him so steadily he could not speak. He also spoiled several business deals for Tom, who remarked angrily one time, "You don't know how vindictive Jim is. If I was blind and holding out a tin cup, he would spit in it."

By the time James Michael Curley had served a few years as alderman, he well understood that if he wanted to rise further, he

would have to outtrick his fellow Democratic ward bosses. Because
they were so firmly entrenched in their individual wards, it would
take a great deal of cunning, double-dealing, promise-breaking, and
sheer audacity to achieve control of city hall—his eventual goal.

Boston was different from almost every other city, where an
ambitious politican could start his own political machine and push
it into the wards surrounding his until he owned a city-wide organization. In Boston, the wards had Chinese walls, and he would
have to play the shrewd ward bosses off against each other, weaken
their power by buying their top aides, spread false rumors, and expose some of their boodling. All the while, he would have to capture
the emotional support of a large Irish following in town, to stick
with him no matter what. But with his abundant Irish charm and
wit that had been released by his successful political life, and with
his gift for turbulence and personal trouble, plus his impudent, winning smile, he expected no problems on this score.

Despite Curley's program, which called for numerous speeches
denouncing bossism, the city's reform movement leaders early in
the century concentrated their efforts on ridding Boston of the seventeenth ward's boss influence in municipal affairs. The reformers'
vehicle for accomplishing this was the successful effort by the Good
Government Association in 1909 in promoting a new city charter
through the legislature to replace the seventy-five man common
council and the nine-man board of aldermen with a single city
council of nine members.

In 1909, the first election of the new city council took place,
with all members elected at-large and without party labels. The
"Goo-Goos," as Curley called the Good Government Association reformers, were certain Curley's support was limited to the seventeenth ward and that a city-wide election would eliminate him.
The truth was that Curley believed this, too, so he attempted a strategy of confusion to win the votes of reform backers throughout
Boston. His technique was simply to print a slick brochure calling
for his own election and listing his sponsors as the "Better Government Association." The name of this nonexistent group was so close
to that of the actual reform organization that thousands of voters
were apparently fooled by it, and Curley was swept into the new
city council.

However, the dismay of the Goo-Goos turned to joy within a
year because Curley announced he was running for the U.S. House
of Representatives. This decision was a sudden one, for Curley's

focus was on Boston politics until a hot summer afternoon in 1910 when he was stretched out for a shave in Mike Fitzgerald's barbershop. Former Congressman William S. McNary walked in, took the chair next to him, and insisted that Curley run against his successor, Joe O'Connell, a Harvard lawyer and the father of twelve children, who had defeated McNary four years earlier. Curley hesitated only until McNary promised to support his candidacy, and once McNary made this pledge, Curley told him, "Okay, I'll throw my 'Iron Mike' into the ring."

But hardly had Curley publicly entered the 1910 congressional race that McNary also became a candidate. Once he got over the shock, Curley saw that what McNary had wanted was a third candidate who would split the vote with O'Connell in Roxbury and Dorchester while he captured his home area in populous South Boston and won the Democratic primary.

Curley recognized that his only hope was to beat McNary in South Boston, and he laid out a campaign to shell the double-crossing McNary daily in his own stronghold. Part of his plan was to rent billboards, but McNary had already leased every one available; and each carried a grinning picture of Iago, as Curley nicknamed McNary, plus the exhortation to SEND A BIG MAN TO DO A BIG JOB.

Because outdoor advertising was considered essential in a Boston election, Curley devised a scheme of ridicule to combat McNary's monopoly. In the dark of night, he had his own lads glue small Curley posters to the billboards that carried the legend: ELECT A HUMBLE MAN, JAMES MICHAEL CURLEY. A laugh at McNary's expense went up in the morning as word of Curley's deed spread.

McNary was also emphasizing his own honesty at every street-corner rally, and so Curley used ridicule to cut him down on this score. A bum appeared in South Boston one day holding a lantern and bearing a sign on his back that read: "I am Diogenes seeking the honest man McNary." Eventually he was arrested, and Curley walked into court as his attorney. When he won the bum's release on the grounds that no man could be imprisoned for calling McNary honest, the newspapers howled in glee, and McNary suffered further embarrassment.

Curley in addition had one of his own boys follow him from rally to rally and interrupt his speech with a jeering, "Why don't you tell us why you spent sixty days in jail?" This invariably roused the crowd to anger at the catcaller and to sympathy for Curley.

When the campaign reached its high-heat stage, Curley learned that Congressman Joe O'Donnell's strength had increased due to the secret efforts of Mayor Fitzgerald. Honey Fitz, as the mayor was called, had promised Curley he would remain neutral, and Curley now stormed into his office, shook a big fist in the face of "Hizzoner," and threatened to pulverize it unless the little mayor returned to his pledged neutrality. The pledge was quickly renewed.

There was little question on election day in 1910 that Curley's showmanship and conniving strategies would make him the winner. But hardly had he arrived in Washington when he learned that McNary had been in touch with old friends in the House to deny him his seat because he had been in jail as a violator of a Federal statute.

This called for action at the seat of power, and good fellow, charming Curley went directly to newly elected House Speaker Champ Clark for aid. Clark, a moose of a man who distinguished himself from other House members by his white vest, coveted the Democratic presidential nomination in 1912, and he believed Curley's claim of political power throughout the Bay State. The result was that Clark pigeonholed the ouster petition and named Curley his New England campaign manager. In addition, Clark put him on the Foreign Affairs and Immigration Committees to give him instant prestige, and Curley purchased a white vest to show his gratitude.

In the hard-fought scramble for convention delegates in 1912 among the Clark, Woodrow Wilson, and William Jennings Bryan forces, Curley gained Clark's gratitude when New England delegations were 2½ to 1 in favor of Clark. But with the two-thirds rule required to nominate, Clark could not rise above a simple majority at the Baltimore convention, and on the forty-sixth ballot, following Bryan's denunciation of Tammany bosses for supporting Clark, the convention nominated Wilson.

Curley had little time for disappointment, for he was himself engaged in his re-election fight for his House seat. Newspaper editors considered him a shoo-in, but he was taking no chances. In the middle of the night before the dawn of election day, he sent dozens of his boys to ring doorbells; and when the sleepy people opened their doors, the Curley crew told them they represented Curley's opponent who wanted their votes. With few exceptions, loud cursing and door-slamming resulted.

Congressman Curley was hardly back in his House seat when

he decided to run for mayor of Boston, the political post that was his true ambition. It had been fun to stand up in the well of the House and denounce Boston Yankees, as in a widely quoted speech in which he had labeled the Boston Tea Party of 1773 as a drunken "beer party," or to detract from the French fighters in the American Revolution by claiming that the best "French" fighters were really Irish. But there was little money to be made in Washington as one of 435 House members; nor was there much time to waste now that he was thirty-nine. As for President Wilson's New Freedom program of tariff and currency reform and antitrust legislation, it was a bore compared with the excitement of Boston politics.

Curley's major problem in running for mayor was popular John Francis "Honey Fitz" Fitzgerald, who was finishing out his second term as mayor and wanted a third. (Honey Fitz's grandson, John F. Kennedy, would one day be President.) As was his approach, Curley took direct action by barging into a hotel dining hall where Honey Fitz was holding a dinner for the city council. When the guests stared at him, Curley calmly announced his candidacy for mayor in the January, 1914, election.

Stunned, Honey Fitz was silent on that occasion, but a few weeks later when Curley met with him in private and threatened to expose his romantic adventures, the mayor agreed to finish out his term and retire. However, Honey Fitz reconsidered afterward and concluded that Curley was merely bluffing. So he enlisted the aid of William Cardinal O'Connell to end Curley's candidacy. The Cardinal called the Congressman to a secret meeting and asked him to let the mayor run for a third term without his competition. O'Connell's chief argument was that Honey Fitz was fifty and Curley only thirty-nine, and a four-year wait would not make Curley an old man.

But Curley would not listen to the Cardinal, nor would he take heed when the Democratic city committee held a meeting to consider candidates and invited him. As soon as the vote of 24 to 1 against his candidacy was announced, Curley upbraided his fellow ward bosses by calling them "a collection of empty eggshells."

Honey Fitz began his campaign with his successful technique used in earlier elections—an off-key rendition of "Sweet Adeline" at street-corner rallies and a stiff-legged Irish jig. But Curley eventually forced Honey Fitz from the race by showing he had not been bluffing. One morning Boston papers carried the following announcement by Curley: "I am preparing three addresses which, if necessary, I shall deliver in the fall and which, if a certain individual had the right to restrict free speech, I would not be permitted to deliver.

"One of these addresses is entitled: 'Graft, Ancient and Modern'; another, 'Great Lovers: From Cleopatra to Toodles'; and last, but not least interesting, 'Libertines: From Henry VIII to the Present Day.'"

Honey Fitz realized when he read this that Curley intended to talk openly about "Toodles" Ryan, reputedly the mayor's girlfriend, and he bowed out of the race. This action made him lose face in his home ward where he was extremely popular, but he felt he had no alternative.

Meanwhile, the other bosses had been daily growing angrier with Curley for his bellowing against bossism. Finally they chose Thomas Kenny, the dull, fifty-year-old president of the city council, as their candidate. The mayor also came out for Kenny as did the Yankees in the Good Government Association, and the struggle against Curley gathered strange bedfellows. This was not lost on Curley who shouted from a speaker's platform, "I invite the opposition of all corrupt ward leaders who have allied themselves with the downtown realty pirates, wealthiest bankers and the New Haven Railroad."

In contrast to Kenny's drab campaign, Curley accentuated their differences with a slam-bang campaign complete with a brass band, loud chorus, and peppy guest speakers. He also had a secret weapon in John L. Sullivan, the "Boston Strong Boy" and former heavyweight boxing champion of the world. John L. was down on his luck and seldom sober, with a free drinking tab at Kerrisey's saloon and a bed of straw in a stable in Curley's ward. But he was still a celebrity, and he was so thankful to Curley for some financial help that he gladly joined him on the campaign platform. The press called Sullivan's appearance on Curley's platform and the other entertainment features "Public theater."

While some of Curley's followers accused Kenny of directing the heavyhanded effort to interfere with their boss' campaign, Curley correctly gauged that his fellow ward bosses were the string pullers. Crowds of toughs and hecklers gathered at Curley rallies to pick fights with the audience and to shout threats and epithets. Curley could not send John L. Sullivan to restore order, for the law said that his hands were lethal weapons. One massive fellow took to showing up and shouting a stream of billingsgate to punctuate Curley's remarks. At one rally, Curley pointed to him after an interruption and called out: "Sir, would you like to ask a question?"

"Sure, I got a question," the rascal replied.

"Fine, my good man," said Curley. "But there are ladies present. So before you state your question, would you remove your hat?"

A moment after the giant did this, one of Curley's boys hit him on the head with a club. He was carried away and was not seen again at a Curley rally.

To the despair of his many boss advisers, Kenny campaigned with dry speeches on the city's budget and tax problems, and refrained from attacking Curley personally. But finally near the end of the campaign, he paused during one such talk and asked, "Where was Curley during the Spanish-American War?"

The next night Curley read the newspaper account of Kenny's talk to his campaign audience in Kenny's home area in South Boston, and when he finished he exclaimed, "Naughty, naughty, Tommy." His audience howled with delight.

The day before the campaign closed, Lomasney came out for Curley after months of leading the attack on his fellow ward boss. But Curley said that the Mahatma was too late and would get no special privileges as a result.

In the end, Curley got 43,000 votes to 37,500 for Kenny. Curley's supporters were surprised that Kenny had done so well, but Curley was pleased that he had won, and this was all that mattered.

"I shall give to this city four years of honest and constructive administration," Curley solemnly pledged.

The Roxbury Tammany Club occupied most of the 2,500 seats in Tremont Temple on that rainy day early in February, 1914, to witness the swearing-in ceremony for "James Hisself." Curley denounced the administration of Honey Fitz, who sat stoically on the platform and suffered through the attack. Then the new mayor walked to his office in city hall, and his first action was to tell the building commissioner to turn in the keys of his office and leave the building.

Curley's reign as mayor got under way in a cascade of public works programs. Tunnels were dug under streets, the electric street-car system was extended, brick-piece city streets were paved by the mile, new parks and playgrounds replaced rat-infested tenements, swamps were filled and beaches came into existence, and hospitals were cleaned and painted.

While all these civic improvements were going on, however, related backstage activities of the new mayor were causing concern in many quarters. The ward bosses fumed like shackled dragons when it became apparent that he planned to ruin them and establish a city-wide machine of his own. Honey Fitz was the first boss hit when Curley swept his predecessor's crew of city employees out of office and for good measure fired anyone rumored to have voted for Kenny. "I have no desire to be ambushed in my own camp," Curley explained.

When emissaries of the ward bosses rode to city hall in their two-horse hacks and one-horse hansom cabs, they learned that Curley would not talk to them. Instead he began a system of holding regular visiting hours each day for any citizen with a problem. As a pleader stood before his desk, Curley's secretary read from a card the name, address, and request, and the mayor disposed of the matter then and there. Usually he took positive action because he needed to build a personal following of undimmed cheerers that extended into every ward. By his swift decisions, he could see 200 persons daily in the allotted hours, or 200,000 persons in his first term. The Boston *Transcript* termed the nauseous scene at the crowded city hall "the spectacle of the corridors." But Curley didn't care what the *Transcript* said, for within a year the ward bosses were, with the exception of Mahatma Lomasney, operating like sick chickens with terminal political diseases.

Yet from the outset and throughout his long career as mayor, Curley was a rather unique type of boss. He was never vindictive, and he never created fear among his opposition that they might be imprisoned, that their voices would be stilled or their businesses ruined, no matter how they fought him.

At first the Good Government Association liked what it saw of the bustling new city administration that was modernizing the city with what appeared to be great efficiency and at moderate cost. But the bills proved sky high; tax rates shot up on banks, newspapers, and businesses; and secrecy from the mayor's office became the rule. Curley granted no personal interviews, he ordered his underlings not to cooperate with the press, and at his daily 11:00 A.M. news conferences he steered the talk to a glib presentation of his own glories. Outsiders who came to discuss city business with him found

Curley was not the loud, smiling, backslapping candidate on the hustings but a loner who was invariably suspicious and wary, a strange double personality.

There was a way to check into the city's activities, and this was through the Boston finance commission, which the state legislature had established in 1907 to act as an independent budget and tax watchdog in city hall. If Curley had any initial fear of the finance commission, he soon dispelled it by his own clever tactic. The commission operated with a thoroughness bordering on slow motion, and when it sent its accountants to check into one program, Curley made use of their slowness by immediately starting a dozen new programs. The commission's investigators uncovered contracts awarded to Curley associates and not to the lowest bidders and showed that low quality materials were used even though contracts called for higher grades. But the commission was so snowed under by hundreds of new Curley contracts that it was soon a decade away from a covering report.

As a result of its own helplessness in dealing with the growing number of city contracts, the commission turned its attention to Curley personally. After his election, he and his wife had assured voters they intended to remain "just folks" and continue living in their simple, frame house in Roxbury. But as mayor, Curley built a large brick Dutch Colonial house on the exclusive Jamaicaway. The new Curley home had a 40-foot-long, mahogany-paneled dining room, 14-foot ceilings, a massive chandelier, gold-plated fireplace equipment for the marble fireplace, and an impressive winding staircase. The Yankee blueblood snobs living on the Jamaicaway did not take offense at their Irish blockbuster until he installed white shutters with cut-out shamrocks.

Once the story of the house became known, the finance commission delved into its high cost to determine how Curley could have bought it on his small salary as a Congressman and mayor. Curley's first testimony in the showdown was that the money had come from the sale of his half interest as a silent partner in the Daly Plumbing Company. But Frank Daly, who was called to corroborate this, insisted that Curley had not received "a nickel" from his company. When the finance commission demanded a new explanation, Curley calmly replied that his high standard of living and ample funds were made possible by the profits he acquired on stock-market tips given him by Nathan Eisman, a wool merchant. Asked where the commission might find Mr. Eisman, Curley replied, "In the grave." Faced with this dead end, the commission gave up its fruitless search into Curley's finances, though it attacked him on other scores, many of which were petty.

Curley had made an enemy of Governor David Walsh by backing his opponent in the last Democratic primary. Walsh, a tall, heavyset man who dressed like a dandy, was the first Irish Catholic to win a statewide political office; and he intended to prevent Curley from becoming the second in this select category. Every request by Curley for patronage was denied, while schemes by the mayor's enemies to weaken his authority were honored by the governor.

In 1914, the Goo-Goos undertook to fight Mayor Curley, and Dave Walsh gave them behind-the-scenes support in pushing a Boston reform charter through the state legislature. Curley found several of its features obnoxious, especially one that would substitute a seventeen-man city council selected by wards for the nine-man council elected at-large. It was obvious that this would strengthen the ward bosses and weaken him. The bill also contained an ominous clause providing for the recall of a mayor through the means of a special election.

Naturally, James Hisself argued strenuously with the legislature and the governor against the charter. But Walsh heard him in cold silence in one face-to-face meeting and then signed the measure. Then to heap further slag on Curley, he also extended the terms of members of the Boston Transit Authority to three years to prevent Curley from putting his own men on the Authority. Little wonder that when the Bunker Hill celebration took place on June 17, 1915, Curley's boys stood on rooftops along the line of the parade and threw stones and bottles at Walsh as he rode by in a barouche. Fortunately, Walsh escaped uninjured. The Springfield *Union* commented, "Jim Curley has about as much use for the governor as a maiden lady for a shaving mug."

Curley gained satisfying revenge on Walsh in 1915 when the governor had to run for re-election. That year, Curley could not prevent Walsh's renomination. But by his agreement with Martin Lomasney, Curley's followers joined the Mahatma's supporters in staying at home on election day. The result was that Dave Walsh lost by the small margin of 6,000 votes to Samuel McCall, a ten-term Congressman, who was his Republican opponent.

Before he left office, Walsh attempted to squash Curley. With his blessings and backstage advice, the Good Government Association undertook a campaign to have the electorate recall Curley in 1915. Curley knew he could count on the Mahatma's help that year to fight recall because he had named his brother, Joseph Lomasney, to the schoolhouse commission. In addition, Curley went to Honey Fitz Fitzgerald, and after assuring Honey Fitz of his support in his next year's intended race against wispy, goateed Senator Henry Cabot Lodge, he induced Fitzgerald to make a strong statement against the recall referendum. Few took note of the incongruity of Honey Fitz's praise of Curley when only a few months earlier he had denounced James Michael as a crook.

How important Lomasney and Honey Fitz were in saving Curley was not measurable. But when the Goo-Goo's recall proposition was defeated at the polls, Curley thanked both bosses.

One of the strange characteristics of the political career of Boston's James Michael Curley was that he could lose an election when he appeared to be invincible yet rise from the graveyard to win an "impossible" victory.

After Curley had become mayor in 1914, he successfully shredded the ward machines of all his Irish ward boss rivals, with the exception of the powerful boss of the eighth ward, Martin Lomasney. Curley gave jobs to the lieutenants of the bosses and thereby undermined their authority, and his big spending program, with employment on the streets and sewers for the city's poor, elevated him to the rare honor of owning Boston's first city-wide machine.

There was little doubt in the mayor's camp that he would win re-election to another four-year term in 1917, and this view was reinforced when twelve Democratic Irish ward bosses promised their support to colorless Andrew J. Peters, a New England Yankee, who was tucked away in Washington's tomblike Treasury Department as assistant secretary.

Curley's smug expression faded only slightly when Mahatma Lomasney's brother Joe quit the post the mayor had given him on the schoolhouse commission. Joe had been awarded the job originally as an effort to neutralize the Mahatma; and when he left, Curley was not surprised that the eighth ward boss was behind the Peters candidacy. Even so, Hizzoner shrugged off the opposition as inconsequential.

But he changed his mind at Lomasney's next move. The shrewd Mahatma blarneyed popular Congressman James A. Gallivan of South Boston into entering the mayoralty contest and followed this with a repeat performance on Congressman Peter Tague of Charlestown. Enraged by this blatant attempt to divide the Irish vote and put the Protestant Peters into city hall, Curley stalked into Lomasney's Hendricks Club and demanded an explanation. "I put them in to lick you," the Mahatma said frankly, signaling his bully boys to surround the visitor.

Curley still believed he would win overwhelmingly, and to ensure this end he used the same format as last time, including well-planned outdoor rallies, denunciatory newspaper ads, fist fights, and the regular inclusion of the great John L. Sullivan, "the Roxbury Strong Boy," in his frontline entourage. But the Mahatma hit Curley with a heavy hand, having Gallivan campaign relentlessly with the false charge that James Michael had said bayonets were needed to prod the Irish-American troops of the Old Fighting Ninth aboard troop ships bound for the European fighting.

Mahatma also led his own personal attack on Curley that gained emotion with every retelling. Charging that Mayor Curley was a crook headed for jail again until Suffolk County's district attorney, Joseph C. Pelletier, refused to take action, Lomasney claimed: "Curley went in to Pelletier, got down almost on his knees, talked of his wife and family, and begged him to stay the execution of the law. 'Hold on, Joe, for God's sake, give me a chance. Think of my wife and family. Think of our party. Think of our people.' And Pelletier did."

The returns showed that Lomasney's plan to split the Irish votes had succeeded, and Peters was elected mayor. Peters had 37,900 votes; Curley, 28,000; Gallivan, 19,400; and Tague, 1,700.

If Curley's surprise defeat in 1917 was not enough to cast a pall on his public future, what he did on the rebound seemed to pound a spike in his political coffin. In an act of revenge he ran against Gallivan, the spoiler, in 1918 for Gallivan's congressional seat. Gallivan dredged up the false story of Curley's alleged maligning of the Old Fighting Ninth as his campaign theme, claimed credit for the large-scale military construction program in the Boston area, and employed almost a battalion of plug-uglies to beat up spectators at Curley rallies as well as Curley's own large crew of "football players." James Michael retaliated by labeling Gallivan a congressional drunk with a degree from the "Washington Institution for Dipso-maniacs." But this was hardly shocking to his audiences, and Gal-livan was easily returned to his third congressional term. It looked as though Curley was finally finished in politics.

Once he was out of the mayor's office, Curley needed money, for he was a compulsive spender, and the spoils he had collected as his due as the city's number one citizen were now gone. The direc-tors of the Hibernia Savings Back on Boston's Court Street solved this problem for him by making Curley the bank's president. This was a shrewd move on their part because Curley's name had great Pied Piper value.

It was also a good move for Curley, for the pay was excellent. However, the job had one bad feature: From his office window, he could look across the alley to city hall and he yearned to return to the high-backed mayor's chair. But by the time the war ended and the troops began to come home, Curley had dropped from political sight, a forgotten man in the postwar world being made "safe for democracy."

In 1921, shortly before he left for Washington to be sworn in as Vice President, Governor Coolidge signed a bill barring any Bos-ton mayor from running for consecutive terms. The purpose of this Republican measure was to prevent any popular Boston Democrat from future fortress-building in that city. But even without this new law, Lomasney and the other ward bosses would not have tol-erated a second term for Peters, the ingrate, who abandoned the city not to them but to his own crooked underlings. As his succes-sor, they chose sixty-six-year-old John Murphy, Mayor Peters' fire commissioner and the former chairman of the governor-appointed finance commission, charged with investigating Boston's public fi-nances.

That Charles H. Innes, head of the city's Republican machine and boss of the state legislature, as well as Curley's frequent politi-cal and business associate, also backed Murphy did not deter Curley from announcing for mayor. Nor did he seem perturbed by the im-mediate opposition to him by all Boston papers except the *Telegram*, the Good Government "Goo-Goos," and the hordes of vocal business-men who had slipped money to Peter's staff for tax rate cuts. In the face of this immense array of power, Curley calmly announced him-self as the reform candidate and set to work with a rush despite the verdict of the gambling element that Murphy was a five-to-one favorite.

From the start, Lomasney and the other backers of Murphy took Curley's candidacy as the dying wing-flutter of a small crow. They laughed at Curley's crude technique of passing out pledge-of-support cards, and they remained complacent when Murphy campaigned in the same tone he used as a sometime lecturer at Harvard on fire department administration.

And while they basked in their self-satisfaction, James Michael connived and maligned and ridiculed. One prime attack was on Murphy's age. Murphy, with his thumbs hooked into his tight vest, enjoyed discoursing on his long public career, and his favorite speech became a chronological listing of the jobs he had held. Curley, a youthful forty-eight, followed Murphy's campaign route on several occasions, and he would totter to the center of the stage, cup a feigned palsied hand over his brow, pretend to peer far out into his audience, and remark in a trembling voice, "I don't see a face of those heroes I welcomed back from the Mexican War."

Besides attacking Murphy for being sixty-six, Curley used religion as a club on his opponent. Catholic audiences gasped in shock after Curley rent the air with the falsehood that Murphy ate steak on Friday and not fish. For good measure, Curley's helpers spread the story that Murphy planned to divorce his wife so he could marry a sixteen-year-old wench. Still another religious attack was the Curley ploy of hiring Harvard students and sending them into Catholic neighborhoods, where the young men damaged Murphy by knocking on doors and proclaiming themselves as Baptists seeking votes for Murphy. In addition, as Curley afterward admitted, he paid $2,000 to a KKK minister named A. Z. Conrad to attack him (Curley) viciously from the pulpit.

Curley's other chief campaign device was the special attention he gave to certain groups of voters. Boston women were voting in their first municipal election, and he catered to them by having his wife join in the campaign. Her stock statement to the ladies, who were pleased to be singled out, was a banal "Mr. Curley and I work together—and play together." Curley liked to set her on one side of him on the platform with an American flag on his other side, and after bellowing out sentimental lines about his love for his nation and his home, he put his arms around the flag and his wife while his shills led the screaming approval.

Curley was well aware that to concentrate on the Irish vote was a mistake, for Boston had acquired sizable numbers of Negroes, Jews, Italians, Poles, and Portuguese. Not only did he attend meetings with solid audiences of these groups but he revealed a special talent for making use of extraneous news events to gain ethnic support. For example, when Enrico Caruso, the great tenor, died, Murphy issued a resolution expressing his sympathy. Curley's response was far more direct and effective: He attended a memorial meeting of 25,000 Italians on Boston Common and cried like a baby from the platform over Caruso's passing.

When the votes were counted on a snowy night, the 8:30 P.M. totals showed Murphy enjoying a 7,500-vote lead. But instead of conceding after newspaper headlines called Murphy the winner, Curley checked with the election commissioners and learned that fourteen precincts he considered favorable to his cause had not reported. When these votes came in, his opposition groaned because James Michael Hisself, the dead politician, was once more mayor of Boston after eking out a 2,696 plurality over Murphy with 157,000 votes cast. There was far more than groaning from three of the ward bosses who lost $128,000 by betting on a Murphy victory. Afterward, a newspaper described the shock of the city's "better" elements at the results of the election: "The city awoke to find the business and financial interests, the bluestocking element, the cultured crowd, had been 'worsted' and the so-called 'lowbrow' element had triumphed."

Curley's second term as mayor paralleled much of the administration of President Warren Harding, a time not noted for honesty in government. But while Harding's cabinet members and lesser officials were hungrily stuffing their pockets at public expense, Curley employed a far more humanistic approach to his personal gains.

"I will leave as clean a record behind me for four years as I did for the four years I was mayor," James Michael assured the citizens of Boston at the outset of his second term. And he did, to the dismay of the Good Government Association.

With successive bursts of energy and purpose, he set the city on an unprecedented public works program. He ordered an enormous expansion of the city hospital, erecting maternity, pediatrics, and pathology buildings, along with a new administrative building and a large structure for laundry work. He also widened a dazzling number of streets, including the pinched area around city hall; built bridges, a tunnel into Back Bay, a stadium, and recreational areas; and dotted the poorer sections with public bathhouses.

An auxilliary benefit resulting from Curley's public works outburst was that the large number of postwar unemployed faded away as full employment came to Boston. Moreover, Curley added to their new good fortune by doubling the wages of city laborers and setting up a retirement fund.

At the same time that Curley was conducting his public improvements program, his own personal fortune rose sharply, even though his salary was only $5,000 a year. The explanation of Joseph F. Dinneen, a Curley biographer, was that "everybody knew there wasn't a contract awarded that did not carry with it a cut for Curley." So James Michael Hisself acted under the theory that so far as public works were concerned he was the city's agent, and all agents collected a fee for bringing buyer and seller together.

Once the street and building projects began, protests did not lag far behind. Businessmen were enraged when they learned they were to be the chief financial supporters. First Curley had their property reassessed at new high valuations, then he increased the tax rate. The finance commission was certain that most of Curley's efforts were fraudulent, but members were so swamped by the sheer number of contracts the mayor had let that they had trouble deciding what to investigate first; and all the while they labored, Curley made fun of them.

When the commission finally issued a few auditor reports, Curley labeled them stupid. One report complained that Curley had spent $28,841 for local parades; another, that he had awarded the Boston Belting Co. $300,000 to call off a contract. In retaliation, Curley went before the state legislature and demanded that the finance commission be abolished and its appropriation used for more public works in Boston. After the legislators rejected this demand, Curley denounced them as "pious humbugs and hypocrites."

With all his spending, Curley was bound to run out of public money. Yet he refused to stop even at this point but instead tried to borrow money against next year's tax revenues. Curley chose the president of one of Boston's great financial institutions to grant him his first loan. However, the banker was an independent Yankee and curtly rejected his proposal. "Listen!" the mayor yelled at him over the phone. "There's a water main with floodgates right under your building. If you don't know where it is, your architect can tell you. You'd better get that money up by three o'clock this afternoon, or those gates will be opened, pouring thousands of gallons of water right into your vaults." The banker complied before three.

Another successful form of Curley blackmail against a banker who did not want to extend credit to the city was the following routine he used in another phone call: "I'll have 600 city employees lined up outside your bank tomorrow with checks for their salaries. That will make a line about a mile long; and I'll advise all of the city contractors who have accounts in your bank to be in that line, too, with any of their employees who have money on deposit to transfer their accounts to other banks. You don't want a run on your bank, do you?"

In addition to his controversial public works program and the numerous charges alleging to his probable dishonesty, Curley managed to dominate the front pages on other scores. There was the constant stream of famous visitors to city hall to have their pictures taken shaking hands with Hizzoner, and these included Admiral Richard E. Byrd, Clarence Darrow, Greta Garbo, and Jack Dempsey. Then there were the numerous trips Curley made around the country to deliver colorful speeches with newsworthy remarks.

Midway through his term as mayor, Curley was struck by the injustice of the state law that would put him out of office when his term expired early in 1926. But there was no hope that a Republican legislature and governor would repeal the act barring successive terms for Boston's mayor. So early in 1924, he began to look about for another political office that would interest him, and he decided to run for governor that year.

The political balance sheet for 1924 showed many favorable signs for a Curley victory, as well as several unfavorable indications. On the positive side, he was well known throughout the state even though this was his first run for statewide office. There was also a deep recession and steep inflation in Massachusetts in 1924, economic conditions that should have reflected on the Republican-ins.

Furthermore, the state's Irish, who had deserted the Democratic fold to support Harding in 1920, were angry with the Republicans, following Harding's harsh stand against intervening in the "Irish Question." Then there was the enormous increase in voter registration since the 1920 debacle—always a Democratic plus.

In addition, David Walsh, who was now a U.S. Senator, was

eager to tie his re-election contest in with Curley's campaign even though they were normally enemies. Another asset was that Mahatma Lomasney was not as formidable a Curley opponent in 1924 as in past elections. Curley had contributed to the weakened status of the Mahatma by changing the ward lines, adding many acres of strangers to Lomasney's domain, and calling the new conglomeration Ward Five instead of Ward Eight.

On the debit side of the ledger, Curley recognized several imponderables. Massachusetts' own Calvin Coolidge, who had succeeded to the Presidency in August, 1923, on the death of Warren Harding, was proving highly popular and might carry any Republican gubernatorial candidate into office in the November, 1924, national election. Curley also saw that the Republicans would tar him in the campaign as a former jailbird and dredge up the matter of his imprisonment for having taken the civil service test for another man. Then there was Curley's image as a rabid Irish Catholic in a state where Yankee votes in the hinterlands were important.

By the time Curley and Senator Walsh were ready to move into their fall, 1924, campaigns, general gloom was beginning to descend on Bay State Democratic politicians because of their national standard bearer, John W. Davis, a Wall Street corporation lawyer whose clients included Standard Oil and J. P. Morgan. Davis was so poorly thought of by Massachusetts Democratic leaders that they advised him not to come into the state after he sent them a list of places and dates for speaking engagements. The Democratic nominee complied. This left Curley and Walsh with the unenviable task of taking on the national as well as the state Republican ticket in their races for governor and U.S. Senator.

Curley's Republican opponent for governor was Alvan T. Fuller, a grade-school graduate who had started politically as a Teddy Roosevelt Bull Moose liberal. But after service as a state legislator, Congressman, and lieutenant governor, Fuller emerged as a reactionary and superpatriotic candidate for governor.

Curley's natural campaign tack would have been to sledgehammer Fuller as a heartless conservative, but the times were against this, despite the recession. Just how widespread was reactionary political philosophy in the early and middle 1920s was discernible by the harsh stand of the AFL against unemployment insurance. In Massachusetts, labor leaders came out strongly against such worker protection at a hearing of the legislature.

Nevertheless, Curley made an early campaign effort to wrap himself in the reform flag when Fuller claimed the banner of "economy and sound administration." Curley condemned Fuller's stand and promised to give the state "Curleyism," which he defined as "a kindly, considerate and humane treatment of the poor, the sick and the unfortunate."

But Curley quickly scampered away from "Curleyism" when the election was a month off. His takeoff point came on the Federal child labor amendment, which was a ratification referendum item on the November ballot. Curley had been an early supporter of the amendment, but after William Cardinal O'Connell condemned it on October 5 Curley let the voters know that he, too, opposed the amendment because it was a "scheme" of the Bolsheviks in Moscow, "which has deluded many good people."

Left without an issue now against Fuller, Curley soon found another—the Ku Klux Klan. The modern rebirth of the KKK in Atlanta in 1915 had witnessed its spread into political power in several states in the next decade. But given a large Catholic population in Massachusetts, the Klan could never rise above insignificance in the Bay State.

Despite this situation, Curley based his entire October campaign on the KKK issue. Night after night in his speaking efforts across the state, at some time during his speech, a fiery cross, symbol of the KKK, could be expected to crackle aflame on a hill near his outdoor rally. And Curley would point to the burning cross and shout in his magnificent voice: "There it burns, the cross of hatred upon which Our Lord, Jesus Christ, was crucified—the cross of human avarice, and not the cross of love and Christian charity!" Then Curley would denounce the state's Republican administration for sending state patrolmen to guard Klan Konvocations.

There were many, including Curley's opponent, Alvan Fuller, who insisted that Curley was responsible for the burning crosses, hiring a crew to set them off. Although the regularity of the flaming Klan symbol at Curley's meetings pointed to a planned effort and James Michael's eloquent response was always the same, the Republican charge could not be proved.

At the same time, while the Republican Party actively sought KKK votes, Curley failed to pin a Ku Kluxer tag on Fuller. For the Republican candidate tirelessly told Boston audiences that his wife was a Catholic and he was a large contributor to Catholic charities.

What irked Curley was that Fuller used his wife as a political plus before Irish audiences. Mrs. Fuller, a trained singer, "warbled" at her husband's rallies, said Curley.

So the campaign between the two antagonists dwindled to Curley's attack on the feeble KKK organization of Massachusetts and Fuller's use of his warbling wife and his repeated chant: "We need less laws." The Republican propagandists went further, charging Curley with graft and wild spending as Boston's mayor; and Frederick Enright, publisher of the Boston *Telegram,* the only local paper supporting Curley in his 1921 campaign for mayor, was now a Fuller adviser and leader of the dirt-dredging press against James Michael.

Chief item in Enright's published dirt was the old story of Curley's imprisonment, with cartoons of Curley in a striped suit behind jail bars for those who might have reading problems. Enright also attacked Curley's family and said that the mayor currently had paid $35,000 to some brokers to avoid a court case that would have led to his second prison term.

Curley acted in character against the sturdy, 6-foot, 4-inch Enright. Encountering him at the site of the Boston Massacre, the mayor sent the publisher sprawling into the gutter with a hard-right smash. Curley also brought a libel suit against Enright, which resulted in the closing of the *Telegram* as well as a fine and a prison sentence for the publisher.

With his own campaign flagging on the dubious KKK issue and his early discovery that President Coolidge's name was synonymous with loyalty to country, Curley still had hope of victory over Fuller because of the statewide enthusiasm of crowds for Senator Dave Walsh in his re-election effort. Unlike Curley, some reporters noted, the tall, dashing dandy from Fitchburg, in north-central Massachusetts, did not show his Irishness but had "class" that appealed even to encrusted Yankees. Women also were enthralled with the bachelor Senator, unaware that he was reportedly a homosexual.

But Walsh's energetic campaign was not enough to give the Senator another term or to pull Curley to victory. For, as the election revealed, the results rested entirely on the degree of Coolidge's sweep over John Davis. Coolidge carried every city and town in the state except Blackstone, near the Rhode Island border. In the wake of the Coolidge vote slide, Walsh did credit to himself by amassing

49.2 percent of the vote for the Senate. Curley, who had led a registration drive to increase the Boston vote by almost 12 percent over 1922, got 59 percent of the city's total vote for governor. But this was not sufficient to overcome the Fuller margin in the rest of the state, and Curley went down to defeat by 161,000 votes.

Despite his trouncing by Fuller, Curley was not again outside the political fence because he still had more than a year left of his second term as mayor. Back once more in city hall, he returned to his favorite sport of feverishly expanding the city's public works, building health units and roads, and taking his cut of the spendings. But he could no longer build as much as he desired, for the state legislature had wisely set a limit on the amount the city could borrow, and his strenuous efforts to raise this statutory limit failed to win sympathy from the Republican majority. So after a time he began to badger individual Boston millionaires to donate money for his projects with his promise to "chisel" their names in the marble. One man gave $5.5 million.

Early in 1925 when the campaign for Curley's successor was the city's chief political topic, Lomasney called a meeting with the mayor and Honey Fitz. The Mahatma's suggestion was that the three end their rivalry and support his protégé, Joe O'Neil, for mayor. This suggestion was treated with hilarity by Curley, despite Lomasney's protestations that he wanted peace and not power.

Following the meeting, Curley put up Theodore A. Glynn, his fire commissioner, as his successor at city hall. But though he saw to it that Teddy Glynn received some campaign funds and a claque, James Michael worked hard behind the scenes for another candidate —a Republican.

This turncoat activity was not without its rewards. Back at the turn of the century, Curley had met Charles Innes, the Republican boss of Ward Seven, a big-time Boston attorney and a successful lobbyist and string puller with the state legislature. Innes conducted a law school in his office, and for a time Curley was a student there. It would probably have been of value for Curley to finish Charlie Innes' courses, because, for reasons never discovered, Innes knew the questions to be asked in bar exams, and an extremely high proportion of his students passed.

Nevertheless, Curley and Innes had become good friends and *sub rosa* allies in politics and business, and over the years they helped each other when called on for aid. It was Charlie Innes, Curley's Republican friend, who proposed a special alliance that would permit Curley to have city hall influence even after he was out of office. Their vehicle was to be dull Malcolm E. Nichols, a Boston accountant and Republican, whom Innes could manipulate without trouble.

Charlie Innes' proposal was that Curley join him in making Nichols Curley's successor and then sharing the spoils of office afterward. James Michael's first reaction was that a Republican did not have a chance, and indeed not since twenty years before when Republican George Hibbard with his polly-parrot beaknose was mayor had Innes' party run Boston. But his second reaction was that Nichols might win if several Irish Democrats became candidates and split the vote.

So Boston was treated to the sight of seven Irishmen put forward quietly by Curley to run for mayor against Nichols, Lomasney's Joe O'Neil, and Curley's announced candidate, Teddy Glynn. The result was a Nichols victory and a massive display of fury by Glynn after he discovered that the mayor had not really supported him. To this, Curley replied in public: "Three of the most famous traitors in history—Judas Iscariot, Benedict Arnold, and Teddy Glynn—had another thing in common—they were all redheads."

During the next four years, about half the persons Nichols appointed were Curley men, and half the contractors were those favored in Curley's regime. Furthermore, it became commonly known that Nichols made no move without phoning Innes, and frequently it was Curley who called him back with instructions.

But despite his influence in the Nichols administration and his own financial security on returning to the presidency of the Hibernia Bank, Curley sorely missed the political hoopla that attended the elected public leader.

It was in 1928, when national interest in the great prosperity was diverted temporarily from its concentration on money-making to President-making, that Curley more than ever missed being directly involved in politics. Domination over the state's Democratic organization had once more fallen into the hands of Dave Walsh, Curley's detracting foe. Walsh, defeated for re-election to the U.S. Senate in 1924, rebounded in 1926 by winning election to the rest of the late Senator Henry Cabot Lodge's term. With this new prestige, Walsh ordered the party's state chairman to resign and reshuffled the Democratic state committee as he wished. Even Mahatma Lo-masney acknowledged the Walsh coup and fell into line. Walsh did not even bother to approach private citizen Curley.

After barring Curley from the state's delegation, Walsh led the Massachusetts Democrats to Houston in 1928 where they supported Al Smith, who won the presidential nomination on the first ballot. Back home again, Walsh established a campaign schedule that froze Curley out of all activities.

But blocked as he was by Walsh, the undismayed Curley em-barked on his own Smith campaign. Across the street from city hall annex was the decrepit Young's Hotel. Curley rented it, renamed it the "Bull Pen," cleaned it, and announced it to the public as *the* Smith headquarters. Loudspeakers blared out pro-Smith plugs to passersby, and every day at noon Curley held a rally for New York's Al that attracted crowds numbering as many as 5,000 persons. Curley also led a campaign to register Democrats by the thousands.

When the balloting came in November, Massachusetts was the only northern state, except for tiny Rhode Island, to support Smith. It was his 100,000 majority in Boston that gave him the state by 17,000 votes, and begrudging Democrats had to admit that the out-of-politics Curley was chiefly responsible.

On the basis of his labors for Al Smith, Curley once again rose from faded political outsider to a potent power. So it was nat-ural that with a mayoralty contest coming up in 1929 he should quickly return to the local wars as a candidate. But if he had a com-pelling need for political life, Curley had still another reason for wanting to be mayor once more. Taken in by fast-talking, high-promising promoters, he was in serious financial trouble from con-game oil stock losses and washed-out heavy investments in a com-pany claiming to have a formula for converting cheap metal to stainless steel and chromium.

Even though he was state Democratic boss, Dave Walsh had no influence in Boston politics. But William Cardinal O'Connell did, and as a man who despised James Michael Curley's political ways, the Cardinal discreetly put forth his own candidate for mayor. His choice was Frederick W. Mansfield, a reactionary labor union attorney, bar association president, and the Cardinal's personal lawyer and chief lobbyist with the state legislature. Despite Cardi-nal O'Connell's failure to endorse Mansfield publicly, everyone in Boston knew that Mansfield was his agent.

With the Cardinal's attorney as his opponent, Curley realized he might be in for a difficult contest. The cleverness of his opposition was soon revealed when Mansfield induced Tom Curley, James Michael's political and prison partner of a quarter century back, to enter the race. The confusion of the two Curley names was bound to cut James Michael's tally, and James Michael remained concerned until Tom Curley suddenly withdrew from the race, even though he still held enmity toward his namesake. However, even this did not make it a two-man contest for Mansfield had yet another stooge on the ballot. He was Dan Coakley, a lawyer disbarred some years before for frame-ups and blackmail activities. Coakley possessed a sharp tongue and could be expected to fire hot remarks at Curley that the staid Mansfield could not.

Curley's ridiculing campaign was as colorful as Mansfield's was dull, and it aroused local enthusiasm as in the old days. "Where were you, furious Freddy, when Al Smith ran for President?" he chided Mansfield frequently at his rallies. Audiences roared when Curley went on, "You were home with your little red slippers on reading the *Ladies Home Journal*." Curley also made reference to Mansfield's outsized feet, a subject painfully embarrassing to the Cardinal's man. As for Coakley, Curley slapped at him incessantly as Mansfield's stooge and hopeful vote-divider. "Dapper Danny, the leprous creature," he named Coakley, and he called his two opponents "Freddy Mansfield and his manikin."

Despite Curley's campaign of ridicule, Mansfield forces believed their respectable candidate would successfully isolate Curley from the organized support of Boston's ward bosses. But Mansfield suffered a severe blow when Mahatma Lomasney dared the Cardinal's wrath by coming out for his old enemy, Curley, "with no ifs, ands or buts." There was widespread agreement with Dan Coakley's description of this event as "a million dollar merger." Then Mansfield suffered further when 25,000 persons jammed Boston Garden to cheer James Michael Hisself, and Honey Fitz Fitzgerald was present to sing his off-key "Sweet Adeline" and do his stifflegged Irish jig.

Mansfield's remaining recourse was to publicize the revelations of the finance commission of Curley's financial misdeeds as mayor. But he was a dreary speaker, and what he exposed were such old cases that they failed to arouse the voters. So there was little surprise when Curley collected 116,500 votes to 97,000 for Mansfield and 2,900 for Coakley, and won election to his third term as mayor.

By the time Curley was inaugurated early in 1930, the Great Depression was already under way across the nation. With Republican Governor Frank Allen approving a bill to permit Boston to borrow beyond its legal debt limit, Curley, the builder, was ready to do his part to fight hard times with large-scale, beneficial public works for the city and appropriate fees for himself and his associates.

Brushing aside red tape, Curley swiftly ordered a breathtaking array of projects. In quick order, his agents had bought the land needed to construct approaches to his projected and badly needed East Boston harbor Summer Tunnel for automobile traffic. Blocks of foul North End slums were torn down to make way for his boulevard, or Prado—"the Curley-inspired beauty spot of the slums," as he proclaimed it—and extensive landscaping was done around sacred Old North Church. Curley also started work on Logan Airport in East Boston's mudflats, closed off Dorchester Bay and constructed seven miles of sand beaches, added wings to the city hospital, extended the subway, widened Cape Cod Canal, and built a new courthouse.

In the past, Curley had been able to becloud his own personal interest in his public works undertakings, but now through a foolish appointment, he laid the groundwork for future grief. Edmund L. Dolan, his short, fat next-door neighbor and bond salesman, had given him free use of his yacht, and when Curley began his third term as mayor he named Dolan city treasurer. Dolan was soon involved in a cloud of activities that fascinated the finance commission.

For one thing, Dolan turned out to be the secret boss of the Mohawk Packing Co., which had a contract to supply city institutions with meat; and it did so at prices a third above those in retail butcher shops. Dolan was also the organizer of the Legal Securities Corporation, a private firm engaged in buying and selling municipal bonds, including those of the city of Boston. As city treasurer, Dolan sold the city's bonds to his company, and as head of Legal Securities he sold investment bonds from other cities to Boston; and his fury of activities—buying and selling to himself in reality—brought him a fee on each transaction.

As guardian of the city's money, Eddie Dolan was also involved in a shady settlement of a damage claim by the General Equipment Corporation. A private contractor on city work had accidentally flooded the basement of a General Equipment building. G.E.'s insurance company had offered to settle with the city for a $20,000 payment, but the amount listed on the settlement was for $85,000. When the finance commission checked the facts, it found that the insurance company had collected only the $20,000. What had happened to the rest was a mystery, but the finger pointed to Dolan and Curley.

Curley had always been able to count on his happy home life to give him respite from his political problems, but serious personal tragedies hit him during his third mayoralty term. His twin infant sons, John and Joseph, had died in 1922, then fifteen-year-old Dorothea passed away in 1925. The sharpest blow of all came in June, 1930, when his wife Mary, mother of their nine children, died of cancer after a long, lingering illness. But if this was not enough grief, twenty-two-year-old James Michael Curley, Jr., then in Harvard Law School and an aide to his father, died only six months later.

In the spring of 1931, Mayor Curley decided to leave the scene of his personal grief and take a trip to Europe. Accompanying him were his twenty-three-year-old daughter, Mary, and City Treasurer Eddie Dolan. Curley took Dolan in order to keep him out of the hands of the finance commission's investigators who were beginning to hit pay dirt in Dolan's mismanagement and crooked deals.

Curley also wanted to get away because of his political frustration. He had counted on a Republican winning the governorship in 1930, so that he could run for that office in 1932. But a Curley enemy, Joseph B. Ely, a Yankee Democrat, won in 1930 and would want a second term.

There was a sojourn in Ireland, a trip to County Galway to look for relatives among the dirt-floor, thatched-roofed cottages, and a contrasting state dinner with the President of the Irish Free State as his host. Then there were visits with officials in England and France before he went to Rome for audiences with Mussolini, the Pope, and the King. With his penchant for raw diplomacy, Curley bearded Mussolini into dropping his plan to dissolve the Catholic Boy Scouts and throw the lot into the fascist Army. Afterward, James Michael told reporters: "As a practical economist, he amazed me."

The trip was good for Curley's ebbing political ego, but his resurgent optimism gave way to gloom as his ship neared the United States in June. There was time to reflect on his declining political career as he boarded the train in New York for Boston. Yet at this low point the Curley luck suddenly made its appearance. By accident, he learned that New York Governor Franklin Roosevelt was taking the same train to Boston. Curley had met Roosevelt only once before—back in 1924—when Roosevelt was just reentering politics after his leg-crippling bout with polio. But politicians have an intra-instant friendship relationship, and when Curley sent his card to FDR's suite, the New York governor asked him to pay a call.

Roosevelt, who had recently started his long haul toward the presidency, was on his way to Massachusetts to discuss and determine the political climate in the Bay State. Little wonder that he plunged immediately into a detailed grilling of Curley about his chances in Massachusetts the following year. Curley bluntly told him that Al Smith would own the state's delegation to the national convention, though he offered the gratuity that Smith could no more win the presidency in 1932 than he could in 1928 because of the large number of bigots who would not accept a Catholic.

As they talked, Curley saw a way out of his lost war with Governor Ely and Senator Walsh. They were rabidly committed to Al Smith—derby, cigar, poor grammar, lower East Side talk, and all. Why not be Roosevelt's man in Massachusetts? "I'll be branded as a traitor for deserting the Smith cause," he told Roosevelt, to give the impression of his self-sacrifice in championing him. Curley later claimed Roosevelt was so overjoyed that he promised him a cabinet post or a political plum of almost equal value.

On the following day, FDR was to attend a luncheon at the home of Woodrow Wilson's private adviser, tiny Colonel Edward M. House, at Magnolia, his estate at Manchester-by-the-Sea on the North Shore. Newspapers reported that the guest list included the two Bay State Senators, Dave Walsh and Marcus Coolidge; Roosevelt's neighbor, Henry Morgenthau; *Atlantic Monthly* editor Ellery Sedgwick; and the editors of three Boston papers. Curley had not been invited to this long-planned meeting, but that morning he received word to come, and he hurried to House's place.

After lunch, the guests were paraded before newsreel cameras. All were vague about the purpose of the meeting, especially Walsh who was solidly committed to Al Smith. However, this timidity ended when it came Curley's turn. "We have been making history here today," he assured newsreel audiences. "Franklin Delano Roosevelt is the hope of the nation." Walsh was outraged.

Immediately after newspapers reported Curley's remark, the mayor's office was flooded with denunciatory letters, and the switchboard could not cope with the number of callers who wanted to tell James Michael he was the Irish Benedict Arnold. Meetings of the Ancient Order of Hibernians resolved without debate that the mayor was a traitor.

Nevertheless, Curley went ahead with his promotion of FDR, using, at the governor's suggestion, Roosevelt's twenty-three-year-old son James as his chief assistant. Jimmy was in the insurance business in Boston at the time and panting for a political career there. To meeting after meeting the two went, and at first Curley was thunderously booed whenever he mentioned Roosevelt's name. After a time, he found he was treated to the ultimate insult to a politician—empty halls.

In the meantime, State Chairman Donahue, acting on behalf of Governor Ely and Senator Walsh, put forth an all-Smith slate to run as delegates to the national convention in the state's preferential presidential primary. This prompted Roosevelt to invite Curley to Albany to ask him to organize a competing Roosevelt slate. Curley bluntly insisted he had a hopeless cause, but he followed orders and watched his group of proposed delegates go down to overwhelming defeat. When the loud brass bands and the cheering crowd of 25,000 persons saw the Smith delegation off for the Democratic struggle in Chicago in June, 1932, the joy of its leaders was complete. For the hated Curley was a pathetically defeated figure without even a pass to get into the Chicago Stadium as a spectator.

But laugh about Curley as they did, Ely, Walsh, and Donahue laughed too soon. Curley went out to Chicago on his own, and talked the delegation from Puerto Rico into letting him be delegation chairman! The result was that Ely and Walsh were amazed to find Curley directly behind them on the convention floor. This turned to shock when the call came from the platform: "Puerto Rico— Chairman Alcalde Jaime Miguel Curleo," and Curley shouted back, "Puerto Rico casts its six votes for Franklin Delano Roosevelt."

With the Roosevelt nomination, Curley was suddenly elevated to insider status, while Ely and Walsh, Lomasney and Honey Fitz were depressed outsiders. This time when Curley returned home to Boston, the twenty-one noisy brass bands and the cheering crowd of 25,000 persons were for him, and no one paid attention to the Smith lovers detraining from Chicago.

But politics had its own scale of values, and only for a short time did Curley retain the mantle of Roosevelt leader in Massachusetts. FDR realized that he needed campaign help from the Bay State Democratic organization if he hoped to carry that state over President Herbert Hoover, for the Republican National Committee was openly boasting that Massachusetts was "safe" for Hoover. So Roosevelt ignored Curley and wooed Governor Ely, who had made the nominating speech for Al Smith.

In the end, after much chasing and pleading, Ely agreed to support Roosevelt. In return, Ely told Governor Roosevelt he would have to have assurances that the Democratic state committee and not Curley would direct the campaign. Furthermore, Curley must not be permitted to reopen his Bull Pen and must agree to leave the state during the first half of the campaign for a speaking tour outside of Massachusetts.

Curley, with his eyes focused on his expected reward after FDR won, agreed to Ely's demands when they were put to him by Roosevelt. But he was back home for the final campaign drive with pounding attacks on Hoover for the worsening Depression and for "shooting down like dogs in our national capital" the bedraggled Bonus Army. And when Roosevelt came to Boston on November 1, 1932, for the big rally at Boston Arena, it was James Michael who introduced him to the full-capacity house.

Roosevelt's election-day sweep across the country on November 8, 1932, gave him a 7 million-vote margin over poor Hoover; in Massachusetts, he got 800,000 votes to 737,000 for Hoover, and there as in the rest of the nation patronage-hungry Democrats began making plans.

Curley was one Democrat entertaining top-level hopes of sitting around the cabinet table in the west wing of the White House, and he chafed until the President-elect finally invited him for their talk at what was to be known as "the Little White House," in Warm Springs, Georgia. Curley took his daughter Mary with him, and after their visit with the affable Roosevelt, the two told friends that Curley had been offered the expected post of Secretary of the Navy; but no announcement was to be made until four months later, in March, 1933, when Roosevelt would be inaugurated.

What seemed to Curley a solid commitment came undone, however, by the time Calvin Coolidge died on January 5, 1933, and James Michael went to his funeral. James Roosevelt, representing his father, was also there; and after the services he broke the news that his father was being forced to withdraw the Navy offer because of opposition of the Methodist Church to the appointment. "But he would like you to accept the post of ambassador to France or Italy," said the President's oldest son.

Curley was unable to make an appointment with Roosevelt until after the inauguration, though Roosevelt confirmed the bad news by phone earlier. This time when they met and discussed the diplomatic appointments, Curley said he preferred Rome to Paris. Roosevelt told him to think over his decision carefully, and they would meet again.

After his visit to the White House, newspapers reported the offer, and opposition developed from many quarters, including that of Cardinal O'Connell, who considered it sacrilegious to send Curley so close to the Vatican. Once more Curley trooped to the White House where a President busy with vast relief programs and New Deal legislation took time off to tell him that Italy was not for him because of objections from the Pope, Mussolini, and the King. Curley recalled that he "stormed out of his office."

Roosevelt's next offer came in mid-April, 1933, when he sent "Dear Jim" a letter telling him that the ambassadorship to Poland was his. Even before the letter came, word of the offer was leaked to the press, with one newspaper quipping: "The President must be anti-Polish"; and another declaring: "If he accepted, he would pave the Polish Corridor."

Curley's reaction was that an appointment to Warsaw was an insult, a four-year exile that should be filled by "a Republican enemy." "If Poland is such a goddam interesting place," he told a hard-selling Roosevelt to his face in rejecting the offer, "why don't you resign the presidency and take it yourself."

By this time, Mayor Curley had developed a deep dislike of Roosevelt; but as every successful boss must be, he was an excellent judge of human political nature. So instead of breaking off all relations with FDR for his too-obvious insincerity in providing him with a political plum, Curley pushed hard and insatiably on Roosevelt for an unreasonably large amount of relief and New Deal project money for Boston. Curley's correct assessment was that Roosevelt was so embarrassed about the way he had treated the mayor that he would yield easily to his demands. This was borne out by reports as 1933 progressed that several Roosevelt aides were complaining that Curley was receiving an unfair share of Federal largesse for his city for river and harbor projects, roads, hospitals, and parks. There was also concern about the proportion of this money that might be going into the bottomless Curley pockets.

Curley's third term was to end in January, 1934, and because he could not legally try for the next mayoralty term, he combined forces once more with Republican boss Charlie Innes to reinstall their stooge Malcolm Nichols as interim mayor until Curley could run again for that office. But Fred Mansfield, whom Curley had defeated four years earlier, was running now against Nichols, and this time Cardinal O'Connell's personal lawyer had His Eminence's open support. More important than the Cardinal's blessing was the fact that Henry Parkman, a popular Republican giant who stood six and a half feet tall and hated Curley, decided to spoil the Curley-Innes alliance by entering the race. Parkman gained most Republican votes and some Democratic ones as well that would have otherwise gone to Nichols, with the result that the Curley-Innes scheme failed and Freddie Mansfield controlled the mayor's high-backed chair for the next four years.

It was unreasonable to expect Curley to retire when he left city hall for private life, even though he would be sixty on his next birthday. Soon he was talking about "the demand of public and press" that he run for governor that year. Governor Ely was retiring after two terms and ready "to take a walk" alongside Al Smith against the Roosevelt New Deal, but the thought that Curley might succeed him led him to devise special action to thwart him. Through his initiative, the state legislature passed a law requiring both political parties to hold pre-primary conventions. This seemed like a harmless measure on the surface. However, Ely and Walsh controlled the Democratic state convention in 1934, and they believed they were ruining Curley's chances by having the convention overwhelmingly nominate General Charles H. Cole as the party's preference for governor. Cole, a high military officer in World War I, was known as "the original Smith man" because of his promotion of the New Yorker before the 1924 national convention.

Curley remained undaunted by the state conclave's handiwork, denounced Ely and Walsh for having "promoted a crooked convention," and set off at a furious pace to defeat Cole in the September primary. It was a bitter campaign for all concerned. Despite his personal dislike of Roosevelt, Curley wrapped himself in the President's glory, shouted with pride about the wonders of the New Deal, and declared he had singlehandedly won the nomination and election for FDR. As "proof," Curley passed out copies of a hastily prepared book by one James H. Guilfoyle, titled, *On the Trail of the Forgotten Man: A Journal of the Roosevelt Presidential Campaign*, which gave overwhelming credit to Curley for the establishment of the Roosevelt Era.

Ely took to the stump for Cole with the theme that Curley was a crook who lived like a millionaire despite his small salary as mayor; Walsh cried out that James Michael was a traitor to Al Smith; and General Cole denounced the Curley campaign with its entourage of singers and comedians along with Curley as a cheap "vaudeville show." Curley's chopping reply was that Ely and Walsh were "instruments of the banking interests" while Cole was "a shopworn nonentity." Moreover, he derided his opposition: Ely was a ventriloquist and Cole his "dummy." Curley also attempted to counter Ely's charge that he was a crooked politician by pointing out he had twice been elected president of the United States Conference of Mayors.

When the primary votes were counted, Curley confounded the so-called political experts by burying General Cole, with a total of 283,000 votes to only 121,000 for Ely's man. But there was no rest for Curley because he now had to run hard against the Republican nominee, Lieutenant Governor Gaspar Bacon, so popular a man that he had been the only member of his party to win high office in 1932. Bacon's father had been a partner in J. P. Morgan & Co. and had served as Secretary of State in the waning months of Teddy Roosevelt's administration. But the son, despite his Brahmin background, had a common touch, and his friends extended into all groups in the population.

Bacon was a man of energy and zest for the battle against Curley, whom he considered an abomination on the fair name of Massachusetts. "Tell us some of the inside details about some of the East Boston tunnel land deals," he lashed at Curley from the platform. "How about some of these contracts given out at city hall, Mr. Curley?" He savagely described Curley's campaign slogan of "work and wages" as meaning "work for the favored contractors and wages for Curley."

There were rumors that the findings of the finance commission of misdeeds during his mayoralty would reach the courts before the election, and this hindered Curley's full attention to his gubernatorial opponent as the campaign went into its final weeks. But he found the best way to stir up animosity toward Gaspar Bacon was to tie him in with J. P. Morgan & Co. even though Bacon had no banking connections. However, anything went—libels and slanders —during a campaign, and Curley's punch pine at almost every political meeting was: "While many citizens of Massachusetts were on welfare lists, Gaspar Bacon was on J. P. Morgan's preferred list." "Aren't you still president of the Hibernia Bank, Mr. Curley?" was Bacon's reply.

But the voters found Curley's false charge more believable than Bacon's true charge. In addition, the Roosevelt tide was running at peak force, and in November, 1934, Curley realized his ambition to be governor when he defeated Bacon by 125,000 votes.

Curley made a gesture of supreme ill-temper on his inauguration day. Ritual called for him to have his oath of office administered by the president of the senate before both houses. The sergeant-at-arms and a joint committee were to escort him into the chamber for the ceremony; and when the national guard gave its twenty-one gun salute on Boston Common, the retiring governor was supposed to walk down the marble staircase through the front entrance of the statehouse, down the more than two dozen granite stairs, and continue through Boston Common to merge with pedestrians as just another John Q. Public.

Curley ignored his part of these rituals entirely. On his big morning, the senate was still wrangling over the choice of its president, and the oath-taking could be delayed several hours. Also, James Michael awoke fuming because outgoing Governor Ely had installed several of his enemies during his final days into positions of power, and they could be expected to cooperate with Mayor Fred Mansfield in pushing lawsuits against Curley and Eddie Dolan. Curley, attired in formal morning clothes and silk top hat, strode angrily into the statehouse and up the stairs leading to the executive chamber. Here he surprised Ely by appearing unannounced in his inner office and closing the door behind him.

Those outside heard Curley's loud, nasty tone as he berated Ely for his appointments. Then there were the sounds of fisticuffs. Afterward, Curley recounted proudly his meeting with Ely: "We were both somewhat disheveled when the door opened." Curley next called in the secretary of state for a quick oath-taking and ordered the cannons on the Common to boom, signaling bruised Ely to quit the executive chamber and begin his lonely walk down into civilian life.

Ely had left behind the insignia of office for Curley—the old Butler Bible, the Book of Governors, and the antique key of the council chambers. But it took people, not insignia, to make Curley feel he was governor. He felt a beginning when he marched into the historic house chamber with its codfish hanging on the wall and received a respectful greeting; and he was engulfed with the realization that he was the state's master when he delivered an inaugural address that evoked twenty-six rousing interruptions for applause.

Curley's term as governor proved a monstrous two years for him and for the state. The poor Irish lad from the cold-water, toiletless, third-floor Roxbury tenement walkup soon discovered an unslakable thirst for pomp and homage. Joseph Dinneen, able observer, noted that "he never moved about without bands, fanfare, salutes, military aides, motorcycle outriders and all the trappings of office." "King James the First of Massachusetts," he was commonly dubbed, while his dazzlingly dressed military aides became known as "General Curley's Golden Soldiers."

In his chauffeured, official twelve-cylinder Lincoln, escorted by spit-and-polish motorcycle officers, James I roamed the city and state like a speed demon possessed, arrogantly ignoring traffic laws and road safety rules. The Lincoln with the S-1 tags became involved in some accidents as a result, and his motorcycle escort had to be replenished because of fatalities in its ranks.

Invited to Harvard's tercentenary commencement in 1935, he arrived with a prancing escort of red-coated cavalry known as the "Dandy Lancers," and the large audience gasped when the governor's group entered Harvard Yard to a deafening beat of drums and a blare of trumpets. Then when it came James Michael Hisself's turn to speak, he gave the best oration of the day, though some present were not amused by his phony Oxford accent.

As the old ward boss and cagey city mayor who had made it still bigger, Curley was unable to shed his belief that in filling state jobs rewards for loyalty were far more important than competence. He replaced the renowned Payson Smith, the commissioner of education, with the Irish school superintendent of a small town. For commissioner of agriculture, he named an Irish grocery salesman who had joined the Grange. Then as civil service commissioner, he appointed his Charlestown boss ally, Tom Green, whom he had once denounced as one of the "James Brothers." Not long after Green's appointment, it became public knowledge that any Curley supporter whom the governor had blessed could pass a civil service exam. Curley owed a special debt to Margaret O'Riordan, an officer in the Hibernian Auxiliary and a member of the Democratic state committee, because she had campaigned hard for him, and her reward was her selection as state librarian. But a stench arose over her appointment when reporters interviewed her and she admitted she owned no books and her reading consisted of *True Romances* and *Spy Stories*.

To those loyal Curleyites who did not want state jobs but craved honors, Curley responded by ballooning the state's voluntary militia, passing out commissions at a furious pace for generals, colonels, and lesser officers. To those who wanted lower-level jobs as their reward, Curley went after Federal money as though it were in never-ending supply. Roosevelt was still embarrassed over the "Curley patronage affaire," and the governor won overgenerous relief program grants that put Massachusett's programs for unemployment aid in a class by themselves. Several times when he believed he needed yet more money, he would write or phone Roosevelt, and on occasion he walked in on the President at Hyde Park and the White House.

There were curbstones paved throughout the state's small towns, and even the parks had curbstones, thanks to Curley's constant nagging at the President. He used Federal money to build a long string of institutions, and when they were completed he staffed them so heavily with his patronage-rewarded employees that some hospitals counted more attendants than patients. When a superintendent complained, Curley ordered him to put some of the attendants to work growing vegetables in the farm field behind. The money was so generous that there were natural concerns whether Curley was up to his old tricks and was skimming off a part for himself. James Michael wasn't telling, though he enjoyed relating the story in a magazine that said that when he rose in the morning and looked at himself in the mirror, he would ask his reflection, "What can I do for you today, Jim?"

Crowds of unemployed surrounded his Jamaicaway home each morning, and when he came out to get into his Lincoln, he handed out cards directing the state employment office to show job favoritism to the bearer. When the sleek car pulled up to the state capitol, there were other crowds seeking favors. The old statehouse with the goldleaf dome stood on the site of John Hancock's pre-Revolutionary cow field. It was a building designed by Charles Bulfinch and contained a hallowed cornerstone laid by Paul Revere and Governor Sam Adams in 1795. Past this cornerstone and all the way up the granite stairs, supplicants for jobs excitedly called to Curley; and inside they blocked the sight of the Revolutionary murals as well as the ripped battle flags along the hall of flags. They were also pleading the length of the marble staircase to the upper floor; and the executive chamber, once a quiet place where an occasional visitor came but dared not speak above a whisper, was now noisily jammed with them as they told their problems to twenty-five clerks who took notes and directed them to possible employment. Within a year, by this chaotic system, Curley gave and created jobs for more than 100,000 persons. The $65 million federally budgeted Quabbin Dam alone gave jobs for almost two years to 25,000.

Besides his hectic effort at job-finding and beating on the Roosevelt administration for funds, Curley managed to find time in his fourteen-hour day to work on the Republican-controlled state legislature for bills he wanted. A knowledgeable logroller, he passed out favors and in return won a reduction in hours in state institutions from seventy to forty-eight hours a week. He was also able to liberalize the Workman's Compensation Law and get the sanction for legalizing horse racing, turning over the job of determining the location of the racetrack to his neighbor, Eddie Dolan. One conspicuous failure was Curley's inability to put over a bill to establish a state lottery. This bill was doomed when Cardinal O'Connell denounced it as "out-and-out gambling," though His Eminence did not object to citizens' betting on the horses, or playing bingo in church.

Although President Roosevelt felt compelled to give James Michael a too-generous share of what Curley derided as the "$4-billion-dollar Roosevelt boondoggle," the President was nevertheless determined to ruin him. According to David K. Niles, who was a member of Curley's "brain trust" and later an administrative assistant to Presidents Roosevelt and Truman, Curley was aware that the national administration had blessed Boston Mayor Mansfield's effort to put Curley and Eddie Dolan in jail. While Curley campaigned for governor, Mansfield had opened the entire available files of Curley's third term as mayor to the finance commission; and a round-the-clock effort was under way to complete the cases and bring the men to trial before the gubernatorial election. But Curley managed to win before the slow-moving legal wheels could pull him into a courtroom.

And once he took the oath of office, he embarked on the tricky task of destroying the finance commission, whose members had been appointed by his predecessor, Governor Ely. The massive job he faced to do this looked impossible: He could not replace any member of the commission without the approval of the nine-man governor's council, an elected body whose chief function was to approve or veto the governor's appointments. The governor's council consisted of five Republicans and four Democrats.

But what seemed impossible was possible to as skilled a politician as James Michael Curley. First, Curley named one member of the finance commission to the bench and won the governor's council's approval for his replacement, who was a Republican friend of Curley's. Then after naming this new member chairman of the commission, Curley brought ouster proceedings against two other members of the commission before the council. Curley charged them with a conflict of interest; and when one Republican voted with the four Democrats, the two finance commissioners were out. Shortly afterward this Republican council member was rewarded with a lush state job, and when he left Curley named a Democrat to succeed him, giving the Democrats a five to four margin on the council. As a result, there was no real argument when Governor Curley sent the names of two of his henchmen for the council's approval as new members of the commission. So it came to pass that Curley controlled both the governor's council and the finance commission.

When the newly constituted finance commission announced as expected that the entire files on Dolan and Curley had somehow disappeared, Mayor Mansfield and the national administration had to admit temporary defeat. But Mansfield refused to quit, and he induced the state legislature to pass a bill establishing a special commission to investigate the city's finances.

Curley was considered eager to veto the bill, but Mansfield was smug in his belief he had the votes to override the veto. However, Curley surprised him by signing the measure, and before Mansfield had time to find the reason, Curley announced the appointment of a chairman for the new investigating commission. The man he named was Eddie Dolan!

Even in the face of such odds, Mansfield refused to end his drive against Curley and Dolan. Without any public attention, he put loyal municipal attorneys to work rebuilding the case against the two while Curley laughed heartily at the ease with which he had supposedly outflanked the Cardinal's lawyer. Curley also sent a warning to Roosevelt by deliberately provoking a break with his son Jimmy, whom the President wanted groomed for a U.S. Senate seat from the Bay State.

Temporarily free of the finance commission and Mansfield, Curley was to reach the height of his statewide popularity in the spring of 1936 when rampaging floodwaters brought on by swiftly melting snow devastated a large part of western Massachusetts and left tens of thousands without homes or food. Curley leaped in to take personal charge of the relief effort, declaring a state of emergency. He dispatched the national guard to maintain order, set up tent cities, sent food, clothing, and medicines, organized reconstruction activities and emergency bank loans.

But he did not take charge from his executive chamber alone. For almost 100 hours straight, he was on the scene of the misery to cheer up the unfortunate and handle specific problems on the spot. Newspaper reporters followed him on his sleepless prowl of the flooded areas, detailing for readers how his presence and sympathy kept spirits high.

There was only praise for the tired governor when he returned to the Boston statehouse in his muddied Lincoln, and James Michael Curley seemed to be in the most secure political position of his life.

In 1936, political observers in the old Bay State were agreed that Governor Curley would be an easy winner in his re-election bid that year. This appraisal was not condemnatory of the voters of the state for ignoring Curley's blatant spoils appointments down to the lowest levels of state jobs; his chaotic administration; his costly trips to Florida with his staff; his high bills for flowers, luncheons, and dinners; and his publicized troubles over alleged bribery payments during his third term as mayor. Overriding all these black marks were his ability to gain enormous Federal outlays for welfare programs in a state especially hard hit by the Depression and his personal effort to help the victims of the preceding spring's heavy floods.

However, it was characteristic of Curley that when things were going his way he felt a compulsion to be a self-spoiler. Nor did he fail this time at this sorry endeavor. Instead of running for re-election to the governorship, Curley astounded his friends and enemies by announcing for the U.S. Senate.

This proved a major blunder, and later Curley assessed the chief blame for his action on Father Charles E. Coughlin, the demagogic priest from Royal Oak, Michigan. Coughlin, a big-lunged, mystic-sounding priest with a huge audience for his weekly radio broadcasts, was an early New Deal supporter. But he broke with Roosevelt over foreign policy and the administration's unwillingness to skyrocket the price of silver, and in revenge Coughlin spewed virulent anti-Semitism and weird theories on monetary policy to his vast army of radio listeners. That the round-collared priest was not a minor figure during Roosevelt's first administration was clearly revealed in January, 1935, when he and Huey Long made radio appeals to flood Senators with telegrams opposing United States membership on the World Court. So deluged by these wires was the upper chamber that what was considered a sure vote turned into a defeat.

Even though Boston's Cardinal O'Connell ordered all priests in Massachusetts not to listen to Coughlin's radio speeches, Coughlin was a hero to most Catholics in Massachusetts, and as Curley observed: "Boston was the strongest Coughlinite city in America." Little wonder then that the practical governor changed his political sights when the silver-loving priest visited him and promised him full support if he ran for Senator instead of a second term as governor.

Curley's announcement that he would try for the seat being vacated by retiring U.S. Senator Marcus Coolidge, a Democrat, produced anger and shock among his supporters, for he would no longer be directly on the scene to handle their personal problems. But with Coughlin's promise of support and the Republican choice of thirty-four-year-old, arrogant Henry Cabot Lodge, grandson of Woodrow Wilson's foe, as his opponent, Curley was not too concerned about the outcome. Lodge had been a newspaper reporter and was just finishing his second term in the state legislature where his name conjured up an emptiness regarding his accomplishments.

But things didn't go as planned. Father Coughlin fielded a new political party in 1936, and the national ticket of his Union Party consisted of one-eyed Representative William Lemke of North Dakota and Thomas C. "Hamburger Tom" O'Brien, a Curley enemy and former Suffolk County (Boston) district attorney. This would have been of no significance to Curley had O'Brien not run simultaneously as the Union Party's candidate for U.S. Senator from Massachusetts. Coughlin's blessing of O'Brien's candidacy was a severe blow to Curley who ran to Hamburger Tom with a bribe offer of $10,000 if he would withdraw. O'Brien refused, and there was later gossip that the Republicans paid him twice that amount to stay in the race.

So Curley lost the "hate" vote; nor was he able to develop his old-time enthusiasm among the poor despite announcements that he gave 20 percent of his salary to charity and had taken out a life insurance policy for $102,385, with the money to be held for 125 years, increasing with interest to $45 million, all to be used at that distant time as "a fund for the needy poor of Boston."

As the campaign limped into its final weeks, James Michael was reduced to answering O'Brien's charge that he was not a good Irishman and to lashing out with ridicule at his Republican Brahmin opponent. "Little Boy Blue," he labeled Lodge, calling him "a boy sent on a man's errand" and never failing to mention that his grandfather had displayed anti-Semitism in opposing Woodrow Wilson's appointment of Jewish Louis D. Brandeis to the United States Supreme Court.

Curley sensed in the homestretch that he had entered the wrong contest. In a year when Franklin Roosevelt trampled Alf Landon, the Republican presidential candidate, by 174,000 votes in Massachusetts, Curley was overcome by the neophyte Lodge by 136,000 votes. How personal the Senate contest had been was shown by the lopsided victory of State Treasurer Charles F. Hurley, James Michael Curley's handpicked choice as his successor in the governor's seat. So the man who could have won again as governor was out on the street.

Curley was shocked by his defeat at the hands of young Lodge at a time when he believed himself at the height of his popularity. And he was slow in recovering his ego. But he was again talking like a man with a future on the last day of his term as governor when he married Gertrude Dennis, a widow. Again he broke tradition as Hurley was taking his oath, for instead of the customary lonely walk down the granite stairs and through Boston Common, Curley was met at the bottom of the stairs by 10,000 cheering admirers who presented him and his bride with a new Lincoln for their honey-moon.

The next year witnessed Roosevelt's unsuccessful effort to "pack" the non–New Deal Supreme Court with men of his persua-sion. While the news media were focusing on this enormous struggle in Washington, a less noticeable event was Roosevelt's cooperation with Curley's enemies to give his career a further downhill kick.

Mayor Freddie Mansfield's term was in its fourth and final year when Curley decided to return to his true love—the control of Bos-ton. With his expected fanfare, he called a news conference where he showed reporters petitions signed by 100,000 persons, who he said were begging him to run for his fourth term as mayor. "A spon-taneous demand," he termed their effort, adding, "These petitions leave no course open for me except to comply. Nothing could justify a refusal."

But Curley's hope for an easy victory was jarred by a double cross comparable to the one Father Coughlin had delivered him the previous year. Maurice J. Tobin, his protégé and lieutenant, now broke ranks and also announced himself a candidate for mayor. Tobin, a likeable young man, was handsome enough to be offered a movie contract later, and glib and fun-loving to a point where Cur-ley had made him a member of his family and a confidant. Now suddenly, he was Curley's formidable opponent for mayor; for as the man in charge of Curley's poll workers, he had quietly organized most into his own personal phalanx.

Tobin's advantage in this respect was furthered by his cam-paigning technique that emphasized the age difference between him and Curley (he was an energetic, clean-cut thirty-seven while Cur-ley was a paunchy sixty-two). But still another factor in his favor was the publicity given to the court action against Curley and Eddie Dolan, his onetime city treasurer, brought by Mayor Mansfield with the support of the White House. Mansfield's strategy was to sepa-rate the charges against the two in order to increase his chances for success. Dolan's case was brought before a regular court, and he was charged with pilfering $178,000 from the Boston treasury. In contrast, Mansfield brought a case in equity against Curley, and although this barred a prison sentence, its advantage was that it would not be tried before a jury where Curley might easily sway members. The claim against Curley was that he and a local attorney had pocketed $50,000 in the settlement of the General Equipment Corporation's insurance claim for water damage against the city. The Curley case came before Judge Frederick Fosdick, an anti-Curley Republican, and despite the ease in which Curley's lawyers got the first of thirty-four continuations for him, the publicity during the campaign was damaging.

However, the worst blow came on election day, which was also the Feast of All Souls, a Roman Catholic holy day. Outside the churches that morning, worshippers found piles of the Boston *Post* that carried the following quotation in heavy black ink at the top of the front page: "Anyone who votes for a person they know to be dishonest or otherwise unfit for office commits a sin" (William Cardinal O'Connell). To those who did not buy the *Post*, Tobin's helpers were on hand to pass out 30,000 free copies.

This was a dirty stunt on the part of Tobin and the *Post*. For the Cardinal had made that remark six years earlier, and it had not been directed against Curley. But it proved to have the force of a religious order to those Catholics who looked to the Cardinal for their thoughts and decisions. Curley quickly tried to get a disavowal from His Eminence, but O'Connell was not available, lending credence to Curley's suspicion that the Cardinal had been in on the plot with Tobin and the editor of the paper. By day's end, Curley was declared the loser, with Tobin winning by 25,250 votes. And there was an extra hurt for James Michael, because he had bet $25,000 on himself.

Curley's severe downhill slide continued into the next year. By now he realized his error in not running for a second term as governor in 1936, and belatedly he tried to recoup his political capital by doing so in 1938. Governor Charlie Hurley, whom he had put into office as his successor in 1936, was now easily overcome in the Democratic primary, but Leverett Saltonstall, the state house speaker and his Republican opponent in the November general election, was far more formidable.

The forty-five-year-old Saltonstall, from an early colonial family, was so reminiscent of his ancestors in his horse face and simple manner that a sagacious observer once described him as a man "whose face hasn't changed since 1630."

Curley foolishly underestimated Saltonstall because he had been defeated for lieutenant-governor in 1936 by a weak Democratic campaigner named Frankie "Myself" Kelley. Instead of ignoring Saltonstall, whose campaign lacked any spark, Curley ignited his phlegmatic opponent by a radio speech in which he jeered: "Saltonstall may have a South Boston face, but he doesn't dare show it in South Boston."

This jibe at Saltonstall was supposed to emphasize that Curley's opponent not only lacked Irish support but would not mingle with them. However, Saltonstall immediately recognized the far-reaching blessing of Curley's taunt. Early on the morning after Curley's remark, Saltonstall went on a walking tour of South Boston and told people along the way, "I may have a South Boston face. If so, I'm proud of it." Crowds collected and there were cheers for "good old Salty," with word passing through Irish communities that Salty of the hoity-toity Protestants was fond of the Irish. From that point on, Saltonstall's campaign came alive.

But if this were not enough to destroy Curley, there were other telling events. Freddie Mansfield, former Governors Ely and Hurley, and other prominent Democrats pledged their support to Saltonstall; and Judge Fosdick chose a propitious moment for Saltonstall during the campaign to render his decision that Curley had "improperly received $30,000" in the insurance settlement case. Curley hastily appealed the decision to the State Supreme Court, pointing out that the chief prosecution witness had indeed given three entirely different versions of the alleged payoff. Nevertheless, the judicial branding of Curley as a crook received wide newspaper coverage and drove off still other would-be Curley voters.

Near the end of the campaign, Curley tried to retaliate by calling Saltonstall's Puritan ancestors thieves, by charging them with being rich mill owners who mistreated Irish employees, and by ridiculing "Stopandstall" as an "apostle of the royal purple." But Saltonstall cheerily and long-toothedly withstood the name-calling and coasted into the governor's executive chamber by the one-sided margin of almost 150,000 votes.

With his losses for senator, mayor, and governor, Curley had now suffered three successive defeats, and it seemed an excellent moment to announce his retirement at age sixty-three. "Many Bostonians have become sick of that grotesque old man," commented reporter John Gunther, who unkindly attempted to bury Curley. But the fighting Irishman bided his time waiting for another political contest to come over the horizon.

An opportunity appeared in 1940. Governor Saltonstall, running for re-election, was vulnerable because he had ruthlessly used patronage to oust Democratic jobholders at the $15-dollar-a-week level. He had also carefully refrained from taking a stand on issues, to the frustration of followers and foes. As a Boston *Globe* headline sneered at this failing: "Saltonstall comes out for Baked Indian Pudding."

But it was Mayor Tobin on whom Curley sought revenge, not Salty. Curley's anger with his onetime protégé had broadened because Tobin refused to appear on the same platform with him. Moreover, the handsome young mayor chose Curley opponents for the better city jobs.

The state legislature made possible a rerun of the 1937 race between Curley and Tobin in 1941 by repealing the law that barred successive terms for a Boston mayor. So the two were soon slashing at each other. This time Curley appeared to be a certain winner coming down to the wire, but the panicky Republican bosses, horrified at this prospect, sent orders to their lieutenants to deliver their voters to the polls to cast ballots for Tobin. Even so, handsome Maurice squeaked through by less than a 10,000-vote margin. Yet it was sufficient to give Curley his fourth consecutive defeat.

And while Curley's friends were bewailing his fate, the Massachusetts Supreme Court ruled three years after Judge Fosdick's decision that Curley would have to pay Boston a judgment of $42,629 in the General Equipment Company's insurance settlement case. A lower court judge quickly set his payment rate at $500 a week for eighty-six weeks and ordered him imprisoned if he failed to meet this schedule. Another lower court judge sentenced Dr. Joseph Santosuosso, Curley's co-defendant, to pay $2 a week for 250 years. As for Eddie Dolan, in a separate suit, he was sentenced to two and a half years in the Charles Street jail for bribing members of his jury.

At this point in his life, Curley was in the midst of financial misery. He held some brewery stock with a par value of $35,000 and a market value of zero. But other than this dubious holding he was broke, for he had invested all his savings in a gold mine in Nevada, and as was his invariable fate in wildcat speculations, the mine had not panned out. Yet the fact that he was reduced to living on loans from friends and wearing old clothes had no effect on the court, which held to its demand for the $500-a-week payment or jail.

Curley went to bed the night after the court's decision, knowing full well he would have to turn himself over to the prison warden. When he arose without hope the next morning, he glanced out the window and there on the pavement leading to his front door stood a long line of people. The newspapers had written of his plight, and the crowd had come spontaneously to help old James Michael. "I figured he could use some dough," one man told a reporter, "so I thought I'd drop by and kind of help him out."

The line of people with coins and dollars continued all that day, and it was back the next morning and every day after that for a month. In addition, the Boston Teamsters' Union held a testimonial dinner to raise money for Curley's fine, and the aging boss was saved.

Scoffed at by rising young Democratic powers, the old war horse Curley still dreamed of a political comeback, and in 1942 he had a surprise for those who considered him politically dead and buried. That year Curley turned to the U.S. House of Representatives for his next place to light. This would be his third term as a Congressman if he won, though the time span was long since his second term victory in 1912.

After looking over the roster of House members from Massachusetts, Curley decided that thirty-five-year-old Congressman Thomas Hopkinson Eliot of the eleventh district was the most vulnerable. Eliot may have been the darling of President and Mrs. Roosevelt and the grandson of Charles W. Eliot, the famed president of Harvard; but apart from a slice of Cambridge his district covered the poor Irish area of Charlestown and wards in East Boston, the North End, and Brighton. Despite the negative point that he did not live in the district, Curley announced his candidacy, counting on his blood ties to overcome this problem.

James Michael ridiculed Eliot for being non-Irish and a Unitarian—"an unfortunate denomination," he said to crowds, and as time went on Tom Eliot found his gatherings grew smaller and smaller. As election day approached, Curley publicly asked his Charlestown supporters "to cast a few votes for Tom Eliot because of his famous name." Curley's sureness was justified, for he battered Eliot on election day with ease and captured his House seat.

But Curley paid little attention to his congressional duties for he had other matters on his mind. Two years earlier and several months before Pearl Harbor he had paid a visit to Washington and was puffing on a cigar in the crowded lobby of the Mayflower Hotel when he was approached by a stranger named James G. Fuller. Fuller introduced himself as a business adviser and said he ran Engineers Group, Inc., which functioned as a know-how organization to bring manufacturers seeking contracts into direct touch with government officials with contracts to award. This seemed like a necessary endeavor to Curley for the papers were filled with stories about a growing chaos in the war goods contracting field. His enthusiasm for Fuller expanded when Fuller named other members of Engineers Group, and the list included Donald Wakefield Smith, the well-respected former official of the National Labor Relations Board, and David Desmond, a Boston stockbroker. He was even more impressed when Fuller told him that his company lacked only a big name as president to become a multi-million-dollar concern, and he begged Curley to accept this position.

Curley accepted the presidency with alacrity; and when asked to put up some collateral, he told Fuller he had only the worthless brewery stock with the $35,000 par value at purchase. Fuller took it, giving Curley a $3,500 check on it to show his own good intentions.

Curley's first indication that something was wrong came when he tried to cash the check and learned that Fuller's account was empty. But Fuller offered a glib explanation that satisfied the money-hungry Curley, and James Michael permitted him to rent a Washington office in his name and print stationery listing him as president.

Afterward, Curley returned to Boston and made only a few trips to Washington before the late fall of 1941, when he demanded his brewery stock and resigned from Engineers Group. During the six-months' period of his presidency, Curley's record revealed that he received no salary or commission and made no phone calls to government officials in behalf of company clients. His only known activities had been to tell three inquiring contractors to talk to Fuller and to phone a bank one time to discuss a loan for Engineers Group.

Trouble over his short association with Engineers Group began in April, 1942, when the defense watchdog committee under Senator Harry S. Truman investigated Engineers Group and called Curley as a witness. Committee investigators had found that Fuller was an ex-convict and that the company had taken money from private firms but had not arranged a single contract with the government. The uncovering in the files of the $3,500 bad check Fuller had given Curley had resulted in the calling of Curley before the Truman committee, and he was quizzed about his association. After the day's hearing, Truman walked over to Curley to tell him he had a clean slate and to forget the investigation.

Not long afterward, Curley heard a rumor that President Roosevelt had been told of the hearing and had ordered the FBI to investigate his role, preparatory to seeking his indictment by a grand jury. Curley quickly asked Congressman John McCormack to go to the White House in his behalf, and the House Majority Leader returned with word from Roosevelt that the rumor was false.

Nevertheless, Curley worried because he was still concerned that Roosevelt wanted him in prison. Back in 1940, Curley had attempted to improve his poor relationship with FDR by coming out for a third term for him; and though the slate for Jim Farley had won the presidential primary in Massachusetts, Curley worked closely with William "Onions" Burke, the delegation chairman, to switch the delegation to Roosevelt once FDR announced his willingness to be the nominee. The single vote they failed to switch belonged to young Joseph P. Kennedy, Jr., grandson of Honey Fitz.

But Curley was uncertain whether Roosevelt had been appeased by his work, and events revealed he had good grounds for his worries. The FBI did investigate Engineers Group, and on orders from the White House Attorney General Francis Biddle told Assistant Attorney General Tom C. Clark to seek a Federal Grand Jury indictment. Curley sought out Tom Clark who told him that if he were Attorney General he would stop the action. Curley also sent McCormack to talk with the President again, and this time Roosevelt's message was that he should concentrate on his House duties.

In September, 1943, the newspapers splashed the story of the indictments of Congressman Curley, Fuller, Smith, and four other officers of Engineers Group on a charge of violating the mail-fraud law. All were accused of "falsely representing themselves as consulting engineers; accepting advance retainers, promising contracts from the War and Navy Departments, the Federal Housing Administration, and the Soviet Government—and securing none." Curley made himself sound like a guilty man when he protested after his arraignment:—"Indictments, threats or pressure of any character shall not deter me from doing what in my judgment is the best for the American people."

Winning a delay in his trial, Curley went back to Boston in 1944 to run for another House term. Again his opponent was Tom Eliot, who graciously did not campaign against Curley as a man under indictment for a felony. Instead Eliot attacked him as a slacker who had avoided military service in the Spanish-American War and World War I. The Normandy invasion of World War II had taken place the previous June, and Eliot hoped to make mileage out of his charge of Curley's alleged unpatriotism. However, Curley demolished him in a debate at a Fourth of July celebration in East Boston when he chided him with—"The young man has told you that I am not a veteran, and left you with the impression that he is. Is he a sailor? Is he a soldier? Is he a member of the Marine Corps? Is he serving in the Coast Guard, or even in the Merchant Marine? What then is he doing in this glorious fight for freedom? He is a member of the Office of War Information, which means he spends a great deal of time in a London bomb cellar having tea and crumpets with Lady Cholmondoley and other members of the British nobility."

This time Curley beat Eliot worse than in 1942, and when the new Congress began, he barged into a White House reception for freshmen members to confront Roosevelt about his indictment. The ailing President was getting ready for the Yalta Conference with Winston Churchill and Joseph Stalin scheduled for February, 1945, and he was careful not to let Curley provoke him. According to Curley, their confrontation went like this:

Roosevelt: "What are you doing here, Jim? You're not a new Congressman."

Curley: "Well, you're not a new President, either. Why don't you have this case against me thrown out of court? You know very well that I am as innocent as you are of any wrong-doing."

Roosevelt: "I am not a dictator. If I were, I would have the case thrown out."

Curley: "You are nearer to being a dictator than any other man who has ever filled the office of President."

A few months later when Curley's lawyer was refused another extension in his criminal suit, Curley took ill and went to the Bethesda Naval Hospital. Federal Judge James Proctor granted a continuance when he received a medical deposition describing

Curley as suffering from a temporary paralysis of an arm and leg. Yet late in May, 1945, he had recovered sufficiently to travel to Boston to sign the necessary papers making him a candidate for mayor that year.

Mayor Maurice Tobin, who had spent the better part of his two terms in city hall trying to find money to meet the huge debts left by Curley's administration, had won election as governor in November, 1944; and as his successor the city council had elected John Kerrigan, the council president. The blight on Tobin's record as mayor was that he had allowed the city to run down. Streets were foul, slums more widespread and degrading, and the port lay in decay. City services had also seriously deteriorated: Police were in business with local vice lords, garbage pickup was sporadic, and fire inspections were poor, even after the tragic fire at the Cocoanut Grove nightclub in November, 1942, in which 491 persons died.

So it was "Curley the Builder," who returned to Boston to campaign once more for his fourth term as mayor, with John Kerrigan as his chief opponent and four others also in the running. The war had ended in August, 1945, with the surrender of Japan, and Curley played on the fears of Boston residents that the cancellation of war contracts might mean another major depression. "Boston will become a ghost town unless I am elected," was the repeated warning from "Curley the Builder." If this scare campaigning were not enough, Curley also hired hundreds of persons to walk about in pairs and exclaim comments such as these in crowded places: "You can say what you want to about him, but Curley gets things done"; and "If Curley was mayor, things like that wouldn't be permitted."

Curley's enemies refused to believe that the sick, seventy-year-old man, soon to be tried on a felony charge, could make a comeback in Boston. But his campaign proved so effective and his supporters so forgiving that when the ballots of November 5, 1945, were counted he had twice as many votes as Kerrigan, the second man, and 45 percent of the aggregate six-man total. With characteristic blarney, Curley announced, "The result cannot be regarded as a personal tribute to me. Rather it is a victory for all of the people of Boston."

Vice President Harry Truman had succeeded to the presidency in April, 1945, upon the death of Roosevelt, and that summer he promoted Tom Clark to Attorney General. During Curley's mayoralty campaign, he had asked Clark to abandon the Federal case against him, but Clark refused, with the comment, according to Curley, that "the pressure from above is too great." So far as Curley could interpret his cryptic remark, Truman had been so closely connected with the odious Pendergast machine in Kansas City that if he acted in Curley's behalf, he would appear to be the champion of all political bosses.

Only three weeks after his victory as mayor, Curley's trial began in Federal District Court in Washington, D.C. Curley's lawyer demanded to know why his client was being prosecuted for mail fraud when he had never written a letter for Engineers Group or signed his name to any sheet of its mail, collected a penny from the company, or charged any of his expenses to it. The prosecution agreed that all these defenses were true, but still Curley's name was printed on the stationery and the office was rented in his name.

In the midst of this bewildering case, the judge called a recess in January so that Curley could go home to Boston for his inauguration as mayor. Then it was back to Washington for Curley and more days of trial.

An FBI investigator testified favorably to Curley, but the prosecution countered by having James Fuller, the founder of Engineers Group and now in jail for passing bad checks, brought to the courtroom each day in handcuffs and seated in full view of the jury. In addition, the lax judge permitted jurors to go home each evening instead of locking them up, cautioning them not to read papers or magazines, listen to radio news, or discuss the case. Then when the jury was trying to reach a verdict, the judge told its members to go home to sleep after nine and a half hours of deliberation. The next day the jury haggled for twelve hours before the foreman told the court that it found Curley guilty of "conspiracy and using the mails to defraud."

Judge Proctor sentenced Curley to prison for six to eighteen months, and when he permitted him to go free on bail pending an appeal, Curley went home to Boston. But instead of being ostracized, he was greeted at South Station by an enormous, cheering crowd, clanging cowbells, and a band playing "Hail the Conquering Hero Comes." A *New Yorker* reporter, galled by this reception, wrote, "Bostonians . . . can see merits in James M. Curley not visible to anyone else." Yet whatever crimes Curley may have been guilty of, those who followed the Curley trial closely generally agreed with the view of John Hanna, the chief analyst of the administrative office of the United States Courts. Wrote Hanna to the *New York Times*: "Few lawyers will doubt that Curley was prosecuted for political reasons and unfairly convicted."

Pending the outcome of his appeal, Curley went to city hall each day, engaged in a host of fruitless efforts to get Federal funds for Boston, and made several speeches a week despite his very high blood pressure, diabetes, and failing eyesight. On frequent occasions he also had to combat political pressures from Joe Kennedy, former ambassador to Great Britain and son-in-law of Honey Fitz Fitzgerald. Kennedy had lost Joe, Jr., his oldest son, who had been killed on a flying mission in World War II; and the elder Kennedy was eager to have John Fitzgerald Kennedy, his next oldest son, begin the political career he had planned for Joe, Jr.

Here was Curley, mayor of Boston, still holding on to his place in Congress, and Kennedy wanted him to resign his House seat. It was unlawful for Curley to hold both offices simultaneously, Kennedy pointed out, and since he obviously preferred city hall to the Capitol in Washington, if Curley quit as Congressman there would automatically be an election within ninety days to choose his successor. It was Kennedy's intention to have Jack run in this election and succeed Curley. But Curley refused to resign until his term in Congress expired in January, 1947, and with House Majority Leader John McCormack on hand to protect him, Curley collected his pay as a Congressman and as mayor throughout 1946. As a result, Jack Kennedy's debut in Washington had to be delayed until January, 1947, after he won the next full term in Curley's district.

On the legal front, both the United States Circuit Court of Appeals and the Supreme Court turned down Curley's appeal in 1946, and the strain of the case proved so great for Curley that he was rushed to the hospital that summer in weakened condition. At one point, a priest was called, and Curley was given the last rites of the church. But Judge Proctor was not to be put off forever, and he finally ordered old James Michael to be brought to his court on June 26, 1947.

Curley was ill, and he had to be brought into the courtroom in a wheelchair. Yet he wanted even more sympathy than his poor condition could evoke from the judge. So for this appearance he purposely wore a shirt with a collar a size too large for his neck. But Judge Proctor was not moved by the wheelchair or the large collar. He refused to permit Curley to read a statement; and when he ordered the mayor taken to Danbury prison to begin his prison term, he appeared indifferent when Curley cried out: "You are sentencing me to die! This is a death penalty!" Proctor's cool reaction was that since this was Curley's second conviction for a felony he was ineligible for probation.

That same day Curley was delivered to Danbury prison in Connecticut, and before sunset his incarceration resulted in hectic political activity back in Boston. Righteous citizens had demanded that Curley's office be declared vacant and a new election called for choosing a new mayor. At the same time, City Council President John B. Kelly was expecting to be named by the council to succeed Curley, in line with past practice. However, that very day, Republican Governor Robert E. Bradford, descendant of William Bradford, the Puritan governor of the Massachusetts Bay Colony, sent the Republican legislature an urgent piece of proposed legislation. An hour later this bill, which became known as "Curley's Law," was passed and signed by Bradford. The measure provided that Curley would retain his office and salary while in jail, and City Clerk John B. Hynes, with a raise in pay and life tenure at his job, would serve as temporary mayor until Curley's return.

There was great speculation regarding the reasons for Governor Bradford's generosity to an imprisoned Democrat. The answer was not complex. In 1946, Curley's lack of support for Governor Maurice Tobin had led to his defeat by Bradford. In addition, Bradford did not want to see the elevation of Council President Kelly, who was then under indictment for demanding bribes in passing out garbage collection permits.

Before Curley went to Danbury, he had asked John McCormack to circulate a petition for a pardon to be delivered to President Truman. All members of the Massachusetts congressional delegation except Jack Kennedy signed the petition. Finally in November, 1947, Truman pardoned Curley in time to be home for Thanksgiving.

So five months after he went to Danbury, Curley was home again in the city of slums, traffic jams, rundown schools, and a population numbering now 17,000 persons per square mile. "I came back ten years younger," the thin, ailing mayor shouted to the noisy, welcoming crowd at Back Bay station after the band finishing playing the Presidential number, "Hail to the Chief!"

Curley the Builder was back with money to spend, for his

friends in the council had sat on almost $40 million in public works projects, saving them for him. Old Curley was also Curley the Moralist attempting to outdo even the notorious Watch and Ward Society in condemning modern art and burlesque shows. But there was a reason for the varied and strenuous activities of an aging man suffering from gall bladder trouble, hypertension, hardening of the arteries, and diabetes. Curley intended to give his city the opportunity to elect him to a fifth term.

Conditions for this seemed excellent in 1949. Even some of the fighting anti-Curley newspapers had accepted with reluctance a sort of institutionalization of James Michael, whose name had grown entwined with Boston; the new Democratic governor, Paul A. Dever, was friendly to Curley who had campaigned for him; and Maurice Tobin, his young-old enemy, had been removed from the local scene by President Truman, by virtue of his selection as Secretary of Labor.

But there was poison in the cup in the form of Johnny Hynes, the city clerk and former temporary mayor. Hynes had announced himself as a mayoralty candidate for honesty and progress; and though Curley derided him as "a little city clerk" and "the Republican candidate from the State Street wrecking crew," there was no erasing the picture of the enthusiasm of Hynes' followers and the tiredness of his own.

Especially galling to Curley was the work of rich, old Henry L. Shattuck, a former Harvard treasurer, who financed a "youth crusade" against him. Led by a young lawyer named Jerome L. Rappaport, about 300 college students of minority backgrounds made door-to-door pitches for Hynes, held large rallies, and wore Pilgrim costumes in political parades. Curley called Rappaport's crew "sunshine patriots" and denounced the lot as a front for scheming, cut-rate politicians. But the college boys worried him.

Even so, until the final days of the campaign, political observers gave Curley an edge over Hynes. However, this forecast was dropped when Secretary of Labor Maurice Tobin came to Boston to speak for Hynes and ask his old political lieutenants to work for Curley's defeat. Tobin's effort doomed Curley, whose vote on election day fell 11,000 below Hynes' total.

When 1950 came, Curley was out of active politics again, though Governor Dever tossed him a bone by making him a member of the Democratic state committee. But the shock of losing city hall was mild compared to his personal grief in February. During his troubles over Engineers Group in 1945, Curley's thirty-two-year-old son Paul had died. Now five years later word came to him that his daughter Mary and son Leo died of cerebral hemorrhages an hour apart in Mary's apartment. This tragedy brought 60,000 persons to the two-day wake, and Curley stumbled about with his two remaining sons, reminiscing about his first wife and seven other children who were dead.

Curley went abroad with his boys, George and Francis, and the Curley political curtain was considered by old associates to have finally closed. But James Michael could not exist without politics, and in 1951 he ran once more against Mayor Hynes. Again Rappaport and his collegiate crusaders rang doorbells, wore costumes, and held rallies. Yet Curley was not as incensed with them as he was with Joe Timilty, who had been his military aide as governor, his police commissioner when Curley was mayor, and owed his success as a rich city contractor to Curley's favors. For Timilty had entered the mayoralty contest, and all his votes would have to come from the Curley pool. Also, like a nightmare from an ancient time, "Hamburger Tom" O'Brien, Father Coughlin's vice-presidential candidate in 1936, was in the race.

Curley called on his hidden physical reserves to denounce Timilty as a renegade and traitor, O'Brien as not half the supporter of Senator Joseph R. McCarthy that he was, and Johnny Hynes as the maker of higher taxes and city debts without the saving feature of creating any of the numerous "Curley monuments" in Boston.

Senator McCarthy, with his scatter-gun attacks on Federal officials, labeling them as Communists, was the newest folkhero in Boston, and Curley wanted all the votes of McCarthy lovers. But this special strategy failed, for Hynes got 107,000 votes; Curley, 76,000; Timilty, 15,000; and O'Brien 1,500.

James Michael Curley celebrated his eightieth birthday on November 20, 1954, but instead of resting he was back in politics the next year when he doggedly ran for mayor once more against Hynes. Johnny Hynes had proved a disappointment in city hall where he showed that honesty and economy did not keep Boston from deteriorating further into squalor and dirt.

But voters of the Eisenhower era were self-centered and incapable of emotional arousement on public issues. There was a don't-care attitude toward politics, and college students, rather than campaign, were far more interested in retirement benefits. Furthermore, the sight of a campaigning octogenarian was distasteful. As Curley afterward described the dull ways of the political campaign scene he had found in the 1950s, "Impromptu speeches, prepared gesticulations, histrionics and other oratorical displays" were out. "Even Daniel Webster would have difficulty holding an audience . . . unless he took time out, every ten minutes, to give away a frigidaire or an automobile."

This was Curley's last campaign for mayor, for he came in a dismal third. However, he had his revenge over Hynes in 1956 when he defeated him in the race for delegate-at-large to the Democratic National Convention.

Afterward, James Michael Hisself slipped into further physical decline. In addition to his various ailments, he broke both shoulders in a fall, suffered a circulatory failure, and underwent an operation for a stomach ulcer. Yet he continued to reminisce about the good old days when bosses like the Mahatma Lomasney, Honey Fitz Fitzgerald, Patrick J. Kennedy, Smiling Jim Donovan, and himself ran the city with Irish humor and an immigrant's drive for power and success. He had still not repeated himself when he died only days before his eighty-fourth birthday in 1958.

Chapter Four

HUEY LONG
A Storm for My Bride

"I can't remember back to a time when my mouth wasn't open whenever there was a chance to make a speech," Huey Long once admitted.

The "Kingfish," as he was commonly called, conjured up a public image of a man on the platform in a white alpaca suit; his arms flailing; a lock of curly, red hair bouncing on his forehead; an impudent expression dancing on his fleshy, pink face flecked with pigmentation; the wide nostrils of his strange, bulbous nose tilting upward in full view; and his heavy, full lips parting and closing as a torrent of abusive, simple words poured forth in a friendly Southern drawl. "That Huey's a cutter," a poor farmer said admiringly. "He sure pours on that poison like nobody's business."

A substantial part of the American public came to view the Kingfish as the champion of the underprivileged rural folk passed over by the goodies of life. He cussed Standard Oil, Wall Street, and the rich the way they did around the potbelly stove in the general store, but the difference was that he had a radio audience of millions and the "big interests" were afraid of the Kingfish. Other Americans saw him as the cruel and ruthless dictator of Louisiana, the boss of a corrupt machine who planned to duplicate his tight control in his home state over the entire nation. "Because you don't read about it in the papers," the Kingfish warned a reporter, "don't think that Huey P. Long ain't organizing the U-nited States!"

Huey knew from experience how to live with chaos, and one of his secrets was his discovery that most other persons could not. So chaos became his prime political weapon for rattling, hamstringing, and destroying his opponents. The higher he rose on the political ladder, the more chaos he created. Endowed with high intelligence, a remarkable memory, an earthiness so primitive that it mocked all proprieties, and a burning desire for power and wealth, the big-nosed, immaculately attired, shouting, abusive, ruthless, cunning Huey Long was more than a match for the stable politicians he encountered. And he puzzled them chaotically, for the more he outraged their sensibilities the more desperate and idiotic were their own countermeasures.

He was the type the comfortable wanted to laugh at but couldn't because they had an uncomfortable suspicion that with his rabble-rousing, never-ending energy and cleverness he might attain the ultimate power he sought. He worried a President, turned U.S. Senate proceedings into total chaos, and made lackeys of all who wanted favors from him. His "Share-Our-Wealth" program and "Every Man a King" theme were continually gaining supporters in the North as well as in the South before his short, wild life was ended at the age of forty-two by an assassin's bullet.

The Longs were Northerners and abolitionists transplanted to the rural South and converted eventually to Southern traditions. The product of several generations of American Longs, John Long, who had a Pennsylvania Dutch grandmother named Huey, moved to a farm at Tunica, in Winn Parish, lying in north central Louisiana, in 1859. The Louisiana parish corresponded to a county in other states, and Winn Parish troubled the rest of Louisiana for it had voted against secession in the Civil War, become a hotbed of easy-money Populists in the 1890s, and elected several Socialists to office in the first decade of the twentieth century.

John Long was a big drinker whose habit was not abetted by his wife, Mary Lee, a militant Baptist who talked religion almost endlessly. One of their sons was a strapping lad named Huey Pierce Long, who stayed close to home until 1892 when he moved with his wife Caledonia and their six surviving children to a 320-acre red clay farm at Winnfield, the parish seat.

It was here on August 30, 1893, that Huey P. Long, Jr., was born in the four-room log house the elder Long had erected. Almost from the time he came into the world Huey Junior showed an inordinate restlessness and precocity.

His father later recalled to a newsman the strangeness of the infant. "Huey walked when he was only seven months old. Even before he could walk he could crawl from the front porch of our home to a gate in front of the house, pull himself up and release the bolt that locked the gate. . . . Huey was a case."

The Longs were preoccupied with their Baptist Church, and all the children were given a heavy dose of Baptist rituals. Little Huey trudged to Sunday School and followed this by attending the regular services; then after dinner came the Young Folks League, and in the evening more services. There was also a Wednesday night prayer meeting plus the numerous funerals where prayers were comforting. "We went to every funeral within ten miles," said Huey. "And most every summer we held a religious revival called a camp meeting, with preaching lasting all day." Huey could not get enough of the brimstone preachers who declaimed at the top of their lungs that the stain of original sin could be cleansed by the power of immersion. After one summer session, he announced he would be an orator when he grew up, but not a poor and raggedy preacher.

There was also a reading from the Bible at home each day. "Most of us read the Scripture from cover to cover," Huey said. In his case, his parents discovered he possessed a remarkable ability to retain whatever he read. Years later he could relate entire pages of the Bible on request, and this became a powerful political weapon for impressing the backwoods people of Louisiana.

But Huey was slipshod in carrying out religious teachings. A farmer who paid him by the pound to pick cotton caught him dropping a heavy watermelon into his sack. His mother's pleading that he take his schooling seriously was ignored. He would not put his superb memory to work on his lessons, and he chewed tobacco before he was ten. Scolded by his father, he ran away from home, but he was caught before he had gone 50 miles.

Huey showed an enormous desire to enter the adult commercial world, and at thirteen he divided his day between school and a local printing shop where he learned to set type. That same year he helped a book auctioneer who came to Winnfield and took his pay in books—works of Sir Walter Scott and Victor Hugo and Ridpath's *History of the World*. From here, Huey joined a friend in their own book-auctioning business, though he admitted that the chief result was their acquisition of personal libraries when they sold few books. But Huey read all his books, and the biographies awakened him to thoughts of becoming a great world leader.

Huey's work as a book auctioneer led him to try out for debating at Winnfield High School. When he was fifteen, he represented the school at the state championship at Baton Rouge, the capital. He did poorly this first time, but he was back in April, 1910, when he was sixteen; then he managed to place third in debate and win a scholarship to Louisiana State University in that city.

Huey repeatedly claimed afterward that he could not go to LSU because the scholarship covered only tuition, and his father was unable to supply him with book money and living expenses. However, his older brother Julius, later his enemy, called this a lame excuse and said he could have worked his way through college as some of the older children did had he really wanted a degree.

As it was, Huey dropped out of Winnfield High, and Harley Bozeman, a local businessman who had connections, got him a job as a drummer, or traveling salesman, selling Cottolene, a cheap shortening made from cotton oil. Huey bought a new suit and shiny buckle shoes, rented a horse and buggy, and energetically made the rounds of his northern Louisiana territory. The company expected him to take orders from grocers, sell Cottolene from house to house, and nail its ads to trees and fences. With the exuberance of a sixteen-year-old who was treated as a man, Huey did all these and more. In the towns and cities on his route, he held baking contests and awarded ribbons and inexpensive prizes to winners.

In Shreveport near the northwestern corner of the state, he awarded the baking prize to seventeen-year-old Rose McConnell for the best "bride loaf cake" made with Cottolene. Taken with the pretty girl, he enrolled that fall at Shreveport High, where Rose was a student. On his first day there, he strode to the front of the room and announced, "Class, I'm Huey P. Long from Winnfield; and I'm here to stay." He went on from his homeroom to the chemistry class where the teacher asked him if he knew what a compound was. "Sure," said Huey, "Cottolene is a compound," and he immediately launched into the peppy sales spiel he used on housewives. During the noon recess, he stood on a box in the schoolyard and recited Henley's "Invictus," roaring out the phrases he loved—"Master of my fate" and "Captain of my soul."

But Huey did not stay long with Rose McConnell in Shreveport High, for the call of the road, money in his pocket, and evenings spent trading dirty stories with other salesmen in hotel lobbies were too strong to resist. Back to the Cottolene trail he returned late in

1910, and in the following summer Bozeman landed him a better deal with a meat-packing firm in Houston, Texas, which assigned him an eight-state territory.

Because he was filling sales books, Huey ignored warnings to keep a detailed account of his traveling expenses. He was stunned one day to learn he was fired for ignoring the notices. Huey had been living it up, and with his last few dollars he took the train to Houston to plead for another chance. When the sales manager refused, he was forced to take odd jobs to stay alive. Finally with his clothes in tatters he rode freight cars to Memphis, Tennessee, where he had heard drummers were in demand. But no wholesale house wanted the seedy eighteen-year-old youth, and he slept on park benches and begged on the streets.

In desperation, he wrote to Bozeman, told him he wanted to go to the law school at the University of Oklahoma at Norman, and asked him to advance the train fare to Oklahoma City. Bozeman, who considered himself the boy's guardian, did this, and on January 2, 1912, Huey reached Oklahoma City. Here his fortune seemed to have changed when a produce wholesaler agreed to give him the sales territory around Norman and let him spend part of his day in law school.

But Huey's troubles were not over. Norman was 18 miles away and he had only 15 cents in his pocket, for he had not dared to ask his new employer for an advance on his commissions. Snow and ice covered the road that he was forced to walk to Norman, and he stayed awake all night after he got there. In the morning, after spending the 15 cents for breakfast, he was a frantic but successful salesman, landing orders for a carload of potatoes.

Huey rushed to a telephone and placed a collect call to Mr. Dawson, his employer, only to have the operator report that Dawson declined his call. In a daze, Huey stumbled to a pawn shop where he sold the new leather purse he had received from home as a Christmas present for a quarter. This time he dropped the 25 cents into the phone box and called Dawson directly with the news of the potato orders. "I'm sorry," Dawson cut in, "we're out of potatoes."

At the end of his rope now, Huey went to the Santa Fe depot to beg. A stranger stopped and Huey poured out his story: "I have walked, I have starved, I have disposed of everything of value I had on the face of the earth." The sympathetic stranger, whose name was R. O. Jackson, gave him $5, and told him his brother-in-law ran a store carrying law books and would give him credit. Mr. Jackson also visited several stores in Norman and asked them to give Long their produce orders.

On such flimsy circumstances did Huey's spirits revive, and he grew even happier when the university agreed to let him take law courses even though he had not graduated from high school. Later, he called the period from January to May, 1912, "the happiest days of my life." He attended classes regularly during this semester, and in his spare time earned $100 a month as Dawson's salesman.

When school let out for the summer, Huey took a job as a salesman with the Faultless Starch Company of Kansas City, Missouri, with the intention of returning to law classes that fall. He did so well his first weeks that the company assigned a crew to work under him with his headquarters in the Gayoso Hotel in Memphis. His family asked him to send money home, and he liked to put on a good show as a generous sport. So in the fall he lacked the funds to return to school and he stayed in Memphis.

In December, when Huey Long took a month's vacation from his company, he went to Shreveport to look up little Rose McConnell. A serious courtship developed, and early the next year, Rose came to Memphis, where Huey borrowed $10 to pay the preacher to marry them. He was nineteen and she twenty; and though he was too young to vote, marriage made him realize he was getting nowhere in life. That summer of 1914, while war erupted in Europe, Huey and Rose made plans for his return to law school. He went out on the road for a patent medicine company, carefully saved a few hundred dollars selling Wine of Cardui, borrowed $400 from lawyer brother Julius, and took his bride to New Orleans, where he enrolled in Tulane University.

With Rose managing their dingy two-room apartment, Huey plunged into law courses. The Tulane Law School gave a rigorous three-year course, and a large percentage of students dropped by the wayside under the burdensome grind. But here was Huey taking a full program for the October through May class period and studying the second and third years' courses on his own simultaneously.

His remarkable memory and ability to read swiftly convinced him after six months in law school that he could pass the bar exam. His professors considered this preposterous because the Louisiana exam was one of the stiffest in the nation, and most law school graduates spent weeks and months after getting their diplomas on special boning-up courses before taking it. But Huey went to see the chief justice of the Louisiana Supreme Court and asked to be given a private exam because he had no money to live on until the scheduled bar exam.

The judge and the bar committee agreed to give him a special exam, though none expected him to pass. But he did exceedingly well, and on May 15, 1915, the twenty-one-year-old former drummer and bum became a lawyer.

That same month he returned home to Winnfield in triumph to go into private practice partnership with older brother Julius, then the local prosecuting attorney. But trouble between the brothers developed quickly because Huey wanted to defend the cases Julius had to prosecute. Julius considered this unethical, and moreover he was growing weary of the unending advice on the law from the fledgling lawyer. So he finally told Huey to move out, and the younger brother collected his three law books and carried them to a tiny room over the Bank of Winnfield that he rented for $4 a month.

Huey had difficulty acquiring law clients until he noticed the high rate of on-the-job injuries in town. Although fellow attorneys called his actions "unethical," whenever he learned that a worker had been injured he raced to sign him up for a workmen's compensation case at a contingent fee of 50 percent.

Huey called these cases his "chip and whetstone practice" to denote its petty nature. Yet in a short time he was bragging that it "approximated, in the number of cases handled, as much as the balance of the bar of Winnfield combined."

But the pattern of his past returned just as his intensive financial worries showed signs of subsiding. A new state law set a low $300 payment limit when a worker was killed through employer negligence, and the large court awards Huey dreamed of disappeared. Realizing he needed political help to change this situation, he went to State Senator S. J. Harper, a radical who had made him his protégé. Harper not only agreed that $300 was too little compensation for a bereaved family that had lost its breadwinner but he also developed a plan to change the law. Huey was to make speeches throughout the state so people could bring pressure on their representatives at Baton Rouge; then Harper would introduce amendments to the workmen's compensation act at the next legislative session, scheduled for May, 1916; and Huey would appear as a witness for the amendments before the committee on capital and labor.

After his series of fiery orations in behalf of unlimited workers' accident benefits, Huey went to Baton Rouge for his first look at the state legislature in action and his talk before the committee. His reaction was sharp. "The formalities, mannerisms, kowtowing and easily-discernible insincerities surrounding all the affairs of the session were disgusting," he said. "Everyone talks guarded, like he was afraid he would slip on something."

At the committee, whenever Huey rose to be recognized, he was ordered to sit down. Following numerous recurrences of this scene, the chairman asked, "Whom do you represent?"

The twenty-two-year-old lawyer replied, "Several thousand common laborers."

"Are they paying you anything?"

"No."

"They seem to have good sense," said the chairman and everyone laughed. Huey never forgot his treatment by the legislative committee.

On his return to Winnfield, his practice improved, but he felt a restlessness to move into public life. There was an opening as Assistant U.S. Attorney at Shreveport, and Huey applied because he knew that many politicians considered this an important first step in their careers. After being told his appointment would merely be a formality, Huey was stunned to learn that the job had gone to another young man. The explanation was that Huey had antagonized several politicians at the capital as well as lobbyists for the large corporations operating in Louisiana, who had been present at the workmen's compensation hearing.

It was Senator Harper who now came to Huey for aid. When President Woodrow Wilson won a declaration of war against Germany from Congress in April, 1917, flames of patriotic emotion fanned the nation; and a witch-hunt was on for subversives. Harper had planned to run for a congressional nomination in the Democratic primary in September, 1918, and to aid his cause he had published a pamphlet: *Issues of the Day—Free Speech—Financial Slavery*. This was a document attacking the war, and in due course the Justice Department had a Federal grand jury indict him for subversion under the Espionage Act. Harper called on Huey Long to serve as his defense counsel.

Huey had listened frequently to Harper expound his radical views, and now before the case started, he read his client's pamphlet with the thoroughness of swallowing it whole. It contained the seeds and much of the arguments and statistics of his later "Share-Our-Wealth" program. With his remarkable memory, he would be able to recite entire sections of Harper's work to excite audience after audience throughout the rest of his life.

Because of the explosive nature of his case, Huey's only hope for winning Harper's freedom depended on which of those on the veniremen's list would serve on the jury. He obtained a copy of the entire list, and by various means he determined which men were unfavorably inclined toward Harper. Then one by one he sought out these prospective jurors, bought each drinks or food in full view of Federal agents; or if this were not possible, he would walk up to one and "talk with him in close, confidential tones, even to the point of whispering in his ear about everything under the sun except the Harper case."

When the jury was being selected, each of these men was asked if Huey had discussed the case with him. The answer was no, but the Federal prosecutor did not believe the truth. The six government challenges eliminated most, and when his turn came, Huey rejected the rest. The jury's eventual verdict was acquittal.

Besides Harper's teachings, Huey Long was strongly influenced by a political novel published first in 1914. This was Samuel Blythe's book, *The Fakers*, which told the story of a demagogue who campaigned successfully for the U.S. Senate with uproarious showmanship plus leather-lunged charges against Standard Oil. "That fellow that put those views and promises into the mouth of a potential candidate thought he was writing something funny, and he was, at that," said Huey. "But he was also writing something of immense value to the man who wants to get somewhere in politics. The people want that kind of stuff. They eat it up. Why not give it to them?"

Huey was twenty-four now, and he thought it time he put into practice some of the winning techniques from *The Fakers*. A roadblock crossed his path before he could decide on the office for which he would campaign. While he cogitated, Uncle Sam sent him notice that his draft number had come up and the army wanted him. But Huey successfully fought off service on the astounding ground that as a notary public he was a public official. "I wasn't mad at nobody," he later explained his decision to remain a civilian.

In his search for a suitable elected post, a discouraged Huey soon discovered that most state offices had minimum age requirements that excluded him. But almost down at the bottom of the list, he finally found there was no age restriction for members of the railroad commission, the state body regulating rates of common carriers, telephone companies, and the utilities. So for this reason, he announced himself a candidate for railroad commissioner for the northern district of Louisiana in the summer of 1918.

Short of funds as usual, he borrowed the $125 filing deposit from younger brother Earl. Older brother Julius became his campaign manager, and Rose's father let them move into his home in Shreveport and use it as their campaign headquarters. Brother Earl also took on the assignment of tacking Huey's picture on barns and posts throughout the twenty-eight parishes in the northern district, while Rose, who had a year-old child and was expecting her second, directed friends and neighbors in mailing out literature.

All this outside assistance left Huey free to travel about the district making speeches and shaking hands. As an old Cottolene drummer in that territory, he knew the farmers liked well-dressed strangers who spoke their slovenly, ungrammatical tongue. So he bought a secondhand car, a linen suit, and a white, striped seersucker suit, prepared his mind to speak the red-neck jargon, and set off to cover one-third of the state. Elect him and not any of his four opponents, said Huey, and he would take care of those "Wall Street money devils" who caused all their troubles. He was tireless, working an eighteen-hour day, making loud and arm-flapping speeches, going from farm to farm in an all-encompassing canvas, hitting at Standard Oil as the boss of "Loozyanna," joking with the farmers at crossroads stores, and kidding with their women.

This was Huey P. Long in his element, fully alive, and where he wanted to be. And for weeks he had a rollicking time until the money ran out. He spent his last dollar on gas to drive to Winnfield to visit his boyhood friend, Oscar K. Allen, and beg him for $500. Oscar took out a promissory note at the bank, and Huey went back to his fun.

Then came the tension of primary day, and the feeling of despair when the tabulation put him in second place, a mountainous 2,000 votes behind number one. But the law called for a runoff when the winner failed to get a majority, and Huey blessed the three candidates behind him who made a second primary necessary.

He still had some money left as he went out again on the vote trail. This time he yelled louder about Wall Street, was a regular yokel again with the yokels, ate meal after meal of potluck with friendly farmers. On election day it was a tense Huey Long who waited for the returns, for he was depending on this job as his springboard to national honors.

At last the votes were counted. He was the winner by the narrow margin of 636 votes. He was on his way.

It was too much to expect that someone whose entire existence had been an unending drama of chaos and conflict through his twenty-fifth birthday could be softened appreciably by success.

Chairman Shelby Taylor and Commissioner John Michel, men twice Huey's age, expected their young colleague to show proper respect and simply vegetate on the job, as they did, after he was sworn into office on the three-man Louisiana railroad commission. The state regulatory agency set intrastate railroad, telephone, gas, and electric rates; and traditionally its dull and crawling pace gave evidence of its cautious nature. But Huey was in too great a hurry to tolerate slow-motion action.

From the start, Huey nagged at his fellow commissioners to expand their activities into the regulation of the oil industry, a frightening concept to them, considering that Standard Oil was the most powerful industrial and political force in the state. But Long had a personal reason for his persistence. When he had moved to Shreveport to campaign, he had opened a law practice again with his older brother Julius, and among their clients were several small independent oil companies in the mammoth Caddo oil strike area in the northwestern corner of the state bordering Texas. Because these firms were suffering a cash shortage, the Long brothers took stock in lieu of fees. In addition, during his campaign Huey had gone into business with Oscar K. Allen, storekeeper and tax assessor, in their hometown of Winnfield, to form the Red Bayou Oil Co., whose stock they planned to sell to the public to cover its wildcatting efforts.

Oil pumped to the surface by the independent Louisiana companies reached a price at the well of $1.55 a barrel as the American economy soared to a record gross national product under the impetus of World War I. However, the status of the independents was chancy, for the path their oil traveled to refineries was through the pipelines owned by Standard Oil of Louisiana and a few other oil giants. As a result they stayed in business solely on the sufferance

of the pipeline owners. The day came shortly after Huey Long took
his seat on the railroad commission that the big three in the oil trust
issued a joint announcement that they would no longer carry the oil
of the independents in their pipelines to refineries.

In this crisis, representatives of more than 100 independent
oil companies met with the big three at the Shreveport Chamber of
Commerce shortly afterward to see if they could arrange an end to
the shipping embargo. Long attended as a businessman, and when
he watched the bored expressions on the faces of the Standard Oil
group as they listened with deaf ears to the pleas, he suddenly
jumped up and yelled at the top Standard Oil vice-president: "And
this is a free country. You've done this before and got by with it, but
this time go do it and see when you hear the last of it!" Huey's
longtime war with Standard Oil was under way.

The big oil companies first learned of the cleverness of their
young opponent when word of a railroad commission executive session of March 25, 1919, became known. Huey had come to this
meeting with a report of the troubles of the independent operators,
plus a recommendation that the commission consider the pipelines
to be common carriers subject to its regulation. Over 99 percent of
the stock of Standard Oil of Louisiana, he argued, was owned by
Standard Oil of New Jersey, which in turn was owned by the John
D. Rockefeller clan in New York. The embargo on pipeline carriage,
he insisted, was merely a replay of the old Rockefeller ploy in other
oil-producing states to ruin the independents and then take over
their property to create a stronger monopoly with even more out-
rageous prices to consumers.

So cruel were the giants in the Louisiana situation, said Huey,
that when a few independents somehow managed to deliver oil to
some small refineries, they found that Standard Oil immediately
offered Mexican oil to those refineries for a third of the going rate.
This was bankrupting those brave independents. At the same time,
Standard Oil had inaugurated a new policy of selling its own refined
oil far below its cost in order to put the independent oil refineries
out of business.

"The oil business in all its phases," Long's report concluded,
"must be recognized as a public necessity, and oil should be produced and transported, manufactured and sold without discrimina-
tion against the producer, the manufacturer or the consumer."

Huey was aware that only the state legislature had the power to increase the commission's authority, but if Chairman Shelby Taylor signed his report it might carry great weight among the legislators. However, Taylor lived in Baton Rouge where he had his law practice, and he knew that Standard Oil, whose refinery there was the largest in the world, could easily ruin his business.

So Huey relied on stampeding tactics. The commission was meeting in an upper-floor office in the state capitol, and Long, who was getting nowhere browbeating Taylor, suddenly ran to the window and pointed to an oil tanker coming up the Mississippi. "Look at that, Shelby!" he bellowed. "There's a ship coming up the river loaded with Mexican crude to go into the tanks where they won't let us pour our oil!"

Taylor stared hard and then reached for his pen. After Commissioner Michel also signed the report, Huey rushed to the commission secretary to engross it as an official commission document and certify several other copies as true copies for distribution to the press.

Early the next morning Taylor ordered Long to return the document he had signed so impetuously so that he could tear it to shreds. But Long informed him mockingly that he had already issued copies to the press, and all had been certified by the commission's secretary. "I've been made a fool of," Taylor wailed in terror.

The day's newspapers across the state gave the report enormous publicity, and Huey's name received its first broad coverage. Lawyers for Standard Oil flooded the commission's headquarters to see if they could still force the withdrawal of the report. But Huey was already a step ahead of them by having sent a request to Governor Ruffin G. Pleasant to call a special session of the legislature to hear his proposal. When Pleasant refused to call a special session, Huey immediately prepared and distributed news releases denouncing the governor as a "weak-backed Democrat"; and newspaper stories featured a David and Goliath confrontation, with bold, young Long declaring, "Thank God, he opposed me when I was running for railroad commissioner."

After only a few short months in office, Huey's attacks on Governor Pleasant and Standard Oil had gained him so much publicity that he was invited to talk on the oil problem at the big July 4, 1919, Democratic meeting at Hot Wells, where all party candidates in that year's primary race for governor had been asked to speak and answer questions.

Huey was still a month short of his twenty-sixth birthday when he spoke at the health spa in the center of the state, and his youthful enthusiasm was electrifying. "A sensation!" one newspaper described his speech, labeling Standard Oil "an octopus among the world's greatest criminals." There was no doubt that he had stolen the show from the gubernatorial candidates.

By the time the rigors of the primary campaign for governor weeded out the fainthearted, only Frank P. Stubbs and John M. Parker remained in the field. Parker, the underdog, was a fifty-six-year-old wealthy cotton planter and broker who had already lost one election for governor, and needing all the help he could get in the 1919 gubernatorial contest, Parker begged Huey, the sensation of the Hot Wells meeting, to campaign for him. Huey later recalled that when Parker promised to help the independent oil producers if he won, "I took the stump for a period of approximately seventy days and went to many places where no other campaign orator had ever reached, traveling at times by horseback." Huey was the crusading railroad commissioner at war with the hated Standard Oil and championing Parker; and his loud, astutely ungrammatical attacks on the trusts in the idiom of the dry, red hill country brought emotional applause.

When Parker surprised the experts and carried North Louisiana—even though by only a 761-vote margin, he won the primary. This was tantamount to election, and in appreciation he sent Huey a warm letter of thanks. However, shortly before his inauguration, Standard Oil lobbyists convinced Parker he would have carried the north without Huey, and he dropped further association with Huey. Not long after this, the governor-elect publicly announced he had reached a "gentleman's agreement" with Standard Oil and was working out an oil program with the help of its lawyers.

When Huey learned about this, his fury was blinding, and the depth of the war that followed between Governor Parker and the lowly railroad commissioner half his age rocked the state. In a showdown Huey led a group of independent oil operators into the state capitol on a lobbying mission to promote a bill declaring the pipelines as common carriers. Despite the plea of Parker's speaker of the house, Huey's lobbying brought passage of the bill by a two-vote margin. It also cleared the senate, though Standard Oil succeeded in weakening most of its provisions. When the bill reached his desk Parker was on the spot for he could not veto it since he was still making speeches as a reformer. But his signature on the bill did not end Huey's warfare against him, for Huey continued to let out a barrage of vicious speeches attacking the governor as a "bought" Standard Oil man.

Parker's goal now focused on destroying Huey. A constitutional convention had been called for March, 1921, to rewrite the old constitution; and in his desire to oust Long from his job, Parker pushed through an ordinance abolishing the railroad commission and transferring its functions to a public service commission. The trickery of Parker's ordinance was that it did not transfer members of the railroad commission to the public service commission.

Long, who was out of the state when Parker made his sly move, heard about the tactic and rushed back to fight the governor. He wrote an amendment to the ordinance effecting a transfer of commissioners, and at a time when several Parker men were absent, Huey's friends won its passage.

Long also warred with Governor Parker on the oil question at the constitutional convention. A state law provided for the collection of a tiny tax from oil companies on the sale of oil brought up from the wells. Huey proposed that this severance tax be increased to 3 percent and be made part of the new constitution.

Before the constitutional convention ended in a wild uproar, it called a special session of the state legislature to meet in September, 1921, to settle the question of the severance tax and other matters still in dispute. The morning of the special session, Long walked onto the floors of both houses and distributed copies of a statement he had written accusing Parker of having "browbeaten, bulldozed and intimidated the legislature" for the benefit of Standard Oil.

When he read the report, Governor Parker was so enraged he issued warrants for Huey's arrest for libel. At the same time, the state house of representatives called a nighttime caucus to impeach Huey.

A friend provided the required $5,000 bail, and Huey hurried to the legislative caucus meeting, barging in, even though he had no legal right to be present. "My opposition was in the majority," he recounted later, "but a few clever parliamentary strategists aiding me kept the caucus in confusion." In the room choked with tobacco smoke and angry arguments, Huey chose a moment of spent turbulence to suggest that instead of impeachment, the legislature should order him and the other two members of the public service commission to resign and run for re-election.

Several members thought this was a fairer solution than impeaching him until one legislator shouted: "Sure Long will [resign], but he's the only one that can be re-elected!"

Screaming arguments again broke out until the house floor leader, who was a Parker man, pounded for order and yelled: "I'm no Huey Long man, but apparently you are not willing for anything to be done here that is fair. I'm taking my hat and walking out of this damn session."

"Near pandemonium reigned," Huey rejoiced. "Any kind of a yell would result in general confusion. Someone gave the yell and that ended the impeachment effort."

But Huey still had to face Parker's legal action on two criminal charges of libel. Fortunately, the judge turned out to be rabidly anti-Parker, and he ruled that Long's written statements were the result of his "impetuous" nature and not a deliberate attempt to revile Parker. On that basis, he sentenced Huey to thirty days in jail, then immediately suspended the sentence, and ordered him to pay a fine of $1. When Long refused to pay, the judge collected 25 cents apiece from Huey's two lawyers and added the final 50 cents from his own pocket.

The court case only served to spur Long on to further and more bitter attacks against Parker and Standard Oil. However, Parker did not sue him again. In fact, when Huey had friends in the legislature reintroduce his 3 percent severance tax on the sale of oil at the well in the spring of 1922, Governor Parker announced he would not oppose it, though he worked behind the scenes against its passage. But Long won the fight when both houses passed his severance tax bill and Parker grudgingly signed it.

Ironically, it was Parker's political status that gained far more from the passage of the bill than Huey's. When he had taken office, Parker had been confronted with a large state debt left him by Governor R. G. Pleasant as well as a current shortage of revenues to carry out his own reform program. But with the revenue from the severance tax on oil and its extension to rice, cotton, and timber, he was able to begin a highway program, develop a site for a modern Louisiana State University, and open a school for the feebleminded in Alexandria.

It was not lost on politicians throughout the Pelican State that Huey Long, operating without a machine and against governors and the strongest economic force in the state, had bested all these groups with his oil legislation. Nor was it lost on them that Long was also drawing torrents of printer's ink because of his activities on the public service commission.

In November, 1921, when Commissioner John Michel died, twenty-eight-year-old Long became chairman of the commission, thanks to the vote of Michel's successor, Francis Williams, of the New Orleans area. A year earlier, over Huey's objection, the commission had granted a requested steep rate increase across the state to the Cumberland Telephone and Telegraph Company. Now as chairman, Huey reopened this phone rate case and ordered new hearings.

Previously a cunning pleader, propagandist, and chaos-maker at hearings of the public service commission, Huey revealed himself now as a harsh presiding officer. One time when the phone company's attorney tried to put something into the record, Long interrupted with—"Don't read the motion. We will not allow it." When the lawyer persisted, Long told him, "You are going to jail if you infringe upon the commission's procedure another minute."

After the bedlam of a hearing, Long, with the concurrence of his fellow commissioners, rolled the rates and charges back to their earlier levels. This led the telephone company to bring suit in the United States District Court to negate the commission's ruling. Huey appeared as chief counsel for the commission, and here was another stage for him. With a dramatic entrance into the courtroom, he tossed his briefcase on top of the counsel table and made judges, lawyers, and spectators stare enviously while he went into the complexities of the case and cited dozens upon dozens of judicial precedents without referring to a note. The court ruled in favor of the commission.

As time passed, a curious Long pattern developed. While his publicized actions were in the consumer's interest, several unpublicized rulings were not. For example, Huey went into court in a successful suit to force the Shreveport Street Car Company to reduce its fare from 6 cents to the old 5-cent fare. In another action, he had the commission hold hearings at the request of the Southwestern Gas and Electric Company, which wanted to increase electric and gas rates in Shreveport. Huey had the commission reduce the light rates by $135,000 a year, and he trumpeted this achievement in speech after speech. Yet without fanfare, he permitted the company to increase gas rates by 38 percent, for an added consumer burden of $500,000 annually. Little wonder that Southwestern Gas and Electric Company became a reliable campaign fund contributor in his future elections.

Chairman Long also enjoyed tangling with Standard Oil now that its pipelines were public carriers. He treated its lawyers to humiliating browbeating, and on one occasion he ordered them to haul the giant company's total business records to his office for examination. The lawyers went to court, and despite an injunction barring him from holding further hearings on the financial affairs of Standard Oil, he ignored the threat of a contempt citation and proceeded with his investigation.

In May, 1923, with the concurrence of the other two commissioners, he chopped $9,120,180.64 from the value claimed by Standard (Oil) Pipe Line Co. for its pipelines. It was from this value that rates were computed. Long also struck down Standard Oil's efforts to evade its changed status as a common pipeline oil carrier. Standard wanted to ban shipments smaller than 100,000 barrels, a level that would prohibit all but a few independents. Long's order required the company to accept oil shipments in quantities of 10,000 barrels or more, store the oil at no cost for 48 hours after it had reached its destination, and exact a maximum charge of 10 cents a barrel for each ten days after that.

But once more, after a victory against an industrial giant, Huey Long lost the war. When lawyers for Standard Oil instituted several lower court cases and ignored the commission's decision in the interim, Long failed to go directly to the state's highest court for a quick decision. Then in 1926 Huey lost the chairmanship when an election put two hostile members against him, and a new commission vote voided Long's earlier order.

In the midst of his fight with Standard Oil, Huey Long expanded his political activity, for he had long harbored a determination to become governor. The Louisiana constitution barred anyone under thirty years of age from filing as a candidate for governor, and he waited impatiently for August 30, 1923, which was his thirtieth birthday. On that day, Huey announced for the Democratic gubernatorial primary set for January 15, 1924.

A major political issue that year was the Ku Klux Klan. Even though Louisiana had a Catholic majority, the KKK had members in almost every town. Louisiana, which many writers compared with divided Ireland, was Creole and Catholic in the south and anti-Catholic, Anglo-Saxon, pro-KKK in the north. How to handle the

Ku Klux problem was a worrisome matter to Huey, for he knew that, in addition to his native north, he had to win support in the south, where only five parishes provided almost a third of the voters.

As his successor, Governor Parker was supporting Henry Luce Fuqua, a wealthy rice, cotton, sugar-cane planter, owner of the largest retail hardware store in the South, and warden of the state penitentiary. Fuqua was also the candidate of the KKK. Among Huey's other rivals was Hewitt Bouanchaud, a lawyer in Parker's administration, who was offering himself as the enemy of the KKK.

Huey's final handling of the KKK problem was to claim to be opposed and in favor of it, depending on who was asking him. Francis Williams, Huey's fellow commissioner, and Francis' twin brother, Gus Williams, a mortgage broker, were prominent Catholics and leaders of the reform Independent Regulars in New Orleans. Huey always called Commissioner Williams "France-Ass," a pronunciation Williams ascribed to Huey's North Louisiana origins, though he sometimes wondered if it were meant as a slur. Nevertheless, he and his brother put their organization behind Long for governor, after he told them he was anti-KKK.

Yet Huey knew that such a stand would harm him in the north, for his hometown of Winnfield had fallen under Klan control; the Eighth Congressional District similarly had its Congressman selected by the KKK; and his new town, Shreveport, had Mayor Lee Thomas, a loud Ku Kluxer. Asked about his stand on the KKK, Huey safely told reporters, "I am for the Declaration of Independence and the Constitution. I have a record," he complained. "Without the Klan issue, the election would be mine by default."

However, he made no denial when the Klan embraced him. In central Louisiana, where his uncle, Swords Lee, was a prominent Ku Kluxer, he stood alongside old Swords and smiled during his fulsome praise. Nor did he bring libel suit when one issue of the KKK publication editorialized: "Huey Long shakes hands with the Great Titan of Orleans Parish. That makes him the Klan candidate, don't it?"

The view of both the Fuqua and Bouanchaud groups was that the race was solely between them and that Huey Long did not have a chance. But their concern mounted as the primary race progressed, for Huey proved a tireless and clever campaigner. In addition, his creativity was especially apparent in the publicity field. At the start, with not a single paper backing him, Huey culled the newspapers for favorable editorials regarding his work as public service commissioner. These he condensed and published as a circular that Mrs. Long, his two older children—Rose and Russell—and workers in his Shreveport law office mailed across the state. The first batch consisted of 100,000 circulars.

As a campaigner, Huey was on the move through north and south without a single day of rest. "I drove my automobile and usually traveled alone," he related in his book, *Every Man a King*, "my car loaded with campaign literature and buttons, which I handed out at my meetings before and after speaking." Sign hanging was another campaign chore he did personally.

The chief worry in the Fuqua and Bouanchaud camps came from spies who told of the huge crowds and prolonged applause Long was drawing. He enjoyed his loudest cheers when he told large audiences, "The New Orleans *Times-Picayune* will report in the morning that there was only a crowd of about 300."

Huey wanted more than city and town votes and he drove, he said, into the bayou and rural country "which never before had seen a candidate for governor," and people traveled miles to "hear this feller, Huey." They were part of his show, screaming, "Give 'em hell, big boy!" and "You tell 'em, Huey"; and he responded in their monosyllabic, illiterate, local colloquial talk with a stream of "He don't know . . . We done that . . . and We'll learn 'em how." He also let out with several "damns" and "hells," as they did in their daily lives, evoked roars of laughter with his great ability to mimic his opponents, and occasionally changed pace with a wildly pompous sentence that impressed the crowd. They loved him when he yanked off his tie, pulled open his stiff collar, and complained that his tight store shoes were biting him. He could make his voice quiver, scream with anger that carried over acres his denunciation of Governor Parker, and sweat as profusely as the most God-fearing revival preacher in giving sinners a chance to be saved.

Farmers in overalls and their ladies in calico dresses, fishermen in blue shirts and their wives cooling their faces with palmetto fans cheered his unrelenting attacks on Parker and Standard Oil, whom he made his campaign opponents instead of Fuqua and Bouanchaud. He promised to abolish Parker's recently established conservation commission and to permit year-round free fishing and hunting. "I'll cut off the tail of the conservation commission right up behind the ears."

Huey also promised free schoolbooks for their children and the construction of more schools, and he castigated Governor Parker for spending money on a new site and new buildings for Louisiana State University and Agriculture and Mechanical College. He told rural crowds he would close the state university "because you'n'me ain't never been ter college, and look at us!" Besides, he went on, "Show me a man who's ever gone ter an agricultural college and then gone home and made a living off the farm, and I'll put him in Ringling Brothers' circus." Of course, said Long, he would pave every country road and reduce taxes at the same time.

Long also talked a great deal about money, for his listeners had the bottom per-capita income in the nation. He told his audiences to take the money his rich opponents—Fuqua and Bouanchaud—were offering to buy their votes. But when they went to the polls, he added in a loud aside, they should vote for him. He frequently moved crowds to tears with recitals of the hardships of farmers, trappers, fishermen, and workers, and when he finished he said he didn't expect them to contribute much to his campaign fund. Yet he always passed his deep hat among them to be filled with their nickels and dimes.

As the campaign moved into its final period, Huey, who believed he had the vote of North Louisiana in his pocket, galloped into the southern Catholic parishes for a saturation speaking tour. New Orleans, a teeming center of vice and political corruption, contained a fourth of the state's population. He pressed hard for votes here, sweating his way through each of the city's seventeen wards.

But he was depending mostly on the rural vote, and on primary day, January 15, 1924, he was dismayed when one of the heaviest statewide rains in years fell. After the first rural box reported late that afternoon, an elated Long worker told Huey, "It's the Clay box. And you got 60 of the 61 votes there!"

"I'm beat," Huey said. "There should have been 100 for me and 1 against me. Forty percent of my country vote is lost. It will be that great in the others."

His prophecy proved correct. Fuqua had a total of 82,556 votes; Bouanchaud, 82,287; and Huey Long, 73,762. The two leaders faced a runoff primary, which Fuqua would win. "It was the rain," Huey complained bitterly. "The great unwashed couldn't get to the polls."

Hardly had Governor Henry Fuqua taken his oath of office than he joined forces with the New Orleans "Ring," or "Old Regulars," Standard Oil, and the utilities in an effort to defeat Huey in 1924 in his bid for a second term on the public service commission. But Huey was so popular in his North Louisiana district that he carried all twenty-eight parishes (counties) and won re-election by an eight to one margin over his opponent. His support also won a third term in the U.S. Senate for Joseph Ransdell and in 1926 a second term for Edwin S. Broussard, who he claimed was his "Couzain Ed."

All the time Huey Long was campaigning for himself and others, he was busy with his public service commission work and his drive to become rich. One railroad case gave him national publicity. This was the famous Galveston rate case, in which the railroads had proposed to the Interstate Commerce Commission new rates for freight that would discriminate against the port of New Orleans and favor Galveston, Texas. Huey did more than condemn this: He caught the train to Washington, and his legal argument before the ICC resulted in a victory for New Orleans. On the other hand, he opposed every attempt by New Orleans to get a new union station.

No conflict-of-interest laws existed to keep Huey from expanding his law practice. In 1925, when he fought an amendment to the Workmen's Compensation Act that would have cut legal fees from their one-third level to 20 percent, a state senator called him "the compensation king of the state" and said Huey had made $40,000 the previous year "from the blood of the workingman."

Huey also made substantial increases in his bank account as the lawyer for the very corporations he was castigating from the political stump. His supporters saw nothing wrong with this, arguing that any money taken from the stingy "big boys" was a neat trick. Three cases he won involved hundreds of thousands of dollars each. In one bragging moment, he claimed, "When the millionaires and corporations of Louisiana fell out with each other, I was able to accept highly remunerative employment from one of the powerful to fight several others even more powerful. Then I made some big fees with which I built a modern home in the best residential section of Shreveport at a cost of $40,000."

In 1926, Huey had additional time to spend on his private law practice because an anti-Long commissioner won election to the public service commission that year. This in itself was not important, but Huey was at odds now with Commissioner Francis Williams, his former campaign manager; and with two votes against him, he lost the chairmanship to Williams. The enmity by Williams had stemmed from Huey's sentencing Francis' twin brother Gus to a day in jail for contempt of the commission. When Huey came to the first commission meeting at which Williams presided, he learned the other two members had barred him from his seat at the head table. "You're welcome to sit here as a spectator," Williams told him.

But even with the loss of his chief propaganda forum, Long was moving confidently ahead toward the 1928 gubernatorial race. He gained much local publicity in 1927 when Secretary of Commerce Herbert Hoover came to Louisiana to assess the great damage caused by the flooding of the Mississippi. At Shreveport, Hoover firmly told gathered state officials that the Federal government would supply the crop-losing farmers with several million cabbage plants. Huey was present in a gleaming linen suit and a loose smile. "You ain't goin'-ter turn Loozyanna into no cabbage patch," he silenced Hoover.

Huey also gained mileage for his contemplated second run for the governorship from his fight for free bridges for New Orleans, a city almost totally surrounded by water. When Governor Fuqua gave a $7.5 million contract for a toll bridge to former Governor Sanders and his associates, Long filed a taxpayer's suit to void the contract.

"Go build the bridge," Huey taunted the toll makers, "and before you finish I'll be elected governor and you will have a free bridge right beside it."

Although a Louisiana governor was barred from running for a second consecutive term, Long planned to run against the record of the Fuqua administration. But Fuqua died and Lieutenant Governor Oramel Hinckley Simpson succeeded him, making Fuqua's record a meaningless issue. Huey's new problem was that Simpson wanted to run for a full term. One way Simpson showed his intention was to pass out hundreds of jobs on the highway commission to his friends. Another way was his theft of a key Huey Long issue —a promise of free bridges for New Orleans. "He has stolen Huey's clothes while he went in swimming," Long's enemies belly-laughed.

The campaign really got under way when three former governors—Sanders, Pleasant, and Parker—met on July 8, 1927, at a self-advertised "better-element" barbecue in Alexandria with the vice-ridden New Orleans "Ring," or "Old Regulars," and lawyers for the absentee Eastern corporations. The purpose of this meeting was to pick a candidate to save the state from what they considered the wild, dangerous radicalism of Huey Long. Governor Simpson was too weak a figure for them, and after much mulling they chose Riley J. Wilson from Huey's hometown of Winnfield. Wilson, a former judge, was serving his seventh colorless term in Congress, and his seat was so safe that he was referred to as being "embalmed" in the U.S. House of Representatives. The better-element barbecuers decided that Wilson would run on his flood-control record in Congress, for want of a more exciting platform.

One month after this porkbake, Huey Long also came to Alexandria to stage his own campaign kickoff. Huey's rally received widespread attention because editors sensed a new political era approaching. The class of planters, merchants, bankers, and absentee corporate owners of the state's resources had elected one of their kind as governor ever since 1877, when they forced the Reconstruction Republican party out of power. Monotonously, their men in office had always treated the underprivileged as if they did not exist and had left them in poverty, illiteracy, and despair over the passing decades. Now in 1927, the political controllers knew they faced a mammoth challenge to their continued rule, and they were frightened.

The crowd at Huey's rally at Alexandria was boisterous and almost hysterically excited, and reporters on the scene labeled the meeting the rally of the "Po' Whites." Banners held high and shading Huey as he strutted through the parade read: "Every Man a King, But No Man Wears a Crown." Huey bluntly admitted he had borrowed this slogan from a 1900 presidential campaign speech of William Jennings Bryan, who proposed a "republic in which every citizen is a sovereign, but in which no one cares or dares to wear a crown."

The screaming crowd assembled before the platform let out a roar of approval when Huey's uncle, Ku Kluxer Colonel Swords Lee, opened the meeting. Then came Huey's speech, whipping the collected po' whites into a frenzy with his choice epithets for the opposition and his declaration that he would make every man a king. With one ridiculing paragraph, he erased Wilson's campaign argument: "So! They seek to elect the gentleman because of his flood record! What is that flood record? Why he has been in Congress for fourteen years, and this year [1927] the water went 14 feet higher than ever before, giving him a flood record of 1 foot of high water to the year, if that's what he's claiming credit for."

Before the meeting ended, Huey announced his running mate, Dr. Paul Cyr, "the tooth puller from Jeannette," whom he had chosen because he came from the center of the Creole-Catholic country. Then Huey Long was off running to his destiny.

It was a time of great national prosperity; yet it was also a time of increasing misery for his po' whites; and Huey never let them forget it. "Every Man a King," he shouted at every meeting, and they took to him as the man who would lead them from the wilderness. He denounced the enemy New Orleans "Old Regulars" and "the self-appointed rulers of the state's money and politics" as "plutocrats, plunderers, blackguards," and he sweated, leaped into the air, grimaced, bellowed, belched, and promised to help his people. He would give them free schoolbooks, more schools, free bridges, paved roads, provide natural gas, make the state prison pay for itself, provide vocational training for the deaf, dumb, and blind, improve state institutional care, end adult illiteracy, and see to it that the state's downtrodden farmers with an average annual income of $627 would have state programs to raise their incomes. Also every capable youngster would be given the opportunity to attend Louisiana State University, even though annual expenses at LSU were $700. And, of course, he would do all this by eliminating the hidden taxes that oppressed them while raising taxes on the "lords, dukes, earls, nabobs, satraps and rajahs who journeyed to Alexandria in special trains."

At St. Martinville, Long was at his best as he stood under a tree venerated by the Acadians and moved the entire crowd when he said: "And it is here under this oak where Evangeline waited for her lover, Gabriel, who never came. This oak is an immortal spot, made so by Longfellow's poem, but Evangeline is not the only one who has waited here in disappointment.

"Where are the schools that you have waited for your children to have that have never come? Where are the highways that you sent your money to build? Where are the institutions to care for the sick and disabled? Evangeline wept bitter tears, but it lasted through only one lifetime. Your tears in this country, around this oak, have lasted for generations. Give me the chance to dry the eyes of those who still weep here!"

All of Huey's enemies were out in force in the immense effort to defeat him. Politicians, newspapers, chambers of commerce, and corporation attorneys joined with the two other announced candidates—Congressman Wilson and Governor Simpson—in ringing a statewide alarm against Huey; but he thrived on exchanging insults, giving severalfold in return, laughing and mocking at the comfortable, naming the dates and places of the misdeeds of his "holier than thou" opposition.

One writer called Huey "the great champion of unrest, fighting everything and promising everything. He gratuitously insulted every previous administration. He attacked the present administration in language that would have barred his speeches from the mail."

A more physical encounter occurred in New Orleans' Roosevelt Hotel where Huey had his headquarters. He had been using former Governor Jared Sanders as a verbal punching bag, and fifty-eight-year-old Sanders picked a fight with thirty-four-year-old Huey in the hotel's elevator. Huey emerged with Sanders' torn sleeve, which he held aloft at a rally that evening. But a *Times-Picayune* reporter claimed that Huey's principal blow came when he "fell on his knees and bit Sanders on the ankle."

Other reporters combined to give Huey a poor press throughout the campaign. One informed the public that Huey's "favorite relaxation" was to walk into his Roosevelt suite, "remove his coat and shirt, pour himself a drink, sit before a mirror, and with half a dozen awed yes-men for an audience . . . indulge in an orgy of boasting." This reporter went on to describe Huey as having "the temperamental sensitivity of a prima donna. Only the most perfectly cooked food could satisfy his delicate palate; his beds must be of the finest down. If anything displeased him, there was a scene often accompanied by a torrent of abusive language."

The primary fell on January 20, 1928, with Huey the picture of confidence, for the weather report for that day was "Fair and Warmer." A record rural turnout cast ballots, and by the end of the day Huey stood first with 126,842. Wilson was next with 81,747; Simpson, with 80,326, was third. A reporter who viewed Huey at the victory celebration wrote: "His face, naturally florid, was flushed a purplish red. His shirt was open at the throat, and his eyes, set deep in his fleshy face, were heavy and bloodshot. Tousled reddish curls tumbled upon his forehead. He held out his hands, clasping those of his comrades—'You fellers stick by me. We're just getting started. . . . I'm gonna be President some day.' "

The election was actually not decisive despite Huey's victory.

Failing to win a majority, he faced a runoff contest with Wilson. However, the hope of Huey's enemies that Simpson would throw his votes to Wilson, collapsed, for Huey convinced the governor that Wilson's backers in the New Orleans "Old Regulars" had counted him out of second place by vote fraud. In addition, Huey promised to give Simpson a state job when his term expired.

When Simpson publicly asked his supporters to back Huey Long, Wilson lost heart and withdrew from the runoff primary. Long was now governor: Everyman's king of Louisiana.

Once there seemed no way to avoid the result of the election, the large corporations and the New Orleans "Old Regulars" machine concluded that perhaps Long's elevation would sober him and end his barbaric behavior. More than a thousand New Orleans businessmen, including the toll bridge owners, attempted to tender him a testimonial banquet. One guest gave him a $2,500 emerald tie pin, and the collective gathering gave him a chest of sterling silverware. "I didn't even know what half the things were for," said Huey about the various sized forks and spoons.

But falling for flattery was not one of Huey's many weaknesses. Before his inauguration, he induced Governor Simpson to operate free ferries alongside the $7.5 million toll bridge, and the bridge company quickly plunged into bankruptcy. "No music ever sounded one-half so refreshing as the whines and moans of the fat, pie-eatin' politicians," Huey said, laughing. And his inauguration on May 21, 1929, shocked the old-style politicians with their facade of Confederate manners. About 15,000 of Huey's people invaded Baton Rouge —the ladies in sunbonnets and lisle stockings, the men in blue work shirts and their churchgoing black felt hats. Huey saw to it that there were plenty of water pails and tin dippers for the thirsty, and he had country music for their entertainment. When Long spoke his inaugural oration, it was with his jacket off and with his campaign threats and challenges as unreformed as ever.

Even so, the old guard continued to court him, in order that he have time to come to his senses and realize it was cozier to play the political game their way. For instance, the legislature elected with him contained only eleven of his supporters in the 100-member house and only nine Long men in the thirty-nine member senate. Yet the old guard let him organize both chambers, electing his man, John B. Fournet, as house speaker and Philip H. Gilbert as presi-

dent pro tem of the senate. Long made swift use of this opportunity to seize total control of the operations of the house and
senate. The New Orleans *Times-Picayune* expressed a wailing alarm,
writing: "The governor has taken control of the legislature, and
named every committeeman, doorkeeper and page."

Once the legislative session began, Huey moved rapidly on his
program. His handful of men introduced bills for paved highways
and secondary schools, free textbooks and bridges, a new school
for the blind, and increased aid for the deaf and dumb, new treatment centers for the insane, and improved charity hospitals. He
also wanted to end the unpopular tax on tobacco and put through a
constitutional amendment for a multi-million-dollar bond issue to
pay the state's existing debt, and meet the highway and bridge
money needs. To pay the costs of his school and textbook programs,
he intended to boost the existing 3 percent severance tax on oil
from the well, and establish a tax of 5 cents a barrel on refined oil.

The session was hardly under way when he revealed his dictatorial approach to browbeat the non-Long majority. He ordered the
legislature to attend caucuses he ran; he walked into committee
rooms while hearings were in progress and yelled at startled members and witnesses; and he took the unprecedented action of striding
into the house and senate chambers to engage in debate on his
bills, glower at opposing speakers, and whisper advice to his stooges.
One senator, beaten by Huey in debate, threw a book at him and
called, "Maybe you've heard of this book. It's the constitution of the
state of Louisiana."

"I'm the constitution around here," Huey yelled back.

But Long knew what interested most politicians, and he hurriedly turned his minority into a majority by giving state jobs to
legislators and their families and by passing out local public works
projects to their communities. Huey openly boasted he had bought
one representative "like a sack of potatoes," and that he "dealt" the
legislature "like a pack of cards."

Nevertheless, despite his tactics his bills failed to win enactment, for the hard-core opposition found a strategy for blocking his
program. This consisted of introducing so many other bills that the
legislative calendar was soon choked.

With precious time disappearing and the session nearing its
close, Huey called caucus after caucus of his legislators to find a
solution. At one meeting, they found one.

The next morning every bill on the calendar was brought up in turn with the speaker recognizing a Huey man who moved for passage without debate. By noon, the entire calendar of more than 300 bills was cleared, with only a few bills falling by the wayside, while the opposition strategists were still trying to find a way to halt the mad rush. Then when all the measures came to Huey's desk, he signed his own bills and vetoed those of the opposition.

So by the time the sixty-day session ended, Long had his appropriations for his program, the increased severance tax on oil, a new tax on the manufacture of carbon black, and his amendment for the bond issue. Among the bills rejected by the legislature was a request from him for a $10,000 appropriation to buy a Rolls-Royce or Isotta-Fraschini automobile for his personal use. But there was one major blow and this had been the rejection of the proposed manufacturer's tax of 5 cents a barrel on refined oil, which Huey had calculated would yield $1.5 million annually for his school program. Although Standard Oil had failed to prevent an increase in the oil severance tax, its lobbying force had fought off this new tax.

Great opposition had initially been whipped up on the free schoolbook issue. Parents of children in parochial schools had united to fight it on the ground that their children would not benefit, yet they would be taxed to help pay for the books going to pupils in the public schools. This was so, as government lawyers pointed out, for the state constitution barred funds to sectarian institutions. A highly creative man, Huey solved both problems by rewording his bill to give books to *children*, not to *schools*, so parochial schools benefited and the constitution was not abused.

But even after the bill became law there was trouble from Huey's old enemy, Mayor Lee Thomas of Shreveport, who said Caddo Parish was so rich the children would have to supply their own books. No amount of name-calling by the governor moved Thomas, but Huey found another way to outwit him. The U.S. Army Air Force had chosen Shreveport for an air field and had been ceded all of the necessary land except 80 acres that belonged to the state. When a city committee visited Huey to ask for the cession, he told them to go home first and "work up them schoolbooks." He also insisted that the city make a public apology for what the mayor had been calling him and that Shreveport's citizens "bow to him [Huey] on the streets and not scowl at him"; and stop "ignoring" him "from public functions." When Thomas finally agreed to call off his war, Long ceded the 80 acres.

While Huey Long was advancing his program through the legislature, he was also involved in ousting the entrenched "Old Regulars" henchmen from the executive branch and putting his own boys into their jobs. He quickly fired all officials whose jobs were under the governor's control, but the task was much more difficult with the many boards and commissions not subject to his authority.

His method for achieving this was often ungentlemanly. For instance, he launched a slanderous war against the highway commission and actually instituted a criminal suit against one member before all resigned. This permitted him to install his own gang under his friend, Oscar K. Smith, and gave him total control of the eventual spending of $100 million under the highway program. He handled the independent levee board by pushing a reorganization bill through the legislature, permitting him to replace all members; and when he did this, he ordered the new men to sign undated letters of resignation. He used identical tactics to gain control of the board of health, and he forced the chairman of the conservation commission to flee from office by calling out the National Guard to remove him.

When Huey failed to get his former fellow members on the public service commission to quit, he slashed its budget to the point where it could do nothing. He also replaced every election registrar at each polling place he had lost in the last election, and forced the head of Charity Hospital to resign by threatening him with jail. But he suffered defeat in his effort to gain control of the courts when the legislature rejected his judicial reform bill, which would have permitted him to "pack" the bench with additional judges.

In the summer of 1928, with almost everything going his way, Huey found time to relax. Harry James, owner of the Frolics, a New Orleans speakeasy, said that the governor frequented his nightclub, danced with the hostesses, became intoxicated on the bootleg whisky, climbed the band platform, and led the musicians while he sang. He sang so much in his off-key voice, said James, that customers took to calling him "the singing fool."

That summer also Long led raids on gambling dens in New Orleans that operated under the guardianship of the corrupt "Old Regulars" and his newly found friends in the "New Regulars"

Democratic faction. In his recent election, Huey had formed an alliance with Robert Ewing, publisher of the New Orleans *Daily States*, and John P. Sullivan, gambler, racetrack owner, and Past Grand Exalted Ruler of the Elks, two of the leaders of the "New Regulars." Huey had given the two over 90 percent of his campaign money to help him in the Crescent City against the "Old Regulars"; yet the Sullivan-Ewing "New Regulars" had failed to increase his New Orleans vote above his 1924 total. This rankled him.

Nevertheless, Huey named Sullivan head of the New Orleans election supervisors as his "reward." But when Sullivan bragged that he owned the governor, Huey wanted to prove he was not under the gambler's influence, and he did this by calling out the National Guard to raid a few gambling clubs. While this gained headlines for Huey, it induced Sullivan to move his "New Regulars" into the "Old Regulars" organization and Ewing to make shrill attacks on the governor, until a state of war existed among the three.

It was also in the summer of 1928 that an ominous shadow fell across Huey Long's political path. Standard Oil had taken Federal court action against the increased severance tax, asking for an injunction to prevent its being made effective. The old severance tax had been a 3 percent charge on the *sale price* of the oil brought up from the well. Huey's new severance tax was based on *quantity*, and the Standard Oil lawyers argued that this was illegal.

The day before the case came to court Huey checked with Attorney General Percy Saint and found he had strangely made no preparation. So Huey hurriedly collected data, boarded the train that night for the 300-mile ride to Shreveport, and after his brilliant argument before the three-judge court the next day, the court denied Standard Oil its request for the severance tax injunction.

But Standard Oil carried the case to the U.S. Supreme Court, which, in February, 1929, reversed the lower court's decision, though promising to reconsider the case again later that year.

The Supreme Court's decision threw Long into a panic, for he was counting on the severance tax revenue to meet his school and free textbook expenses. To take up this money void, he called a special six-day legislative session on March 18, 1929, to consider once more his 5-cents-a-barrel tax on oil refined in Louisiana, a bill rejected in the regular session.

Huey Long had secured pledges from two-thirds of the legislators to vote for his refining tax in advance of this special session.

But the Supreme Court decision on the new severance tax and Long's request for the passage of the refined oil tax bill galvanized Standard Oil to work like demons for its defeat. By the time March 18 came, many of the legislators appeared to have a great deal of spending money, and when Huey checked he found that the two-thirds army who had pledged to vote for his bill had faded to a small minority.

So the six-day session got under way with Huey aware that his refining tax had small chance. Nevertheless, he was at hand at the outset to try his in-person methods of patronage-bribing, urging, and threatening. But members were no longer afraid of him: one demanded that the chamber be cleared of "visitors"; another, that the governor be condemned for "vote-trading." Dr. Paul Cyr, the lieutenant-governor, was also making loud cursing sounds against Huey. Cyr had recently broken with Huey when the governor refused to commute the death sentences of his friends, Dr. Thomas Dreher and Mrs. Ada LeBoeuf, found guilty of drowning Mr. LeBoeuf.

Two days after the short session began, Huey failed to get the necessary two-thirds vote to suspend the house rules, which he needed if he hoped to bring the refining tax to a vote before the session quit. But instead of letting the session die a natural death at the end of six days, he blundered by adjourning it after two days and then calling an immediate fifteen-day session to give him more time.

His blunder was soon apparent, for house members in this new special session took turns attacking him relentlessly. On March 25, with the house in a warlike mood, Huey smelled personal danger and asked his floor leader to move for adjournment without pushing further for his tax on refined oil. Shouting arguments took place when the motion came, yet Speaker Fournet ignored the outbursts to order an adjournment vote. The house used push buttons for this: when a member pressed his "yes" button, a red light showed up after his name on a board over Fournet's head; a green light if he voted "no."

On this particular call, despite the overwhelming opposition to adjournment, only red lights showed on the board. "The machine is fixed," members screamed as the riot began, with the gallery shrieking and members yelling, cursing, fighting—tearing clothes, bloodying noses, upsetting furniture. Huey's men sneaked out, but those who were left called their own roll, and the vote against ad-

journment was 71 to 9. A *New York Times* story compared the goings-on to a "frontier saloon" brawl.

The next morning the house took up a bill of impeachment
with nineteen counts against Huey. "Two-bit charges," he exclaimed,
saying it was all the work of Standard Oil, which had passed out
enough bribe money "to burn a wet mule." Among the nineteen
counts were charges that he had asked his bodyguard to kill a house
member opponent, that he carried a pistol, that he illegally pardoned an embezzler, that he used public money to buy law books
for his personal use, that he tore down the old executive mansion
without permission and used part of a $6,000 appropriation ear-
marked to entertain the governors' conference to buy a car for himself, that he fired a telephone operator for being slow, that he held
a scantily clad hula dancer on his lap at a nightclub, that he entered
into business on the legislative floor, passed out jobs to legislators,
and treated public officials to violent abuse—using words such as
"hell" and "damn."

The cockiness of the anti-Long forces was epitomized by a
mass rally Standard Oil staged in Baton Rouge. More than 6,000
turned out to listen to attacks on Huey and to the sixty-piece
Standard Oil band. Huey was reported as depressed and sobbing
into his pillow in his Heidelberg Hotel suite, and he himself acknowledged his sadness when he called Senators Ransdell and
Broussard in Washington for aid, and neither would come to the
phone, even though he had helped elect both.

Highway Commission Chairman O. K. Allen saw him in this
condition and scolded him. "Hell, you gotta fight fire with fire," he
bellowed. "Get them circulars goin'. Get up a mass meetin' and get
it up quick." Robert Maestri, New Orleans furniture dealer and
realtor, known as "Red-Light Bob," because of his extensive ownership of property in the Tenderloin section, came forward with
$40,000 to pay for 100,000 circulars and for an April 7 mass rally
for Huey in Baton Rouge.

Huey used state highway patrolmen to carry the circulars to
towns across the state, and readers were implored to save their
governor by coming to the April rally and "don't take time to dress
up." The response was awesome. They came by the thousands jam-
ming the city of "lying newspapers" for the all-day mass gathering.
Their hero, Huey, stood before them, sweating, screaming, sobbing
into the microphone for two hours: "What's all this bribery about?
Yes, bribery so that the school children might have free textbooks.

. . . They say I tried to have a little numbskull murdered." The crowd grew hysterical with rage when he expanded on his controversy with Standard Oil: "I propose a little tax on the sacred Standard Oil . . . and they told me they would impeach me." There was hardly a dry eye when he finished with his favorite poem, Henley's "Invictus": "Out of the night that covers me . . . My head is bloody, but unbowed . . . I am the master of my fate: I am the captain of my soul."

While the house continued its impeachment hearings, Huey raced across the state arousing the people with his fiery talks against Standard Oil and his ridicule of the charges. "They said I tore down the governor's mansion that had been there since 1856, and one of our citizens said that if our governors had lived in it since 1856, he couldn't see why I couldn't live in it. It's like the old lady who said to a roomer when he complained of a dirty towel, 'Why, there's been a hundred men's used that towel before you, and not one of them has complained.'"

But Huey's mass meetings, his circulars, speeches across Louisiana, and free time over his friend W. K. Henderson's Shreveport radio station KWKH had no influence on the house. On April 26, 1929, the house impeached Huey, and a trial was set in the senate for May 15. Long's removal from office seemed assured.

Pondering his fate, Huey knew that a two-thirds vote of the senate, or twenty-six of the thirty-nine members, were needed to oust him. One morning before the trial, he telephoned fifteen senators and sent fifteen limousines to their homes to bring them to his office. With promises of lucrative rewards, and threats of defeating them in renomination primaries, he finally induced them to sign their names in a circle on a document pledging them to vote him innocent "by reason of legal irregularities" in the house charges. Because their signatures were arranged around a circle to hide the order of signing, the document became known as the "Round Robin."

After the trial began in the state senate, Long's man, President pro tem Philip Gilbert, handed the secret Round-Robin manifesto to the presiding chief justice. A hurried conference took place among Long's opponents. Their faces showed total shock. There was no point continuing the trial, and they voted for an immediate adjournment. Long the politician had saved himself.

Once Huey Long finished celebrating his escape from being ousted from the governor's office with three days of fishing and drinking with the fifteen Robineers, other legislators, and friends, he set to work to tighten his organizational control over the state and especially in New Orleans. He had state trucks carry much of the governor's office furniture to New Orleans where he opened an office to combat the powerful, local "Old Regulars" machine. There he started his Louisiana Democratic Association, creating a detailed ward organization in the city and a looser parish machine elsewhere. He also fired every state employee known or rumored to have favored his impeachment, including janitors and bridge tenders, lavished patronage on his Robineers and other loyal Long men, started recall suits against opposing legislators, and bypassed "disloyal" towns in his road-building program. In addition, he launched his own weekly newspaper, *Louisiana Progress*, collecting 20 percent of each state employee's pay for one month to begin his rip-roaring attacks on his enemies.

Huey had always been a screaming, sobbing, flailing-arm speaker with a reputation for total seriousness. But an event in February, 1930, altered this picture indelibly. This was the morning he was lounging in green, silk pajamas, with his reddish hair uncombed, when the German consul and the commander of a German cruiser anchored in the Mississippi paid him a courtesy call. The visitors' protest to the press regarding his attire won front-page play across the country and a pat on the back for this great democratic governor who clowned against rituals.

Huey enjoyed this favorable national publicity—the first he had received—and he decided to cultivate this picture of himself as a character. When General McCoy of the Fourth Corps Area came with his aides in full dress for a meeting, Huey wore his B.V.D.'s. One time when he dressed formally, he told reporters, "I got a collar so high I had to stand on a stool to spit over it." On past occasions, when Huey was in parades he went almost unnoticed, but now things were different, with photographers turning out by the dozens to snap his picture for the front page. In one parade, he led a 150-piece band along New Orleans' Canal Street while he "strutted a cakewalk" and yelled at the traffic cops, "Make way for the Kingfish!"

This nickname of "Kingfish" was also a major publicity catcher. "A lot of 'em [the national public] wouldn't even have heard of Huey P. Long, if it hadn't been for the 'Kingfish' and some tomfoolery," he explained to a reporter.

As for the origin of the nickname, Huey said, he "used to listen to them blackface fellows on the radio," to a program called "Amos and Andy," which had a blowhard character named "Kingfish." "Somehow I got to callin' one of my gang 'Brother Crawford' and he took to callin' me 'Kingfish.' I took it up myself. . . . Long, or Huey P. Long, is hard to get on the telephone. But when I picked up the receiver and said, 'The Kingfish speaking,' everybody in Loozyanna knew who was talking."

On the hustings and over the radio, he called himself "the Kingfish" now instead of "Huey P. Long," and he laughed and clowned, ridiculing his opponents with jeers and grins as he lambasted them as "trashy mouth," "pie-eating sons of buzzards," "gutter-snipers, alley-rats and till-tappers," and in the case of a woman enemy, "tarbrush" and "nigger-baby."

The Kingfish had several political breaks before the next legislative session began in May, 1930. The U.S. Supreme Court, for instance, handed down opinions upholding his oil severance tax and free schoolbooks; and Huey now had a few million dollars for his educational program. At the same time, he brought an end to much of his warring by signing a secret pact with the leading industrialists of the state. He pledged he would not promote further his bill for a 5-cents-a-barrel tax on refined oil, while the oil companies pledged they would accept the severance tax, and chemical manufacturers promised to build a new $20 million chemical plant in the state.

In addition, through his ceaseless efforts, twenty-one house members who had voted for his impeachment had been "converted" in the interim into allies. The opposition was shocked to discover this on the occasion when the Kingfish's speaker, John Fournet, was re-elected 55 to 44 instead of being easily ousted. Huey again owned all committee chairmen and stacked the committees as he chose.

For his increasing political machine, Huey needed money, and the means he sought to acquire a sizeable sum he expected from his proposal for a $68 million road bond issue. The bond issue required a constitutional amendment approved by two-thirds of the legislature before going to the people for a vote. Always on the aggressive, the Kingfish ran onto the house floor to direct the fight, and one time he had to scurry out of the chamber when the sergeant-at-arms gave chase. He also had his gun-carrying bodyguards stare down

menacingly at members from the galleries (one carried a submachine gun in an open paper sack), and several of the burly crew
picked fistfights with the weak physical specimens in the house.

Yet just when Huey acquired his necessary two-thirds in the
house, two members died suddenly. But failing here through fate,
he swiftly changed tactics and had his men introduce a bill calling
for a constitutional convention, which needed only a simple majority. This bill sailed through, though in the senate, Lieutenant Governor Cyr organized a filibuster that successfully ran to the end of
the sixty-day time limit on the life of the session. So Huey did not
have his money after all and had to settle for revenge in the form of
vetoing bills providing appropriations for Dr. Cyr's expenses, the
salary of Attorney General Saint, and a $100,000 payment to banks
to defray the cost of his impeachment.

When the legislature adjourned, the Kingfish made his next
major political move. Insatiably hungry for continuing political
power, he knew he would be on the outside in 1932 when his term
expired because the constitution barred successive terms for a governor. There was a way out of his dilemma, and he took it on July
16, 1930, when he announced he was running for the U.S. Senate
in the September 9 Democratic primary against Senator Ransdell.

This was a campaign long talked about in the state afterward.
All state employees were assessed 10 percent of a month's salary
to get the business moving, and the Kingfish celebrated by purchasing two sound trucks for an estimated $60,000, a bargain despite
the fact that the Depression had begun.

Insiders called it a precision campaign, even though Huey was
"loose" with rambling stories. He had a card catalogue of every
known voter in the state with his voting record, plus the number of
campaign circulars various individuals had pledged to distribute.
State convicts painted his posters; government stenographers typed
his circulars, letters, and envelopes; highway trucks speedily delivered his campaign literature and were alerted to take voters to the
polls.

There were also friendly radio stations giving him hours of
free time, and he had a way of developing huge listening audiences
with his slow opening that went like this: "Hello, friends, this is
Huey P. Long the Kingfish speaking. And I have some very important disclosures to make. But before I begin I want you to do me a

favor. I'm gonna talk along without saying anything special for four or five minutes, just to keep things goin'. And while I'm doin' that, I want you to go to the telephone and call up five of your friends and tell 'em Huey P. Long is on the air and has some very important revelations to make."

One of his sound trucks was an advance station, moving ahead to towns with blaring music and the good news that the Kingfish was coming soon. When he did come with his second sound truck, he had his Bible to thump on, two pistols laced into pockets, and a leather-lunged voice that boomed over the amplifying system. Efficiency was his byword. He also had a baby service consisting of paid youths who tended children—even changing diapers—so mothers could hear him speak at his outdoor rallies and give him their undivided attention. For those in his crowds who dared interrupt Huey with shouts of disapproval or ask mean questions, he had his plug-uglies who enjoyed punching troublemakers in the mouth and nose—because of the ease with which blood flowed from that area.

The Kingfish's campaign used other techniques. Highway employees were sent to almost every town to pound red flags in the ground, as indication where new roads would go if Huey won the election. In the Protestant northern parishes, Huey attacked Roman Catholic, wet Ransdell as an exponent of "Rum, Romanism and Ruin," a take-off on the 1884 Blaine-Cleveland presidential campaign when Blaine's friends charged the Democrats with "Rum, Romanism and Rebellion." For the labor vote, Huey had a letter in his favor from AFL's President William Green, and when he addressed workers, he assured them they need not fear the loss of their jobs in the Depression because "the Long Plan" would prevent this— "When it goes into effect, there won't be a jobless man in America." Unfortunately, he never gave any details of the Long Plan.

He had a special campaign for New Orleans. His machine passed out money freely to buy election officials and ward workers, and he had a pat spiel to arouse crowds—"I have a plan that will take New Orleans out of debt in 24 hours." But like his full-employment plan, he told no details. The "Old Regulars," led now by Mayor T. Semmes Walmsley, were in agony every time his cortege swept into the city, for the governor's highway patrolmen tried to direct city traffic and had numerous fistfights with unwilling city police.

Down to the final week of the campaign, Huey seemed a shoo-in over the tired veteran of thirty-two years in Congress. However, the desperate anti-Long Democrats found a live issue that could upset their enemy. Sam Irby, a shoddy, little schemer, who was the uncle of Alice Lee Grosjean, Long's pretty, twenty-five-year-old secretary, had lost his job in the highway department after an argument with her. Huey allowed Miss Grosjean a great deal of political power. Irby had testified at a hearing about Long's shenanigans in the department and how after Miss Grosjean, the "sparkling baby-doll brunette with a hard mouth rouged to Cupid's bow coyness," as a reporter described her, had Mr. Irby fired, Mrs. Irby left her husband. At this point, Irby announced he planned to sue Huey for having encouraged his wife to leave him; and young Jimmy Terrell, the former husband of Miss Grosjean, also came into the news with a statement that he planned a lawsuit against "the person who broke up his home." This was interpreted by newspaper readers to mean the governor.

Huey realized that if the two did any more talking to reporters, it would damage his chances in North Louisiana, and he took swift action. Irby and Terrell were in their beds in a Shreveport hotel when the Kingfish's men kidnapped them. Headlines and accusations greeted this event; then a few days later, after state and Federal searchers failed to bring them to light, Huey made a radio speech in New Orleans, declaring he had a telegram from Irby and Terrell with a message that they were "just where they wanted to be."

While the uproar over their disappearance continued, Huey celebrated his thirty-seventh birthday a week late with a resounding victory over Ransdell, by more than 38,000 votes. In St. Bernard Parish, with only 1,900 qualified voters, Huey's men controlled both the voting list and the polls, and the St. Bernard vote was 3,979 for the Kingfish to 9 for Senator Ransdell. Now with their potential for trouble over, Irby and Terrell were released, after confinement on Grand Isle, a remote island in the Gulf of Mexico that had once served as headquarters of the pirate Jean Lafitte.

Hardly was Huey elected to the Senate when he began thinking about a higher office. Former President Calvin Coolidge visited Louisiana, and when a photographer took a picture of Coolidge and Long together, Huey exclaimed loudly, "Sonny, you've just taken a picture of an ex-President of the United States and a future one."

Despite his election to the U.S. Senate, Huey made no move to resign the governorship in 1930. Instead, he said he would remain as governor until his successor was elected in January, 1932. When newspapers charged that this would deprive Louisiana of half its Senate membership, Huey shouted back that with Old Feather-Duster Ransdell in the Senate, the seat had been vacant anyhow.

The Kingfish's chief reason for holding on to the governorship was that the despised Lieutenant Governor Cyr would replace him if he went to Washington, and he could not countenance this. So he remained on as governor, and by the time he called a special five-day session of the legislature for September, 1930, he could rejoice in Dr. Cyr's frustration and his own growing power in the state. The legislature on convening was a rubber-stamp body, and even New Orleans Mayor Walmsley, his hard foe, came hat in hand to plead for constitutional amendments permitting a $4.5 million bond issue to pay off the city's debts, $7 million for another bridge across the river, and $700,000 for street paving. Huey was agreeable because his generosity now meant a temporary end to warfare with the New Orleans machine, and he sandwiched the proposals among his own, which included a $75 million highway bond issue amendment and a 1 cent gasoline tax increase.

The legislature gave him what he wanted, though he had trouble in the house over his proposal for a new $5 million, thirty-three story capitol on the bluffs over the Mississippi. His younger brother Earl, peeved at Huey for keeping him out of his inner circle, successfully lobbied the defeat of the measure on one ballot, but Huey engineered a second vote that brought passage.

The Kingfish governor-Senator-elect moved ahead on many fronts after that. Among his hectic activities, he completed the governor's mansion, appointed Miss Grosjean secretary of state, and undertook to expand and modernize Louisiana State University in Baton Rouge, including building the "Huey P. Long Field House" and a magnificent medical school located in New Orleans.

Enrollment at LSU leaped from 1,600 students to 5,000 in two years, but while the Kingfish took pride in the growing academic standing of the institution, he was primarily interested in the football team. He handed out a large number of football scholarships, charged highway contractors for the cost of sending chartered trains to games, and became emotionally involved in the team. Spectators took to watching him instead of the team as he ran up and down the sidelines, shouting orders to the quarterback, jumping into the air when a play succeeded, and falling on the grass when there was failure. Players dreaded his expected appearances in the dressing room between halves. "Go in there next half and kill those bastards," he exhorted the boys in the Tulane game. "What the hell do you care if you break your legs while breaking their necks?" When the Pacific Coast college league would not invite LSU to play in the Rose Bowl, he started his own post-season game in New Orleans and called it the Sugar Bowl.

Huey wanted academic as well as political recognition, and he was furious when Tulane rejected his proposal that he be granted an honorary LL.D. degree. But he talked Loyola of New Orleans, a Jesuit university, into granting him one in February, 1931. He listened fondly to the outpouring of exaggerated praise, and when some of it was in Latin, he yelled, "What the hell did the damn Latin mean?"

After Huey showed no signs of claiming his Senate seat, Lieutenant Governor Cyr started a campaign to force him to give up the governorship. The Kingfish considered himself a "prisoner" because Cyr had said he would take over the governor's powers any time Huey left the state. One time Huey was in Jackson, Mississippi, when he heard that Cyr was speeding toward Baton Rouge to take over. So the Kingfish made a mad race across the line and telegraphed the statehouse that he was in home territory.

Finally, Dr. Cyr's patience gave out one day, and he took the oath of governor at Shreveport. Huey mobilized the National Guard at Baton Rouge and gave them and the state highway police orders to arrest Cyr as an imposter if he tried to enter either the mansion or the statehouse.

Then Huey declared the office of lieutenant governor vacant, and he swore in Senator Allen O. King, the president pro tem of the upper chamber, as Cyr's successor. Huey's actions went to a Shreveport court, where a friendly judge declared that he had proved in his 1½-hour argument that Dr. Cyr had given up his own office when he was sworn into another office that had an occupant. So Huey was rid of his pest for good.

At the same time the Kingfish battled Dr. Cyr, he was involving himself for the first time in national problems. In June, 1931, he had become national committeeman from Louisiana. Huey was more than a chairwarmer, as he revealed that summer when he wired all Southern governors, Senators, and Representatives, to meet with him at a New Orleans conference on his plan to end the engulfing Depression among cotton farmers.

A large crowd attended and greeted enthusiastically Huey's proposal that their states prohibit cotton-growing in 1932 because of the heavy cotton crop of 1931 and ruinous current prices. Huey predicted that with the "drop-a-crop" law, cotton prices would soar in three weeks to 20 cents. The Bible, he said, gave him the idea: "The Lord told us to lay off raising these crops one year out of every seven to let the people have time to consume them."

The success of Huey's plan depended on the affirmative action of the Texas legislature, for that state was the largest cotton producer. After Governor Sterling of Texas insisted that Louisiana act first—"It's Governor Long's baby; let him wash it first"—Huey called a special session, appeared in the chambers in a starched white *cotton* suit, and later signed the approved bill in a white *cotton* nightshirt. When Governor Sterling still delayed taking action, undiplomatic Long attacked him and the Texas legislature, with the result that his plan was voted down. As one reporter appraised matters, "If the plan had been put over and had resulted in 20-cent cotton, the Democratic Party might have nominated Huey Pierce Long at Chicago instead of Franklin Delano Roosevelt."

With his own term as governor running out, the Kingfish put up his old friend, Highway Commissioner O. K. Allen, for governor in the January, 1932, primary and House Speaker John Fournet for lieutenant governor. Allen, his boyhood friend, moneylender, first law client, and business partner, was the most loyal and subservient of all Huey's associates; but he created a problem, as Huey once admitted, because "he is the hardest man I have ever seen to make look as though he has ability."

This campaign aroused deep interest throughout the state for Huey's brother Earl was challenging Fournet, and the entire Long clan condemned Huey for not showing family loyalty. "I don't care if they run every brother and sister I've got, and my father, I'll stand by Fournet," Huey spat back. "I have three brothers and five sisters, 5,000 cousins and three or four uncles. When I run a family ticket, I'm gonna run a full ticket, and not half a one." Earl told reporters that Huey was the "yellowest physical coward that God had ever let live," and Julius Long added from the speaker's platform that Huey was "the greatest political burglar of modern times."

All these family epithets continued until primary day when O. K. Allen and Fournet were elected by a substantial margin. Now that he had men to finish his program, Huey announced he was leaving soon for the U.S. Senate. In a review of his accomplishments as governor, the Kingfish proudly pointed to his free bridges; 2,000 miles of concrete roads, 1,000 with asphalt, and numerous rural gravel roads; an increase of 25 percent in school enrollment since the free textbook program began; night schools for adults that lowered the state's 238,000 illiterates to 140,000; the improved port at New Orleans and the bringing of natural gas to that city; and the construction of the new showpiece capitol.

Huey came swaggering into Hoover's Depression Washington in an expensive gray suit, dazzling polka-dot tie, and a saucer-size gladiola on his extra-wide lapel. Reporters flocked to his suite at the Mayflower Hotel where he greeted them in his green silk pajamas and with a host of colorful thoughts on a variety of political and economic issues. "I'm a small fish here in Washington," he told them while puffing on a cigar and running a razor down a lathered cheek. "But I'm the Kingfish to the folks down in Loozyanna."

With his entourage applauding from the Senate gallery, Huey Long strolled onto the Senate floor at noon on January 25, 1932, to be sworn in as a member of the upper house. Reactionary Senator Broussard approached to escort his Louisiana colleague to the rostrum, but Huey was his sworn enemy since Broussard had not aided him in his impeachment troubles, so he told "Couzain Ed," as he called Broussard in an earlier campaign, to get lost. Senator Joseph Robinson of Arkansas, running mate to Al Smith in 1928 and now Democratic leader of the Senate, was appalled at Huey's violation of Senate rules, and to end the tense moment personally escorted Huey to the rostrum for the oath-taking. He was further annoyed when Huey lit up a cigar in violation of the no-smoking rule, but Robinson said nothing. And afterward he blinked in shame at the sight and sound of Huey scampering about the chamber, yelling to members, "I'm the Kingfish. Who are you?" He pumped the hand of old Senator William E. Borah, the "Lion of Idaho," threw an arm around Republican floor leader Jim Watson of Indiana, and pinched the wrist of white-thatched Hiram Johnson of California. To florid Senator Bob Reynolds of North Carolina, the Senate's admirer of Adolph Hitler, Huey yelled, "I know you! You were running the skating rink in Baton Rouge when I was selling swamp root." Unabashedly, Reynolds replied, "You were a medicine man selling herbs and berries, and the fastest skater at my rink."

Two days later, he violated the unwritten rule that freshmen remain silent for two years and delivered his maiden speech. This was a screaming attack on an appointment to the Federal Trade Commission by President Hoover. Huey later called on Hoover at the White House and told reporters as he left, "For the mis'able party he represents, I guess he is about as good as any of 'em."

After his opening taste of Washington politics, Huey was determined to take charge of the Senate and the Democratic Party. He told reporters that Democratic leaders suffered from "political paralysis" at a time when the nation cried out for help. "This was one of the most sorrowful things I found in Washington," he said in a sad tone. While the Senate Democratic leadership was cooperating with the big business Republican administration, Huey told the Senate, "I have come here with only one project in mind, which was that I might do something to spread the wealth of the land among all of the people."

When Huey had first come to Washington, he had declared that Senator Joe Robinson was one of the favorites for the presidency. But when Huey introduced an amendment to the tax bill, calling for the confiscation of incomes in excess of $1 million a year and inheritance above $5 million, war broke out between the two Senators.

Robinson acridly commented that Huey was really asking for the end of the free-enterprise system. Huey pounded on his Bible and shouted, "I'm advocatin' what the Lord gave Moses! What is a man going to do with more than $1 million?" His face brick red by now, Huey roared at Robinson, "There has got to be another leadership responsible to the American people in the Democratic Party. And here we have a Democratic leadership in the House and Senate that is comin' out for the sales tax instead of laying taxes on Baruch, Rockefeller and the like."

The battling between the freshman Senator and the Senate Leader raced along in the wake of Huey's continuing effort to ridicule Robinson and reduce the upper chamber to chaos. Joe Robinson should be Hoover's running mate, said the Kingfish, because both were "trying to impose starvation, pestilence and disease upon the country." Robinson, Huey told the Senate, was a crook who used his office to collect law clients for his legal firm back in Little Rock. "The Senator's law firm represents every nefarious interest on the living face of the globe." Robinson's weak replies proved to be no match for the Kingfish.

Huey's first session of the Senate belonged to him, in terms of the amount of time he spent in possession of the floor and the anarchy he produced. A typical display came the last day, June 10, when Congress expected to pass the tax bill before adjournment so that Republicans could go to their national convention scheduled for June 14. Huey's "confiscate the wealth" amendment received only a few votes, and to punish the majority he filibustered against the finance committee's low tax rate bill. This proved to be a three-hour attack on Senate leaders, until they agreed at 10:00 P.M. to adjourn and quit town without completing their work.

All the while the Kingfish was pacing up and down the U.S. Senate's center aisle in his numerous speeches, he was ruling Louisiana with a club in his hand. He made excursions back to Baton Rouge aboard the *Crescent Limited* to trod the state house and senate floorboards that spring to put through a bill to increase taxes on cigarettes, soft drinks, insurance premiums, corporate franchises, and gas and light bills. Louisiana needed new revenue sources, for Long had spent money wildly in his years as governor and the state was deep in debt. Members worried about re-election if they raised taxes, but Huey had the votes because of patronage promises and threats, and the tax bill passed easily after the hearing.

Back again in Baton Rouge after his Senate filibuster and congressional adjournment, Huey took up his state headquarters in Allen's office. O. K. Allen, selected by Huey as governor because of his subservience, was proving so totally servile that Earl Long aptly described his mechanical role: "A leaf blew in the window of Allen's office and fell on his desk. He signed it." Huey was sitting alongside the governor at his desk one day. "Oscar," he said, while reporters were in the room, "go get me those goddam bills we was talkin' about." When O. K. Allen continued work on another chore, Huey screamed, "Goddam you, Oscar. Don't you stall around with me. I made you and I kin break you. Get me those goddam bills and get 'em quick!" Oscar left on the run.

On one of Huey's quick trips back to Baton Rouge, he had called a meeting of the 104-member Democratic state central committee. The purpose was to choose a delegation to the Democratic National Convention in Chicago in June, and he arranged to serve as delegation chairman with total control of Louisiana's twenty votes. For a century, a statewide convention had selected the delegation, but in 1928 Huey had broken precedent by having the state central committee take on this function, and now in 1932 he repeated it.

Huey's old enemies among Louisiana Democrats, led by former Governors Parker, Sanders, and Pleasant, called their own convention in Shreveport and elected a delegation to represent the state in Chicago. The Kingfish publicly jeered at this "bunch of Ex-es," but he was concerned they might win seating from an anti-Long credentials committee. So to confuse the issue and create a smoke screen of chaos, he ordered some of his stooges to stage a convention, choose a third delegation, and select a favorite son other than himself.

A few months earlier, Huey had opposed the nomination of New York Governor Franklin D. Roosevelt, but Senators Burton K. Wheeler and George Norris worked on him and Roosevelt himself sent Huey a clinching letter, declaring, "You and I are alike for the rights in behalf of the common man of this country."

When Huey and Norris made a simultaneous announcement for FDR, Jim Farley, the governor's campaign guide, phoned Huey to go early to Chicago to help collect Southern delegations for Roosevelt. Huey stepped off the train in the convention city a week before the Democratic powwow was scheduled to begin. He had four pongee suits to carry him through the hectic period he hoped would make him a President-namer and the father of a national Share-Our-Wealth plank in the Democratic platform. "Hey," he told reporters, while fanning his red face with a gleaming white hard straw hat, "no, I'm not running for Vice-President. I wouldn't be a vice anything. Huey Long stands second to nobody."

With his reddish hair falling in ringlets, he set off to get delegations to drop favorite-son candidates and move onto the Roosevelt bandwagon. Jim Farley and Edward J. Flynn, Democratic boss of the Bronx and co-convention manager for Roosevelt, could see 663 votes for their man, but they needed 768 of the 1,154 delegates to nominate FDR. Huey was up all day and most of the night roaming the convention hotels with his bodyguards in search of Roosevelt support. Heywood Broun, renowned reporter of that era, tried to follow Huey on his lobbying work but failed because of almost total physical exhaustion after a short time.

The fight over which Louisiana delegation to seat went to the national committee, the credentials committee, and the full convention. Huey told the national committee: "The Democratic Party in Loozyanna? I am the Democratic Party in Loozyanna." Ed Flynn, who heard Huey at the credentials committee, wrote afterward: "Never in all my experience have I listened to a finer or more logical argument." The only bad moment there came when a spectator booed Huey, and the Kingfish told the chairman, "Brother, I can give you a man to take care of that disturber." The offer was declined. Huey won the committee's vote for seating his delegation, but the issue was renewed before the entire convention. The final vote after a long debate favored Huey's delegation 638 ¾ to 514¼.

After Roosevelt's nomination, Huey took no vacation but spent his time adding to his power. Mrs. Hattie Caraway had been appointed to the Senate seat of her late husband, Thaddeus Caraway, by the governor of Arkansas on her promise not to run in 1932 for a full Senate term. When Joe Robinson announced his own candidate for her seat, Huey induced her to break her promise and run. Mrs. Caraway was considered a sure loser in the Democratic primary, but Huey borrowed four sound trucks from the Louisiana highway department and campaigned for her through thirty-nine of Arkansas' seventy-five counties. She won the primary with as many votes as her six opponents combined.

Afterward, Huey had to return home to collect still another Senator in his network when he put John Overton, his old friend and lawyer, into the Louisiana primary against Senator "Couzain Ed" Broussard. To meet campaign expenses, Huey ordered all state employees to hand over 10 percent of a month's salary, and again he borrowed highway trucks and state printing presses.

"Broussard's been one of Wall Street's own, and you just watch us clean that bird's plow," Huey boasted. "Why, Edwin Broussard dassn't blow his nose without orders from Wall Street. He sits in his office about a block away from the Senate, and when it comes time to vote, they punch a bell and Edwin meets a feller in the hall, and the feller says, 'Vote no this time, Edwin,' and Edwin goes in and he votes no. . . . After a while the bell rings again, and the feller in the hall says, 'Vote yes this time, Edwin,' and Edwin, he votes yes.

Once in a while they punch the bell and they ain't no feller in the hall. When that happens Ed just waits and watches how I vote, and then he votes the other way!"

Broussard didn't have a chance, but he fought back. "Long has been preaching a doctrine of division of wealth," he advised audiences. "When he comes here you ask him to divide with you." Broussard would then launch into an accounting of Long's mysterious wealth, including his expensive house, his pocket wad of paper money, and his travel in special railroad cars.

Overton defeated Broussard overwhelmingly in the September 13 primary, triumphing in almost all parishes. However, Huey's machine resorted to widespread dishonesty, even though none was necessary, and Broussard entered a charge of fraud with the U.S. Senate election committee. One of his prime examples was the old story of St. Bernard Parish with its 2,510 eligible white voters who cast 3,176 votes for Overton and 13 for Broussard. In some other contests in the primary, Huey had put up as many as nine dummy candidates in order to control polling precincts, for each candidate was entitled to polling place officials.

When a Senate subcommittee came to Louisiana to hold hearings on the election, Huey made their lives miserable. He served as counsel to Overton, forced all hearings to be public, and packed the room with his henchmen who applauded and booed on signal. The subcommittee declared the primary had been corrupt, yet it raised no objection to the seating of Overton.

Besides the primary contests in Arkansas and Louisiana, Huey campaigned strenuously for Roosevelt in the fall of 1932, after the nominee invited him to Hyde Park where he charmed him. Jim Farley gave him the Midwestern area of the Dakotas, Minnesota, Nebraska, Iowa, and Kansas, states Roosevelt believed were bound to be Republican. But when all those states voted for Roosevelt, Farley commented, "We underrated Long's ability to grip the masses. . . . He put on a great show and everywhere he went, we got the most glowing reports of what he had accomplished for the Democratic cause."

Following Roosevelt's victory in November, 1932, Huey was photographed visiting the President-elect at Warm Springs, Georgia, where Roosevelt and his "Brain Trust" were mulling over approaches to the vexing domestic problems, and Long was quoted as telling Professor Raymond Moley, the chief adviser: "There never was a wise man who did not have to see someone wiser at some time, and I'm available to you at any time you want to come." Moley's judgment of Huey Long was that he had a superb brain but used it "so erratically he seemed a great deal of the time to be insane."

What camaraderie seemed to exist between Huey Long and Franklin Roosevelt proved short-lived. Four days after FDR's inauguration on March 4, 1933, Huey dropped in at the White House oval office and had a friendly chat with "Frank." But hardly a month later their warfare was in full flower. When Roosevelt began his famous "Hundred Days" with an economy wave, a big business banking bill, and a setting aside of the antitrust laws, Huey was among his most vitriolic attackers. He blasted the administration for cutting veterans' benefits by $300 million; roared at the Glass-Steagall banking bill that made Federal funds readily available to banks instead of nationalizing them and prohibited banks from paying interest on checking accounts; and denounced the National Recovery Administration, which gave trade associations of individual industries authority to set up codes limiting competition and production and determining selling prices and labor conditions. Huey claimed that Wall Street and impractical dreamers had taken over the New Deal.

After his opposition to the New Deal was in full swing, Huey discovered that Roosevelt was retaliating. Federal patronage in Louisiana was being given to his home-state enemies, and the Bureau of Internal Revenue was investigating Huey and his lieutenants for income-tax evasion. But Huey was not frightened on the latter score, for he believed Roosevelt was bluffing. This served only to fill him with greater contempt for the court circle, and the Kingfish took to ridiculing members of the administration: Roosevelt was "Prince Franklin . . . liar"; Secretary of Agriculture Henry Wallace was "Lord Corn Wallace . . . ignoramous of Iowa"; and Secretary of the Interior Harold Ickes, "the Chinch Bug of Chicago."

In June, 1933, Jim Farley arranged a meeting at the White House between Huey and Roosevelt in an attempt to settle their differences. Farley later recalled: "Long kept his hat on during the conversation. At first I thought it was an oversight, but soon realized it was deliberate." The only times Huey removed his hat came when he leaned close to the President to "tap him on the knee or elbow to emphasize one of his finer points. . . . Roosevelt was enjoying it immensely." Afterward, Huey bawled at Farley, "What the hell is the use of coming down to see this fellow? I can't win any decisions over him."

By this time, the Kingfish had begun to consider seriously running for President. "It was easy to conceive a situation," said astute Farley, "whereby Long might have the balance of power in the 1936 election." Huey's first step in this direction came in August, 1933, when he collected financial assurances in New York to expand his weekly newspaper, *Louisiana Progress*, into a national publication called *American Progress*. Then in October came his autobiography, *Every Man a King*. Following this, Huey laid plans to establish his own national political organization.

Huey was well aware, however, that without a solid base at home in Louisiana, his national ambitions would founder. He had no trouble, of course, with the governor and the executive branch, but Mayor Walmsley of New Orleans, with whom he had established a nonaggression pact, was showing signs of restlessness.

The truth was that Walmsley was only one of many politicians and private citizens in the state who had lost their fear of him. This was the result of the notoriety Huey picked up at the Sands Point Club on Long Island, New York, in the late summer of 1933. Following several drinks, Huey danced with a girl at an adjoining table and allegedly made an ungentlemanly remark to her. Afterward, in the men's room, the girl's escort punched Huey in the eye and drew blood.

The next day papers across the nation wrote up this "sock in the eye," and Huey's enemies rejoiced. When he went home for some speech-making, listeners in the crowds started taunting him about Sands Point. "How about that Long Island affair?" would come one taunt, followed by—"Why weren't you in the war?" At Hammond, he was hung in effigy with the title: "Long Island Huey"; and at Alexandria he was not only bombarded with catcalls but with "a shower of eggs, rotten oranges and stench bombs." Huey found himself in the unusual position of being on the defensive, and he took to repeating that Wall Street had hired Al Capone's boys to waylay him. But his explanation served chiefly to draw more scoffing laughter.

It was in this atmosphere that Mayor Walmsley declared his independence and told Huey to get out of New Orleans' political affairs or face his political death. There was a mayoralty election coming on January 23, 1934, and Walmsley ordered Huey to steer clear of it. But the Senator responded by issuing a pamphlet entitled *No Combination with Rats and Lice*, in which he attacked the mayor and the "Old Regulars" machine. In addition, he put up a candidate against Walmsley and boasted he would also defeat District Attorney Eugene Stanley who had won convictions against three Long election commissioners in 1932 for fraud.

As the New Orleans campaign moved into its final weeks, emboldened Walmsley challenged "Long Island" Huey to a fight "any place, any time," and said he would force the Kingfish to "swallow every insult" even if he had to "drag him out of the hotel or trail him to Washington." Despite these and other taunts Huey was suffering on the local campaign trail, he did not quit as Walmsley expected he would. Instead, he stepped up activities in behalf of his candidates, and at one point he rushed to Washington to replenish his shrinking prestige with another publicized visit to the White House.

When Walmsley defeated Huey's candidate and the district attorney also won re-election, the aura of invincibility that had surrounded Huey seemed to be gone for good. The New York *Herald-Tribune*'s appraisal of the New Orleans election was that the decline of Huey's machine "rapidly is assuming the proportions of a collapse."

But just when the politicians were writing Huey off as finished, he came roaring back stronger than ever. The Louisiana legislature was to hold a regular session in May, 1934, and the "Old Regulars" plus the reactionary former governors looked forward to a resumption of their old-time control. However, Huey blithely commandeered the desk in Governor O. K. Allen's office, bought off key legislators with patronage, and issued the Huey P. Long program for the legislature. He would end the $1.00 poll tax so his "po'-whites" could flock to the polls (Negroes were barred by a law of 1898 from voting in Democratic primaries); institute a state income tax law to balance another law exempting the first $2,000 of assessments on houses from taxation; cut license-plate costs on inexpensive cars; take liquor-control power away from localities (courthouse rings) and centralize it in the state government; and establish a futures tax on trading on the New Orleans Cotton Exchange, plus a tax on gross receipts of private newspapers. He was daily on the house and senate floors, pushing his program with yells and epithets (and without any demands that he be expelled). On one of his bills, when a member refrained from voting, Huey ran to his seat and screamed, "This man votes yes!" There were no objections, and the vote was included.

Flushed with the success in getting his twenty-eight-bill program through the state legislature, the Kingfish went back to the Capitol in Washington where he found that the Sands Point incident was now forgotten. As of old, he took to the Senate floor to produce more chaos and step up his ridicule of the upper chamber. In one speech, he exposed in detail the behind-the-scenes logrolling among members on the tariff bill; another was a tirade against the Rockefellers and Standard Oil, whom he charged with fomenting war between Paraguay and Bolivia over the disputed Chaco border area. He also tried to peg the New Deal as antifarmer—"Them city slickers are takin' the country boys for a snipe hunt."

But Huey's mind was on gaining revenge on Mayor Walmsley and New Orleans, and he soon concentrated on this job. His first step involved the election of two Congressmen from the New Orleans districts, who were up for re-election in the September, 1934, primary. Walmsley had permitted Huey to name these men during their earlier truce, but now the mayor expected to eliminate the two with ease since he controlled the registration rolls and election machinery.

To re-elect his boys, Huey put on a wild show to gain control of New Orleans. Back in February, 1934, Huey had quietly ordered one of his stooges, District Judge William O'Hara of New Orleans, to empower him to investigate "wide-open gambling" in the Mardi Gras town. But it was not until July that he made use of this unusual authority. He caught Mayor Walmsley by surprise when he announced that unless the "lottery kings, racketeering ward bosses, dives and bawdy-houses" were immediately wiped out, he would do the job himself. Walmsley cursed his audacity, declared he lacked any authority as a U.S. Senator to act within the state.

But the Kingfish flashed his grant from the judge, and eight days later he ordered Governor Allen to declare martial law in New Orleans and dispatch 3,000 National Guardsmen to fight vice there. Walmsley in a public address denounced Huey as a "Caligula, Nero, Attila, Henry VIII and Louis XI rolled into one. . . . I warn you, Huey Long, you cringing coward, that if one life is spent in defense of this city, you shall pay the penalty as other carpetbaggers have done before you."

Huey's answer was to send the troops at night to seize the office of registrar of voters across the street from city hall, in order "to prevent election frauds." From the sanctity of the "Old Regulars" sanctuary at the Choctaw Club, the mayor called Huey "a political degenerate, moral leper and Al Capone." But Huey, enjoying his trickiness, laughed at "Turkey Head Walmsley," who, he said, "sent his police running down into the red-light district to warn the prostitutes to hide."

The city fell into turmoil and fear with Huey's army and Walmsley's police force, both armed with machine guns and bayonets, facing each other in the downtown area and noting each other's presence in other parts of town. The mayor in desperation appealed as a New Deal supporter to the White House for Federal action under the Constitution to guarantee a state's republican form of government. When Roosevelt decided not to involve himself, Huey chortled, "Roosevelt is no damn fool. . . . He knows his place."

A few weeks before the election, Huey had Governor Allen appoint him a special attorney general with authority to hold hearings in New Orleans on "the direct corruption of the mayor, the mayor's brother, all city commissioner's, the police chief." Citizens were soon reading about Senator Long, the local prosecutor, questioning madams from the "Storeyville" red-light district about alleged police payoffs and promising to end the terrible vice he claimed was overrunning the town.

By election day in September, 1934, the Kingfish seemed to be everywhere in New Orleans. The papers were filled with his investigation; the streets with his soldiers; and on the hour for five minutes all day Huey delivered a political sermon. His two Congressmen won easily.

With his success in shattering the "Old Regulars," New Orleans now belonged to Huey. However, he revealed the sham of his drive against vice a few months later when he met secretly with Frank Costello, the New York rackets leader. The two arranged a deal whereby Costello was promised Huey's protection in installing slot machines in New Orleans. Costello later testified that in return he was to pay Long for each operating machine, the money allegedly to go for "a certain kind of relief to the poor, the blind. . . ."

To win acknowledgment of his strength, the Senator did not remove his 3,000 bivouacking troops from the city until New Orleans' top businessmen abjectly cringed before him and thanked him for "ending vice" there. But having had a taste of victory over the mayor with the election of the two Congressmen, Huey was determined to go further and reduce Walmsley to mayor in name only.

U.S. Senator Long called the state legislature into a series of special sessions during the rest of 1934 to make himself the dictator of New Orleans. One law shifted the police and fire departments to state control; another took away the city's authority over voter registration books and election machinery, and barred the police from interfering in elections; still another throttled the city financially by removing its power to impose and collect taxes, an authority transferred to the state tax commission. Senator Long also ordered banks that had extended credit to the city to call their loans, with the unhappy result that city workers went unpaid and garbage lay in the streets for weeks.

The Kingfish concluded after his successful ending of home rule in New Orleans that it was time to extend his dictatorship in other directions. At a further special session, he ended home rule privileges for other cities. A reporter on hand described Huey in the legislative chambers, ". . . a jumping-jack a self-motored ping-pong ball, one minute at this member's seat, whispering, now consulting the speaker, now in the aisles, laughing, shouting, bellowing with strut and grimace—half like a straw boss with a chain gang, partly like an Elk on initiation night." He showed up at a legislative committee meeting with thirty-five bills just off the press and unread by members. "Before I explain these bills, I want to hear any comments by opponents," he dared the crowd of twenty members. He railroaded all bills through with little debate and said after a string of uncontested measures, "Make that vote 19 to 1."

As for his municipal legislation, he made it necessary for all police and firemen to get state commissions; slashed the salary of his enemy, the district attorney of Baton Rouge; barred all district attorneys from naming more than three assistants and barred sheriffs from naming more than five deputies (the state would name additional personnel); gave himself (through the governor) power to remove the mayor of Alexandria—an act of revenge against the place where he had been pelted with eggs and oranges during his "Long Island Huey" days; and terminated all local self-government for Baton Rouge, the authority to run the city going to the governor.

But the dictator's thirst was far from being slaked. Other bills barred the courts from interfering with the governor's use of the militia; established a secret police force answerable only to the gov-

ernor (Huey), with authority to arrest in every locality; removed
the bar association's power over admissions of new lawyers to the
bar; ordered the purchase of the powerful radio station WDSU os-
tensibly for LSU but actually for Huey's personal use; and took
Federal funds from Roosevelt-appointed administrators in the state
and put the spending into the governor's hands.

Senator Long also had Governor Allen appoint him special
attorney to the public service commission, giving him control over
electric and gas rates. In addition, Huey signed a contract with the
state tax commission to serve as its boss of tax frauds and delinquency. Huey was to get one-third of all the money recovered.

One bill caused trouble, and this was Huey's insistence on the
passage of his 5-cents-a-barrel tax on refined oil, the legislation
that had led to his impeachment in 1929. Standard Oil immediately
laid off 900 employees of the 3,800 employed at its Baton Rouge
refinery and denounced Huey. Company workers and an outside
group of young men outraged by Huey's oil tax and other legislation
formed the Square Deal Association and demanded the repeal of
"all dictatorial laws." But Huey used his secret police and the state
militia to suppress them, and effected a new agreement with Standard Oil to reduce the state refining tax from 5 cents to 1 cent a
barrel.

Once his home base was secure, the Kingfish began in earnest
his move toward the presidency of the United States. This was to be
an effort based not on working within the framework of the Democratic Party but through his own organization.

The pattern was determined back in February, 1934, when
Huey's *American Progress* announced in fiery red headlines: "Share
Wealth Move Begun: People Will Set Up Local Organizations
Throughout Nation." As the chief organizer and manager of his
"Share-Our-Wealth Clubs," the Kingfish chose the Reverend Gerald
L. K. Smith, a big-nosed, hard-eyed, blond heavyweight and a
fourth-generation Disciples of Christ preacher, who ministered anti-
Semitism to his Shreveport flock. That Huey would tolerate an anti-
Semite as his second in command was odd considering that his
closest friends and henchmen were Seymour Weiss, Abe Shushin,
Al Danzinger, Jules and Joseph Fisher—all Jews. But Huey consid-
ered how each person could be useful to him, and he saw no conflict
in having opposing aides.

Reverend Smith in his sweaty blue shirt and booming voice

that remained strong for hours had a gift for arousing poor little people, and as Huey put it, "Next to me, Gerald Smith is the greatest rabble-rouser in the country." When someone once compared Huey and Smith to Hitler and Goering, Huey turned the question into another direction, as he so frequently did, and replied, "Don't liken to me that sonofabitch! Anybody that lets his public policy get mixed up with religious prejudice is a plain goddam fool."

Smith was a good organizer, yet his task was simple, for with no dues or contributions expected of members and with Huey Long as the man on horseback, the rolls grew quickly in the Share-Our-Wealth movement. Huey's program had to be popular with the bulk of poor Americans because it included a promise to seize large fortunes, grant every family a homestead allowance of $6,000, a guaranteed $2,000 annual family income, "adequate" old-age pensions, a short work week, universal free education, and government purchase of agricultural surpluses. It was the message of a Depression Messiah.

At the beginning of 1935, Smith claimed, there were already 30,000 Share-Our-Wealth Clubs with 4.5 million members and a 7.5-million-person mailing list. Huey had to add fifteen girls to his Washington staff to handle the growing mountain of letters that daily blocked the entrance to his Senate office. Everytime Huey or Smith went out on speaking trips, membership and the mail grew. One of the few rules Huey enforced was that Negroes could not become members. As one of Reverend Smith's aides told the large audience among the loblolly pines at one village, "Now all you niggahs quit crowdin' up here, stand back in the rear theah. Y'all ah welcome to stay or go on home jest as you likes. An' jes' don't sign none o' them Share-Our-Wealth cards. Them's fo' white folks."

Proud forty-one-year-old Huey composed his campaign song for 1936, "Every Man a King," and after he sang it over radio a few times, he came to Washington in January, 1935, to touch off his campaign for President in earnest. For this large goal, he announced he had become a teetotaler and daily woodchopper, though his face was flabby and purplish and his stomach bulged. He led off by taunting the administration as the "greatest cesspool of evil" and said he was going "to put the facts on the barrel head."

While the administration expected a sledgehammer attack on the President, Huey decided not to take on FDR directly. Instead, he concentrated his fire on Roosevelt's chief campaign strategist, Postmaster General and chairman of the Democratic National Committee Jim Farley. Demanding a Senate investigation of Farley, Huey in loud, ranting floor speeches accused him of throwing post office construction contracts to the General Builders Supply Co. of New York, with whom he had previously been connected. The Kingfish also charged that Farley was in a "wire service" racket with gamblers; had given $80,000 in new stamps to friends; used Reconstruction Finance Corporation money for election purposes; and was responsible for "slime, filth and rottenness in government."

For two months Farley made no reply, nor did his friends in the Senate come to his defense. Finally at the beginning of March, Farley issued a written denial to all the Long charges except that dealing with stamp-giveaways. Farley claimed this "was a practice of seventy years' standing." With Farley on the defensive, Huey hit at him again, won approval of a resolution calling for a Senate committee investigation of his charges, and brought Interior Secretary "Honest Harold" Ickes into the scene by declaring that his department was investigating Farley. Ickes could "go slap-damn to hell" for ignoring him in passing out public works goodies, said Huey, promising to "nail his ears back" for this and for having ridiculed him as "the Emperor of Louisiana."

With the Kingfish apparently too facile with words for the likes of Farley and Ickes, Roosevelt chose General Hugh "Iron Pants" Johnson, former head of the National Recovery Administration, to lash out at Huey over nationwide radio that same March. This was a blunder even though Johnson hilariously mimicked his voice, mocked his Share-Our-Wealth program, told one of Huey's "nigger" stories, and tied him and radio-spouting anti-Semitic, Roman Catholic priest Charles Coughlin together as "Pied-Pipers." Added Johnson, "Hitler couldn't hold a candle to Huey in the art of the old Barnum Ballyhoo—a new sucker born every minute!"

Roosevelt advisers considered the entire performance a mistake because Johnson's speech served chiefly to give Huey additional publicity and lent credence to the rumors that the administration feared him. Furthermore, Huey parleyed his publicity by demanding and winning free radio time for a coast-to-coast rebuttal. With a far warmer radio personality than the general, Huey easily bested him, ridiculing him, ripping into Roosevelt and his administration, and spending most of his time explaining his Share-Our-Wealth program. The Roosevelt crew was "gunning for me," he said. "They think Huey Long is the cause of all their worry. They are like ol'

Davy Crockett who 'fired and fired' at a possum only to discover that it wasn't a possum he saw at all in the top of the tree, but a louse in his own eyebrow." As for the big American fortunes, he promised to "cut them down to fryin' size."

Afterward, when Huey's talk brought him about 25,000 letters a day for several weeks, Roosevelt tried to stem his growing popularity by sending Congress a "soak the rich" tax proposal. But though this deflated Huey temporarily, the Kingfish was not weakened. Instead, the tax bill hurt Roosevelt, for it marked the point of departure by much of the business community from its support of the New Deal.

In the Senate, Huey's attack on Johnson and on financier Bernard Baruch, who was Johnson's employer, finally moved Majority Leader Joe Robinson into engaging in a screaming match with the Kingfish. Robinson said that "anywhere else than in the Senate, Long would be called a madman." Among his own remarks in this tussle, Huey threatened to retire Robinson as well as Pat Harrison of Mississippi to private life. "I'm a-goin' to beat Pat and Joe," he warned the two Senators who were up for re-election in 1936.

In preparation for the 1936 presidential contest, Huey went on a series of speaking trips in 1935. At the capital in Georgia, he spoke to 10,000 hysterical admirers and gave the impression he would welcome Governor Ol' Gene Talmadge as his running mate. With mounting political support in Louisiana, Georgia, Arkansas, Alabama, and Mississippi, Huey talked his way through parts of Texas and the Carolinas. More than 40,000 South Carolina rednecks signed membership cards in his clubs after his brief appearances in that state. Huey also went North, donning overalls and traveling with a hillbilly band as far as North Dakota. At Des Moines, Iowa, he moved the crowd to roaring cheers with his attack on the administration's farm policy.

In 1935, the Kingfish exerted some influence on legislation in the Senate for the first time. He was partly responsible for the popular opposition that defeated approval of the World Court. His build-up of public pressure also brought the defeat of the St. Lawrence Seaway measure, and his radio appeal brought a lobbying response that almost succeeded in overriding a Roosevelt veto of the highly inflationary soldiers' bonus bill that called for the issuance of $2 billion in greenbacks.

On June 13, 1935, Huey made the longest speech of his career, a U.S. Senate filibuster lasting almost 16 hours against an administration bill to provide a skeleton NRA after the Supreme Court had declared the original act unconstitutional. Huey ate up the evening and night by relating recipes for fried oysters, potlikker, coffee, and turnip greens; going through the Constitution section by section; and telling the life stories of Confederate Cabinet member Judas P. Benjamin and Huey's hero, Frederick the Great. At dawn, he quit, after eighty-five pages worth of talk in the *Congressional Record*, and the Senate passed the bill. But another filibuster on August 26, 1935, the last day of the session, was more effective because he talked until the agreed-upon adjournment time, and the Senate could not vote on the important supplemental appropriations bill.

Despite the growing membership in Huey Long's Share-Our-Wealth movement and his pervasive dictatorship over Louisiana, the Kingfish was well aware in mid-1935 that his personal situation was not as secure as it appeared on the surface. For one thing, Huey was obsessed with the notion that his enemies were planning to assassinate him. For another, he knew that Louisiana was crawling with treasury investigators out to pin income-tax frauds on him and his top henchmen.

For personal safety, Huey increased the number of his gun-carrying bodyguards, and they accompanied him wherever he went in Washington and back home. His suspicions bordered on hysteria. On one occasion, the Senator had just begun to talk when a photographer's flashbulb exploded. "I've been shot!" Huey screamed, running from the room.

Another time, Huey Long told the Senate on August 9, 1935, his agents had eavesdropped on a meeting of plotters at the De Soto Hotel in New Orleans, and among those planning to kill him was Baton Rouge District Attorney John Fred Odom. Odom admitted later he was there, but said that although "violent expressions against Long were voiced, these were far from constituting a murder plot." Huey's secretary insisted that the records of the hotel meeting showed that one of the participants was Dr. Carl Austin Weiss, a Baton Rouge eye, ear, nose, and throat specialist. "They drew straws to kill the Senator and Weiss lost," said Earl Cristenberry, Huey's secretary.

Besides his fear of assassination, Long was somewhat concerned about President Roosevelt's determination to put him in jail.

It was during the Hoover administration that the first investigation of Huey's finances was made. But by the time Hoover's term expired, there was not sufficient evidence to indict Long and his associates, so the job passed on to the Roosevelt era. It was not until January, 1934, following FDR's public break with Huey that Treasury Secretary Henry Morgenthau, Jr., ordered Elmer Irey, the Treasury's enforcement branch chief, to push the Long investigation to its conclusion. "We already knew that Long and his gang had collected millions in graft in the course of spending state loans that Huey had systematically raised to an even $100 million. Technically we were uninterested in graft payments but concerned only with the fact that taxes had not been paid on these bribes," said Irey.

Irey's "T-Men" conducted an in-depth investigation of 232 persons, 42 partnerships, and 122 corporations, and by early 1935 were ready to start indictments. The program called for testing a Louisiana jury's reaction to dealing with Long by starting on a lesser light in his organization and then working up to Long himself if all went well. The chosen guinea pig was state Representative Joseph Fisher, nephew of state Senator Jules Fisher, the shrimp cannery king and fur-trapping monopolist.

The grand jury was not afraid to indict Joe Fisher for failure to pay Federal income taxes on "commissions," as he called the money he collected on state highway projects. Another jury found Fisher guilty in April, 1935, and he was sentenced to eighteen months in Atlanta.

Higher-ranking Long associates were harder to imprison, though indictments came readily, and several years were required to complete this task. Among this group was Abe Shushin, a New Orleans merchant, who made a fortune selling merchandise to state institutions during Huey's reign. Huey named him president of the New Orleans levee board, and when the board built the immense and modern airport, Huey saw to it that it was named the "Abe L. Shushin Airport." Irey found that Shushin received a personal commission on each cubic yard of dirt to fill in swampland between New Orleans and Lake Pontchartrain. The T-Men had proof that he received over a half-million dollars in bribes without paying a tax. Shushin was indicted and found innocent; but he was later tried again on another charge and sentenced to two and one-half years, with the city of New Orleans spending $30,000 to erase his name from dozens of fixtures at the airport.

Then there was Seymour Weiss, second in command in Huey's state machine. The Kingfish had helped him rise from manager of the barber shop in New Orleans' Roosevelt Hotel to owner of the hotel and of the New Orleans Pelicans baseball team of the Southern Association league. For friendship's sake, Huey lowered the hotel's tax assessment drastically and wrote off a half-million dollar debt the hotel owed the state. Irey found that Colonel Weiss, known as "the best-dressed man in New Orleans," had sold a hotel and its furniture to LSU for $575,000 and then collected an additional $75,000 afterward for the furniture. For this, he went to jail for two and one-half years.

Robert "Red-Light Bob" Maestri, so free with his money to help Huey fight his impeachment in 1929, had been rewarded with the job of commissioner of the state conservation commission. Evidence showed that he permitted William Helis, a poor Greek, to operate oil leases on state property and become "the richest Greek in the world." For this Maestri was given free stock in Helis' company that was worth $1,157,161. A poorly written fraud law saved Maestri from prison, but he was forced to resign as mayor of New Orleans, a post he had held for six years without being elected.

Huey's handpicked president of LSU was Dr. James M. Smith, who was plucked penniless from a tiny school for this job. "There's not a straight bone in Jim Smith's body," Huey was once quoted as judging his educator. He was right. The treasury found that Smith milked the university's money accounts of hundreds of thousands of dollars. Smith fled to Canada, was extradicted, and jailed for embezzlement.

Robert Leche, another Long crony, who was later boosted into the governor's office by the Long machine, was so contemptuous of the Treasury that he once filed a tax return with the statement: "Other Earnings, $90,000." Leche had been a young lawyer whom Huey made into a state judge. Investigation revealed Leche had used WPA labor and materials to build a house, and had taken a $67,000 bribe in an oil case. In total, Leche accepted $450,000 in graft in three years. He was sentenced to ten years in jail.

Dan Moody, former governor of Texas, had been sweet-talked by President Roosevelt into undertaking the huge job of prosecuting the Long machine cases. Moody did not envision a Louisiana jury convicting Huey on an income-tax charge. Nor did he see any possibility of a conviction on the basis of the testimony of Huey's brothers, Julius and Earl, that one time they had seen an agent of the Electric Bond and Share Co. slip $10,000 in new banknotes in Huey's bathrobe pocket, and another time witnessed agents for Union Indemnity Insurance give Huey rolls of banknotes so large "they made his pockets bulge out and spoil the fit."

However, Moody saw pay dirt when agents dug up details of the "Win or Lose Corporation." The company, formed in 1934, gave Huey thirty-one free shares; Governor Allen, twelve; and Lieutenant Governor Jimmy Noe, thirty-one. In one deal, Allen sold an oil and gas lease on state property to a private operator and put the proceeds into the company. Allen also slipped twenty proved gas fields belonging to the state to Win or Lose, and these were sold to private firms for $320,000. On the basis of Huey's connection with Win or Lose, Dan Moody decided on September 7, 1935, to go before the October grand jury and ask for an indictment of the Senator.

However, events moved too swiftly for this. In the late afternoon and evening of September 8, Huey Long, just past his forty-second birthday, met with his lieutenants in the state capitol to discuss his legislative program and examine possible candidates to succeed Governor O. K. Allen when his term expired.

After four hours of talk, Huey headed for the house chamber with his burly bodyguards, Supreme Court Justice John Fournet, and other aides. Suddenly a thin, bespectacled young man stepped from behind a marble column, and Huey automatically put out an arm for a political handshake. Instead, a shot resounded, and the Kingfish doubled over slowly in pain. In the next few seconds, sixty-one bullets were poured into the body of the young man, who, it turned out, was Dr. Carl Weiss, reputedly a De Soto Hotel conspirator and son-in-law of Judge B. F. Pavy, whose political career Huey was in process of destroying. A puzzling aspect of the shooting was that the dead Weiss had a .22 caliber pistol in his hand while the bullet in Huey Long was a .45 caliber missile.

Huey was rushed to a hospital and given a blood transfusion. Those on the scene said he wailed, "O, Lord, don't let me die for I have a few more things to accomplish."

But early in the morning of September 10, the Kingfish, who once poetically said, "I was born into politics, a wedded man with a storm for my bride," was dead.

Chapter Five

GENE TALMADGE
Wild Man in Red Galluses

O L' Gene Talmadge, fifty-one years old and serving his second term as governor of Georgia, was expected any minute now to come round the bend and cut through the crowd to the platform for one of his humdinger, rabble-rousing speeches. On that broiling summer day in 1936, the large audience of city folk and poor wool hat farmers, their wives, and barefoot children stood strewn out before the hastily erected stand in the town square with an air of excitement despite the heat of cotton picking time.

This was a bad time in the history of the state and the nation, what with the Depression and drought, farm and business bankruptcies, unpainted barns and patched old clothes, and a dim, dull future. Ol' Gene stood out like a strong-handed helmsman in all this disaster, fighting and screaming all the time the way he did in the capital about the "big boys" in Georgia and up North. What if he fired people illegally and seized the powers of the legislature to do whatever he thought needed doing? Didn't he say you had to be a dictator to be a leader?

"You farmers in Geo'gy ain't got but three friends in this round wide world," a city feller in the waiting crowd told some red-necked wool hats. "An' they're Jesus Christ, Sears Roebuck and Company and Gene Talmadge." Another man agreed: "They tried to stop Ol' Gene in the cotes. They abused him, they fought him, they tried to block him. You'n me know who the nigger in the woodpile was. It was those sons-uh-bitches in Rooshia."

An ascending shout went up while they were agreeing, and

two Georgia mules hove into sight pulling a buggy with the governor at the reins. Ol' Gene's presence electrified the crowd, and the cheers were a roar by the time he stood on the platform. Then he spat a tobacco spray on the wood floor and screamed, "Wait a minute, listen to this carefully, my countrymen!"

While the applause continued, he flipped off his cream-colored, wide-brimmed Stetson, and his trademark lock of wiry black hair flopped over his forehead. The sight of the floppy lock brought still another cheer. He held aloft his thin arms and watched the throng through glazed, dark eyes that were fronted by Harold Lloyd-style round horn-rimmed glasses.

"Wait a minute!" he yelled again, and the cheering subsided somewhat at his stern appearance. "Now can you people out there on the edge of the crowd hear what I say. . . . Now listen carefully." But before he said another word, he shucked his baggy suit jacket and revealed his red suspenders. A sudden gasp passed through the crowd at the sight of his red galluses, and men who also wore suspenders snapped them to show they were his staunchest followers.

Finally he started his speech, and there were tidal waves of cheering and clapping to punctuate the rundown of his accomplishments in combatting the "big boys" and "nigger-lovin' furriners." While he shouted praise of himself, his wife, a freckled lady with discolored teeth and wearing cotton stockings, a 10-cent straw hat, and a dollar dress, moved persistently through the crowd to drum up additional cheers for Talmadge. Talmadge said that "Miss Mitt," as she was commonly known, was his "wool hat guinea pig," because she sensed even better than he the rhetoric that would please the ignorant Georgia crackers, as well as the wild illogic that could get them to oppose a cause which they really favored. Then on the hustings, as she was doing now, said a reporter, Miss Mitt could frighten nonsupporters of her husband to applaud him by "a-weavin' in the crowd a-givin' it to 'em where she can look 'em in the eye." But this was merely an extension of her own activity as overseer of 5,000 acres of farms where she stood on tree stumps, calling orders to farmhands because "if ah didn't get out heah with 'em, these han's'd nevah get the crop o'nuts gathuhed."

"Tell 'em about so-and-so," one of Gene's shills, perched high in a tree, boomed out when Talmadge began slowing down. Ol' Gene waved a hand and called back, "I'm acomin' to him, boy."

When he finished shredding this opponent, another of his plants volleyed, "Gov'nor, what about the old-age pension?"

This was Talmadge's chicken pie after the candied yams, fried eggplant, baked smokehouse ham, squash, and cornbread. For Ol' Gene was a master at bringing out the bigotry in his listeners to spoil a liberal program. "Yeah, what about the old-age pension?" He stretched his suspenders and caused the lock of hair on his forehead to bounce. "Listen, my countrymen. I been studyin' the pension act of the New Deal. I find they's mo' niggers in Jawjah that would git the pension than there are white folks. They's mo' niggers past sixty-five than there are white people. An' listen to this: Eve'y nigger that got his pension would be suppo'un a passle of young niggers able to work. The white people wouldn't git the pension, but they'd be taxed to pay the niggers. An' listen to this—listen to this carefully. You wouldn't be able ta have a nigger plow-hand, a nigger washwoman or cook 'cause they'd all be livin' high on pensions."

Leaving his listeners confused on this subject, Ol' Gene went on to attack Franklin Roosevelt, the Federal income tax, and creeping Federalism. Then he was finished and ready to move on to the tune of final cheers from the puzzled, tired, and worried farmers. Ol' Gene's four body lifters now elbowed their way through the crowd to the platform, raised the governor to their shoulders like a winning football coach, and delivered him to his buggy. Then to the awe of onlookers, he slapped a fly off a mule's ear with a jet stream of brown tobacco juice and set off for his next town to conquer.

From small town to small town, from farm to farm, over much of Georgia, Gene Talmadge rode, exhibiting his tobacco spray, red galluses, horn-rimmed glasses, the unruly shock of hair on his forehead, his ham-brown complexion, and the phony backwoods cracker accent that gave him his immediate identity and rapport with his people. "Gene has spat and snapped his way into the hearts of the voters," said one Georgian.

Talmadge's "wild-man-from-Sugar-Creek" style of stump speaking; the vague Robin Hood image he projected as the champion of the poor against the rich; and his unrelenting straw-man attack on the cowed, semislave black population of Georgia united his following. "I want you to pray for me to have the strength to endure," he entreated his crowds, " 'cause I'm advocatin' somethin' for the common people." Yet in all the time Gene Talmadge exercised dictatorial control of the state, his "something for the common people" never became tangible. The high illiteracy rate, poor health, poor roads, poor housing, sharecropper totals and misery, sparse bank credit, and large proportion of unskilled workers showed no easement during his reign.

There were times when his wool hats grew impâtient with him, but he knew he could always spit his way back into their good graces. One newspaper story that increased his popularity related to the occasion during a campaign when he was talking to the neighborhood's well-off farmer while dozens of poorer folk listened. At one point in the conversation, Ol' Gene suddenly spat a stream of tobacco juice in the interior of the farmer's new car that adjoined them. Afterward, a reporter for the Atlanta *Constitution* asked him the reason for his spitting. "These farmers like it," Talmadge said seriously. "It lets them know I don't give a damn about these expensive cars."

The Talmadge clan, hailing from England in 1631, lived in New Jersey until Gene's great-grandfather moved to Georgia in 1815. Gene's father, Thomas Talmadge, Jr., was a well-to-do-farmer, owner of a cotton oil mill, and chairman of the county board of education.

The staid and comfortable Talmadges did not bargain for the kind of child they produced when Eugene, the second of their six children, was born on September 23, 1884, at The Cedars, the family home near Forsyth in Monroe County. They had named him for Mrs. Talmadge's father, who was a quiet man, but the namesake turned out to be the opposite in temperament. Neighbors considered the boy to be harebrained because of his continual escapades that kept his elders in a state of perennial concern. One time he did a balancing act on the point of the barn roof; another time he barely escaped from the mushy bottom of an abandoned well while on a frog hunt. On still another occasion, he leaped on the back of a snorting colt that had never known a rider and went flying around the turn of the farm road out of sight of horrified onlookers. "Now doan you all worry 'bout dat boy," Uncle Alec, one of the Talmadge's freed "darkies," said assuringly. "He gwinna stick on de top o' dat hoss longs de hide stay on!"

Well-to-do planters, such as Thomas Talmadge, erected special buildings on their plantations to be used as schools, and neighboring planters were invited to send their children for lessons in the McGuffey Readers. A Mrs. Toney taught at the Talmadge plantation, and Gene soon won recognition as the pupil with the quickest mind and loudest voice. This reputation followed him into town when Forsyth opened its first public school in 1896, and he enrolled there at the age of twelve.

Between punishments for misbehavior by the male teacher, Gene gave initial evidence of his later firebrand public speaking ability when he competed in the Forsyth School's oratorical contest and won with an emotional recitation of Patrick Henry's "Give Me Liberty or Give Me Death" speech.

Mischief-making, good schoolwork, and a natural bent for speaking were not all of Gene Talmadge's talents. When his son reached his teens, the elder Talmadge was pleased when the lad revealed a deep interest in farming the red clay acres. The land produced cotton, corn, pecan groves, and the pine trees that kept the lumber mill busy in Forsyth; and Mr. Talmadge proudly taught Gene the details and fine points about seeds and fertilizers, plowing and harvesting, drainage and erosion problems, and proper animal care—especially of stubborn mules. This interest and knowledge of farming was of vital importance to Gene in his later political career, for it was the farmers who felt kinship with him and became the hardcore base of the 100,000-vote machine he owned.

Still another important part of young Talmadge's existence was his inordinate interest in Georgia's history and politics. This did not stem from his father who was not directly involved in local courthouse politics. However, the elder Talmadge had a close friend named Hugh M. Dorsey, who was then at the beginning of a political career that would carry him to the governor's mansion. Dorsey frequently visited The Cedars, and young Gene was a good listener. But for current information on the turmoil inside the Democratic Party, Gene's best source was the Forsyth courthouse square political gossipers. And what they were saying was being mouthed at every county courthouse square throughout the one-party state. What it boiled down to was that the Bourbon business-minded faction, in control of Georgia since the early 1870s, was facing competition from a rising leader of Georgia's long-ignored farmers.

The farmers' champion was Thomas E. Watson, and he became Gene's hero and model. Watson, the vice-presidential nominee of the Populist Party in 1896, fought Henry W. Grady, publisher of the Atlanta *Constitution* and chief exponent of an industrialized

"New South." Watson's Utopia was a world of happy, healthy, small farmers. Gene was twelve years old when he first heard him, and he was spellbound watching Ol' Tom "gesturing with whirling arms, swaying body, and tossing his head that loosed a lock of hair which punctuated his periods," while he denounced those who kept farmers poor. The "Wild Man of Hickory Hill," as Tom Watson was known, was a deep student of successful rabble-rousing; and Gene, who intended early to follow in his footsteps, was a keen observer of his hero's techniques, such as the lock of hair bouncing on the forehead and the manner of speaking in order to ignite listeners. On this latter point, Watson once wrote: "The power of the orator lies in the sympathy between him and the people. When it is struck, thousands burst into tears or rouse into passion, like a single individual."

With Watson's speeches ringing in his ears, Eugene Talmadge boarded the train to Athens and enrolled at the University of Georgia at the age of seventeen. He had already trained a lock of hair to fall on his forehead in imitation of the great Populist, and he was in for a fit of anger when upper classmen cornered him during initiation week and proceeded to shave his head. But the hair grew back quickly, and a new cowlick was trained to do its forensic duty.

Despite his obsession with Watson, Gene found time to disturb the school authorities with his continuing array of pranks, including firing off the double-barrel Confederate cannon that was a feature of the Georgia campus. He also gained excellent grades by his ability to cram; won the freshman debater's medal and the public-speaking silver cup in his sophomore year; played varsity football on the Georgia Bulldogs eleven, even though he weighed only 127 pounds; defeated heavyweight boxers in prizefights; and was elected president of the Athletic Association.

The Talmadge whirling dervish got his law degree in 1907 when he was only twenty-two, and after passing the Georgia bar, he set off for Atlanta to capture the legal world. But a neat office, a cowlick, and a head filled with Tom Watson speeches were not the ingredients for a successful law practice, as he bitterly learned. Yet with his father continuing to send him expense money, he did not go hungry or wear threadbare clothes. Nor did he sit and brood over his sad lot, for the old city hall and the Indiana limestone state capitol were close by, and the political talk was far superior to what he had heard at the Forsyth courthouse square.

It was late in the following year, after failing to acquire a single client, that Gene decided to move to a rural area where a young lawyer would not face the competition of an Atlanta, with its ratio of one lawyer to every 250 men, women, and children. Not wanting the continued charity of his father, who would have been pleased if he had returned home to practice in Forsyth, Gene chose a small town in the wire-grass and piney woods section of Montgomery County, about 100 miles southeast of The Cedars. Here he rented an office and moved into a boarding house run by Mrs. Matilda Thurmond Peterson, an enterprising young widow.

Meeting "Miss Mitt," as Mrs. Peterson was known in the neighborhood, was a vital event in Gene's young life. Tom Watson may have preached relentlessly that women were not meant to involve themselves in business and political matters, but Miss Mitt was a shining exception to this rule, so far as Talmadge was concerned. Not only was she raising her son John to be a proper youth, but she was also running the boarding house, managing a large farm, engaging in animal trading, and serving as depot agent and telegraph operator for the Central of Georgia Railroad that came down through Atlanta and Macon and connected with Savannah, the major seaport city. Miss Mitt, a big-boned woman, spent much of her time in overalls, for she was an active farm foreman and a practical boss at her other enterprises. Local folk called her a "trash-mover" because she would not tolerate less than a full day's work for a day's pay. Yet for all her business world abilities and her lack of interest in feminine attire, Miss Mitt had been raised on a plantation similar to The Cedars, near Modok, not far from the Georgia border in Edgefield, South Carolina.

Gene's luck in attracting law clients was almost as bad as it had been in Atlanta, but he was able to support himself by working almost full time as a horse, mule, and stock trader. His earnings were only a tiny part of what Miss Mitt took in. Nevertheless, the fact that he had a bankbook gave him the courage to court the wealthy, hardworking widow, and she married him in September, 1909, two weeks before his twenty-fifth birthday.

The newlyweds bought a large farm on Sugar Creek, near the town of McRae in Telfair County, two counties to the west of Montgomery; and they built a showplace twelve-room, two-story colonial residence snug among the pines on a hill. But Miss Mitt had no intention of becoming a passive housewife. So she told Gene to farm the Sugar Creek acreage in competition with the adjoining farm, which she bought and managed. Gene accepted the challenge, though he was never able to outproduce his wife.

In addition to growing cotton, corn, dewberries, watermelons, peaches, and pecans, Gene also ran a sawmill in the fall and winter, went fox hunting on the hills with his neighbors, shot quail in the bottomland, and tried to put in Saturdays in the one-room law office he rented in McRae. The town, which was the seat of Telfair County, was surrounded by dense, long-leaf pine forests and was often a smelly place because of the smoke billowing from its many stills, where resin from the slashed pines was cooked into crude turpentine and hard rosin. Despite the odor, farmers of the wire-grass country liked to congregate there on Saturdays to do some buying and selling, gossiping, whittling, chawing cut-plug tobacco, and discussing possible lawsuits with the town's half-dozen lawyers. Gene's advantage was that he was a farmer, unlike the other attorneys, and besides, he was a walking encyclopedia on Tom Watson. So he soon had a law practice, though he grumbled because it interfered with his competition with Miss Mitt.

McRae had a courthouse gang that had ruled the town for a quarter of a century, and Talmadge's request that he be permitted to join the group was met with muttered comments about the arrogance of newcomers. However, his desire for a public role would not die, and Gene turned to his father for help in 1917. The elder Talmadge's friend, Hugh Dorsey, was now governor of Georgia; and when apprised of the McRae ring's blacklisting of Gene and the young man's desire to enter the local political scene, Dorsey appointed Gene solicitor of the city court in McRae. When the news reached town, the county commissioner and his gang were outraged to the point that they refused to acknowledge his existence. More than that, after reflection, they took the train to Atlanta and held conferences in the state capital. New word regarding Eugene Talmadge reached McRae: The state legislature had taken the drastic action of abolishing the city court.

Now in his mid-thirties, Gene Talmadge found himself a fairly successful farmer, a small-bore lawyer, and a total failure in the political field. The odds appeared overwhelmingly against any significant change in his future.

Post-World War I Georgia was hardly the shining model of democracy that Woodrow Wilson might have cited at the Paris Peace talks of 1919 for peoples newly risen from oppression. The Ku Klux Klan, in a violent rebirth after decades of quiescence, had lighted a fiery cross atop Stone Mountain outside of Atlanta, and from a Georgian base it was soon to spread its eyehole-sheeted savage terror and bigotry across the nation.

It was no accident Georgia was the godmother of the new KKK, for by 1920 the statewide obsession was not with industrial progress or agricultural development but with keeping the one million blacks within her borders in a constant existence of subservience, squalor, and ignorance. By then, no white voice in the land of the crackers was heard to propose political and economic equality for the dark-skinned third of the state's population. Negroes were the house servants, street day laborers, and sharecroppers (only 2 percent of rural blacks owned the land they worked). They lacked proper housing, food, clothing, education, and mobility and were deprived of the franchise by being barred from voting in the Democratic primary of a one-party state.

This racial bigotry was a physical, emotional, and mental paralysis that prevented the citizens of the state from turning their chief attention and abilities to the pursuit of the best in life. From the wool hat white farmers and sharecroppers and the blue-collar city workers to the middle-class—especially those in the forty counties where blacks were a majority—and even to the highly reputable Atlanta *Constitution* and Atlanta *Journal,* a vigilance against the blacks' becoming more than "pickaninnies, coons and niggers" had to be maintained no matter what the cost.

The pity of the debilitating effect of Georgia's racism was that even without it, the state had so far to travel to catch a glimpse of the American dream. A land of gracious hospitality and love of relatives, midday dinners at home and evenings on the porch, Georgia was nevertheless a depressed state in the post-World War I era. The boll weevil descended on the state in 1921 bringing economic havoc to the one-crop farmers who planted cotton all the way to their screen door. The red clay soil had been misused and abused, rutted wagon wheel roads hampered deliveries from rural areas, and discriminatory freight rates kept Georgian shipping to the North at a minimum. In an agricultural economy in which the average gross income of farmers was under $100 a year, much clothing was made of flour sacks; a diet of fatback, cornbread, and molasses made pellagra commonplace; electricity was a rarity on the farm; ninety-day a year one-room schools could not stem illiteracy; and a $1 poll tax kept about 85 percent of otherwise eligible voters from casting ballots.

Yet despite this sorry environment for most Georgians, politics remained their engrossing subject, and for Gene Talmadge it was the breath of life.

In 1920, when Talmadge was thirty-six, he had his first opportunity to test the local Democratic machine after the courthouse lords made known their choice for county commissioner in the Telfair County primary. For want of a campaign issue, the courthouse dynasty's candidate declared his first action on taking office would be to fire old Bill Harrell, the courthouse janitor who, he said, had not swept the building in months. Talmadge knew Old Bill had relatives by the dozens throughout the county, and when Talmadge learned further that J. C. Thrasher, the 350-pound county convict warden, who rented out prisoners to the mills and other private operators, had been told by the dynasty he would be replaced at the end of the year, he felt he was on to something.

It took little urging from Gene to convince Thrasher he should seek revenge for losing his job by running for county commissioner, and that he should let Gene run his campaign. Both actions roundly amused the McRae clique, but Talmadge was serious, even though the odds were oppressive.

Old Bill Harrell's angry and vocal army of relatives all over the county, plus his friends, were willing to pay the $1 poll tax and vote for Thrasher on the assurance that Harrell could continue as janitor. Talmadge made this promise, and on election day the dynasty blinked at the news that obese Thrasher had upset their man. The blinking was even harder when word came that Thrasher had appointed Talmadge county attorney.

When Thrasher turned out to be a lazy sort, there was angry consternation because Talmadge assumed his duties as well. But though the dynasty seethed at the effrontery of the substitute county executive, two years passed before it managed to arrange a grand jury investigation of the Thrasher-Talmadge regime. The chief finding of the grand jury's probing was that the county's $15,000 in assets when the two took office had become a $90,000 deficit. The conclusion of the jury was that further legal action was necessary because the two officials were guilty of "inefficient and questionable transactions."

Talmadge offered no apologies or excuses, and when it became apparent the county attorney did not intend to prosecute himself or resign, the dynasty took its usual action. A quiet trip to the state capital in Atlanta led to quick passage of legislation abolishing Telfair County's offices of commissioner and attorney. In their place, the chief county officer would be the "ordinary," a peculiar Georgian institution in which the probate court judge took on the county's executive duties.

Twice the victim of a legislative write-off of his political jobs, Talmadge was again outside the political gate by 1923, at the very time he wanted to be active. The Harding-Coolidge era in Georgia seemed to cry out for a second Tom Watson, leader of the wool hats, who had died in 1922 while serving in the U.S. Senate, and Talmadge believed he was destined to pick up the fallen hero's baton.

The spreading boll weevil destruction had yet to produce a seller's market, and the postwar price of cotton had spiraled downward from 30 cents a pound to 8 cents. Farmers burdened with mortgages written when cotton was at its peak price lost their property, and sharecroppers already living in unpainted, flimsy shacks with their several children in "poverty, ignorance and disease" sank deeper into the mire of misery. Then as the cotton depression widened, its effect was felt in the watermelon, peach, and pecan prices as well.

The KKK with its message of hate gave the wool hats an opportunity to let out steam. But anti-foreigner and anti-Negro cursing failed to raise crop prices a penny, and with no other form of relief in sight the poor farmers took to cursing the state department of agriculture, which was adding to their agonies.

At the outset of World War I, Georgia's department of agriculture had been small, but its commissioner, J. J. Brown, a large, heavyset man with a wide, drooping mustache, engaged in empire building under the name of wartime emergency. By the twenties, Brown directed hundreds of employees and developed dozens of new duties until he was running a formidable organization. J. J. Brown's army of inspectors had jurisdiction over the fertilizers that could be sold. In addition, their authority extended to food, drugs, livestock, gasoline, plants, fowl, and even bees, "J. J.'s" men were in every town, and no farmer or producer of the long list of items under their jurisdiction could escape their surveillance.

Brown's office was elective, and his inspectors doubled as his campaign helpers and rural lieutenants. Because of their continually increasing numbers and authority, Brown's help was wildly sought by candidates for all state offices, and it was generally assumed J. J. was biding his time until he decided to run for governor. The Atlanta *Constitution* called Brown and his regiment of inspectors "the slickest political machine in modern Georgia."

As a farmer and as a lawyer, Gene Talmadge had a double interest in Brown's department of agriculture. Despite the poor economic situation in Georgia, the Talmadge farms prospered through Miss Mitt's astute management, though the profits would have been higher if the acreage had not crawled with J. J.'s inspectors. Besides their numbers, the general incompetency of the lot was such that Talmadge later said he "wondered how bankrupt storekeepers, third-rate schoolteachers and tombstone peddlers managed to blossom out as veterinary surgeons, chemists, agronomists and whatnots, simply by virtue of the commissioner's appointment."

What angered him more than their incompetency was the fact that the fertilizers and gasoline they were supposed to have inspected were inferior to the specifications on their labels. Because cotton growing required large quantities of high-quality fertilizers, the thin varieties certified by the inspectors as better-grade products were adding further to the burdens of Georgia's farmers.

A growing number of lawsuits began against the fertilizer frauds, and in Telfair County, lawyer Talmadge became active in these cases on behalf of himself and his neighbors. As his reputation for success grew, his fertilizer cases took him into the justice courts of several other counties. Wherever he went, he sat around in his spare time with the farmers in their tattered overalls on courthouse lawns, joining them in their cussin', whittlin', and chewing cut-plug and listening to their condemnation of J. J. Brown and his inspectors.

By early 1925, Gene was throwing out the rhetorical question that someone decent should run against Brown in the 1926 Democratic primary. Soon some of the tobacco-juice spitters began suggesting he undertake the race, and after a time he started conversations by asking others if they would support him if he campaigned against J. J. in the statewide contest. Even the McRae dynasty, adamantly unwilling to let him hold any local office, said it might support him. Yet despite his galloping ambitions, Talmadge held back, and it was not until a few minutes before the filing deadline that he paid his fees as a candidate for Brown's job.

Reporters who came to the splendid Sugar Creek residence of Eugene Talmadge were amused at his self-characterization as "just a plain ol' dirt farmer"; and they smiled at the heading of his campaign stationery, which read:

A REAL DIRT FARMER

Talmadge Against the Machine

EUGENE TALMADGE

CANDIDATE FOR
Commissioner of Agriculture

J. J. Brown, too, thought Talmadge to be of no consequence, and at the outset of the campaign, Brown proposed that Talmadge join him in a debate at the big Fourth of July barbecue at McRae, on Gene's homeground. Brown would make the first speech and Gene would have a turn to answer; then J. J. would be given a rebuttal period. Although this arrangement was grossly unfair, Talmadge acted swiftly to accept it. Brown then graciously agreed to a later debate with the same arrangements in Brown's hometown of Elberton, across the state near the South Carolina border.

The great day finally came: The big turpentine stills in McRae were closed, and the smoke instead came from the barbecue pits "out in a thicket of long-leaf pines and under a sky ablaze" with a hot July sun. When the time came for the "debate," the two candidates mounted the platform. The older Brown was a large, dominating figure, and his walrus mustache added to his look of old authority, while Talmadge was a nondescript, slender, youthful man with unruly, black wiry hair and outsized horn-rimmed glasses. "Talmadge did look a sorry nubbin in comparison with his handsome opponent," said Allen Henson, later Talmadge's secretary.

Brown turned out to be an excellent speaker, with a ready stream of funny stories and what sounded like an undemolishable defense of the agriculture department. By the time he sat down, reporters agreed he was a hard act to follow.

But Gene was ready for him. "My countrymen!" he bellowed at the mammoth audience of wool hats. "I'm a-goin' ta pull a pretty big bunch of politicians off their high perches in the department of agriculture, an' I'm a-goin' ta put that department ta work for the

Geo'gy farmers instead of the big interests, an' if these politicians keep on lobbyin' laws through the legislature to protect corporations they're a-goin' ta have ta look to these corporations for their salaries —not ta you!"

His opening remarks electrified the crowd. "By God!" someone shouted. "He's game." Others noted his resemblance to Tom Watson. He threw his head back the way he recalled Ol' Tom had so that a lock of hair fell over his forehead, and he employed the same exaggerated arm gestures. Then as he continued speaking, he used some of Watson's exact sentences and phrases to punch at Brown. Finally he moved into a long list of charges against the way Brown was running his department. He railed about the short-weight, watered fertilizer and the low-grade gasoline; he insinuated that the inspectors were forced to kick back part of their salaries to Brown and declared that the entire group was a patchwork of little politicians untrained for their duties. Someone in the crowd interrupted with a loud inquiry about Brown's need for 200 oil inspectors. "I'm a-comin' ta that, boy!" Gene shouted back. He called these inspectors "oily boys" and derisively referred to Brown's veterinarians as "hoss doctors."

At one point, Talmadge, soaking wet with sweat, tore off his suit jacket, and a man far back among the pines yelled out, "Red galluses! By God!" An immediate uproar of approval followed this display.

When Gene finished, J. J. Brown's expression revealed that he had made a blunder in offering to debate him. Given his time to rebut Talmadge, unhappy Brown refused and quickly left the scene. Political reporters agreed that Talmadge had "eaten Brown alive." The *New York Times* reporter in Georgia offered the comment that Brown had "picked a tartar in Talmadge by debating him."

The effect of the Talmadge explosion in the McRae debate was to make him quickly known throughout rural Georgia, and a clamor arose for his appearance at dozens of barbecues and fish fries. In fact, because of him, interest in the race for commissioner of agriculture soon far exceeded the much more important contests for governor and U.S. Senator.

As a result, in hot August of 1926, these candidates for higher office found only small audiences to greet them as they tore into each other. Yet the crowds on the wheel-rutted dirt roads along which

Talmadge's campaign Ford jalopy chugged and the acres of people at his meetings showed what the people wanted.

And Gene didn't disappoint them. Posing as the "po' man" who understood other "po' men," he pulled out all the stops of his imitation of Tom Watson's fire and antics. The wool hats loved the way he encased his speeches with wretched grammar, his call for "Old Time religion," and his frequent use of Biblical quotations as he ripped at J. J. Brown and his department. The display and snapping of his red suspenders made crowds delirious, and the way he could knock a fly off the platform railing with a jet of tobacco juice was a matter for cheering.

Even so, J. J. Brown did not lose his political calm because a half-dozen candidates were in the field besides him and Talmadge, and he expected the divided opposition to give him the necessary winning margin. But when all these straw candidates dropped out of the race, Brown, in desperation, tried to paint his sole remaining opponent as a dangerous liberal. "The fight against me is a fight for Al Smith," he screamed at bewildered audiences, trying to tie Talmadge to the Catholic Democratic presidential figure. At his second debate with Talmadge in his hometown of Elberton, he had none of the assuredness of a winner, and gave the appearance of a doomed candidate.

On primary day in September, 1926, Talmadge was an easy victor, and his parting comment to the losing Brown effort was: "The people of Georgia have disposed of machine domination."

Hailed by a part of the press as the David who slew Goliath and as a reformer anxious to install his program, Commissioner of Agriculture Talmadge proved a total disappointment to his wool hat followers throughout the sixty-day biennial legislative session at the beginning of 1927. However, he had no alternative. He had campaigned strongly with the promises to fire most of the inspectors and see to it that fertilizers were properly labeled. But he was an instinctive politician who shrewdly realized if he fired any inspectors while the legislature was in session he would precipitate unending rows that would destroy him, for Brown still had many friends in the state capitol.

So he bided his time until the legislature quit. Then once the capitol was quiet, he fired every Brown inspector. None offered resistance, but when he turned to the department's professional staff, there was less willingness to quit offices. Brown had retained several newspaper reporters on the department's payroll, and when the new commissioner fired an anti-Talmadge Atlanta newsman, the reporter struck back with a news story. The headline read: "The Wild Man of Sugar Creek," a name that stuck with Talmadge the rest of his life.

Emboldened by this incident, the fired veterinarians and agronomists refused to leave their offices. Talmadge retaliated first by halting their paychecks and refusing to pay their expense vouchers. Finally he asked some of his muscular friends from Telfair County to walk into their offices, drag them through the halls, and toss them into the street. Then he had locksmiths install new locks on their doors.

The removed professionals took him to court with a tangle of lawsuits in an effort to retain their jobs. When several writs of injunctions crossed his desk, he shoved them off into his wastebasket. In time, a judge ordered the sheriff to arrest him, and Talmadge was sentenced to a year in jail for contempt of court. But Talmadge appealed to the State Supreme Court where he was saved from serving the sentence, and the cases by the professionals were voided.

Afterward, he built up his own corps of inspectors and "hoss doctors" and evolved a political machine across the state personally loyal to him. Another Talmadge move to solidify and increase his political strength was his publication of laudatory articles about himself in the *Market Bulletin*, a magazine put out by the department of agriculture and sent to all farm families in the state.

But Talmadge knew his recently acquired political authority would not last if he failed to live up to his campaign promises, and it was not enough to fire Brown's inspecting army. He established strict rules for inspecting fertilizers and penalties for manufacturers who failed to meet specifications stapled to sacks. His inspectors soon gained a reputation for toughness. "Why," said a fertilizer company sales manager, "if you move a carload of that guano of yours through any Georgia town at midnight, that damn fellow Talmadge, or a gang of his inspectors, will bounce out of bed smelling that ochre filling which you substituted for cotton seed meal!"

In 1928, when Talmadge ran for renomination in the Democratic primary, J. J. Brown considered him too formidable an opponent and put up one of his henchmen ·G. C. Adams, as a sacrificial lamb. And Talmadge, using the same campaign technique, swamped him at the polls on primary day.

During his second term, Talmadge added to his political power by hard work and showmanship. No issue of the department's *Market Bulletin* failed to carry either a bragging editorial by the commissioner or an adulatory article about him. But he gained the most publicity from his short war with the Chicago hog market. The big slaughterhouses had consistently downgraded Georgia's peanut-fed hogs on the ground they "killed soft" compared with Midwestern corn-fed swine that "killed hard," and on that basis they paid lower prices for Georgia hogs. Talmadge insisted this was sectional prejudice, and Georgia's hogs had just as firm meat. To prove his point that Armour and Swift in Chicago merely wanted to keep Georgia hog prices low, he induced farmers to let him act as their seller, and he sent eighty-two carloads of their porkers north to East Coast markets. His theory was that if he could sell the hogs at higher prices than those set by the Chicago market, Armour and Swift would be forced to raise their prices for Georgia hogs. However, at the Baltimore stop the price offered him was no higher than the quoted Chicago figure, and he pushed on with mounting frenzy and anger to other markets. Finally, he ended a dismal failure, selling the eighty-two carloads for a loss of $11,000 that his department was forced to absorb.

With this black mark on Talmadge's record, J. J. Brown believed the time ripe for a comeback, and he returned from hibernation to run against his successor in the 1930 primary. Brown's campaign was pitched largely on the wandering eighty-two carloads of hogs and the charge that the state's taxpayers had to foot the bill for the misadventure of the "Wild Man from Sugar Creek." But even when Brown implied that Talmadge was a thief, he lost ground. "Sure, I stole. But I stole for you, my countrymen," Talmadge replied to resounding cheers from every farm audience.

In this popularity contest, Talmadge drubbed his rival by a vote of 148,000 to 58,000. But Brown still had several reporter friends and a host of powerful allies in the legislature, and he determined to ruin Talmadge. Soon newspaper stories began cropping up reporting that Talmadge made yearly visits to the Kentucky Derby, where he was reportedly a substantial better as well as a drinker of prohibited alcohol. While several ministers in Georgia professed public shock, Talmadge made no denial.

This was just the first of the attacks on him. Reporters also pictured him as a belligerent creature, unhappy unless he was involved in lawsuits. Then in the legislature, he was attacked for turning the *Market Bulletin* into a public relations journal for his own benefit. This led to the passage of a resolution forbidding the *Bulletin* from carrying any editorials.

Next came legislation to put his department's budget under the control of the governor. At the time, the prevailing system in Georgia made each department independent of the governor in preparing its budget and in its spending. Although there were sound administrative reasons for putting the entire budget and executive expenditures in the hands of the governor, the reorganization act of 1931, sponsored by Governor Richard B. Russell, Jr., which did so, was motivated by the desire to curtail Talmadge's power.

All these actions were just a warm-up for what now developed. A senate committee announced it was investigating Talmadge, and it made its chief scrutiny an examination of the eighty-two carloads of hogs incident. "You're charged with using $14,000 of the state's money to buy hogs," the committee chairman told Talmadge when he was finally called to testify.

"You're wrong," he replied. "It was $80,000. I bought the hogs for that from Georgia farmers and shipped them north because those Chicago packing houses were bidding 4 cents a pound under their own market. I reckon it took around $80,000, but I got back all but ten thousand—but I learned them Chicago packers some sense. They put the market back where it ought to be, and I saved Georgia farmers more than a quarter of a million dollars, and I don't regret losing the ten thousand. Do you?"

The committee had him return a second time because his story did not jibe with what he had said after the hog incident. But when it called him back a third day for further testimony, he refused to appear.

Little time passed after this before the house undertook impeachment action against Talmadge, and the senate set a day to sit as an impeachment court. But Talmadge was just beginning to fight back. With his inspectors acting as rally managers, protesting letters came by the thousands from rural Georgia to the desks of the senators. A large percentage were marked with an "X," and many others were scrawled on butcher paper and filled with misspelling.

But if the flood of mail was not enough to give the senators pause, Talmadge had a sure way to end the impeachment trial. Stealing a leaf from Huey Long, who had used the same stunt in

Louisiana two years earlier, he foiled the would-be impeachers by getting eighteen of the fifty-one senators to sign a Round-Robin statement, declaring they would not vote to find him guilty under any circumstances on the charge of misusing public funds. Since thirty-four senators were needed for a guilty verdict, without the Round Robineers there were only thirty-three other senators. When the Round-Robin statement was made public on the day his trial was scheduled to start, Talmadge's enemies immediately ended the proceedings.

Governor Richard Russell was unable to cope with the growing problems of the devastating national Depression as they affected his state. Unwilling to raise taxes appreciably or increase the state's deficit in order to give relief to the fast-growing hordes of city un-employed and to the one-crop cotton farmers thrown into agony by 6-cents-a-pound cotton, Russell battled privately with legislators to pare to the bone the budgets the independent departments submit-ted for approval. The highway board, in control of half the entire budget, found itself bound temporarily by legislative orders to end all construction. No school construction was permitted, and the measly $35 a year spent per white pupil and $6 per black child were further slashed. The 20,000 schoolteachers went unpaid for months, even though many received only $90 a month in the one-room schools open ninety days a year. With public health care trimmed to the brink of nonexistence and thousands of families without even outdoor toilets or running water, it was little wonder that malaria, hookworm, rickets, and typhus were on a steep rise.

In April, 1932, when the senior U.S. Senator from Georgia died, Russell saw a way to escape these problems. After naming an interim appointee who would not oppose him, he announced he would run for the four remaining years of the Senate term.

Now an enormous battle got under way among those who wanted to succeed him as governor. Former Governor Tom Hard-wick said he wanted the job, and so did Abit Nix, who claimed to represent the "best element." Then seven others also became con-tenders. Talmadge, who had considered waiting until 1934 before making his next move, became the tenth candidate now. Ordinarily, a politician who had so recently been pommeled by the state legis-lature would have been given little chance for success. But the news-paper publicity concerning his impeachment troubles had favored him as the little man who had defeated the governor and a majority of the legislature.

On July 4, Talmadge opened his campaign at the McRae barbecue. "My countrymen," he bellowed, when there was a pause in the cheering. He ripped off his jacket and snapped his red galluses, and this was a signal to hundreds of male supporters who had come wearing suspenders to snap their elastics loudly.

Governor Russell came under his attack for advocating a sales tax. "A sales tax is a tax on the poor," Talmadge got off to a fighting start. "And if the legislature passes it, I'll veto it," he said firmly. Then he poured out his program—to legislate a halt to the spreading bank failures, reduce the state debt, cut the ad valorem state tax, pay pensions due Confederate veterans, lower utility and freight rates. But none of these drew a fraction of the cheers that broke out when he leaned over the lectern and screamed, "You can't afford to pay from $13.50 and up for automobile license tags. Three dollars is plenty—and I'll cut it to three dollars!"

He had found his campaign issue, and he knew it from the roar of approval. "And don't worry about your schools," he added. "They'll operate and your road buildin'll start up. I'll pay every dollar we owe: to schoolteachers, Confederate veterans, and everybody else. And I'll do it without raisin' your taxes one thin dime!"

Dicky Russell's contest for the Senate seat against Charles R. Crisp, the dean of the Georgia congressional delegation, had hardly begun to heat up when Gene Talmadge's promise of $3 auto tags made the gubernatorial contest the prime race in 1932.

Talmadge also had a master plan for the campaign. As he put it, "I'm only gonna campaign in counties where the streetcars don't run"—and for good reason. What Talmadge really meant was that thanks to old Tom Watson, Georgia did not use the popular election system. Instead, it operated a thoroughly "rotten-borough" election and representation system to thwart the popular will and give rural counties tight control over representation in the state legislature and Congress.

It operated in this fashion: Principally through Watson's influence, the existing counties were divided and redivided until a total of 159 emerged, a larger number than in any other state except Texas. The purpose of this effort was readily apparent, for the election law of 1917 provided that each county, no matter how tiny its population, must have at least two county-unit votes. The candidate winning a plurality of the popular vote in the county—not even a majority—would get all the county's unit votes.

With a total of 410 county-unit votes, a winning candidate in a statewide election needed 206 for victory. The small counties, or those "where the streetcars don't run," became vital in this undemocratic system, for 121 of them were given two county-unit votes apiece; the next thirty larger counties, four unit votes each; and the eight most populated, six each. This meant that fifty-five small counties with a combined population less than Fulton County (Atlanta) with its 400,000 persons had 110 county-unit votes while Fulton had only six! So in two-unit-vote Echols County with a population of 2,600, each unit vote represented 1,300 persons compared with Fulton County's unit vote standing for 67,000; or for purposes of election, one person in Echols County was politically the equal of fifty-one persons in Fulton County.

Nor was this county-unit vote abomination the sole undemocratic feature of Georgia's election system. Each county's representation in the statehouse was set at half its county-unit vote. This meant that the smallest county had one legislator and the largest county only three! In addition, since Negroes were barred by law from voting in Democratic primaries, 1,071,000 of Georgia's 2,908,000 citizens were excluded from effective political participation. Then there was the poll tax to slash the eligible list still further, plus a requirement that the vote was restricted to those who owned a minimum of forty acres or $500 worth of property.

Further, the county courthouse clique made it difficult for undesirables to register. Courthouse tests might consist of complex constitutional questions, or the registrar might be continuously "absent" to them. The list was cut again by the fact that in rural counties voters marked their ballots in the open with candidates and their watchers looking on. Little wonder with all the restrictions that Burke County along the Savannah River with its 24,000 residents in 1932 and four county-unit votes cast only 492 ballots that year. The average throughout the state found only 16 percent of those over twenty-one casting their votes.

Talmadge's small-county campaign for governor in 1932 came complete with more than his usual trappings. Gene hired top country entertainers to put on a lively show at the political barbecues and fish fries before he pulled off his jacket and let the charges fly. Also in Talmadge's entourage were the "Tree Climbin' Haggards Family from Danielsville." The Haggards' specialty was to scale pines to dizzying heights, bounce on swaying branches, and shout, "Tell us about Tom Hardwick, Gene" and "What about them three-dollar tags?" Talmadge always answered with a crowd-pleasing yell, "I'm a-comin' ta that, boy." Poor as the wool hat small farmers and tenants were, Talmadge never ended a political meeting without passing out fruit jars and pails for contributions. Nor was a barbecue complete without his entertainers letting go with his campaign song:

> *I gotta Eugene dog, gotta Eugene cat,*
> *I'm a Talmadge man from ma shoes to ma hat.*
> *Farmer in the cawnfield hollerin' whoa, gee, haw,*
> *Kain't put no thutty-dollah tag on a three-dollar cah.*

Down the road a piece, when he passed through a small town, he would stop to talk with the banker, for the man who controlled the loans was generally the man who controlled the votes. He also paused at the general stores between stops for an ungrammatical exchange with the old boys on the front landing.

Talmadge considered his chief opponent to be former Governor Tom Hardwick, and Gene's lieutenants sought ways to ruin Hardwick's speeches. On one occasion, Hardwick held a major rally at Carrolton, a place with busy textile mills and a surrounding area of solvent farmers. Shortly after Hardwick began talking in the courthouse square, Talmadge men set fire to acres of dry grass on the outskirts of town. The excitement of the crackling blaze and the clanging fire-truck bells triggered a race by the crowd to the fire, and Hardwick was soon alone at his rally.

At last came the fateful September primary day. Talmadge's total was only 117,000 votes, or slightly more than 40 percent of the 279,000 cast. But this was not important. The small two-unit counties where he had centered his campaign were chiefly responsible for giving him twice as many county-unit votes as all the other candidates combined. He was now governor of the largest sized state east of the Mississippi.

In January, 1933, when Talmadge took office and moved into the governor's mansion in Atlanta with his wife, Miss Mitt, their son and two daughters, and Miss Mitt's son by her first marriage, political reporters expected him to push hard for his program during the sixty-day legislative session. But Talmadge had made a nose count and found that the majority of the legislators did not feel friendly toward him. The result was he repeated his action as commissioner of agriculture and waited for the legislature to end its session.

So while he dutifully sent his program to the capitol's leaders, he made no real effort to promote his bills. Nor did he offer strong objections when the "midnight" appointments of outgoing Governor Russell were saddled on his administration by the quick-to-confirm senate.

Instead, while reporters puzzled, Talmadge went about establishing himself as "just a plain ol' dirt farmer" character in the governor's chair. Newspapers carried pictures of the barn and chicken house he had ordered built on the grounds of the governor's mansion, and they quoted him as saying he would suffer from insomnia in the big city if he didn't hear the familiar mooing and cackling of his beloved farm animals. Miss Mitt, whom he called "the best farmer in the wire grass," brought her favorite dairy cow to the mansion grounds, where it grazed on the lawn and supplied the milk for her family. Store milk was just too unsatisfactory, she declared.

Talmadge also fogged over his academic training by announcing that no top government official should be appointed if he went past the eighth grade. It would be an excellent idea, he said, if the Henry W. Grady School of Journalism at the University of Georgia were abolished because writers were "born," not "made." He declared himself a born writer and said, "I can write anywhere, and even with telephones ringin'." Talmadge had a big brass spittoon set beside his desk, and when farmers visited him, he chewed tobacco instead of his expensive cigars and rang the brass bell on the floor with regularity and accuracy. He kept himself so suntanned his face was ham brown, and he told farmer visitors they could guess his occupation from his tan. He also let them know what he read, pointing to the only three volumes on his desk: The Bible, the latest Sears Roebuck catalogue, and the Georgia Financial Report.

In talks to farmer visitors and on the campaign trail, Talmadge's language was a jumble of grammatical errors and slurred consonants. All this was a condescending put-on that held his support in line, for when he met with bankers or a university group, he was extremely careful about the proper choice of words. His secretary, Allen Henson, compared his boss with Apostle Paul, who, he claimed, specialized in a similar manner in "fitting his language to his audience." Said Henson: "Paul spoke as the great scholar on Mars Hill, but he harangued the rabble in Jerusalem in the unpolished language to which they were accustomed."

Talmadge's lack of legislative aggressiveness during the Depression session of the winter, 1933, legislature gave the impression he planned to be a docile governor. But this was to change savagely as soon as the unfriendly legislators adjourned in early March, and he emerged as a dictator.

First evidence of the real Talmadge came with his proposal for $3 auto tags. The three-man highway board's strong testimony against this measure had led to its being pigeonholed by the general assembly's ways and means committee. But within minutes after the legislators quit the capitol, Talmadge signed an executive order lowering the price of tags for all vehicles to $3.

This brought a sharp protest from the head of the licensing division of the department that he was usurping a legislative function and lacked authority. All this was true, but Talmadge boldly proclaimed he was merely putting into effect an old state statute (whose number and year he failed to supply), which empowered the governor "to suspend or reduce taxes at his discretion."

When the official still refused to sell tags at the Talmadge price, the governor fired him, put a new man in charge, and told "my people" to apply for tags at the new price. The following day enormous lines of people queued up at the Atlanta tag window in an atmosphere almost as exciting as the "gold rush." Farmers who previously had been too poor to buy car tags for their jalopies, because the price was based on weight of the vehicle, now scraped up the $3 to make themselves mobile again along the state's wretched dirt roads. But with the roads clogged with untrustworthy vehicles and drivers, the accident rate immediately skyrocketed.

While Talmadge was hailed as a "statesman" by the wool hats and the city poor because of his $3 tags, the biggest bonanza from his executive order went to bus and truck firms. The new tag price was a tiny fraction of the previous prices.

Angry with the elected highway board for having lobbied against his $3 tag proposal and for opposing his executive order, Talmadge decided to go after the board itself. Russell's reorganization act, which put the budgets and spending of the departments

under the control of the governor, and which had come into existence specifically to control Talmadge as commissioner of agriculture, became effective in 1933, in time for Talmadge to use it
against the elected highway commissioners.

When the quarterly budget of their department reached Talmadge's desk for approval, it was expected that he would sign it per-
functorily. But he wielded a blue pencil like an ax. On one project
listing twenty-eight civil engineers, he crossed through twenty-seven
names. He "x'd" through other projects entirely, and he drew his
pencil throughout the document across all employees with names
the same as state legislators.

The day he sent the slashed budget back to the highway commissioners, they returned it to him quickly with a note demanding
he approve it as originally submitted. When he cut further into the
money requested this time, the board decided on a plan to bring
public pressure to bear on him. It announced that since the governor was depriving the board of needed money, it would not accept
his proffered half-loaf but would stop paying all salaries, wages, and
other bills, thus eliminating essential work and payments to private
contractors.

Talmadge realized letters of protest would soon pour into his
office from all sections of the state, and to head off this attack he
issued another executive order. Because the commissioners had rejected money and were not handling their business, he proclaimed,
they had "abandoned their offices." On that basis, he said, their offices were vacant, and he would name replacements. Declaring an
emergency existed, he dispatched elements of the National Guard
immediately to take charge of the offices and files and to see to it that
once the highway commissioners were escorted out of the building,
they were barred from returning.

By now, Talmadge saw how easy it was to boss the state by
issuing executive orders as though the state lacked a legislature. He
signed one order cutting the state ad valorem tax from four to three
mills, and he drew up a plan to get rid of the elected public service
commission by the same scheme he had used on the highway department.

In mid-July, 1933, while his National Guard units were in
charge of the offices of the highway department, he ordered the five
members of the public service commission to appear in his office.
When they arrived, Talmadge denounced them for "aiding and abet-

ting Georgia Power." Then by another executive order, he fired the five elected officials and named their successors.

All the departments soon fell under his total domination. He continued to make even the smallest detailed decisions for the department of agriculture, ran the highway department with close scrutiny, and installed loyal henchmen throughout the state government. All employees came to realize they served at his whim. "I'm against civil service," he explained. "It ain't neither civil nor a service. If a man knows he can't be fired, he won't work."

Talmadge's expressed philosophy also included the tenet that "the only way to have an honest government is to keep it poor." He trimmed every department's budget in order to pay off the state's debt to teachers and Confederate pensioners, though in doing so he slashed state relief and health activities to the bone. He wrote one county's public health budget for the next year as a $2.75 expenditure. But Talmadge's philosophy of a poverty-stricken government stopped at his own shoreline. With great fanfare he ordered all officials driving state automobiles to turn them in, and quietly he increased the number for his own use. At the same time that all department budgets were curtailed, the governor's budget almost tripled.

In March, 1933, when Talmadge was in his third month in office, he was among the forty-eight governors invited to Washington to participate in the inauguration of Franklin Roosevelt. The new President considered Georgia his second home, for he had organized the Warm Springs Foundation to treat polio in 1927 and spent part of each year there at the foot of Pine Mountain near the western end of central Georgia. Roosevelt knew the state and its problems quite well, and in conversations, he referred to Georgia as "the unfinished state," because it lagged so far behind its human and resources potential.

Talmadge and the Georgia legislative leaders, who were flown to the capital on a navy plane, were accorded special treatment in Washington. Talmadge was given easy access to the new President's "brain trust" advisers, and the speaker of Georgia's lower house was loaded down with legislation Roosevelt wanted passed by the state legislature. It was a tense time in the nation's history, with a deepening Depression, a declared bank holiday, and the closing of the New York Stock Exchange. But Roosevelt was affable, found time to talk privately with Talmadge, and invited the governors' conference to a meeting in the East Room on March 6, 1933, where to loud cheers he promised large-scale Federal relief aid for their masses of unemployed.

Instead of enjoying his trip to Washington, Talmadge returned to Atlanta in a fury. He despised the idea of playing second fiddle to any man, even a President, and he felt blind hatred for the condescending Roosevelt brain-trusters. Yet he bided his time before coming out as a seething Roosevelt-hater because he recognized the New Deal's enormous political usefulness to himself. On the one hand, he could cut state spending beyond rational limits and reap the praise of businessmen and farmers. On the other hand, by acquiring large amounts of Federal money to take up the state gap, he would appear as the miracle man who did so much with so little.

So when Congress passed the National Industrial Recovery Act (NRA) to establish codes of fair play in various industries for business and labor, Talmadge rode a Georgia mule down Peachtree Street in the Atlanta NRA parade, even though he opposed the legislation. But he balanced off this street display when he vetoed the state banking reform bill that the Roosevelt crew had given the Georgia house speaker.

Talmadge soon found himself with a great deal of Federal money plus a patronage gold mine. With almost no Federal supervision at the beginning and with a free hand to determine where the Federal funds should go, Talmadge gained an immediate boost in power. And when he wanted more than the generous Roosevelt had provided, he made frequent trips to Washington to get it.

However, although the money was good, Talmadge had difficulty containing his personal dislike of the New Deal crowd. Nor did it keep his blood pressure down when he grew convinced Roosevelt planned to use the Depression as an excuse to change the racial way of life in Georgia.

The incident that gave him "proof" of Roosevelt's intentions toward the blacks involved the arrest of a Talmadge friend who had a large highway building contract. The charge against the contractor was that he had violated the wage and hours provisions of the NRA construction industry code by paying his workers far less than the minimum and holding them on the job far longer than the permitted maximum hours. Since almost all the pick and shovel workers were Negroes, Talmadge smelled a plot, and he gave loud, verbal battle with the Federal government. "Why, we built our own roads, good roads, too, for a maximum of 13 cents an hour," he told the press. "The government figures should be in line with wage scales in local communities," he warned Roosevelt. "The NRA is taking labor off the farm and making it hard to get crops harvested." For political peace, Roosevelt ordered a cut in NRA wage rates in Georgia to meet Talmadge's objection, but he lost some of his initial friendliness toward the boss of the "unfinished state."

This chilliness increased when Talmadge in July, 1933, referred to the Civilian Conservation Corps boys in forest camp projects for unemployed youth as "the CCC bums and loafers," and two months later ridiculed Roosevelt's efforts to end deflation by telling reporters that a better method would be that of "printing money and dropping it from airplanes as a means of creating inflation."

He also found something sinister in the proposal by Relief Administrator Harry Hopkins to use Federal funds to put Georgia's unemployed rural schoolteachers, a large proportion of whom were black, to work combating adult illiteracy. When Talmadge rejected the offer, Hopkins said, "All that guy is after is headlines. He never contributes a dime, yet he's always yapping. Some people just can't stand to see others making a living wage."

Talmadge's run-ins with Interior Secretary Ickes, who insisted on a close accounting of public works spending, made several news stories before Ickes abruptly cut off the entire program in Georgia in April, 1935. Ickes, a master at name-calling, dubbed Talmadge "His Chain-Gang Excellency," following a Talmadge defense of ball-and-chain treatment of prisoner road-gang workers. Another time Ickes coined the word "eneciable," which he defined as meaning "constant fever," to describe the Georgia governor.

Talmadge also carried on open warfare with Secretary of Agriculture Henry A. Wallace. "I would end all government aid to the farmers. He can work out his own salvation," Talmadge told audiences. With little purchasing power in a Depression-burdened nation and with cotton facing huge surpluses and low prices, Governor Huey Long of Louisiana had in 1931 called for a one-year moratorium on all cotton growing in 1932. Shortly afterward, Talmadge, then Georgia's commissioner of agriculture, had come out for a similar scheme.

But to the Roosevelt Agricultural Adjustment Act (AAA) of 1933, which was based on creating scarcity and raising farm prices, Talmadge made an about-face and offered shrill objections. He said the AAA's restricted land-use program, with payments to farmers who let their land stand idle, was monstrous; and the AAA's processing tax on turning raw cotton into products was a fiendish plan, even though the proceeds were used to pay farmers "parity benefits." Parity was designed to give them the purchasing power equal to the level farmers enjoyed in 1914. Talmadge charged that the AAA took $53 million from Georgia's cotton processing mills and paid $47 million of this to Georgia farmers who had not worked their land; and for these reasons, he said, he was bringing suit against Secretary of Agriculture Wallace before the U.S. Supreme Court. It was in January, 1936, that Talmadge enjoyed his revenge when the court, by a 6 to 3 decision invalidated the restricted acreage and processing tax provisions of the AAA and ordered the Federal government to return $200 million to the processors.

Roosevelt and the rest of his administration early suffered their fill of the governor. In January, 1934, he removed Talmadge's authority to run the Federal relief program in Georgia and ordered the dissolution of the Georgia civil works and relief board under Talmadge's stooge, Donald Ransom, an Atlanta banker. Then as Federal administrator of the Georgia relief program, Roosevelt named Miss Gay Shepperson, who had come from Virginia and had worked six years in the state welfare office.

Talmadge fumed at the selection of Miss Shepperson, denounced her as "a crabbed old maid," and charged her with threatening to "freeze some of the relief money or hang it on the hook until Talmadge did this or that." He also sputtered over the number of women she hired as local relief administrators, and hit at Miss Shepperson and her staff as "furriners." Some were "furriners," he said, because they came from other states. Others were Georgians who had "been to Northern and Eastern colleges long enough to get 'de-Georgianized.'" These latter individuals were the worst, he pointed out, because they had "ideas that are contrary to the established traditions of Georgia."

Talmadge had to stand for re-election in 1934, and Roosevelt wanted him retired. Major and former Senator John Cohen, Democratic national committeeman, proprietor of the Atlanta *Journal*, and Roosevelt friend, made a search for a suitable opponent and announced his support early that summer for Circuit Judge Claude C. Pittman of Cartersville. Not to be outdone, Talmadge decided to take out insurance by dividing the New Deal vote, and his friends talked Atlanta City Councilman Ed Gilliam, another New Dealer, into joining the race for the September primary.

That year, no one could have defeated the man who delivered on the promise of $3 tags. Like Tom Watson, Talmadge had begun publishing his own newspaper (*The Statesman*), and he used it to pump up the $3 tags to the importance of winning a major war. The masthead of *The Statesman*, aimed at his wool hat followers, noted: "Editor—The People. Associate Editor—Eugene Talmadge."

While the campaign was in its early stages, Pittman hit on two chief issues for his speeches. The first was the "pardon racket," for the record showed that Talmadge was issuing pardons at an annual rate of about 500. "A good strong man has got no business sittin' around a jail," Talmadge offered one explanation. "What we need is a whippin' post in a man's own town in the case of smaller crimes, such as gaming or wife beating." Since Pittman could not prove that any money had been given Talmadge for his pardons, he had a weak issue indeed.

Pittman's second issue was the strong attacks made by Talmadge on women administrators, the CCC forest project boys, and relief workers. But a recital such as this could not evoke as many cheers as Talmadge could collect by approaching a well in his shirt-sleeves and red suspenders at a country barbecue and drinking water from a gourd. And when Gene bellowed his braggings, the crowds yelled themselves hoarse—"They said Talmadge couldn't reduce the price of tags to three dollars." He pounded on the flag-covered speaker's box. "They said it'd bankrupt the state. Well, my countrymen, Talmadge did it! What happened now? After Talmadge reduced the tags to three dollars, mo' gas, mo' tags and mo' automobiles was sold in the state than ever befo'. Boys, I reduced the farmer's taxes. [Few wool hats paid taxes.] I put money in his jeans. I cut the utility rate. They said a lot of things Talmadge couldn't do. But he done 'em."

Talmadge's victory was a county-unit landslide. In the popular vote, he managed to double Pittman's showing, with a total of 178,000 ballots in his favor. But the shrewd man who campaigned where the streetcars did not run won 394 county-unit votes to Pittman's pitiful 16, and he carried 156 of the 159 counties.

It was after this resounding county-unit victory that Talmadge concluded ambitiously in 1934 that his defeated foe had been Roose-

velt and not little Pittman. Bolstered by this contention, he decided
to take on FDR himself in a fight for control of the national party
that would rival Huey Long's war against the President. "The New
Deal," he told the nation, shortly after his second term was assured,
"is a combination of wet-nursin', frenzied finance, downright communism, and plain damn-foolishness. President Franklin D. Roosevelt isn't a Democrat. The real fight in this country is Americanism
versus communism, mixed up with some kind of crazy gimme!"

To let the country know he was superior as an administrator
to the President, he made a newsreel for movie theaters across the
nation, in which he said pointedly, "We cut out the frills in Georgia."
Then to infer on another occasion that Roosevelt had surrounded
himself with dangerous, foreign advisers, he said, "If you will take
jockies like Tugwell, Hopkins, Wallace, Mordecai Ezekiel, Morgenthau, and other names I can't spell and can't pronounce out of the
saddle, you will see the American horse representing business and
work come to the front."

This and other remarks were shouted on the speaking tour he
made into New York, Chicago, New London, Connecticut, and other
Yankee strongholds. Everywhere, he promised his audiences that
Roosevelt would lose in 1936 against any Republican opponent,
vowed that he would personally keep FDR from winning the Democratic nomination because he was now Democratic national committeeman from Georgia, and showed no modesty at the news that
the first "Talmadge for President" Club had been organized in Rye
Patch, Georgia. "If elected," he declared, "I'd tear down a lot of
buildings in Washington and make beautiful parks. Let the government quit lendin' to anybody. I'd cut relief to the bone. I'd put 'em
to work. Why I could end relief in Georgia in three months." To an
urban New York audience, he ripped repeatedly into the government's farm program with simple anecdotes. "The one-horse farmer
with a potato patch is scared white," he told the cheering nonfarm-
ers. "He don't know whether to plant potatoes or to wait until someone comes around and tells him what to do."

But if Talmadge gained many admirers by appealing to prejudice and ignorance, he damaged himself severely by attacking the
President's physical infirmity. "The greatest calamity in this country
is that President Roosevelt can't walk around and hunt up people
to talk to," he attacked FDR for having crippled legs. "He can
only talk to those his secretaries and assistants allow to come in to
see him, and 90 percent of the crowd is the gimme crowd. Why, if I

stayed in my office like that, never going out to meet and talk to people, I'd mildew. So the next President who goes into the White House will be a man who knows what it is to work in the sun fourteen hours a day. That man will be able to walk a two-by-four plank, too!"

Besides his continuing attacks on Roosevelt, Talmadge lost little time after his 1934 primary victory endearing himself to mill owners and businessmen whose financial support he wanted for his national effort. He did this by fighting labor unions for them.

During the 1934 primary campaign, Talmadge had given state AFL leaders the impression he was sympathetic to labor. But when the United Textile Workers called a nationwide strike in September, 1934, and 44,000 of Georgia's 60,000 millworkers walked picket lines to win recognition, a pay boost, and a ban on night work for women and children, Talmadge denounced them first for interfering with "the right to work." Then he sent state troops to keep open the Goodyear mill at Atco, and two days later he proclaimed martial law and dispatched 4,000 soldiers with guns, bayonets, and tear gas to 100 mills. At Newnan, troops arrested 200 pickets at the eight large mills, hauled them off in army trucks to barbed-wire internment camps near Atlanta, where they were beaten and generally mistreated before the strike ended on October 8. Six months later, when hosiery and textile workers again struck, Talmadge ordered the militia to seize twenty-two of the labor leaders and intern them at Fort McPherson.

All the newspaper attention Talmadge was getting reinforced his belief he had presidential stature. When Huey Long was assassinated in September, 1935, Talmadge concluded he was now the undisputed leader of anti-New Deal Southerners. This in turn fed his dictatorial appetite at home. Brave souls hung him in effigy in stealth at the state capitol on November 29, but only a few newspapers dared speak out against the governor inside Georgia as fear of his dictatorial rule was spreading.

Talmadge reached the height of autocratic power within Georgia in 1935 when he tangled with House Speaker Eurith Dickinson "Ed" Rivers over the appropriation bill for the next fiscal year. Rivers wanted an amendment included to remove the school system's appropriation from the governor's control, and when Talmadge would not budge the session ended without any appropriation bill for the entire operation of the state government.

Politicians expected Talmadge to call a special session and

iron out his differences with Ed Rivers because the various departments could not function without money. Instead, Gene announced
he had no intention of calling a special session but would run the
state without appropriation legislation.

Great tension developed in the capital over Talmadge's decision to usurp the ultimate legislative function—the power of the
purse. The test came when he sent bills for payment to Comptroller
General William B. Harrison and State Treasurer George B. Hamilton, both of whom were elected officials. After some fumbling, Harrison and Hamilton declared they could not pay the bills because
state law required warrants, and warrants had to be based specifically on appropriation legislation.

True to form, Talmadge fired both men. When they said he
lacked such authority, he sent Adjutant General Lindley Camp and
a contingent of troops to take over their offices. However, they refused to leave, and the soldiers had to drag them out and throw
them into the street. When Talmadge then learned that the time
locks on the great steel vaults had been set seventy-two hours
ahead, he sent experts to cut through the thick steel doors and
"blow" the safes' mechanisms. Afterward, there were several lawsuits against the Talmadge seizure, but none restrained the governor.

Talmadge received what he hoped would be an over-the-top
push toward strong national status when some of the most conservative big businessmen in the country contributed money for a "Grass
Roots Convention of Southern Democrats" for Talmadge, to take
place at the end of January, 1936, in Macon, Georgia. Many of the
contributors were encrusted Northern Roosevelt haters, but the
principal underwriter of this Talmadge clambake was a seventy-five-
year-old semi-illiterate Texas lumber and oil millionaire named
John Henry Kirby, a close friend of Vice President John N. Garner.

Shortly before the Macon Convention, Talmadge went to Washington where his negative ballot spoiled an otherwise unanimous
vote of support for Roosevelts' renomination by the Democratic National Committee. Then on January 28 he showed up at Macon to
greet the expected 10,000 delegates from seventeen Southern and
border states to whom old Kirby had sent red, white, and blue invitations with a stars and stripes masthead.

The *New York Times* described Talmadge as "truculent" and
"biting a cigar," and well he might be, for a snowstorm hit the city

on opening day, and only 2,500 delegates were on hand in the municipal auditorium. On each seat in the auditorium was a copy of the *Georgia Woman's World*, which featured a photo of Mrs. Roosevelt and a Howard University black faculty member and student. As Vance Muse of Kirby's Southern Committee to Uphold the Constitution described it: "It was a picture of Mrs. Roosevelt going to some nigger meeting with two escorts, niggers, on each arm."

As the speeches unfolded, the theme of the redundant speakers was that it was "the Christian duty of white voters of the South to uphold the Constitution." When it was the hero's turn, Talmadge was introduced as "a plumed knight on an errand for the Republic," even though he was dressed in a tight, green double-breasted business suit with a sapphire pin sticking in his black tie. His theme was: "We should stop nine-tenths of the Federal activities in America." His black hair bounced on his forehead as he screamed, "You have to help in this fight to see that no Communist or Socialist steals the Democratic nomination. Let's don't allow a bunch of Reds to have four more years in office."

The convention voted afterward to ask Talmadge to accept its nomination for President of the United States. But Talmadge sensed that the seventeen-state meeting had failed miserably to serve as his expected springboard because of the small turnout and he would not accept, hedging that he would have to consider it carefully. His national candidacy was no more, though he still intended to bedevil President Roosevelt at every opportunity.

After the dismal Macon Convention, Roosevelt wanted a showdown in Georgia between himself and Talmadge, and he asked his friend Clark Howell of the Atlanta *Constitution* to arrange for a statewide presidential preferential primary. While Talmadge mulled over his possibility of defeating Roosevelt in such a contest, two local primaries showed Roosevelt the winner over Talmadge by a very large margin, and on that basis Talmadge decided there would be no statewide primary. Moreover, as controller of the state Democratic executive committee, he said he would choose the entire delegation to the National Convention. But when Clark Howell persisted with his request for a presidential primary, Talmadge then attempted to thwart him by setting the entrance fee at $50,000 for each candidate. However, this did not prove to be a bar for the pro-Roosevelt forces, and when Talmadge did not put up $50,000 in his own behalf, Roosevelt's name was the only one in the presidential primary. The result was that instead of an all-Talmadge delegation being handpicked by the governor, a pro-Roosevelt delegation went to Philadelphia in June for the Democratic National Convention. Then in one of its early actions, the delegation ousted Talmadge from the national committee, replacing him with Clark Howell.

Besides the Macon and presidential primary debacles, 1936 dealt another harsh blow to Talmadge's ambitions. The state constitution permitted a governor to serve two consecutive two-year terms but barred him from seeking a third term until four more years had passed. This meant that Talmadge was approaching the end of his political career unless he ran for another office.

Early that summer, he made his course known: He would run against Senator Richard Russell who was up for re-election that year.

Although Russell was a white supremacist with a strong distaste for the New Deal, he was shrewd enough to run on Roosevelt's coattails, for all signs pointed to a Roosevelt sweep that year. This left Gene with a loud, repetitious tirade against the President and the New Deal, and it gave him an uphill struggle even though he was personally far more popular than Russell. As the Atlanta *Constitution* gauged the primary between Talmadge and Russell: "A vote for Talmadge is a vote against Roosevelt."

With House Speaker Ed Rivers running for governor on a "Little New Deal for Georgia" platform, the campaign catchphrase contest belonged to Talmadge's opposition. The battle of the slogans went additionally against him when the state was flooded with auto stickers reading: "R R R," easily translated into "Roosevelt, Russell, and Rivers."

This was a test of Talmadge's physical endurance, racing from barbecue to fish fry to roar about a New Deal plot to end Georgia's cheap black labor situation. Every small county was to see Miss Mitt "a-weavin' in the crowd a-givin' it to 'em where she can look 'em in the eye," while Ol' Gene was "a-rantin' in piney-wood language."

While Talmadge was proceeding like a tornado against "the rubber stamp of the Washington bureaucrats," as he labeled Russell, the Senator carried on a slower-paced campaign whose key features were a plank, a box of ten-penny nails, and a hammer. "I'm going to nail Ol' Gene's lies," he promised each audience, and while he called out a Talmadge statement and declared it a falsehood, he pounded a long nail into the plank for emphasis. In a fighting mood, he might drive in a half-dozen nails or more. And when the votes were counted, the far more popular Talmadge won only 16 counties in the Democratic primary while Russell carried 143.

Following his defeat, Talmadge still refused to believe he had really been in a popularity contest with the President, and he fell back on an excuse he had voiced during the campaign. "I'd like to suspend the poll tax," he had confided to friendly reporters. "I could do it by executive order, pending the next session of the legislature. My fellows—the little farmer, tenants and sharecroppers—didn't make a crop last year. They're sufferin'. They can't pay the tax and they can't vote for me. But I reckon I won't do it. If I do, all those damn boondogglin' lazy workers'll be able to vote against me."

For the first time in a decade, Talmadge was out of politics, and except for the continued publication of his *Statesman*, he was strictly the farmer of Sugar Creek and the lawyer at McRae. But just when his enemies began talking about him as a former politician, he was back in full regalia on the hustings.

Angry with several Senators for opposing his court-packing plan in 1937, President Roosevelt was determined to oppose, or "purge," those who came up for re-election in 1938. One of these was the senior Senator from Georgia, Walter George, a stocky, white-haired, dignified man in a dark blue suit and thick-lensed glasses, who called himself an "80 percent New Dealer." Roosevelt's support went to Lawrence Sabyllia Camp, the young U.S. Attorney at Atlanta, and Talmadge announced his candidacy because he believed George and Camp would destroy each other.

The surprise in this campaign was that in the early returns on September 14, 1938, Talmadge owned a comfortable lead. By midnight with the lead still holding up, his campaign workers held a victory party, and Gene went on radio to claim he was the winner. But during the night a large number of small two-unit counties sent in word that "a lot of missing boxes showed up late," and a stunned Talmadge woke up the next morning to find that George had swept into the lead with 141,922 votes and 246 unit votes to his 102,464 popular votes and 148 unit votes. Camp had only 78,223 votes and 16 unit votes.

Talmadge was convinced he had been "counted out" with the aid of large sums of money having been passed out in more than thirty counties to give George the late and necessary lead. But he was unable to get recounts.

Gene Talmadge's strong showing against Senator George presaged his early return to political power, and this became a statewide conclusion in the spring of 1940 when he asked friends to organize "Georgia Needs Talmadge" Clubs in several streetcarless counties. A short time later Talmadge announced that he could not withstand the pleas of so many of "my countrymen," and he would run once more for governor in the Democratic primary.

In the four years that Talmadge had been away from the state capitol, Ed Rivers had served as governor of the "Little New Deal," with a generous financial assist from Washington. Under his smaller version of the national program, Rivers extended the lower grades' school year to seven months, provided free textbooks for public schools, moved the health department from a basement room in the capitol to ample quarters, and with a large budget in the new six-story state office building, he installed a state old-age pension system and extended state parks and rural roads. But he was an abominable administrator who overstaffed agencies and squandered money recklessly.

Such an abysmal showing by Rivers led the Atlanta papers to forget their previous strong dislike of Talmadge and offer no objection to him now. This meant that when the New Deal Democrats chose Columbus Roberts, a wealthy dairy farmer and businessman, as their gubernatorial candidate, they could not even count on big city newspapers to support their man.

When Abit Nix, the self-styled "best-element" candidate, joined the field, the campaign began. Despite the general belief that he could not lose, Ol' Gene ran "scared." Instead of conducting his campaign as though other candidates did not exist, he agreed to some joint meetings of the three Democrats speaking from the same platform at that summer's political barbecues. But he staged his arrival while either Roberts or Nix were already speaking; and at his approach, said one reporter, the "cheers shook the ground and drowned out his opponents." Later the thunderous sound was "found to be a record of crowd noises on an amplifying system."

The "scared" campaign of Talmadge revealed itself in other

ways. When he learned Abit Nix wanted to drop out, his friend supplied the Nix headquarters with funds to continue, in order to split the opposition vote. Also, the master at crowd domination came up with a new gimmick in 1940—a touch of humility before he shed his jacket, pulled his red suspenders, and let the lock of hair bounce on his forehead. "I want you to pray for me to have the strength to endure," he called to his wool hats.

What dampened to some extent an otherwise rousing campaign for governor that summer was the fall of France to the Nazis and the Battle of Britain in the skies over the British Isles. But these had no effect on the outcome of the primary. Ol' Gene won election to his third term by amassing 346 of the 410 county units, though his popular vote was barely more than half the 261,000 ballots cast.

"Ol' Gene's back!" the loyal wool hats congratulated each other as they watched Talmadge's long inaugural parade down Peachtree Street in January, 1941. Ol' Gene was back, and the show of humility he had displayed in the campaign vanished as soon as he reoccupied the governor's office. He told the legislature Ed Rivers had saddled the state with a $29 million debt, and with this as an excuse, he asked for passage of a measure that would give him a total appropriation authorization figure without any detailed strings on how to spend it. When both houses gave their approval, Talmadge was swiftly installed with dictatorial spending powers, and the legislature was left helpless.

By the time his opponents awakened to this state of affairs, Ol' Gene had already slashed vital services by his money-starving of various departments, had cleaned out every executive branch nest of Little New Dealers, and had begun paying off the state debt. Questioned about his acquisition of legislative power over the purse and his ruthless tactics, Talmadge scratched his ham-brown face and told reporters: "Did you ever know anybody who did any good that didn't have a little of the dictator about him? You can't run a state or anything else by a committee."

By cutting the debt without increasing taxes, he found that almost all newspapers in Georgia were willing to condone his grab of one-man authority. A fourth term in 1942 was his for the asking as the state settled down to a general acceptance of Talmadgeism.

But at this point Ol' Gene proceeded to ruin himself. The man who kept saying he was cutting out frills and restoring honesty to government was himself caught with his hand in the till. In a court case involving the Tattnall prison farm, evidence was revealed showing that cases of eggs, hams, vegetables, and chickens had been delivered to "Honest Gene" from the 980-acre prison farm near Reidsville. "A governor can live well if he knows how to manage it," Talmadge admitted.

However, the free Tattnall food caused only a minor uproar compared with the Cocking Affair. Even though Gene and his son Herman had received their bachelor and law degrees at the University of Georgia, Gene maintained a deep animosity toward that institution. This longtime smoldering hatred finally burst into the open in 1941 with the excuse that "nigger-lovers" were trying to subvert the state's segregated higher education system, and Talmadge said he had a sworn statement to prove it.

A Mrs. Scylla T. Hamilton, who had been fired as an instructor of physical education in the university's college of education, had an opportunity to gain revenge. She arranged an interview with Talmadge, and with his encouragement she signed a paper charging Dr. Walter D. Cocking, dean of the college of education, with favoring the mixing of white and black races in schools. The governor also got the name of President Marvin Pittman of the State Teachers' College at Forsyth as another advocate of bi-racial education, and Talmadge decided to take action against both men, despite his dubious evidence. With the state known to be warped in its concern with maintaining white supremacy, Talmadge saw a new high in his popularity from the favorable publicity that would result.

But the opposite happened. In the spring of 1941, eager Talmadge, as an ex-officio member of the state's university system board of regents, attended its annual meeting at Athens. Dominating the proceedings, he demanded that Cocking, the "furriner" from Iowa and former employee of the Yankee-interfering Rosenwald Foundation, be fired. The intimidated board of regents did his bidding at its morning meeting, but in the afternoon session they voted to retain Cocking.

At this show of independence, Talmadge reshuffled the board, firing a sufficient number and replacing them with his own henchmen so that it was his mindless puppet. However, Cocking demanded a public hearing before the new board had voted on him, and Talmadge, envisioning a steady stream of pro-Talmadge news stories, agreed.

The trial was held in the state senate chamber in July, 1941, with a large crowd of newsmen and educators in attendance. Talmadge found himself repeatedly hooted; his only evidence, with which to confront the even-voiced denial by Cocking, was the statement of Mrs. Hamilton, the fired instructor in Cocking's department. At the conclusion, Talmadge's wincing friends were of the opinion that Ol' Gene had blundered. Nevertheless, the governor's arranged vote resulted in the discharge of both Cocking and Pittman. "I appointed men that would give them a fair hearing," Talmadge said unconvincingly. "I done it to stop them furriners from preachin' that niggers and whites should get together."

Unfortunately for Talmadge, the Cocking Affair did not end at this point. A statewide outcry came when the Southern Association of Colleges and Secondary Schools removed Georgia's seventeen-institution university system from its accredited list. This caused consternation among parents of college students because their degrees would not be recognized outside Georgia. Thousands of students hurriedly transferred out of state, and a similar exodus of high school teachers took place. In some towns, high school students had to take over classrooms. Even the alumni association, hitherto interested chiefly in the football team, denounced the governor, and some wool hats with ambitions for their children had unkind things to say about their hero.

An early climax of the opposition came when a large number of angry college youths formed a motor caravan and paraded the 75 miles from Athens to Atlanta, where they strung up and burned an effigy of Talmadge on the statehouse grounds. Then when Talmadge showed up at a football game, the boos were thunderous.

At this time, Talmadge felt his life might be in danger and he fled Atlanta for the safety of his fenced acres, his dogs, and his twelve-room colonial house on top the pine thicket hill south of McRae. When reporters found him and asked why he didn't return to Atlanta, he asked, "Do they think I'm a damned fool?" "Well, governor," one newsman piped up, "some think you're a damned fool, some think you're a dictator, some think you're a demagogue, and some think you're just a plain crook. A lot of others think you're just as mean as hell." Talmadge frowned. "I am. I'm just as mean as hell."

The uproar over the loss of accreditation failed to subside, as Talmadge believed it would after the initial excitement. Nor did the entrance of the United States into World War II, following the sneak attack by Japan on Pearl Harbor on December 7, 1941, and the declaration of war by Germany and Italy four days later, close the subject. In fact, it gained additional force as a political issue that same month when the accrediting agencies set forth two basic demands: Dr. Cocking and Dr. Pittman had to be reinstated and the university system must be made independent of the governor and the legislature. As an implied political threat to Talmadge, there would also be another examination of the situation in Georgia in October, 1942, shortly after the next gubernatorial primary.

Within an hour after the accrediting committee expressed itself, Talmadge had an opponent for 1942. Ellis Arnall, Talmadge's thirty-five-year-old attorney general and former boy protégé whom Ol' Gene had made house floor leader in 1933 when Arnall was only twenty-four, announced himself a candidate for governor with the avowed purpose of reaccrediting Georgia's schools. The short, pudgy Arnall, blessed with a conscience, high intelligence, and ample campaign funds from his relatives who owned most of the prosperous textile mills at Newnan in Coweta County, had changed from a reactionary to a liberal New Dealer and saw himself as the man to lead Georgia into the twentieth century.

Talmadge desperately wanted to win re-election in 1942 because the law had been changed so that the next governor would serve four years instead of two. Yet he failed to take "Little Boy Blue," as he referred to Arnall, with any degree of seriousness. So minor did he consider Arnall that he did not have his friends promote another New Deal candidate into the race to divide the opposition. As Talmadge discovered too late, this man-to-man contest was a major mistake.

Both campaigns opened on July 4, 1942, with near disasters at Arnall's barbecue in Newnan and Ol' Gene's fish fry at Moultrie. Arnall had already begun his statewide radio speech when the muscles of his right arm suffered severe spasms. Somehow, while continuing to speak enthusiastically, he motioned to an aide to approach him, and in a momentary respite while the crowd cheered, he asked him to get medical help. A nurse was rushed to the platform and massaged his painful limb just as he swung into a rousing denunciation of Talmadge. The next day's newspapers, showing Arnall in pain at the microphone, called him "the game little fellah."

Although Arnall gained sympathy from his opening-day trouble, Talmadge could not from his own. Ol' Gene had chosen Moultrie in southwestern Georgia for his political kickoff because it was symbolic not only for the tight lid it kept on its "darkies" but for its excellent farms that produced watermelons a yard long with a two-foot diameter.

On his drive to Moultrie for the fish fry and speech, Talmadge stopped to use an outhouse, and it was his misfortune that a black widow spider lurking under the seat hole bit him when he sat down. When he staggered out, he was deathly pale, sweated profusely, and appeared to be going into a coma. But within a few hours, he insisted he had recovered sufficiently to go to Moultrie for his noon-time speech.

The large, cheering crowd at his arrival grew uneasy after a few minutes of Ol' Gene's listless voice limping into the radio microphone. But it was not a long ordeal for the entire affair came suddenly to a close with an enormous cloudburst that sent the crowd scurrying for shelter, ended his speech, and ruined the barrels of fried fish and hushpuppies.

Besides getting the better of the campaign kickoff, Arnall's organization proved far superior to Ol' Gene's. By the thousands Georgia's women had registered and paid their poll taxes to swell the Arnall cause, and the varied vote-getters were a new phenomenon in Georgia. College boys and girls and young drafted soldiers in Georgia's camps made house-to-house and farm-to-farm doorknocking pleas for him. In the older generation, women's clubs, PTA's, and teachers' organizations pitched in to pass out Arnall literature and make phone calls.

Arnall was also helped by special events. A signal break came when Adjutant General Sandy Beavers, Talmadge's boyhood friend and chairman of the board of regents, deserted the governor to tell the state, "I would crawl on my belly to restore recognition of the schools. The governor is depriving children of a college education." Then there was the small but effective role played by Roosevelt who had the selective service issue a report showing that 30,000 Georgians had been rejected by the draft for illiteracy.

With the large-scale doorbell-ringing campaign, the popularity of Arnall's themes of reaccrediting the schools, his effective championing of "democracy versus dictatorship," and his promise to raise the level of life so that "Georgia will no longer be the laughingstock of the nation," Gene Talmadge's camp took on an air of desperation. Ol' Gene's literature spoke of "irresponsible young jackanapes and painted-faced little girls who think they know how to run Georgia"; and some of Talmadge's secondary speaking crews were reported by Arnall to be yelling in Gene's behalf, "Niggers, niggers. All teachers is nigger-lovers. All newspapers is subsidized by nigger-lovin' Yankees."

Too late, Talmadge recognized that his campaign was in jeopardy. He stepped up his pace, took on a harsher tone, and dropped the vaudeville aspects of his small-county tour. He hurled invective at native blacks; warned out-of-state Negroes who opposed the local Jim Crow laws to keep out of Georgia; denounced the Atlanta, Augusta, Macon, and Savannah newspapers for "trying to get me"; and produced checks he claimed totaled $48,000 paid out by former Governor Rivers, who had made Arnall attorney general, to Atlanta reporters for "part-time" state work.

On September 9, 1942, the election turmoil ended, and by the close of that day Arnall had won the Democratic primary with 261 county-unit votes to 149 for Talmadge. Unwilling to accept defeat gracefully, Ol' Gene pointed out that had he won fewer than 60 additional votes in only a third of the counties, he would have been the victor instead of Arnall. "I didn't run a scared race," he offered a postmortem. "I didn't think the public would change during the war. And I was too busy with government business. Also I started the race too late."

World War II pushed high the price of cotton, corn, pecans, lumber, and tobacco; and from the heights at Sugar Creek, Gene Talmadge watched the profits rolling in and kept a hateful eye on the little man who had chased him out of the governor's mansion.

With the victory of Ellis Arnall over Ol' Gene, the Southern Association of Colleges and Secondary Schools had pronounced its reward by reaccrediting Georgia's university system in 1942. Arnall had then followed this with legislation removing the board of regents at the university level and the state board of education at the secondary level from control by the governor or legislature. In addition, Arnall gave teachers a 50 percent salary increase and stretched the school year.

Arnall also won the abolition of the poll tax, an action which he claimed would add a half million votes to the existing 600,000-vote base and decrease the possibility of a future demagogue's winning the governorship. In an obvious slap at Talmadge and to reward his army of youthful helpers in the 1942 campaign, Arnall also won approval for a cut in the voting age to eighteen, as well as the nation's first soldier-voting law.

There were more Arnall actions and issues that aroused Talmadge and kept his political ambitions alive. New laws pointed a gun at Ol' Gene's administrative tactics by barring the governor from firing the state treasurer and department heads, from serving on any commission that operated a department, and from getting into day-to-day budgetary activities of state agencies.

He also disliked Arnall's broadcasted remarks, such as "Let's bring Georgia back into the United States," and "Let's get off Tobacco Road." Nor did he enjoy Arnall's one-man effort to "prove" Georgia stood for more than depravity, poverty, and illiteracy by going on nationwide radio as a participant in the so-called highly cultural quiz program known as "Information Please." Nor did he find pleasure in Arnall's continuing personal attacks on him even though the election was over. In a book, *The Shore Dimly Seen,* Arnall thinly veiled the "charlatan" and "demagogue" he described, calling him "avid for power . . . painting upon his face the symbols of a painful and righteous indignation and stomping like the dickens . . . in despair he uses the tricks of mountebanks . . . promises a vague Utopia, flanked by jackals who drain the state treasury, he attacks a racial or religious group and loads its back with the sins of the people. . . . Always he dresses himself up as the little man, the common man come to life, grown to Brobdingnagian stature and becomes the 'Leader,' or maybe, 'Ploughboy Pete.' He knows the tricks of the ham actor, the gestures, the tones of voice that can arouse passions."

At the beginning of 1946, Talmadge was ill with a liver ailment, but events were developing that would push him headlong into a strenuous campaign for governor that summer. He was furious in January when Arnall's packed Democratic state executive committee rescinded its seventy-five-year code provision that barred nonwhites from voting in the party's primaries. But it was still only minor compared with his internal boiling in April when the U.S. Supreme Court reaffirmed the decision of the state committee and ruled that it was a violation of the constitution for a political party in Georgia to bar blacks from primaries.

It was this Supreme Court decision that galvanized Ol' Gene into political action. Within the week, he announced himself as a candidate for a fourth term as governor and promised to restore the white primary. Bluntly, he warned Georgia's 200,000 blacks not to vote in the primary, and he assured whites: "Elect me and I'll put inspectors at the state line to look into every sleepin' car and see that there's no mixin' of the races."

With Roosevelt dead and no longer available for a David and Goliath act and with the hordes of returning GI's demanding a better existence, Talmadge found it politically wise to become a latter-day New Dealer. With a broad, liberal catch-all program, he promised higher pay for schoolteachers, increased old-age pensions, a modern road system, a local hospital construction expansion, guarantee of collective bargaining rights for labor, a steep increase in rural school building, a GI home-building program, free business licenses, and higher market prices for farmers. For the icing on the cake, he said he would accomplish all this while eliminating the more than $30 million state debt Arnall had run up and without raising taxes.

At the outset, many newspapers refused to take Talmadge's candidacy seriously because they did not believe Georgia's voters were so dense that they could not see through his promise to deliver trainloads of goodies at no cost. Others expressed the opinion that this was 1945, and his flamboyant campaign style was antiquated. "Vaudeville is dead," scoffed one headline.

But Ol' Gene Talmadge was counting on his loyal wool hats, now freed from the poll tax, and on other Georgians frightened by the recent inroads into white supremacy. Moreover, he took additional heart when former Governor Ed Rivers became a candidate in addition to young James V. Carmichael, a former legislator, running as Arnall's protégé, for now he visualized a split in the opposition vote.

Then again, Talmadge had picked up a superb campaign manager in the person of former House Speaker Roy V. Harris of Augusta. What doubled Harris' value was that he was bent on revenge against Carmichael, whom Arnall was backing instead of Harris, the mastermind of Arnall's 1942 campaign for governor against Talmadge.

Despite Talmadge's apparent ill-health, Harris charted the most rigorous campaign of Gene's career, a total of 272 speaking stops with dozens of barbecues and fish fries where he would show his red galluses, drink water from gourds, and make his listeners' hair stand on edge with dire predictions of what the "niggers" would do in Georgia unless he were elected. "My countrymen, my people, now listen to this here!" would be his repetitive cry while Confederate flags waved and known Ku Kluxers walked about the crowds, and he raised his voice to a frenzied pitch railing against "Henry Wallace, Red Russia, Harlem, carpetbaggers, and the FEPC [Fair Employment Practices Committee]."

Gasping and pressing on his stomach between political meetings, Ol' Gene, the old pro, forgot his pains when he stood before his people for an old-fashioned harangue. He knew he still had the power to drive crowds into hysteria when a gang left one of his gatherings and destroyed a black church at Soperton. And he knew Roy Harris was a man of imagination when he hired a young white man who resembled Carmichael and sent him on a drive through Georgia accompanied by two jet black companions. At their frequent stops, the two Negroes would be puffing on cigars while the young man smilingly introduced himself as Jim Carmichael, Talmadge's opposition.

Unlike the Carmichael campaign, the Talmadge setup was an opulent show, financed, said insiders, by mill owners, the Georgia Power Company, and the crew of Coca-Cola millionaires, numbering a thousand in Atlanta, according to author John Gunther. There was ample money to buy off the county bosses in a dozen small counties where a price was normally set for a winning margin, and there was money for a first-rate survey that showed Talmadge ahead in only seventy-five 2-unit counties, necessitating a further expenditure of funds and Ol' Gene's energy in thirty other small counties.

So the race came down to D-Day in September, 1946, with Carmichael's likable personality and his support from Arnall casting doubt on the combined efforts of Talmadge, Harris, the Georgia Power Company, Coca-Cola, and the mill owners. But Carmichael's popular appeal proved unequal to the task of overpowering the rotten-borough county-unit vote system. Carmichael's popular vote total was 314,000 to Talmadge's 297,000 and Rivers' 67,000. In the unit-voting, however, which controlled the outcome, Talmadge had 242 county-unit votes while Carmichael lagged far behind with the rest, or only 148.

After he was acknowledged the winner, a tired Talmadge said

prophetically, "Yes, I won. But it's going to cost me ten years of my life."

He was an old sixty-two on his September 12, 1946, birthday, and he went off on a hurried vacation to Hollywood, Mexico, and Florida. He was in Jacksonville when his liver ailment flared up, and he was rushed to a hospital where he was found to be suffering from cirrhosis and stomach hemorrhages. But by mid-November, he was pronounced fit enough to travel, and he returned home to McRae.

On Thanksgiving Day, Ol' Gene felt so good that he went hunting. Afterward, he ate a large meal as though he were starving, and then he drove himself to Atlanta to enter the Piedmont Sanitarium. Doctors expressed concern with his deteriorating condition, but a week of bed rest brought on a gain in strength. A visitor confided to him, "Governor, you are the first man in the history of Georgia to cause every single person to pray at the same time—half of 'em praying for you to get well and half of 'em praying you won't."

"I'll bet a lot of them haven't prayed in years," Gene replied with a thin grin. "Probably made their knees sore."

On December 15, he suffered a relapse, and blood transfusions inflamed his liver cells. He died six days later.

Huge crowds came from all over Georgia to view the remains of the "Wild Man of Sugar Creek." There were wool hats by the thousands, businessmen, and a few curious blacks; and among the many wreaths the most impressive was one with KKKK printed on the ribbon—a memorial from the Knights of the Ku Klux Klan. On December 23, he was buried in lonely McRae cemetery. But the imprint of the Wild Man of Sugar Creek would remain deep in Georgia's future.

Chapter Six

TOM PENDERGAST
Missouri's Compromiser

MARCH 27, 1934, was a local election day in Tom Pendergast's kingdom, otherwise known as Kansas City, Missouri. An estimated 50,000 to 100,000 fake registrations were on the books; all these meant votes for Tom's candidates. Yet taking no chances, the Pendergast machine went all-out with its roughest manners.

In the streets that morning, long, black limousines cruised slowly past voters on their ways to the polls and created an atmosphere of fright, for none of the cars had license plates and their passengers looked like gangsters. One of the cars did more than cruise. When it rolled past the opposition's headquarters in downtown Kansas City, seven shots were fired through the big window, though miraculously no one inside the crowded office was hit by a bullet. Another car pulled up at the ninth ward center of the opposition, and its passengers rushed inside to beat several persons with blackjacks.

As the day lengthened, mayhem and murder grew commonplace. A Kansas City *Star* reporter witnessing repeat voters being driven from one polling place to another was severely beaten, and his car ventilated with bullets. Reports from various polling places told additional gruesome stories. At one, a Negro precinct captain was killed when he attempted to stop a gang from beating a Negro election judge; at a second place, ten men terrorized men and women voters by brandishing guns and swinging baseball bats; at a third, an oppositional clerk and challenger were felled with bats. At day's end, the Associated Press story sent across the country read: "Big Tom Pendergast's Democratic machine rode to overwhelming victory today after a blood-stained election marked by four killings, scores of sluggings and machine gun terrorism."

The Pendergast bossism had its start not with Tom but with his older brother Jim, who came to Kansas City in 1876. Jim had only a few dollars in his pocket, no trade or job, but at age twenty, he possessed a chest like a brick wall, shoulders and arms to match, and a determination to make his way in this exciting, new place so that he could bring his parents and six remaining brothers and sisters from the little family house in St. Joseph, 60 miles up the Missouri River.

For five years Jim worked as a puddler in an iron foundry, and he faced a dreary dead-end existence. No way out of this situation appeared until a warm day in 1881, when Jim went to the Sunday racetrack and bet his entire wad on a longshot named Climax.

With his substantial gains from the horse's surprise victory, Jim bought a barrelhouse—a combination rooming house and restaurant—and a saloon that he naturally named the Climax.

Even though Kansas City had 200 saloons for its 57,000 residents, the Climax prospered. The saloon offered excellent giveaway food, and Jim didn't care how much his customers ate while buying only a nickel beer. He also took a deep, personal interest in those who came regularly to the Climax, almost all of whom were factory or railroad workers. He cashed checks without charge and refused to serve heavy drinkers. In addition, Jim found jobs for the unemployed, sent food and clothing to his impoverished neighbors, and gave advice on family problems. Nightly he stood on his side of the bar, thoughtfully flattening his thick, black mustache while he listened to pathetic, personal tragedies; and his reddish, round face would light up with a wreath of a smile when he offered a solution in his fatherly, soft-spoken, tenor-baritone voice.

It was in 1884 that Jim found that the success of the Climax was transferable to politics. Leander Talbott, a friend of his, was running for mayor, and Jim asked his saloon customers to vote for him. When the ballots were tallied, Talbott had won in Jim's ward by a plurality fourteen times that of the winning candidate for alderman. Afterward, party leaders began trekking to the Climax to ask his support for their city and Jackson County candidates. Jim also started attending ward "primaries," or conventions, and was easily elected a delegate of the first ward to the Democratic city conventions. Then in 1892, he won election as an alderman. When his margin over his Republican foe was five to one, the Kansas City *Star* gave him a title that remained until his death—"King of the First."

Jim truly was King of the First, and within a few years he would be King of the Second as well. The second ward, which abutted the first, included the old levee district on the lower side of the Missouri River where steamboats docked shortly after the Big Muddy shifted from its north-south to a west-east course on its way across the state to St. Louis. Here in the dingy North End, where the West Bottoms poor had been moving in increasing numbers in recent years, he opened a second saloon in 1891. This new saloon lay near the courthouse and city hall, and a block from Market Square where, in the glamor of past decades, its saloons and faro tables had been frequented by folk heroes such as Wild Bill Hickok, Wyatt Earp, Bat Masterson, and Doc Holliday.

The Main Street saloon fared even better than the Climax, and Jim brought his brothers and sisters to Kansas City. Youngest brother Thomas Joseph Pendergast, sixteen years his junior, called Tom, or T. J., was born on July 22, 1872, and had been only four years old when Jim left home. Now eighteen, Tom stood 5 feet, 9 inches tall, but he was so big-boned and heavily muscled that he moved slightly sidewise when walking. He had shrewd blue eyes and his hair was light, but his most distinctive quality, apart from his powerful body, was his enormous head and outsized features that made people gulp on meeting him. Young T. J. also had a rumbling bass voice that sounded like summer thunder, and fists that struck like bolts of lightning.

Tom, who was Jim's favorite brother, lived with him in the smelly West Bottoms when he first came to Kansas City, until Jim married a widow named Mrs. Dorr. One of Tom's assignments from Jim was to serve as bookkeeper and cashier for the Climax and the other Jim Pendergast enterprises, and when Jim was not present, he was in charge of maintaining order. Saloon troublemakers tested him on occasion to their black and blue regret.

When the horse-racing season was on, Tom also worked as cashier at Jim's liquor concession at the Elm Ridge track. This was unfortunate because Tom started taking an occasional $2 chance on a nag. In time, his betting became a regular daily event, and eventually it developed into a sickness that enveloped his entire existence.

By far, Tom's most important function in brother Jim's world was to help him in politics once Jim won election as an alderman in 1892. Even before Tom could vote, Jim named him a precinct captain in the roughest part of the first ward, and from the patient guidance he gave his younger brother, it was readily noticeable that Jim was grooming him as his political heir-apparent rather than brother Mike.

But just as Jim was gentle, Tom was brutal, invariably using his fists to settle arguments that arose. Jim worked to change this incorrect approach, and in time the lesson sank home that it was service to voters that won their political hearts and not a welt on the head. What Jim kept emphasizing to Tom was his favorite home-made axiom: "You can't saw wood with a hammer." Years later, Tom told a reporter for the *New York Times* what he had absorbed from his brother Jim: "I know all the angles of organizing and every man I meet becomes my friend. I know how to select ward captains and I know how to get to the poor. Every one of my workers has a fund to buy food, coal, shoes and clothing. When a poor man comes to old Tom's boys for help we don't make one of those damn fool investigations like these city charities. No, by God, we fill his belly and warm his back and vote him our way."

The basic tenet in Jim's code of ethics was that when a man gave his word he was honor-bound to keep it. There was nothing more unmanly and dishonest to him than a person who broke a promise. As Jim's lieutenant, Tom adopted this theme, and it became as important a rule in his political career as another basic tenet prescribing total loyalty to the boss.

Once Jim acquired a taste for political life, he soon grew dissatisfied with the restricted power of a ward boss, and he determined to control the entire city and county. This was easier vowed than done, for two strong opponents stood in the path of his enlarged ambition. The first was William Rockhill "Baron Bill' Nelson, the despotic publisher of the Kansas City *Star* and energetic city beautifier. The second was Joseph Shannon, a wily Democratic politician with an insatiable appetite for power and spoils.

Although Baron Bill kept up a running war over the years against Jim Pendergast for being the champion of the saloon and gambling interests, all his efforts to dislodge him from the city council failed. Moreover, Nelson sometimes tempered his attacks on Jim to offer editorial praise for the first ward alderman's support of his own public works projects.

Tall, good-looking Joseph Shannon, the Pendergasts' crafty Democratic rival for local power, was a master at dirty election tactics and possessed enormous ability to walk away with more patronage than his small army of followers merited. As boss of the heavily populated ninth ward, Shannon held one-fifth of the delegates to Democratic county conventions, and through tricks, threats, and deals, he frequently gained control over his party's nominees for local office.

To distinguish between their factions of Democrats, the Pendergasts took to calling themselves "Goats" and the Shannons adopted the label of "Rabbits." As for the origin of the titles, one newsman in the Gay Nineties wrote that in the last election "the Pendergast crowd voted everything in sight, even the goats on the hillsides; while the Shannon men flocked to the polls like scared rabbits after hunters had beaten the bush." Another story had it that Shannon told a reporter one time that he had rabbits on every corner to let him know when they saw the governor enter Kansas City that night. Jim, on hearing this story was supposed to have suggested the nickname "Goats" for his crowd because he owned and liked goats, and besides, many of his followers in the first ward lived on the West Bluffs where they raised them, too.

Only eight years after he won his first election as alderman, Jim Pendergast, the Goat boss, had his first mayor. In 1900, fearful that Shannon might outmaneuver him and name the next Democratic nominee for mayor at the Democratic convention, Jim won approval from the party's central committee to choose the nominee through a Democratic primary. And because Shannon could not compete with Pendergast on the open-voter market, Jim's man, James A. Reed, whom Jim had put into office as county prosecuting attorney two years before, now swept the Democratic mayoralty primary.

Reed's victory in the general election made 1900 a banner year for Jim Pendergast. The new mayor's agreement for Pendergast support was to give Jim control of the city's patronage, and Jim already had a long list of deserving Democrats to replace Republican city hall clerks, streetworkers, firemen, policemen, and department heads. To solidify his new power, Jim also started his own political club. This was his Jackson County Democratic Club with headquarters in the Navajo Building on Delaware Street, complete with lunch rooms, a pool hall, bar, and auditorium. Jim had wisely insisted on a first-floor headquarters so that when fights broke out and individuals were thrown through windows, their chances for survival would be greater.

Part of Jim Reed's payoff to the Pendergast Goats in 1900 was his naming young Tom as superintendent of streets. This in turn put Tom in a position to hire 200 workers and buy materials and equipment for an expanded paving program. The more streets he paved, the greater was his patronage as well as praise from Baron Bill Nelson, who was bursting with eagerness to modernize the city. "Tom Pendergast is more than a battler; he is a man of marked ability," the *Star* hailed him. Tom also became a candidate for the first time in 1902 and won election as county marshal, though he lost two years later chiefly because of the vote-stealing by Joe Shannon.

It was Shannon's never-ending aggressive Rabbit tactics against his Goats that finally led Jim Pendergast to the conclusion that the Republicans were the principal beneficiary. So he finally sat down with Shannon and, like two foreign ministers jockeying over an international peace treaty, they agreed to what became known as the "Fifty-Fifty" accord.

Under Fifty-Fifty, he and Shannon were to meet before the primaries and hammer out a unified Democratic slate. If one or the other could not swallow acceptance of particular candidates, each would run his own choice in the primary, but both would back the winner for the general election. In addition, the arrangement called for dividing patronage equally between the two factions. So Shannon made up for his minor faction by clever footwork, and Fifty-Fifty remained in effect until 1916.

Following two defeats for county marshal, Tom Pendergast still craved public office, and when Thomas T. Crittenden, the Goat choice for mayor under the Fifty-Fifty deal, won election in 1908, he named Tom to his second stretch as superintendent of streets. Goat control over the mayor showed itself one time when police tried to arrest two Goats in a saloon. Tom happened to be there, and he threatened to thrash the officers if they did not leave. Newspapers got wind of the scuffle that took place, and editors demanded that the mayor punish him for obstructing justice. A reporter was present when Crittenden publicly dealt with Tom in a face-to-face meeting.

"Now, Tom," said the mayor, "you know you lost your temper or you wouldn't have used all those cuss words. But you are a mighty good superintendent of streets."

Even before Crittenden's term, Jim's health was gradually declining. He had contracted Bright's disease, then a terminal kidney ailment, and on top of his physical troubles, his wife died and his stepson Frank moved in with relatives. Growing steadily more tired, Jim turned over most of his political work to Tom, and he explained to reporters, "Anything the doc'ie [doctor] says goes with Jim . . . Tom's out this morning working like a bird dog. He went down to the stockyards on a handshakin' expedition. Goin' to make a house-to-house canvas."

By 1910, Alderman Jim was weak and wan. "If I run again," he said, "it won't be under packin' house rules. I'm too old. Now take Brother Tom," he added, "he'd make a fine alderman, and he'll be good to the boys—just as I've been. Eighteen years of thankless work for the city; eighteen years of abuse, eighteen years of gettin' jobs for the push is all the honor I want."

He asked brother Tom to run in his place for alderman in 1910, and when his hard core of supporters elected Tom to the city council, Jim seemed at peace. He died on November 10, 1911, and after the wake and the burial in Mount St. Mary's Cemetery with Father Bill Dalton giving heaven notice that a good man was on his way, Jim's sobbing Goats took up a collection for a lasting monument to him.

This became a lifelike bronze statue of their Jim seated in a chair; and when the city donated a small piece of land for the setting, Jim belonged to the ages, sitting in Mulkey Square on "Irish Hill," overlooking his beloved West Bottoms.

Tom accepted the fallen leader's baton with a sureness that belied the Rabbits' early assessment of him as an "oaf." There would be none of that sentimental slush that was part of Jim, who had never climbed out of the maudlin nineteenth century. Tom was a twentieth-century man, as modern as the Kansas City *Star,* which wrote about women aviators as early as 1911. He had shaved off his thick, blondish mustache, put his heavy arms through the sleeves of a belted-back jacket, shortened his collar, and purchased a car as proof of his "today" character.

As for the Goats, the twentieth century in Tom's view required a political organization run with businesslike principles and similar to an in-step army with total loyalty to the top general. If there were to be kind deeds, they would have to serve a calculated political purpose. There would be no more of Jim's quiet charities, as in the great river overflow of 1903 when Jim was up days on end directing rescues and resettling refugees at his own expense. And no more of the modesty that was Jim's when he begged reporters on that occasion, "Boys, it was my own money I spent, and the public is not interested in how I spend my money."

Where Jim's broad face would break into a pained expression when he was double-crossed, Tom impressed culprits that the pain was theirs if there was dirty-dealing. For instance, one time after a fellow alderman voted the opposite of the way he had promised, Tom asked him to stop by his office. A reliable reporter wrote up their encounter and said that the official "could not escape until Mr. Pendergast got tired of hitting him." Policemen, who were members of the Goat faction, could also expect a private beating for failing to carry out his orders.

Another basic difference between the old Goat and the new Goat regimes lay in their differing efforts to win elections. Both Tom and Jim social-worked with baskets of food, coal, and clothing and Christmas dinners to gain votes; but Jim would not stoop to vote frauds if such catering to voters proved insufficient. He was outraged when poor Republican losers charged him with paying the expenses and a fee for citizens from the state of Kansas to cross the Missouri boundary into Kansas City and vote for him. "I never needed a crooked vote," he said. "All I want is a chance for my friends to go to the polls." Tom, on the other hand, employed a philosophy that was a surer road to victory: "The important thing is to get the votes—no matter what." A chronicle of local elections over the years would reveal the ingenious techniques Tom Pendergast used to come in first.

The beginning of Tom Pendergast's six-year stay as alderman saw two further changes in his life. On January 25, 1911, a *Star* headline asked: "Is T. J. Pendergast Married?' Two days later the paper answered itself: "It's True." On the excuse that he had to go to Cincinnati on business, Tom, thirty-eight, and Carrie Snider, twenty-seven, were married at Belleville, Illinois, said the *Star*. When they returned to Kansas City, Carrie began agitating for a house outside Tom's run-down ward. But it was not until he quit the city council in 1916 that he moved to a new house at Fifty-fourth and Wyandotte Street, miles south of Jim's old constituents.

The second change in Tom's life when he became an alderman

was his intense determination to combine his politics with efforts to enter the millionaire's ranks. His various business activities were to develop and expand so rapidly that he picked up the habit of reducing conversations to a few words or expressive facial contortions. He bought three saloons on Twelfth Street, including the biggest money-maker in downtown Kansas City, the three-door saloon at 5 West Twelfth Street. Then there was the Pendergast Wholesale Liquor Company, which had a meteoric expansion when other saloonkeepers were warned they faced trouble unless they bought their wet goods from the alderman. Tom also operated the Hasty-Speedy-Hurry Messenger, Automobile, Transfer and Livery Company, and he signed several leases for downtown business properties, renting each place at high profit. In addition, he collected big packages of currency from those who wanted favors from the city council, such as the Metropolitan Street Railway Company, for whom he pushed through a thirty-year franchise in 1914.

All these operations and more, plus his political control of the Goats, he directed from a small office off the lobby in the six-story Jefferson Hotel, a second-rate place near Market Square. Joe Shannon, the super-wily Rabbit chief, had "discovered" Thomas Jefferson in the course of his wide readings, and his study of the writings of the master of Monticello became his major interest outside of his political plotting. His insatiable reverence for Jefferson made his law office look like a secondhand bookstore, and he needed only a few more clay busts of his hero to open a museum. The result was that he was moved to outrage when he heard that Tom Pendergast had purchased the Jefferson Hotel. The Goat should have renamed it the Jackson Hotel, he argued, for Tom and Old Hickory were alike in their simple thoughts and brutality.

Do-gooders considered the Jefferson a sin hole where drinkers, gamblers, and prostitutes gathered. This was true, but the attitude of those who patronized the bawdy and poker floors of the Jefferson was a lusty "So what!" Ranchers depositing their cattle in the Kansas City stockyards after the long trip from the Texas range hailed the Jefferson for having the best night life between Chicago and spots south of the Rio Grande. The most popular place in Tom's hotel was the cabaret in the basement, which some social historians claimed played a large part in starting the "Jazz Age." Here Tommy Lyman, the first "crooner," invented the term "torch song." One time in a crusade against Tom Pendergast, the *Star* sent a reporter to the Jefferson cabaret to describe the evil place. But he had a good time, for he wrote: "Cabaret entertainers wandered from table to table, singing sensuous songs. Midnight passed and the crowd of underworld habitués became hilarious. . . . The Jefferson hotel has police protection and is free to ignore the closing law."

When Tom Pendergast took over the Goats from Jim, he set his sights on gaining one-man control over the 250,000 citizens of Kansas City. But this seemed remote in 1911, for it ran counter to the plans of Herbert Hadley, Missouri's Republican reform governor. One of Hadley's principal intentions was to break up bossism in Kansas City just as his predecessor, Democrat Joseph "Holy Joe" Folk, had pitchforked the crooked aldermen-businessmen combine in St. Louis. Holy Joe's efforts in St. Louis had led to prison terms for several boodlers and flights by night across the border by a large number of other scoundrels.

While Tom considered ways to make himself the city's boss, Hadley moved on him by appointing Tom Marks, a Republican lawyer, as police commissioner of Kansas City. Marks' orders were to check into voter registration frauds in Tom's North End and to establish himself as Pendergast's challenger for political control in that area. With money and a large staff, Marks moved ahead swiftly, and in a short time his investigators found thousand of names on the registration books of persons listed as Democrats who did not exist or were dead or no longer lived in the West Bottoms and North End. However, when Governor Hadley ordered their names removed from the registration lists, he failed to take the next logical step, which was to bring the perpetrators to trial.

Nevertheless, the sharp curtailment of the registration rolls was a severe blow to Tom Pendergast's ambitions and a threat to his many business enterprises that depended on his political success. But he was not a man given to panic, and he calmly laid plans to thwart Governor Hadley. So while Tom quietly repadded the registration lists, he set out to make an ally of Republican Tom Marks, assure Joe Shannon that Fifty-Fifty was still being honored, and undertake the new development of a strong Goat machine in the South Side's middle-class wards.

Shannon proved too clever for Tom when the 1912 elections rolled around. He agreed with Tom that each would name eight alderman candidates, and both would support these choices in the sixteen wards. But he couldn't quite see Tom's right to name the mayoralty candidate, and when the Democratic primary was over, Henry Jost, one of Shannon's Rabbits, was the surprise nominee. Then while Tom pondered the Goat course in the general election, Shannon conducted a whirlwind campaign for the "Orphan Boy Mayor," as he referred to Jost, letting his voice crack with just the right degree of emotion to win crowd support for his thirty-seven-year-old candidate.

It was after Jost was sworn in, and Tom saw from his city council seat that the Orphan Boy Mayor did not express an opinion without prior consultation with Joe Shannon that he lost his coolness. Then, walking through city hall and the county courthouse, he spied Rabbits at most of the desks, and his fury increased. The final blow came when he learned that the new Democratic governor, Elliott W. Major, who had succeeded Hadley in 1913, had agreed to give Shannon patronage control over police and election commissioners.

In this crisis, Tom called in older brother Mike, who first ranted and roared that the Pendergasts should never have agreed to Fifty-Fifty and then accepted Tom's plan for outwitting Shannon. Besides continuing his political work in the tenth ward, Mike was to organize the Goats in the rural part of the county to nip Shannon's growing power there. This was not a strange area to Mike, for he had been the county license inspector for a time on a job that held life and death determination for businesses that needed a county license to operate. A large number of Jackson County businessmen had become indebted to him because of his generous treatment, and with this good will as a starter, Tom believed Mike would soon pen the Shannon Rabbits in the county.

In addition, Tom Marks, the Republican sent in by the governor to destroy the Goat Democrats, was amenable to Pendergast's suggestion that they combine against Joe Shannon. When this working arrangement was later publicized, the *Star* denounced the Marks faction as the "Democratic Aid Society." But Marks was not thin-skinned about newspaper attacks after the many jibing stories the *Star* had printed on his proposal to fight vice by containing it. While serving earlier as police commissioner, Marks had voiced the opinion that vice was a natural human trait, and he proposed restricting it locally to one defined area, rather than permitting it to be "scattered like measles along our boulevards."

For unpublicized rewards, Marks had his Republicans cross

party lines and vote for Tom Pendergast's Goats in the Democratic primary. But the Goat leader did not gloat over the victory of most of his slate, because the margin over the Rabbit candidates was small. This meant that if Shannon's boys later stayed home on general election day, the Republicans would sweep into office. So again, Tom Pendergast asked Joe Shannon to meet with him for a renewal of the hated Fifty-Fifty. What was hardest to swallow was that Shannon's man Henry Jost became mayor once more.

By 1916, Tom Pendergast's hard work had won him a majority of the forty-one members of the Democratic county committee and the Democratic city central committee. His strength was revealed when he dictated the choice of delegates to the Democratic state convention, to be held in St. Joseph in March, and he barred a place to Joe Shannon. A newsman reported the triumphant arrival of the Jackson County delegation at Tom's birth city with state leaders on hand to greet Tom and his boys and their live goat mascot:

> The Goat Special over the Kansas City, Clay County and St. Joseph trolley line got in at 10 o'clock, bearing about 500 stalwart Pendergast men. In all there were five carloads. Each man wore a button . . . a picture of a goat rampant.

Tom knew that Governor Elliott Major yearned for the vice-presidential slot with President Woodrow Wilson in the coming summer's Democratic National Convention. So he led the loud chorus at the state meeting to endorse Major for Vice President. And the governor said, "Thank you," to Tom by telling him that the Kansas City police and election commissioners patronage awarded in 1913 to Shannon now belonged belatedly to the Pendergast Democrats in 1916.

In the city elections that year, Shannon employed desperate tactics to prevent his being swallowed alive by the Goats. Jost, his Orphan Boy Mayor, was running for a third term against Tom's Goat Boy, R. Emmett O'Malley, in the Democratic primary; and when cocksure Pendergast told Tom Marks he didn't need Republican cross-voting, Jost won the nomination. Then at the Democratic city convention, Jost and Shannon threw out a sufficient number of Goats so that they had freedom to name their own candidates for aldermen in all the wards.

However, Shannon failed to browbeat Tom into submission, for the Goat leader took independent action, put up his own candidates for aldermen and loudly told all good Goats to vote in the mayoralty contest for George H. Edwards, the Republican candidate. Tom was still in bed on election day when one of his henchmen came to his house with bad news. Mayor Jost had collected all Pendergast policemen and sent them out of town for the day. Then Jost-Shannon policemen had raided the flophouses and mission centers where Pendergast counted on a substantial number of repeater votes and whisked hundreds of the derelicts off to jail.

But these final acts of Shannon desperation failed, for Edwards carried fourteen of the sixteen wards, Tom had five aldermen, and the Republicans the rest. A few months later when the county primaries were held, Tom came out with a Goat county committee.

So by the time World War I arrived, Tom Pendergast was the most influential Democrat in Kansas City and Jackson County. He lacked his own mayor, though he owned the police and the election commission, and he believed Kansas City would soon be his, if only Joe Shannon would drop dead.

Tom Pendergast had to make a major decision in January, 1920, when prohibition came to the nation. Unwilling to clutter his political ambitions with illegal speakeasies and Federal agents, he padlocked his saloons and closed his wholesale liquor company. The picturesque Jefferson Hotel also shut its doors for good, though T. J. reaped profits from this closedown when his lieutenants in the city government gave him a high price for the property on the ground that it was needed in a street-widening project.

Tom was far from poor, despite the effect of prohibition. He still held several leases on business property he rented, was still part owner of the crooked Ross Construction Co., which cheated on construction contracts, and was in business with brother Mike in the Eureka Petroleum Co., which concentrated on selling oil to city and county government departments. Most important, T. J. began the Pendergast Ready-Mixed Concrete Co., in time a multimillion-dollar business with a stranglehold on government contracts locally. His Ready-Mixed Concrete was one of the first in the nation with trucks lumbering along while stirring concrete en route in huge revolving drums.

With the Democrats across the nation engaged in mild civil war, 1920 was apparently going to be a Republican year, and T. J. wanted a friendly Republican governor in Jefferson City. But despite the frenetic efforts of his pal, Tom Marks, and his Republican Democratic Aid Society, a prohibitionist and heavy churchgoer from Trenton, Missouri, named Arthur M. Hyde won the Republican gubernatorial nomination and the general election that year. Once in office, Hyde stripped T. J. of his say over the selection of Kansas City's police, elections, and excise commissions; sent Tom Marks' Democratic Aid Society into political oblivion; and ordered a continuing effort to catch Democratic politicians in dishonest transactions.

In the postwar era, T. J., trying to avoid trouble with the governor, also began a major effort to take over the county government apparatus. Jackson County elected three county judges, a presiding judge and a western and eastern district judge, who were really county commissioners and not courtroom presiders. The county judges ran county agencies, levied taxes, and overseered the road and building construction programs, activities presenting many opportunities for graft, patronage, and contracts for a political boss.

It was in his sweep for control of Jackson County that T. J. had two Goats in as county judges in 1922—Henry F. McElroy, who would be his closest co-worker in the future, and Harry S. Truman, twenty-three years later to be President of the United States. Truman was to lose re-election in 1924 when Joe Shannon had his Rabbits support the Republican candidate. But in 1926, Truman was elected presiding judge and dominated the county outside Kansas City for T. J. for the next eight years.

Shannon's success in 1924 in combining with the Republicans to defeat Truman in the county was equally effective in the city where his Rabbits were instrumental in defeating Tom's candidate and putting Republican Albert I. Beach in as mayor. Yet from these depths, T. J. was soon to leap into undisputed bossdom thanks to the good government reformers in town.

Local clamor by the Kansas City Civic Research Institute and the Charter League for a clean, nonpartisan, scientific city-manager form of municipal government led to voter approval in 1924 for the establishment of a group to write a city-manager charter. This charter was to be voted on in February, 1925, and support for its passage came from the chamber of commerce, ministers, women's organizations, and Mayor Beach. Another champion, the Kansas City *Star*, editorialized staunchly in its favor as the best means to rid the local political scene of bosses such as Pendergast and Shannon.

Under the city-manager charter that was written, the city would have a council of nine men instead of the current two-house council of thirty-two. A mayor would be one of the nine, with special functions limited principally to presiding at council meetings and attending to ceremonial affairs. Members of the council were to run as independents, not as Democrats or Republicans, and they would elect a city manager, who would take administrative control of the local government.

It did not take Joe Shannon long to denounce the proposed charter, for he saw it as a boss-breaking move, just as the reformers did. T. J.'s joking reaction before he read the document was that the charter had to be worthwhile if Shannon opposed it. Then he dubiously read the charter, examined its provisions from every angle, and his happy conclusion was that it was made to order for him. He saw clearly that if he could land only five Goats on the city council, he could then name the city manager, and Kansas City would belong to him.

When Tom announced that he favored the charter's passage, the reformers grew suddenly concerned that perhaps the city-manager plan would not kill the Goat and Rabbit machines as they had hoped. But they were reassured when Shannon publicly declared that T. J. was stupidly "signing his death warrant."

On the day of the special charter vote in February, 1925, T. J.'s Goats sent their people to the polls to vote with the reformers, and the charter passed by a four to one margin. Nonpartisan candidates were now expected to announce for the individual council seats and mayor. First there would be a primary with the top two candidates for each place engaging in a runoff election in November, 1925.

However, T. J. made a mockery of the reformers' hopes for nonpartisan candidates by putting up a Goat slate headed by Ben Jaudon for mayor. Shannon also announced a Rabbit ticket, and when Mayor Beach led a slate of Republicans, the old party politics swallowed the charter. The Shannon team lost in the primary, leaving the voters to decide between the "Jaudon group" and the "Beach group," as the *Star* persisted in calling the Goat and Republican slates, in order to maintain the fiction of competing nonpartisan candidates. But everyone in town knew what had happened.

On election night of November 3, counting of the ballots was not completed, and the job was put over to the following day. Disputes arose regarding the counting, and days passed before the officials began to issue the results. Mayor Beach was declared the winner over Jaudon, and then three Republicans and four Goats were announced as new councilmen. With a four to four split it now became obvious that the entire election's outcome had narrowed down to the victory or defeat of George Goldman, a Goat, in the final contest for a council place. When the figures were eventually released, they decided T. J.'s fate. By the paltry margin of Goldman's 304-vote majority, Tom was now the boss of Kansas City.

It came over Beach that had only 153 of Goldman's votes gone the other way, the Republicans would have held a five to four margin in the council instead of Pendergast. Immediately, he charged a vote fraud and began collecting evidence of Goat shenanigans. But T. J. quickly dispatched his lawyers to Jefferson City where they induced judges on the State Supreme Court to order the Kansas City elections board to declare Goldman "properly elected."

Now T. J. took the offensive, charging Beach with having defrauded Jaudon out of victory as mayor, and while Beach was enveloped in this Goat smoke screen, T. J. announced who would be his city manager. The man he chose was Henry McElroy, who had served on the county court with Harry Truman.

Once the reformers' government officially began in Kansas City under Pendergast-McElroy auspices in April, 1926, T. J.'s personal stranglehold on the city was not broken until thirteen years later when Franklin Roosevelt ended his reign.

The Pendergast-McElroy rule of Kansas City was a mutually satisfying one for both men. T. J., as the political boss who held no public office, set the broad outlines of what he wanted, and McElroy, as the city manager in charge of running the city government, carried out the orders without the faintest reproach from Tom for anything he did. "Tom and I are partners," McElroy explained their relationship to reporters. "He takes care of politics and I take care of the business. Every Sunday morning, at Tom's house or mine, we meet and talk over what's best for the city."

Henry McElroy, who was tall and sturdy when he began as city manager, in time grew thin and round-shouldered, despite the fun he had and the graft he collected for himself as T. J.'s spokesman at city hall. He had come from Dunlap, Iowa, where he had had only a few years of schooling and some experience as a bookkeeper. In Kansas City, he ran a successful bakery business and then went into the real estate business where he gained a reputation for shrewd, sharp operations that he continued in his tour as county judge and then as the city's administrative dictator. As a businessman, McElroy achieved a small fame among the chamber of commerce crowd for trenchant witticisms, and this trait he later carried over into politics with rather shocking results. He was also known for a time for his eagerness to use his fists to settle disputes, but he later relied entirely on his tart tongue and superb acting ability. Some claimed he lost his appetite for fisticuffs the day little Miles Bulger, formerly county judge and leader of a minor Democratic faction, accosted him and gave him a faceful of bruises and cuts. McElroy insisted afterward that Bulger caught him by surprise when his big hands were stuck in his tight pants pockets. Nevertheless, "Old Turkeyneck," as McElroy's detractors referred to him because of his long, wrinkled red neck, changed his combative style following his encounter with flyweight Bulger.

On taking over the supposedly nonpartisan post of city manager early in 1926, after T. J.'s five puppets on the city council outvoted Mayor Beach and his three Republican council members, Old Turkeyneck brought dying gasps to the charter reformers by declaring he would run the city as a Democrat. He also let it be known that he considered the elected mayor and council to be his lesser creatures.

One of McElroy's first destructive battles was with Mayor Beach, who proved no match for him. On a spring morning, the mayor came to city hall and found that the city manager had taken physical possession of his office for his own use. Caught by surprise, Beach failed to carry on like an outraged elephant with the result that the coup succeeded admirably and Beach found himself sitting in a tiny back room. McElroy also ordered the mayor's free limousine and chauffeur transferred to his own use, and he spread the message that Beach's remaining functions as city greeter of notables and chief speaker at civic events were now the prerogative of the city manager. For a while, Beach fought for his rightful place as greeter of Queen Marie of Rumania and radio's blackface white comedians, Amos n' Andy, but McElroy embarrassed him so much at these and other occasions with his edging, pushing, and talking that eventually he defaulted to Old Turkeyneck.

A chief mission that McElroy carried out for T. J. was to give city employment to thousands of loyal Goat ward workers. McElroy's passion and workmanship in this area resulted in a turnover of city jobs to 6,000 Goats and a payroll in the millions, part of which was reclaimed in the form of kickbacks received by McElroy and T. J. Of those Goats on the payroll, *Star* investigators were to claim that 2,000 were "pads," or persons who did no work or never reported to the job. McElroy used a variety of preposterous reasons for firing city department heads who were longtime technicians and not political appointees. In the case of the health department director, Old Turkeyneck blamed him for the color of the walls in the new nurses' hall at city hospital. Anyone who had approved that ghastly color, said McElroy, must lack judgment on all other matters.

One of McElroy's big efforts was to win support for the Goats from the business community. A surefire weapon in his arsenal was his selective lowering of tax assessments on the homes and company property of influential businessmen. Among firms neutralized in this fashion were the Kansas City Power and Light Co., the Kansas City Terminal Railroad Co., and the Kansas City Public Service Co. In contrast, businessmen who would not join T. J.'s ranks suffered from steep increases in tax assessments and uncollected garbage. Roy Roberts, the 375-pound managing editor of the *Star*, who frequently supported T. J. but on occasion found fault, moved his home across the river into the state of Kansas when his property assessment soared.

Businessmen who might have opposed T. J. before he became all-powerful were lulled by McElroy's claim that as city manager he was giving them good government at a reasonable cost and without going into debt. When he took over Mayor Beach's office, the city had an acknowledged inherited budget deficit of $5 million left by the previous administration. McElroy announced that to solve this problem he had immediately put into effect the bookkeeping system he had learned back in Iowa. You take some figures from this side of the balance sheet and put them on the other side; then a few from the other side go on this side; and presto, half the debt has vanished, and only the addition of a small tax boost was needed to eliminate the rest. "It's just a little country bookkeeping," he said smugly.

Businessmen might have asked at that time for a detailed explanation of this mysterious "little country bookkeeping," but no one did except the head of the Civic Research Institute, somewhat of a laughingstock now because T. J. had turned inside out his nonpartisan city-manager idea. Several years later when some civic-minded citizens demanded to see the books, McElroy abruptly informed them they could not because the financial records were his responsibility. So what McElroy collected and spent for the city, T. J., and himself did not become known until a major milking of municipal monies had already taken place.

While McElroy concentrated on the duties Pendergast assigned him, T. J. was busy pushing his organization into control in every ward in town. Remnants of minor Democratic factions plus brave objectors were beaten, threatened, bought, or swindled. Chief among T. J.'s convincers were "Terrible Solly" Weissman and Bob Hawkins, each a 300-pound brute. As for the John Doe voters, these were cunningly studied to give them reasons for supporting Pendergast candidates in the future. In the poor wards, the old tried and true programs of Christmas food baskets, bushels of soft coal, rent payments, free clothes for the kiddies, court assistance, and construction jobs for unemployed males were intensified. In the middle-class wards where the Coolidge inflationary prosperity was ostentatiously evident, T. J.'s program called for the establishment of year-round political club buildings where the neighbors were invited for parties, dances, and card games; and the children joined social clubs and were organized into baseball, football, and basketball leagues. Older brother Mike Pendergast helped add support for the machine by strolling through neighborhoods and passing out tickets to the games of the Kansas City Blues, the local minor league team.

To handle his voter programs, T. J. employed an army of ward and precinct workers. Their jobs involved keeping personal records on occupants of every house, offering a "Welcome Wagon" type of service to new arrivals, operating emergency help for others, getting out the vote on election day, and ferreting out potentially dangerous dissident elements through an elaborate spy system. For all these tasks the machine had an average of twelve Pendergast workers operating in each of the city's 458 precincts, and those who were not given city government sinecures were helped with jobs in private business. In addition, their morale was kept high by frequent meetings in the ward Democratic clubs where the beer flowed freely despite prohibition, and gambling was common. On occasion, the meetings turned into brawls, but these were considered a cleansing process.

As insurance, should all efforts fail to bring out the coddled voters in required numbers for victory, T. J. fell back on the boss' prerogative of voting the names on gravestones, stuffing ballot boxes, and keeping the opposition vote small. One T. J. brainstorm for election-day use was to hire hundreds of derelicts, intersperse them with hard-punching Goats and have the lot form a double line at the polls hours before opening time. His purpose was simple. The lines never moved forward during the entire day. While known T. J supporters were permitted to slip past the lines and go inside to vote, all others were stopped, jostled, and told, "Get in line and wait your turn!"

T. J. professed to see nothing illegal or immoral about his tactics. "You've got to have boss leadership," he told one reporter. "Now look at me. I'm not bragging when I say I run the show in Kansas City. I am boss. If I was a Republican, they would call me 'leader.'" Another time he told a *New York Times* newsman: "I'm the boss. The reason I'm the boss is because of my ability. I know all the angles of organizing and every man I meet becomes my friend."

An important tool for winning popularity and acceptability for the Pendergast machine was the *Missouri Democrat*, T. J.'s newspaper that he established at the end of 1925. His ownership was steadfastly denied, for the paper pumped up the wonders of T. J. and his candidates with never-diminishing enthusiasm, and such admission would have reduced its impact immeasurably. To make it more credible, the *Missouri Democrat* shrewdly ran favorable articles on local businessmen, many of whom had kind words to say afterward about T. J.

T. J. was firmly convinced that Kansas City should be a wideopen, lively town, even though he detested speakeasies and made certain he rested his massive head on his blue pillowcase by 9:00 P.M. for the night. As his agent, McElroy looked the other way while an enormous bootlegging industry spilled over into speakeasies, houses of prostitution, and gambling casinos and joints.

Kansas City high livers were supplied with a dog track complete with a speedy mechanical greyhound; open slot-machine operations were in every neighborhood; and dope and rotgut bootleg products were readily available. One student of Kansas City pointed out that the city was "responsible for the production of most marked cards and loaded dice," while in the larger area of hard crime the developing national epidemic of kidnappings of wealthy citizens had its start in Kansas City along with the practice of disposing of individuals by "taking them for a ride." T. J. brought hard-core sports fans to town by introducing racetrack betting on the horses, a pastime prohibited twenty years earlier through the efforts of Governor "Holy Joe" Folk. T. J.'s lawyers were able to legalize this pastime again by getting a majority of members on the State Supreme Court to declare that individuals could "contribute" money at racetrack windows "to improve the breed of horses." This was correctly interpreted by T. J. to mean the blessing of placing bets and led to the establishment by him and some friends of "Pendergast's Track," or as it was legally called, "Riverside Park Jockey Club," a few miles out of town where as many as 15,000 persons showed up at a day's meet to "contribute."

Along Twelfth Street and neighboring side streets in downtown Kansas City, at least fifty speakeasies with raucous crowds and top-notch jazz bands did a big business. At the Reno Club, customers who came for gin and dancing listened to Count Basie and his "Kansas City Seven" pounding and blowing out their frenetic, happy notes. Darrell Garwood, a local historian, reported: "It was possible at one place to order a 65-cent highball and have it brought to you by a waitress completely in the nude, or to see four striptease acts in the course of a noon lunch." Edward R. Murrow, then a young reporter, described Pendergast's metropolis in this fashion: "If you want to see some sin, forget about Paris and go to Kansas City. With the possible exception of Singapore or Port Said, Kansas City has the greatest sin industry in the world." On a drive through the extensive red-light district, Morrow said that "in every window, upstairs and down, were women. When the cab drew near, the women dropped whatever they had in their hands, seized nickels and began to tap furiously on the window pane. A steady stream of tapping accompanied the cab up the street. We swung into a street where most of the window tappers were Japanese."

T. J.'s effort to make Kansas City the leading swinging city was not accomplished without hard work. For a time, the chief roadblock was his lack of control over the police. By law, the governor appointed Kansas City's police board, which in turn picked the police director; and, of course, with a Republican governor, T. J. might control the city council and city manager, but the Republicans ran the police force in Kansas City, and John L. Miles, the city's Republican police director, was a thoroughly honest and conscientious man.

Open warfare erupted when Miles arrested gamblers and speakeasy owners. T. J.'s judges quickly won releases for them, but Miles was so persistent that he made a hundred raids in about that number of nights on a single place even though judges monotonously undid his work. Yet Miles remained an obnoxious pest to T. J., and the Goat boss utilized other means to discourage him.

Since the city paid the expenses of the police department, T. J. had McElroy slash its budget. Miles' expense account was also studied, ridiculed, and then rejected. McElroy's harshest blow was his foot-dragging in paying the low wages due policemen. When checks failed to be distributed for more than four weeks to the men, several of their wives wrote pleading letters to McElroy for funds to feed their hungry children. "Let them eat castor oil," the city manager replied. Miles finally took the city to court over the nonpayment to his men, and McElroy spent $50,000 of the taxpayers' money in his losing legal fight. By that time, however, many policemen had succumbed to bribes and payoffs by the crime element and were no longer worthy officers of the law.

Harassed, Miles finally resigned. "I did it because I thought it would take McElroy's pressure off the police department," Miles told this author in 1960. "I wasn't afraid that I might be murdered." It was not until 1932 that the State Supreme Court ruled that Kansas City should name its own police director. But this was just a formality, for after Miles left, the police marched to McElroy's music.

Another disruptive force in T. J.'s operation of a wide-open city was James R. Page, a Goat who was elected county attorney in 1926 when Harry Truman became presiding county judge. Page specialized in railing at the leniency of judges and said, in effect, in a speech, that they were fostering a permissive society, or a "crime-forgiving society."

McElroy was Page's pet target, and he hit at him again and again as the friend of the vice lords. "I refuse to get into an endurance contest with a skunk," McElroy brushed him off. The two tangled over the slot-machine jungle that the city had become, and when McElroy ignored his demand that owners of shops containing the "one-armed bandits" be arrested by the police, Page took charge of sheriff raids inside the city. But the city manager outwitted him by having the sheriff turn over the slot machines to his police and then ordering their destruction. As a result, Page's cases were then

thrown out of court for "lack of evidence." Despite his war with Mc-
Elroy, Page won T. J.'s support for a seat on the circuit court in
1932, but the mystery was never solved regarding the reason Tom
tolerated him.

So long as McElroy was on the scene, righteous citizens came
out second best in attacking the Pendergast machine for corrupting
the city. When aroused parents complained that school children
were throwing their lunch money into the one-armed bandits in
stores near schools, McElroy told them, "I will not remove them
[slot machines] from small, independent stores. Why? Because they
are keeping small, independent stores in business. Furthermore, I do
not believe slot machines corrupt children. Their parents corrupt
them."

To a group of women who came to talk with him about the
growing crime rate, McElroy used himself as a prime example of
what they should do as interested citizens. He spoke in hushed
tones about his "old Presbyterian mother who taught me to avoid
gambling in all its forms along with alcohol and nicotine." He proposed that there should be a more positive home life and greater effort by the churches "as a bulwark against evil influences."

While the city manager ignored the goings-on along Twelfth
Street, he did attack and take action against what he declared to be
"evil" undertakings. For instance, the El Torreon Ballroom held a
walkathon, with the last couple still awake on the dance floor the
winner of a money prize. Large crowds paid to watch the suffering
twosomes, with Red Skelton, a budding comedian, entertaining the
audience as master of ceremonies. The walkathon was a highly
popular venture for three weeks when McElroy sent men to the El
Torreon to end it. Asked on what grounds he took such action, Mc-
Elroy snapped, "Coffee grounds."

That T. J. had squelched his local opposition was apparent as
early as the fall of 1927 when he and his family went on a lavish
three-month tour of Europe. At various stops, he sent a single post-
card back to his Goats, as at Tours, France, when his message began: "As it is impossible to write to all members, I am taking this
means of letting you all know that I think of all at some time or
other on my trip. . . . Paris is a wonderful city. I found no evidence
of bitterness or price gouging."

Home at last, when he stepped from his railroad car into Union
Station, the welcoming crowd was so large that it choked all traffic
outdoors, and T. J. was presented with enough flowers to bury sev-

eral Chicago gangsters in style. "A reporter met me on the ship in
New York," T. J. responded to cries of "Speech! Speech!" . . . "and
told me of the awful state of affairs out here. He did not scare me
one bit. I told him I would bet any odds he liked to name it was just
the outs trying to put ignominy upon the ins, and that I had played
that game myself many a time. I get home and find things fine."

The nerve center for the world of T. J. was a most improbable
setting for such a pervasive enterprise. Beginning in 1926, he established permanent headquarters for the Jackson Democratic Club on
the second floor of a yellowish brick building over a cafe and wholesale pillowcase and bedsheet store at 1908 Main Street. The building was in a shabby part of the downtown business district about a
mile and a half from city hall, and clanging streetcars rolled past it
throughout the day.

At the top of the creaking staircase, the club occupied three
rooms. One was an unkempt hall large enough for meetings of the
top layers of the organization, the second a waiting room lined with
chairs, and the last the private office of the "Chairman of the Executive Board," as T. J. titled himself. The meeting hall walls held pictures of a trio of staunch Democrats—Tom Pendergast, Woodrow
Wilson, and U. S. Senator Jim Reed—the waiting room smelled of
old paint over rotting wood, and the inner sanctum of the leader
contained on old rolltop desk on a wall-to-wall, frayed, faded green
12-foot-square rug, a few chairs, a brass spittoon, a yellowing
framed *Star* cartoon on the wall of his brother Jim holding a ballot
box, and pictures on his desk of his wife and their children, Tom, Jr.,
and daughters Marceline and Aileen. There was also a black up-
right phone on his desk for barking orders to his lieutenants around
town.

Once T. J. was firmly in power, an enormous number of persons craved favors from him personally, and he made himself directly available to them on a first-come, first-served basis. It was not
uncommon to see a governor or Congressman waiting patiently for
hours and not being accorded priority over a derelict who had
climbed the stairs before them.

T. J. rose every morning at 4:30 A.M., ate a plain breakfast,
and then went by limousine to 1908 Main Street, where he entered
his office through a secret entrance. His arrival—usually by six
o'clock—was noted by Cap'n Elijah Matheus, a tall, muscular man
who had once been a steamboat pilot and was now the majordomo

of T. J.'s waiting room. Cap'n Matheus knew the order of appear-ance of each of the 200 or 300 persons who showed up daily to choke the anteroom and flood into the hall, and when Pendergast was ready to begin, Matheus led the first person into his office.

T. J. sat in a comfortable swivel chair behind his desk during his public hours and always motioned the visitor to take the little hard chair facing him. Tom wore his gray flannel hat in the office and doffed it only when a woman visitor entered. But neither sex dared hope for an exchange of amenities. He would slide to the edge of his chair, his eyes never leaving those of his guest, while his voice boomed, "Well, what's yours?"

Impatient hand gestures ordered the visitor to hurry imme-diately to the reason for his call. If anyone hesitated or started to stray, T. J. rudely demanded a straightforward, short statement, and when the issue was clarified—the need for a job, desire for a hand-out, or a plea for political support—T. J. would then restate the re-quest and give his decision. It could be a flip of a half dollar to a bum, an assurance of "I'll do that" to a political hopeful, or a scrib-ble on a piece of paper torn from a brown grocery bag ordering a city official to give the bearer a job or handle his problem without de-lay. Seldom did a visitor get more than five minutes of T. J.'s time, and as he opened the door to leave, T. J.'s loud voice would come through to Cap'n Matheus: "All right. Who's next?"

T. J. frequently held political business meetings in his office. Once when County Judge Harry Truman found himself involved in a snarling crisis with top-level Goats because he would not approve their dishonest county contracts, T. J. ordered him to come to 1908 Main Street.

"I went," said Truman, "and there were all the crooked con-tractors that caused the scandals: Boyle and Pryor and Ross." Ross was T. J.'s partner in one construction company. "These boys tell me you won't give them contracts, Harry," T. J. began the meeting.

"Ross as spokesman," said Truman, "demanded that the con-tracts go to local bidders. They gave me the old song and dance about being local citizens and taxpayers and that they should have an inside track to the construction contracts."

When Ross finished his browbeating effort. Truman failed to collapse. "You can get contracts if you're low bidders," he snapped at Ross. "But you won't be paid for them unless they come up to speci-fications."

Before Ross and the others could lambast the upstart further,

Pendergast let out an immense laugh. "I told you, Bill," he said finally to Ross, "he's the contrariest man on earth."

"I'm not being contrary," Truman remembered contradicting T. J. "I was just proceeding in the legal and business manner."

T. J. brought the meeting to an abrupt close. "Get out of here," he ordered his lieutenants. And when they were gone, he assured Truman, "You carry out your commitments."

At the time—and even years later—Truman claimed that this showed T. J. would stand with a man who was honest. But, in truth, the chief Goat was feeling no pain. No matter who landed the contracts T. J. had to be the winner. For it was understood that every road had to be made of Pendergast's Ready-Mixed Concrete, and every old, country road had to be topped with oil from Tom and Mike Pendergast's oil company. Had Truman questioned this rule, he would have quickly learned of Tom's angry reaction.

By lunchtime, Tom's public hours were over, and after Matheus brought him soup and salad from the cafe below, he finished his meal and went to his Ready-Mixed Concrete Co. office a few blocks away to take care of business matters. Ready-Mixed was a gold mine netting him $500,000 a year, chiefly because all holders of city and county contracts found it wise to use T. J.'s concrete. In addition, he had gone into a lucrative insurance business with Emmett O'Malley, whom he had unsuccessfully promoted for mayor a decade earlier. Businessmen flocked to buy their insurance from him, and drugstores promoted the cigars produced by another company he and O'Malley owned. T. J. also owned a thriving softdrink bottling firm. When reporters came snooping about for evidence that T. J. was using his political power for business favors for his own companies, he was incensed. "I live here, am a businessman here, own property here, pay all my taxes here," he told one reporter. "Does any man say I have not a right to make a living here?"

As a rule, T. J. ended his workday in time to reach his home before dark, for he believed his enemies had paid killers hovering in the shadows. Outside of a love for expensive tailor-made suits, the best automobiles, and trips to Europe, his wants were simple; and he did not drink, smoke cigars, chase after women, or play golf or cards. Nor did he belong to country clubs or enjoy night life, for he customarily went to bed at 9:00 P.M.

However, he did crave luxury in his physical surroundings at home, in contrast to 1908 Main Street; and those who visited his

$150,000 French Regency style mansion at 5650 Ward Parkway in the exclusive part of town talked about it afterward with some awe. The interior was elegant Louis XV with paneled walls on the first floor and rugs like a thick lawn. The second-floor bedrooms had special color schemes, and T. J.'s, for example, had blue wallpaper, blue drapes, a blue bedspread, and blue sheets. His wide closet held enough suits to bury a few dozen Goats.

T. J. lavished material splendor on his wife and children in the form of cars, clothes, and jewelry, and he employed several servants to cater to their whims at home. Just how doting a father was T. J. was revealed in 1929 when his house was burglarized. Mrs. Pendergast estimated that she had lost jewelry costing $150,000, and daughter Marceline was robbed of forty dozen pairs of silk hosiery. Safe was the paper money roll of $3,000 that T. J. had tucked under his mattress. Mayor Beach, now reduced to a pathetic figurehead, told reporters after the robbery, "Among the jewelry taken was a six-inch bar pin worth $10,000. That is more than my house cost."

T. J.'s protective attitude toward his family was legendary. One time when he received a phone call with the false report that his son, Tom, Jr., had been kidnapped, he ordered two of the city's leading underground figures to come immediately to 1908 Main Street. When they arrived, he gave them two hours to retrieve his boy, and in his anxiety knocked one man down with an uppercut and punched the other through a glass door. Young Tom was finally located at Rockhurst College, where he had been attending classes that day.

The first big test the Pendergast machine faced after gaining undisputed political authority came in 1930 when county and city elections were held. T. J.'s brother Mike had died in 1929, and County Judge Truman claimed priority as his successor in rural Jackson County in controlling the 11,000 Goat vote there. T. J. never gave him this title officially, but he treated him with increased friendliness afterward. In the county, Truman was running for his second four-year term as presiding judge, and even the Republican Kansas City *Star* was supporting him because of his successful and honest road program.

In the city elections, Mayor Beach found his prime target in T. J.'s use of his bossdom to become a concrete-making millionaire. Regarding Pendergast's enforced monopoly for his concrete, Beach cited "a certain big building where there was a refusal at first to buy Ready-Mixed Concrete. The builder was forced to tear out footings installed . . . because it had been claimed it [sic] had been damaged by 'frost.' The result was the builder then bought Ready-Mixed." A grand jury, obviously composed of Goats, was assigned to check Beach's charge. Its report was that no evidence existed of T. J.'s wrongdoing and that Beach's accusation had "a distinct political aspect."

Had Beach been more aware of T. J.'s other business monopolies, he might have added stories about Pendergast's Midwest Asphalt Co., Midwest Paving Co., Midwest Pro-Cote Co., Kansas City Concrete Pipe Co., Sanitary Service Co., and Standard Sales Co. But T. J. had hidden his ownership in these corporations so carefully that he felt he was completely safe in not listing the profits from any of them in his income tax returns.

T. J. knew from reports by his lieutenants and from the fawning of the business community that his continued control of the city would be reaffirmed in the election; and if he had any lingering doubts, he had only to reread the strange editorial in the *Star* that said: "For the last four years, with all its faults and failures, Kansas City probably has had the most efficient city government in its history."

But despite his sure thing, T. J. was so prone to an overkill policy that he could not refrain from old Goat election tactics. On election day, when his boys brought word to him that the Republican chairman of the county planned to announce evidence of fraudulent voting in the city, T. J. had his lads kidnap the man, treat him to a painful beating, and hold him prisoner until after the vote was counted.

The results of the vote count surprised no one: T. J.'s team won all eight city council seats, and Tom's choice for mayor, Bryce B. Smith, rich breadmaker and Rotarian leader, won easily over Mayor Beach. The first order of business of the Goat nine was to continue Henry McElroy as city manager. He made his acceptance speech at the council meeting before they actually took their vote, causing his daughter Mary who was present to upset the decorum by laughing hysterically.

In this election also, T. J. finally got rid of Joe Shannon's Rabbits for good. Shannon was sixty-three now, and he was quick to accept Pendergast's offer to put him into the U. S. House of Representatives. So Joe Shannon went to Washington as an errand boy for T. J., a spokesman for the chamber of commerce, and as champion of his hero, Thomas Jefferson.

The election was hardly over before Tom Pendergast gave his blessing to the "Kansas City Ten-Year Plan," a large-scale public works program. Two years earlier, his reputation had been temporarily damaged when McElroy's $28 million bond issue failed at a special election. But now with the entire city council and mayor in his possession, he didn't see how the Ten-Year Plan could lose.

The plan called for an expenditure of $40 million, including $8 million for Truman county projects, and its coverage was so extensive that William Allen White, the "sage of Emporia," hailed it in his *Gazette* as "the monument to the Depression." Under McElroy's direction, the city would gain a block-square auditorium, a skyscraper city hall, a courthouse, a police station, parks, playgrounds, hospital wings, sewer system expansion, and a new road system "second only to Westchester County, New York."

The Ten-Year Plan bond issue passed by a four to one vote, and once the bonds were sold, T. J.'s pocketbook never had it so good, despite the worsening Depression. His Ready-Mixed Concrete trucks were scurrying all over the county, and to keep up with the demand he had to add to his fleet. But not satisfied solely with worthwhile projects, his desire for profits led to his involvement in one scandalous program. This was his paving of Brush Creek, an anemic little stream that traveled through the city. At completion, Brush Creek was found to possess an eight-inch underbed of Ready-Mixed Concrete that was 80 feet wide in some areas.

Individuals who had been suspicious of McElroy's country bookkeeping and contract letting in the past were even more suspicious of the way he was handling construction under the Ten-Year Plan. But McElroy fought off all their attempts to see his records, and it was not until 1939 that accountants found that fully a fourth of his contracts had not been let according to the rules.

T. J.'s victory in the 1930 city and county elections soon cast a long political shadow over the state government and the Missouri members of the U.S. House of Representatives. The "Show Me" state's slow rate of population increase compared with other states, as noted in the 1930 census, cost Missouri three of its sixteen seats in the U.S. House and forced a remapping of its congressional districts. However, when the Democratic state legislature and Republican Governor Henry Caulfield failed to agree on a redistricting plan, all candidates for the U.S. House in 1932 had to run as statewide candidates-at-large instead of from single districts.

After the at-large campaigning became inevitable, all would-be House candidates reached the same conclusion: The man in the upstairs room at 1908 Main Street in Kansas City held the balance of power. For T. J. could give a candidate 50,000 to 100,000 votes, enough to offset the results in the rest of the state. Little wonder that Cap'n Matheus saw the anteroom fill daily early in 1932 with politicians from every part of the state who had come to ask for Tom's blessing. Some he annointed; others he bluntly told to get out; and in time when he had the thirteen men he favored, he handed his slate for the Democratic primary to the *Star,* which printed it on June 5, 1932.

T. J. had choices, too, for judges on the State Supreme Court and lower courts, for U.S. Senator and Governor. Harry Truman yearned for the governorship, but T. J. considered his aspiration ridiculous. He gave his support instead to his old friend Francis M. Wilson.

T. J. also had his own choice for President. He had been to New York where Al Smith glumly put it on the line to him that the Irish should support each other. Jim Farley, who was Governor Franklin D. Roosevelt's advance man, had come through Kansas City, where he spoke straight from the shoulder from one Irishman to another to win support for FDR. Then there were the friends of U.S. House Speaker Jack Garner who wanted T. J.'s help to keep the East from running the party. But T. J.'s answer had been to clasp aging Jim Reed to his burly chest as his man for the White House. Since 1900, when Jim Pendergast made Reed mayor, the machine had been instrumental in making him a three-term U.S. Senator. However, although T. J. dominated the state convention, and selected a slate of thirty-six Reed delegates to the national convention, he was shrewd enough not to approve an order to the delegates to remain frozen on Reed until the end of all balloting. He also showed the state convention his physical strength had not waned when he knocked an arguing delegate unconscious with a short slap on the cheek.

Late in June, 1932, T. J. came to Chicago with an entourage of 400 Missouri Democrats, including Judge Truman, whom he had refused a delegate's seat. Academic graduate studies later purported to prove that T. J. was for Franklin Roosevelt. But only after Roosevelt's victory became certain on the fourth ballot did T. J. hurriedly assemble his delegation before the final count was announced and give Missouri to the winner.

T. J. had a thermometer reading of his immense statewide power when all except one man of his home-slate candidates won in 1932. The single loser was Charles M. Howell, Jim Reed's former law partner, who ran in the primary for the U.S. Senate against Bennett Clark, son of former House Speaker Champ Clark. Tom gave Howell 90,000 votes in Jackson County to only 8,000 for Clark. But even this could not overcome Clark's 187,000 lead in the rest of the state, and Clark won by 95,000 votes.

In another contest, T. J. had been forced to make a change in his slate. Four weeks before the general election in November, 1932, his old friend Francis Wilson died of stomach cancer, and T. J. had to scramble for a new gubernatorial candidate. Despite the appeal of top Democrats for his approval, Pendergast reached far down into the local political scene in Platte City north of Kansas City and plucked unknown Circuit Court Judge Guy B. Park for the honor and put him into the governor's mansion.

So early in 1933, T. J. had a chorus of helpers in the U.S. House of Representatives and political control of his state, county, and city. His power was so awesome to newsmen on the scene that they were soon referring to his little room on Main Street as the "state capitol" and the structure in Jefferson City, housing the state legislature, as "Uncle Tom's Cabin."

Like a boulder cast into a stream, T. J. was to make a big splash beyond this parochial area during the next few years. Despite his failure to hop aboard the early Roosevelt boat, the new administration realistically assessed Missouri as the property of Thomas Joseph Pendergast and gave him a major share of New Deal patronage and money in his state. While Roosevelt barred Reconstruction Finance Corporations loans to Kansas City and Jackson County, almost every other Federal program was made available to the Goat boss, who played a major role in the selection of state administrators, the distribution of Federal money, and the determination of which unfortunate citizens would be helped. T. J. was fond of saying, "You can't beat $5 billion," to note how the New Deal money availability had overwhelmed and outmoded the techniques of the old-style local boss, who passed out food baskets and pails of coal. But T. J.'s words formed a smoke screen for his own increased power under the New Deal.

The largest power maker for T. J. was the various Federal relief programs. In one program alone, the Civil Works Administration (CWA), Pendergast's Missouri *Democrat* boasted that the machine had found jobs for 200,000 Missourians. The paper failed to mention how much Ready-Mixed Concrete this army used. T. J. also had control of the state's Works Progress Administration (WPA), the Federal work relief program succeeding CWA. State WPA director was Matthew Murray, who had worked previously for the Ross Construction Co. and as an assistant at city hall to City Manager McElroy. The large number of district WPA directors under Murray soon learned they were expected to spend much of their time "encouraging" those on work relief to vote for Pendergast candidates.

One Federal relief administrator continually wary about cooperating with the Missouri boss was Secretary of the Interior Harold Ickes, who also directed the Public Works Administration. McElroy was able to obtain over a million dollars from WPA to help complete the Kansas City auditorium, but Ickes would not accept the Ross Construction Co. bid and ordered new ones. An outside contractor won it this time, and Ickes ordered scores of inspectors to roam the site during construction and safeguard Federal money from T. J.'s skulduggery.

If T. J. ever gave thought to what was the ideal period of his life, no doubt he would have picked 1927 or early 1928. For his political power was solidly entrenched and expanding; his wealth from his various businesses had made him a millionaire; and his horse-race betting was still moderate and fun. But by mid-1928, an upsetting factor had made its appearance, and his name was John Lazia. Lazia was a gangster.

When T. J.'s wife had prevailed on him years earlier to move out of the run-down North Side to a stylish neighborhood, Tom's top political lieutenant and business partner, Mike Ross, personally took over the Goat organization there at T. J.'s request. Like T. J., Ross lived on the South Side, but he had a way with the "Eyetalians" in the North Side's Little Italy, and he kept the Goat votes coming by handing out jobs as ditchdiggers to the Sicilians who crowded the mean ghetto and by taking care of many of the problems of the poor self-employed who peddled fruit and vegetables from horse-drawn wagons.

Mike Ross made a practice of enticing the brighter sons of the Italian immigrants into his Democratic Club, using them to keep a watch on their voting elders and do the necessary legwork in delivering food baskets and the votes. The brightest and most aggressive of these youngsters was Johnny Lazia, son of a street laborer. Born in 1897, Johnny quit school after the eighth grade to get on with the business of life.

For a time he worked as a clerk in a large law firm, but in 1915 when he was eighteen, he turned to crime as the fastest route to success. However, he was caught after his first robbery.

It took Mike Ross' sly intervention with the lieutenant-governor when the governor was away to win Lazia's parole; and after serving only eight months of a fifteen-year sentence, Johnny was back on the streets of the North Side. He told Mike now he was going straight; and while Ross gave him one small political assignment after another, Johnny quietly went into the bootlegging business and started gambling. By the mid-twenties, he was a good-looking, sallow-faced young man, soft-spoken and generally smiling, a dude in style and dress, whose appearance was marred only by the large wad of gum he slowly chewed. His sharp outdoor attire included a big, gray felt hat, kid gloves, a cane and sometimes a concealed revolver, though he generally depended for his safety on Big Charley Carollo, his bodyguard.

All the while Lazia was learning the techniques of neighborhood political control from Mike Ross, he and his followers in the Young Sons of Italy grew more resentful that an Irishman—and an absentee one himself—was the boss of Little Italy. The explosion came in May, 1928, on the day Kansas voted down City Manager McElroy's first proposed bond issue for public works. This was the day Lazia chose for his power fight with Ross over the control of the North Side, and early that morning his gang of young hoodlums captured Ross' lieutenants and ward heelers and took over the polling places. After the voting ended and Lazia determined the vote totals, he sped in his curtained sedan to Ringside Hall where his faction had gathered to celebrate. At his entrance, the crowd chanted, "Johnny! Johnny!" and the brass band played, "Here Comes the King."

When Lazia sent notice to 1908 Main Street that he was now the boss of the North Side, T. J. told reporters that Johnny was a little punk and Mike Ross was still his lieutenant there. But Mike did not dare set foot in Little Italy, and a few days after the bond issue election T. J. called Lazia to a meeting. Lazia turned out to be a youthful thirty-one with a vocabulary that showed he used the dictionary and a gum-chewing habit that seemed to taunt and mock others in his company. T. J. took a practical appraisal of the situation on the North Side: There were too many thousands of votes in his old home territory he would lose if he offended Lazia. As for Mike Ross, they would still be partners in construction and cement.

So Ross was sacrificed within a week and forced to the shame of attending a rally of the North Side Democratic Club where he publicly endorsed Johnny Lazia as his successor. It did not take long after that before T. J. found Johnny so useful that he made him his top lieutenant, and they developed a warm friendship. The Goat machine became the Pendergast-Lazia organization, despite the outcry of Cas Welch, T. J.'s allied boss of the sixth and eighth wards, and Welch's hoodlum associate, Joe Lusco.

If Kansas City was a wide-open town before Johnny Lazia took charge of its organized vice, it was a crime haven afterward. Johnny had a few legitimate businesses to which he could point when the accusations started to fly that he was a gangster, but even these legitimate activities were run in a mobster's fashion. For example, Lazia owned a company producing a softdrink called Golden Mist. Retailers promoted it to top selling status in the softdrink field when Lazia set purchasing quotas for them and threatened them with bombings or arrest if they failed to keep up with their buying. Once when the circus came to Jackson County, Lazia ordered trucks to jam the unloading platforms until the circus manager agreed to buy a certain amount of Golden Mist.

Lazia was a superb organizer, and he claimed he learned about bookkeeping in his eight months in prison. Both attributes were given wide play, for on the basis of being Pendergast's top lieutenant, he moved swiftly and with authority to organize his own crime syndicate. He controlled the slot machine and numbers rackets, prostitution, bootleg liquor distribution, gambling joints, and the most profitable nightclub speakeasies. One of his enterprises was the giant Cuban Gardens gambling casino adjacent to Pendergast's racetrack north of town in Clay County. His casino was protected by heavily armed hoods, though at intervals Lazia let the sheriff stage nonevidence-gathering raids to satisfy the antigambling crusade of the local clergy.

Where T. J. would reward a ward heeler with a political job, Johnny rewarded his lads by putting them into his vice businesses. A select few were given the jobs of tossing stinkbombs where Johnny thought they were needed and taking certain individuals for a ride; others became his toll collectors who called regularly on businessmen and fellow racketeers for "insurance" payments that permitted them to stay in business. Federal investigators later estimated that smiling, gum-chewing John Lazia was earning $2 million a year from one of the many rackets he ran.

It was chiefly for Lazia's benefit that T. J. and McElroy undertook to discourage the Republican-appointed police director, Major John Miles, and drive him into retirement in the late 1920s. Then to put an end to outside control of the police department, T. J.'s lawyers tried to get the state legislature to grant authority over the police department to the city and remove the governor's jurisdiction in this area. When this effort stalled, T. J.'s attorneys brought suit on behalf of City Manager McElroy to the State Supreme Court to give the city home rule over the police; and finally the court obliged Pendergast by declaring the existing statute unconstitutional.

Old McElroy now named Eugene C. Reppert as police director after Lazia gave his approval, and Johnny expanded his activities to include the direction of the police director. Over seventy cops were later found to be Lazia appointees and many others were former convicts. Private citizens reported that on occasion when they phoned Police Chief Reppert, Lazia answered at the other end of the line. McElroy's expressed view on the relationship of Lazia to the police was that Johnny helped keep the crime rate down.

A world atlas of 1930 referred to Kansas City as "the largest marketing and wholesaling center for hay, stock hogs and stock and feed cattle in the U.S." However, the view of Kansas City by the St. Louis *Post -Dispatch* was of another side of the metropolis. "The underworld has got the upper hand," the newspaper noted. "Organized lawlessness is the law. An irresponsible political machine concerned solely with spoils is in full, terrifying control."

Rather than attempt to fight Lazia, T. J. took the easier route of denying that Kansas City was a criminal's paradise. "I have been around quite a bit," he confided to a *Star* reporter. "There are all kinds of people in a political organization, just as there are in the world. Among them are the best and others who take advantage.

"In recent months I have been in New York, Philadelphia, Chicago and other places, resorts and otherwise. I say there is more gambling in these cities than there is in Kansas City. So far as rackets are concerned, I can say advisedly that Kansas City is freer from racketeering than any city of its size in the country. I say that Kansas City is the standout city of the country so far as the protection of its city by the police is concerned."

Of course, T. J. knew better, but he was increasing his horse bets by that time and to help pay off some losses he had started to get a "cut of the lug," as Lazia's income tax on gambling racketeers in town was called. Nor was he in the dark about Lazia's kindly gesture in inviting big-time gangsters on the lam to use Kansas City as a vacation spot without concern about police troubles. Johnny had assured T. J. that despite his invitations his vice guests would not involve themselves in "messy crimes" while in town, and with few exceptions they were exemplary guests.

Having failed to gather the needed evidence to jail mobsters for their criminal activities, the Hoover administration had developed the technique of prosecuting them for income tax violation; and one of the Hoover legacies to Roosevelt was the tedious amassing of data on Johnny Lazia's record of undeclared income that finally led to his indictment in March, 1933. But T. J. interceded with Jim Farley, Roosevelt's chief political aide, and the U.S. district attorney in Kansas City announced he was laying the case aside "on orders from Washington."

"My Dear Jim," T. J. had written Farley, "Lazia . . . has been in trouble with the income tax department for some time. I know it is simply a case of being jobbed because of his Democratic activities. . . . I wish you would use your utmost endeavor to bring about a settlement of this matter. I cannot make it any stronger than to say that my interest in him is greater than anything that might come up in the future."

Soon after his tax troubles were aired, there was a kidnapping that gained Lazia much favorable publicity. Mary McElroy, daughter of the city manager, was kidnapped on May 27, 1933, and reporters found her father hysterical, with T. J. unable to console him. McElroy, always imperious and rude to the press, now wept and moaned trancelike, "Mary, Mary, my Mary."

This became a job for Johnny Lazia, who went to work raising the ransom and arranging for her safe release. Then he led the search for her abductors. Three of the four were quickly apprehended; and the ringleader had the dubious honor of being the first American sentenced to die for kidnapping. Mary McElroy was the most tearful pleader for the life of one of her abductors because she had fallen in love with him while in their clutches.

From Lazia's efforts in the Mary McElroy kidnapping and others, Kansas City residents were aware that their city had a one-man army to combat such crimes. But on the morning of June 17, 1933, the city became equally aware of the savagery of gangsterism within its boundaries in what became known as the Union Station Massacre. This led to an angry reopening of the income tax case against Johnny Lazia by Attorney General Homer S. Cummings.

According to Federal agents in a later recounting, Johnny Lazia had requested Pretty Boy Floyd and killer Adam Richetti to meet with gangster Verne Miller on the night of June 16. Verne Miller wanted the meeting because he had received a phone call for help from the wife of Frank "Jelly" Nash. Nash, who had escaped from Leavenworth three years before, had been caught, and the FBI was returning him to jail. His train was scheduled to reach Kansas City at 7:00 A.M., and he was to be transported from Union Station by car back to Leavenworth. The three men, Miller, Floyd, and Richetti, all of whom were on the FBI's "most wanted list," worked out a plan to liberate Nash, and it seemed simple for men of their bravado.

The next morning seven officers led manacled Nash out of Union Station to the parking lot where they put him into the front seat of a car. Five of the officers were about to climb in when Verne Miller, toting a machine gun, approached and ordered them to release Nash. Similarly armed and standing behind Miller were Pretty Boy and Richetti, and the logical action by the officers would have been to comply. But one fired his gun, wounding Pretty Boy Floyd in the shoulder, and the three criminals opened fire. By the time the three fled the scene, four officers lay dead, two were seriously wounded, and Nash had fallen over the steering wheel, accidently killed by his rescuers.

In the days following the carnage at Union Station, an outcry of fright and shame was heard in Kansas City. Nor was the massacre kept local, for newspapers across the nation condemned the city as a bossed town in league with criminals. In a public relations rejoinder, Pendergast had McElroy and Police Director Reppert issue statements insisting that the Union Station outrage had been the work of "outside" criminals who would have used any other city for their action if Nash's train had stopped there.

But this failed to stop the growing crescendo of rumors that Lazia had been involved, and two months later T. J. took it upon himself to squelch these stories in an interview with reporters. "I have made it a policy to find the good in everyone, not the bad," he said. "I believe some have been charging Lazia with many things he had nothing to do with or any knowledge of." T. J. also argued that Johnny was not a dominating Goat. "At no time has Lazia tried to dictate the policy of the organization, or has he been given any privileges by the organization."

But T. J. had hardly begun his campaign to make Lazia look respectable when Johnny was in the papers again with more bad news. By accident in August, 1933, Jackson County Sheriff Tom Bash rode into a movieland-type gangster scene one night on Armour Boulevard. Some of Lazia's mob, led by Charles Gargotta, had just "rubbed out" rival gang leader Joe Lusco's lieutenant, Ferris Anthon, by submachine gun bursts. Bash captured Gargotta after the thug emptied a pistol point-blank at him first. Thanks to the perjured testimony of a Kansas City policeman who said Gargotta did not have a gun, Gargotta was not thrown into a cell, but Anthon was dead, and more whispered fears about Johnny Lazia spread through town.

When Lazia's income tax case was reopened in the late summer of 1933, T. J. again tried to use his Washington contacts to head off prosecution. But he failed because President Roosevelt demanded action. Henry Morgenthau, the President's neighbor who became Secretary of the Treasury in January, 1934, confirmed later that when he took office "there were five famous gangsters on the intelligence unit's list of men to get." Lazia's name was at the top of that list.

Lazia finally had to stand trial at the beginning of 1934, and there was concern among his friends because he was shuffled to the court of Federal Judge Merrill E. Otis, noted for the severity of his sentences. But Otis surprised onlookers in February when he sentenced Johnny to a mere year in jail and fined him only $5,000 for income tax evasion. Then when Lazia got out on bail pending an appeal, it seemed reasonable to his persistent lawyers that by asking for endless continuances they might keep him from ever going to prison.

T. J. was especially pleased that Johnny's services were still available to him because the municipal campaigns for mayor and the eight city council spots had begun, and he was edgy about the results. The Union Station Massacre had given a boost to the National Youth Movement (NYM), and Pendergast didn't like the college brats of Kansas City's middle- and upper-income classes in the NYM who were screaming about ridding the city of his machine. Ordinarily, he would not have cared about the noise they were making. But they had the nerve to join with anti-Pendergast Republicans and Democrats to form a political party—the Citizens-Fusion— and not only had candidates to oppose T. J.'s slate but also a 3,000-ward worker force to promote their cause door-to-door. An equally great blow to T. J. was that the influential Kansas City *Star*, which had never really attacked his machine on a sustained basis, now stood unwaveringly behind the upstarts.

However, T. J.'s concern was totally unwarranted. At his order, puppet Governor Guy Park had named Tom's choices as election commissioners, and these Goats had given their approval to a huge registration swindle devised by T. J.'s lieutenants. The total registration as approved was suspicious even on the surface, for it contained 244,000 names of Kansas City voters, a preposterous figure considering that the city had only 399,000 men, women, and children. Then within this figure, T. J. knew there were from 50,000 to 100,000 "ghost" voters for his slate, including thousands of cemetery names and Goat rounders who had registered as many as thirty separate times. Some of the addresses of registered voters were vacant lots, while from single rooms in boardinghouses, 100 persons were listed.

Nevertheless, T. J. was so much in need of the money he earned from his bossdom that he would take no chances. The Citizens-Fusion mayoralty candidate was Dr. A. Ross Hill, the former president of the University of Missouri and currently a Kansas City real estate operator. McElroy could turn his scathing tongue on the elderly Hill and defend T. J.'s helpless and functionless Mayor Bryce Smith, who was running for another term, However, T. J. believed he also needed the talents of Johnny Lazia to make victory certain on March 27, 1934.

That day started poorly for Tom Pendergast, who had always taken pride in being the first to vote at his eighth ward precinct place. Shortly after dawn with the temperature reading 22 degrees, he reached his voting place only to find several NYM girls already in the line; and no matter how much the frightened precinct officers begged and threatened, they refused to step aside to let the boss vote first and keep his record intact.

However, the rest of the day went his way. T. J. had set high quotas of votes for each precinct, and his word to his machine was that the election "has to be won or else!" Lazia, acting like a general, saw to it that T. J.'s order was carried out. By nightfall the city had witnessed its most savage election, with killings, shootings, stabbings, and clubbings occurring in all parts of the metropolitan area.

As the beatings and shootings of Fusionist voters multiplied, Fusionists demanded that Police Director Reppert give them protection. When he refused, they sent telegrams to Governor Park, pleading that he order troops out "to stop further murder and bloodshed." But Park, the puppet of T. J., replied that he was confident such aid was unnecessary, that the local police would handle the situation. Reppert's men did take some action: They arrested four Fusionists.

At day's end, with four persons dead and dozens in hospitals, little Mayor Smith was announced the re-elected winner over Dr. Hill by 60,000 votes, and T. J. also won six of the eight council seats. But the price was high because the election was publicized throughout the nation.

In the public furor that developed after this brutal 1934 city election, T. J. tried to let some of the air out of the opposition's bag by ordering Police Director Reppert to resign and replacing him with Otto P. Higgins, a former *Star* reporter. A few policemen and detectives were noisily reprimanded and fired, and the police force undertook some highly publicized but petty raids against minor vice merchants in order to focus attention on its hard work in behalf of honest citizens.

Within two months after this odious 1934 city election, T. J. had to move on to the job of naming his choice for the U.S. Senate in the Democratic primary; and despite the local stench, he believed this was his year to have a U.S. Senator because of the national Democratic trend. Missouri's encrusted reactionary Republican Senator Roscoe Conkling Patterson, whose six-year term was expiring, had to stand for re-election, and T. J. considered him a sure loser in November.

In going through his assortment of possibilities, T. J. thought first of his old hero, Jim Reed, even though Bridlewise Jim had campaigned for Bennett Clark for the Senate in 1932. But Reed disagreed with his optimism and coldly turned him down. Then Tom offered his support to Joe Shannon. But Shannon was nearly seventy, and he didn't want to give up his safe House seat for a hard primary fight in which he would have to carry the stigma of T. J.'s foul city election of only some weeks earlier. T. J. next offered his backing to Jim Aylward, his attorney and chief political adviser. Again his offer was rejected, for Aylward also believed he would be defeated by angry Democrats across the state because of the city election scandal. On his fourth try, T. J. pulled a "Guy B. Park" out of his hat, and his name was County Judge Harry Truman.

T. J. gave a variety of conflicting reasons for promoting Truman for a skyhigh political office when he had previously refused to make him county collector. One man quoted T. J. as saying: "Frankly, it was a matter of pride to me to name just any man and beat Bennett Clark's candidate." Truman was now secretly an officer in a savings and loan bank, and T. J. told a fellow officer in that bank, "I want to put him in the Senate so I can get rid of him." To a Truman friend, Pendergast pessimistically said, "I don't feel that Harry Truman has a chance." Yet he optimistically told a reporter that Senators represented big business interests in their state, and "he decided he wanted to have his own emissary there." Later he changed "emissary" to "office boy."

By coincidence, Truman's campaign opening speech came only a few days before Johnny Lazia's ending. Shortly after midnight on July 10, Lazia, his pretty wife Marie, and menacing "Big Charley the Wop" Carollo, after a visit to one of the downtown Kansas City nightspots Johnny owned, headed for the Park Central Hotel on Armour Boulevard where the Lazias had a glittering apartment. When the car reached the hotel, Johnny the gentleman climbed out first and kept the door open for his wife. Immediately, a submachine gun rattled off, and Johnny dropped to the ground. Tough Johnny was only thirty-seven and in excellent health, factors that kept him alive twelve hours. "Doc," he cried out, "why would anyone do this to Johnny Lazia, who's been the friend to everyone?" His last words reputedly were, "Tell Tom Pendergast I love him."

Out on the campaign trail, never-say-die Harry Truman carefully worked to combat the effort of his opponents, Congressmen John J. Cochran of St. Louis and Jacob Milligan, sponsored by Senator Bennett Clark, who were tying him to Lazia through Tom Pendergast. "I live in Independence, not Kansas City," Truman said loudly. "I've never voted in Kansas City in my life." Spunky Truman worked himself thin in an intensive speaking tour of sixty counties, and he revealed himself a sad campaigner with a voice that was a cross between an Ozark twang and the slurred, hurried cry of a mule auctioneer.

But nothing mattered except the audacious dishonesty of the sponsors behind the candidates. On primary night in August, 1934, the vote outside of Jackson County showed Cochran had 235,000, Truman 139,000, and Milligan a few hundred votes behind him. St. Louis Democratic boss, Bill Igoe, whose machine backed Cochran, was ready to celebrate, for even though Jackson County's votes were not yet in, Jackson County had given Cochran 100,000 votes two years earlier when he ran his at-large race for the House.

However, there was a reason why Kansas City and the rest of Jackson County waited until the entire vote of the rest of the state was known before announcing its own results. T. J. had to be absolutely certain how many votes Truman needed to overcome any lead by his opponents. He knew Igoe's vote was as crooked as his own, and he had no intention of letting the St. Louis boss outmaneuver him. When the Jackson County totals were finally announced, Truman had 137,000, Milligan 9,000, and Cochran the tiny ripple of only 1,500. Truman was declared the statewide winner by 40,000 votes and Igoe was in no position to complain.

In November, 1934, when Truman beat Republican Senator Patterson by 262,000 votes, T. J. seemed to have risen again to a new plateau of power. The strongest boss in the nation, newspaper editorials called him. But events were building up that made T. J. uneasy.

With Lazia underground, T. J. had an opportunity to sever his ties with racketeers. However, when "Big Charley the Wop" Carollo took over the Lazia empire, T. J. continued as before, accepting both a "cut of the lug" on forced payoffs and Carollo's political assistance.

T. J. had an excuse for doing so. According to one of his associates, shortly after the municipal election of 1934, Pendergast bet $10,000 on a long shot in a horse race and won $250,000. This single race was to prove his eventual ruination, for from that point on, what had been his chief avocation now became a compulsive obsession.

In the morning he began driving to the Riverside track in Platte County to watch the horses work out at sunrise before he went to 1908 Main Street. He still had his remarkable powers of concentration, and during the morning he conducted his first-come, first-serve meetings with favor pleaders just as he had before. But after lunch, instead of going directly to his office at the Ready-Mixed Concrete Co., he would yell out to Cap'n Elijah Matheus, "Where the hell is Offut?"

Roy Offut was his personal tout, and Roy came each day when T. J. was in town. In the quiet of the little room, the two would pore over racing sheets covering that day's handicaps at the various tracks. In addition, T. J. frequently was telephoned by jockeys and other touts around the country who called in their tips for a price; and when all this racing intelligence about the condition of tracks, horses, and jockeys was hashed over and restudied, he would determine the horses he would back that day. In a single afternoon, he could bet $50,000, with $5,000 on one race, and in a twelve-month period the betting might come to $2 million.

R. J. Brewster, one of Pendergast's attorneys, offered the following picture of T. J.'s miserable obsession: "He told me that when the afternoon was here, he would go into a little room, and there he would take the form sheet, and with the advice of a friend he would handicap these horses, and then he would sit with the telephone at his ear and he would hear a call, 'They're at the post!' Later: 'They're off!' And so over that telephone by ear and not by eye, he watched those horses run to the finish line—all the thrill that can ever come to any man for that which possesses him and which he cannot down."

In his own businesses or in politics, T. J. would never have tolerated a Roy Offut because he seldom delivered. But in racing, Pendergast was remarkably forgiving. At a thirty-day meet in New York in 1935, Offut's misguided selections cost T. J. $600,000. Yet he went on with Offut instead of dropping him.

Other tipsters who worked the bettors on tracks from the Atlantic seaboard to the Pacific had a code name for the Missouri boss —"America's Number One Sucker." They flocked about him like vultures when they heard he was outside of Kansas City, and they created bedlam offering him sure things. On one occasion when Senator Harry Truman and his secretary, Victor Messall, visited T. J. in his twenty-ninth-floor suite at the Waldorf-Astoria in New York, Messall reported the folly that was consuming America's Number

One Sucker. "T. J.'s penthouse looked just like a stockbroker's office," said Messall. "It was a madhouse with ticker-tape machines bringing him racetrack news and results, and the place was filled with jockeys and bookies. He told us that some jockeys had double-crossed him with wrong tips and he almost killed a few of them."

Even though his political activities were never known to have worried his family, T. J.'s racing craze did. At his Ward Parkway mansion, evenings turned into a tedious repetition of pleas by his wife, son, and two daughters that he quit his gambling; and as often as not T. J. agreed to do so. "You're right," he would say. "I swear I'll never bet on another horse again." But the next day as track time approached, he would yell for Offut once more.

To a man of T. J.'s large income, his sizeable bets would have been no cause for alarm had he won even a third of the time. But the relentlessness of his losses soon endangered his entire empire. First there was the considerable profit from his Ready-Mixed Concrete and other Pendergast construction products concerns. T. J. had also been smart enough to turn in his liquor supplies at prohibition time to the Federal government for warehouse receipts instead of pouring them down the drain; and as soon as the Eighteenth Amendment was repealed in 1933 by the Twenty-first Amendment, T. J. got a jump on competitors by trading in his receipts for liquor and re-establishing the highly successful Pendergast Wholesale Liquor Co.

However, the profits from all these endeavors were not sufficient to meet the continual need for cash that his betting required. As a result, Charley Carollo had to increase T. J.'s cut of the lug to 40 percent. In addition, City Manager McElroy had to engage in some more country bookkeeping to cover T. J.'s diversion of tax money, and Pendergast's business partners were forced to give him large cash advances on their future business. Bill Boyle, one of T. J.'s partners, frequently roused John Pryor, another partner, in the middle of the night to get $10,000 to $100,000 in cash for T. J. by the next afternoon. "I told Boyle that T. J.'s craze for betting was going to get us all in trouble," Pryor was reported to have complained. "Boyle said we had to come through. I told Bill several times that giving T. J. all that money would ruin us and T. J. both."

T. J.'s need for cash seemed never-ending as he retained his title as America's Number One Sucker. This search for betting money was to lead him into a major blunder in January, 1935, when he set the stage for what was to evolve into a $750,000 bribe for himself from a group of 137 fire insurance companies doing business in Missouri.

The story had its beginning fifteen years earlier in 1922 when the Missouri superintendent of insurance reduced fire insurance rates 10 percent. The companies fought this through state and Federal courts to the U.S. Supreme Court, where the ruling went against them. Despite this, they raised their rates 16 2/3 percent in 1929, and when the state insurance superintendent rejected this increase, they again went to court. In this new action, a Federal judge permitted the companies to continue collecting these excess premiums but ordered the money put in escrow until a final determination could be reached. By 1935, this impounded money was almost $10 million.

At T. J.'s request, his puppet governor, Guy Park, had appointed as state insurance superintendent Emmett O'Malley, whom Pendergast had unsuccessfully run for mayor back in 1916.

Shortly after the start of 1935, O'Malley took a trip to St. Louis where he asked Alphonsus Logouri McCormack, president of the Missouri Insurance Agents Association, if the fire insurance companies were interested in a favorable settlement of the escrow fund matter, and if so what would they be willing to pay for this kind deed.

McCormack's response was to arrange a meeting in some rented rooms at the Palmer House in Chicago between T. J. and Charles R. Street, vice president of an insurance company and the tough representative of the fire insurance combine. Street, who was known as a hard-as-nails executive, was not the least bit awed by the political boss for he knew about his gambling mania and looked upon him as a pleader. A fair bribe would have been perhaps the sum of $2 million. But under the circumstances, Street offered T. J. only $200,000. When T. J. called this ridiculous, Street raised it to $500,000 without taking a breath, and Tom accepted it. During the negotiations, T. J. asked to use a phone and he placed a call to Kansas City. "Bet $10,000 on 'Flying Dere' to win," he barked into the mouthpiece and hung up. Later, the fire insurance companies weighed what might happen if they held T. J. to Street's stingy bargaining, and they raised the bribe to $750,000.

T. J. kept his part of the bargain. Not long afterward, O'Malley handed Governor Park a settlement document that would give the insurance companies 50 percent of the money held in escrow (almost $5 million), plus another 30 percent to cover the cost of law suits against the state and policyholders. The remaining 20 percent, or less than $2 million of the $10 million, was to be distributed among the thousands of policyholders.

When Park sent the proposed agreement, as the law required, to Attorney General Roy McKittrick, even though he was a loyal Goat, McKittrick gulped at this sell-out and recommended its rejection as a bald steal. Park reacted by telling him, "Yes, you're right. I am a lawyer myself and I can see flaws in the document." But an hour later, after Park phoned T. J., the governor hurriedly signed the settlement into law, setting off roars of anger by representatives of the policyholders who denounced it as the "Second Missouri Compromise."

The catastrophic blunder T. J. made in entering into the Second Missouri Compromise was that too many individuals were privy to the role he played. But T. J. thought he was safe because he had not signed any papers, and he insisted all payments be made to him in cash. But if any of the parties involved talked, T. J. would be in peril. As matters turned out regarding the bribe, the fire insurance combine paid T. J. only $450,000 of the $750,000, and of his take he gave $135,000 to O'Malley and McCormack to split. Of the $315,000 he retained, the entire amount soon vanished in bets on horses. In a short time, he had none of it left, while rumors were beginning to spread in Missouri about an alleged half-million-dollar payoff to T. J. in the one-sided insurance settlement.

T. J. was sixty-three in 1935, and though he continued with his long daily schedule of politics, business, and betting without letup, friends saw that he suddenly looked sick. It was not the insurance payoff that was on his conscience and affecting his health, for his stomach and chest pains stemmed from real physical ailments. Nevertheless, he would not lighten his routine in the slightest. The crowds in the anteroom guarded by Cap'n Matheus were as large as ever, and one of those waiting to see Pendergast early in 1935 was Lloyd Crow Stark, who wanted his backing for governor in 1936. Three years earlier T. J. had rejected him outright for this same post.

T. J. prided himself on an unerring instinct on human character, and he felt there was something repulsive about the young man so eager for his favors. Stark came from a highly regarded Missouri family, possessed an excellent military record as an Annapolis graduate and World War I army artillery captain, and he made a good physical impression with his straight back, tall, muscled body, and strong jaw. As for his family, the Starks owned the Stark Brothers Nurseries and Orchards Co., the largest in the world, and "Stark's Delicious" was a heavily advertised apple. Yet T. J. saw him as a man with cold, unfriendly eyes and a calculating expression. Friends said that T. J.'s disbelief in Stark's sincerity was best expressed by his opinion of a similar gentleman of whom he said, "When you walk in his front door, you walk into his backyard."

In reality, T. J. was looking for a docile candidate who would serve as his stooge just as Park was doing. Stark did not appear to be this sort despite loud professions of loyalty; and if the law didn't bar a governor from serving successive terms. T. J. would have chosen Park again. As for Stark, T. J. told him frankly he was not his man.

But Stark was too ambitious to quit. He went to Washington where he became friendly with Senators Harry Truman and Bennett Clark. Pendergast and his wife were scheduled to take the *Normandie* on her maiden voyage to Europe that summer of 1935, and Stark prevailed on Truman and Clark to take him to New York when they went to pay homage to T. J. at the Waldorf before sailing time.

Here in the suite cluttered with bookies and jockeys, the two Senators put in a plug for Stark, who also did some boosting for himself. Truman recalled afterward that T. J. said repeatedly, "He won't do, Harry. I don't like the sonofabitch. He's no good." Yet after the two Senators kept pushing Stark, T. J. reluctantly agreed, said Truman, "that if Stark would get some country support he would support him."

This incentive was all Stark needed. Truman had a list of names of important rural political powers in each of the state's 114 counties that he had used in his Senate race in 1934, and Stark quickly borrowed it. Every person on that list was soon showered with bushels of fruit and requests for letters of endorsement. In October, Stark paid a call on ailing T. J. after sending him a bushel basket of endorsements, and he held Tom to his word. With continued distrust, T. J. reluctantly consented to support him, and in making the announcement the boss told reporters: "Ten spoke for Stark when one spoke for all other Democratic candidates "

Before the Democratic National Convention and the Missouri primaries got under way in mid-1936, T. J. wanted to have a long holiday. So in the spring he and his wife went to Europe with return reservations aboard the *Queen Mary* on her maiden voyage to New York. While he was abroad, the first crack appeared in the cover-up of his insurance bribe when the Internal Revenue Bureau made a routine investigation into the income tax records of the late Ernest Hicks, who had been a partner in the Chicago law firm of Hicks and Felonie. R. J. Felonie had been the chief attorney for the fire insurance companies in the Missouri Compromise, and in going through his and Hicks' records, Internal Revenue agents found that the law firm had received $100,500 in checks from fourteen insurance companies. All the checks had gone from the firm to Charles Street, the spokesman for the fire insurance companies; and in checking Street's income tax records, the agents found he had not included the money in his income tax statements. Confronted with this information, Street said he had passed all the money on to "someone." Pushed further, Street said he would not divulge the name of that "someone" until "at least before the *Queen Mary* comes in." He also said that the person involved "was high in political circles in Missouri."

Treasury agents immediately checked the passenger list of the ship that was heading for New York at that moment with a June 2 docking date. Among the passengers in the elite section was the listing "Mr. and Mrs. Thomas J. Pendergast." However, Street could not be intimidated further; and to head off possible prosecution, he submitted an amended tax return for 1935 and included the $100,500, paying a tax of $47,093 plus $2,825.60 in interest. Afterward, the Treasury Department put the entire file on the insurance company checks into dead storage, and luckily for T. J. the first installment paid him in the insurance bribe was not brought into the open.

In the meantime, T. J. reached New York and made arrangements to commute daily between the Waldorf and Philadelphia's Convention Hall when the Democratic National Convention began on June 23, 1936. He went that first day and presided as head of the Missouri delegation in the happy atmosphere of a sure Roosevelt nomination and victory in November. But during the hot afternoon, he developed such pains in his abdomen that Senator Truman, who was a delegate-at-large, accompanied him back to New York and then called in doctors. The diagnosis was that he had suffered a coronary thrombosis, and he was ordered to take a complete rest for six months.

While T. J. lay in bed at the Waldorf, the convention nominated Roosevelt for a second term, and back home in Missouri the air was rent by speeches as the August primary approached. "I guess the people at home are saying I have stayed back here to dodge a fight," he told a visiting *Star* reporter who noted that T. J. had lost about 40 pounds. But sick as he was, T. J. worked out a detailed set of instructions to his lieutenants, and Tom, Jr., was entrusted with taking the plan back to Kansas City by airplane. One of T. J.'s orders was that there must be no violence as in 1934, and the boys complied. But they exceeded even his figures regarding the size of the vote in the Democratic primary. For instance, they arranged matters in the second ward so that Lloyd Stark received 19,202 votes to only 12 for William Hirth, his Democratic opponent!

A few days after the successful primary in which Stark and all his other candidates won, T. J. suffered such biting abdominal pains that he was hurried to a hospital. Here tests showed he had a malignant intestinal obstruction, and without delay surgeons operated. The cancer was successfully removed, but in doing so his rectum had to be closed. As a substitute, a tube was placed in his side, connecting with his intestine.

"If he had died there in New York," said ever-loyal Harry Truman, "he would be remembered as the greatest boss this country ever had." However, heart attacks and cancer could not stop T. J.; and within a month he was back at 1908 Main Street, seeing visitors, planning for the general election in November, and calling for Roy Offut.

T. J. was also working hard to quell the uproar that had developed over the vote frauds in the August primary by which Stark had won the nomination. Ungrateful Joe Shannon, certain that T. J. would never leave New York alive, had come from his congressional office back to Missouri during the primary campaign to support Lawrence McDaniel, a well-known St. Louis lawyer, for the State Supreme Court against T. J.'s man, Ernest S. Gantt. When Gantt won the primary, Shannon immediately set off a charge that the election had been "a disgrace to American civilization." In his recital of particulars, Shannon pointed out that while the total population of Kansas City's second ward was 18,478, the Goats had given Gantt 19,201 votes.

Rather than let Joe Shannon's blast at T. J. die, the *Star* assigned several top reporters to investigate registration irregularities, and shortly before the November general election gave prominent play to their findings. The *Star*'s activity also led Maurice Milligan, brother of Jacob Milligan, a Truman opponent in the 1934 Senate primary, to examine the 1936 election.

Maurice Milligan had been appointed by President Roosevelt in February, 1934, as U.S. attorney for the western district of Missouri to combat the crime in Kansas City, and this was his first close look into the Pendergast organization. So fruitful was his preliminary scratching that on December 14, 1936, Federal Judge Albert L. Reeves, instructing a grand jury to delve deeply into registration and voting frauds, told its members: "Gentlemen, reach for all, even if you find them in high authority. Move on them!"

T. J.'s reaction to Reeves was to tell the press: "I have' been investigated for forty years. If Reeves and Milligan can find anything wrong, I'll not squawk." In Washington, Harry Truman had this to say of this challenge to the boss: "The registration was crooked, and this was what made Stark governor. I don't believe Tom Pendergast knew anything about it or that he was involved in that sort of thing. It was due to overzealousness of his workers."

The grand jury also took this view, and only those far down in the Goat hierarchy were indicted and put on trial, with charges no different from those that could have been assessed in 1934 or earlier: Repeaters had been registered as many as thirty times; precinct captains had nailed long lists of "ghost" voters to walls of empty buildings to help them keep their records straight. At one polling place, a Goat official had been overheard complaining, "I'm all in. Some of those damned Republicans marked their ballots so hard it was all I could do to rub them out."

The trials of the indicted 278 Goat defendants took almost two years. At one point, Judge Reeves, angry because T. J. and his top lieutenants had escaped the dragnet, taunted them to accept the blame for the misdeeds and "rid literally hundreds of poor people of being humiliated and punished for doing their bidding." But T. J. would not accept responsibility, and 259 persons were convicted. The reaction of some Pendergast Goats was to call Judge Reeves in the middle of the night and threaten him and his family. Telephone callers to Milligan warned him "to keep off the highways after sundown."

When Milligan's term as U.S. Attorney expired in the midst of the court cases, Roosevelt swiftly reappointed him. This led Senator Truman to voice bitter denunciation of Milligan in T. J.'s behalf on

the Senate floor. Judge Reeves called it the "Speech of a man nominated by ghost votes, elected with ghost votes and whose speech
was probably written by ghostwriters."

T. J.'s gnawing suspicions about Lloyd Stark were realized
soon after Stark took over as Missouri's governor. There were reports of the stylish governor's acceptance by the aristocratic President and his frequent invitations to White House affairs, and
there was evidence that Roosevelt was transferring some of T. J.'s
patronage to Stark. Jim Farley pointed out, for example, that when
Senator Truman recommended a man for U.S. Marshal in Missouri,
Roosevelt told him to clear it first with Stark. Farley tried to clarify
things by explaining to the President that Federal appointments
were controlled by members of Congress and not by governors. But
Roosevelt insisted on having his way, and Truman had to oblige
him. Within the state, Stark ignored the fact that T. J. had made
him governor and chose people for state jobs without consulting
the Kansas City boss.

Doctors were warning T. J. about possible complications from
the tube in his side and further trouble with his heart if he failed to
keep his emotions in check. But Tom's frustrations over his meager relations with Stark were raising his blood pressure, and in July, 1937,
he decided on a showdown by asking Stark to meet him in Colorado
Springs on the governor's way back from an Alaskan vacation.

At this get-together, T. J. asked him bluntly to appoint a
"friendly" election board, retain O'Malley as insurance superintendent, and increase the Goats' patronage. Stark was just as blunt in
saying he would name anyone he pleased to the election board and
would keep O'Malley on trial for one year before deciding his fate.
But Stark agreed to permit T. J. to name the state liquor control
supervisor.

However, Stark fired O'Malley in October and the liquor supervisor shortly after that, and he named three anti-Goat men to the
four-man election board, with instructions to purge the Kansas City
registration rolls of all ghost voters before the March, 1938, municipal election. These actions were a clear declaration of war to T. J.
The governor was an "ingrate," he declared. "I still say that
O'Malley is the best superintendent of insurance Missouri ever had,
if not the best in the country."

By the time the municipal elections neared in March, 1938,

Lloyd Stark was gloating. The legislature had approved his permanent registration law, and his election board had struck out more than 60,000 ghosts from the Jackson County registration lists. The collapse of T. J.'s machine appeared imminent.

But there were many in Kansas City who were indebted to the machine for favors received; and others felt resentment with this major effort to topple the boss by a governor who had used the machine to win election. In addition, clever pro-labor actions by T. J. and McElroy in mediating disputes in the building trades and their siding with CIO efforts to organize the city's Ford plant, after T. J.'s many years of anti-labor activities, pushed another large segment of the voters their way.

Astonishment rocked the state when T. J.'s Mayor Bryce Smith won by 40,000 votes and seven of the eight city council members were T. J.'s boys. "If it is true, as the Kansas City *Star* and the Coalition speakers reported," T. J. gloated in the flush of his greatest victory, "that the Democratic President of the United States was against us, that the governor of the state of Missouri was against us, that the independent Kansas City *Star* newspaper was against us—I think under those circumstances we made a wonderful showing. . . . The Democratic organization which I represent will do its utmost for the best interests of Kansas City now, and for all time in the future." As for the punitive action taken by Stark against him, T. J. noted, "Let me say that Stark will have to live with his conscience, the same as the rest of us. If his conscience is clear—I know mine is. I now say: Let the river take its course."

Early in 1938, a Missouri employee of the Internal Revenue Bureau, who had recorded the details of the 1936 investigation of the $100,500 in checks from insurance companies to the Hicks-Felonie law firm, their transfer to Charles Street, and the cryptic Street remark about the *Queen Mary* passenger, quit his government job. Afterward, he phoned the Washington correspondent of the Kansas City *Star* and spilled the beans to him about the material in the dead file at Internal Revenue. Then, because he had no way to confirm this obvious Pulitzer Prize winning story, the reporter related it to Governor Stark.

Stark took an early train to Washington where he called on Roosevelt and told him what he had heard. The President in turn phoned Treasury Secretary Morgenthau, said he was sending Stark to see him and that the Treasury was to conduct a full investigation of the subject the governor would relate. Stark then phoned U.S. Attorney Maurice Milligan back in Missouri to join him in the Treasury meeting, and the prosecution of T. J. was on.

Investigators received bad news at the outset when they learned Street had died a few months earlier, in February, 1938. But Street's financial records were available, including a special account in which he had deposited $330,000 in checks from fire insurance companies, in addition to the $100,500 he had deposited, exchanged for cash, and paid to someone in 1935. Even so, Treasury agents would have been unable to go further had it not been for two notations of payments totaling $30,000 to a Mr. A. L. McCormack, a St. Louis insurance executive.

Milligan now moved onto the scene, demanding that McCormack tell what he knew of all the checks and where the money had gone. When McCormack held to a story of innocence and ignorance, Milligan called a Federal grand jury in March, 1939, under dour Judge Reeves who had heard the 1936 Kansas City primary election fraud trials. For three days, McCormack spun his repetitive lie to the grand jury; but after Milligan threatened the heads of the nation's largest insurance companies with prosecution unless they convinced McCormack to be truthful, McCormack agreed to tell what had really happened. And the story of the insurance bribe and deal involving T. J., O'Malley, Street, and himself poured out.

Through his numerous spies, T. J. soon became aware of the grand jury and the prying investigation of his resources by Treasury agents. One of his friends said he had originally realized something bad was happening because he had started to have remarkably good fortune with his horse bets. With concern, Tom dispatched Police Director Otto Higgins to Washington to ask Roosevelt personally to end the massing effort against him and Emmett O'Malley. Higgins stayed a week, but he failed to get an appointment. In guarded optimism, Mrs. O'Malley wrote her son in Washington, "Truman will fly back Thursday and try to use some influence." Then four days later she wrote, "Jimmy [Pendergast] is flying to see our big friend (?) in Washington tonight."

While T. J. desperately tried to use his puny influence in Washington, a battle was also developing between the Justice and Treasury Departments. Justice wanted to indict T. J. immediately for the insurance bribe while Treasury wanted a thirty- to sixty-day delay until it completed its twelve-year investigation of T. J.'s other financial deals that it knew would lead to a far more severe prison sentence.

From its preliminary findings, the Treasury agents were amazed at the complexity of T. J.'s personal bookkeeping system. The work of a genius, they concluded. He hid his ownership of several companies by registering his stock under the names of employees and filled out their tax returns to include the dividends, though he took all the money. Cap'n Elijah Matheus, impresario of his waiting room, was listed as owner of a large bundle of Ready-Mixed Concrete stock with annual dividends of $30,000. Confronted with the fact that he had no savings and owed a bank $400, the old captain lied, "Well, I was just nigger-rich and threw my money away." But fearful he might be prosecuted, he finally admitted he was merely a front for T. J.

To avoid income taxes, T. J. also listed the names of fictitious persons as employees and pocketed their salaries. Frequently, his companies' records showed officials borrowing large sums of money, when in reality what they did was to issue checks to themselves, convert them to cash, and hand the money over to T. J. He also took bribes and other payments in cash, and when he needed money on his travels, he had money orders sent to him under pseudonyms.

In the end, the Justice Department, eager for a quick kill, prevailed over the Treasury. On April 4, 1939, beetle-browed, red-headed Attorney General Frank Murphy and FBI Director J. Edgar Hoover were in Kansas City for talks with Milligan, and the decision was made. On April 7, the grand jury indicted T. J. and O'Malley. The charge was restricted to income tax evasion on the insurance bribe.

That same day T. J. reported to the U.S. Marshal's office to be arraigned, even though it was Good Friday. Paul Fisher, a *Star* reporter, noted that T. J. put on a dignified, unruffled show until it came time to be fingerprinted. When one of his battery of lawyers took hold of his overcoat to help him out of it, he growled, "I'll take it off. There's nothing the matter with me. They prosecuted Christ on Good Friday, and nailed him to the Cross."

When the deputy marshal asked if he minded having news photographers take pictures as he was fingerprinted, T. J. barked in anger, "Hell, they have a million."

He was also required to answer personal questions. "You are 5 feet 9, aren't you?"

He feigned a chuckle. "I was. I've grown shorter. They say, you know, that age shortens a man.

"Your hair is gray."

"What's left is gray."

He had to put up a $10,000 bond, and when he left the marshal's office, he seemed unperturbed by his indictment. But a friend said he appeared to be in a state of shock after he was away from newsmen.

Senator Truman was on his way back to Washington from Kansas City that day when a reporter told him about T. J.'s indictment. "Pendergast has been my friend when I needed it," he commented loyally. "I am not one to desert a ship when it starts to go down."

It was not until May 1 that T. J. and O'Malley stood before Federal Judge Merrill Otis and pleaded not guilty. T. J. had been indicted a second time for income tax evasion, and there were rumors he would be indicted further. He saw only additional trouble if he maintained his innocence; so on May 22 he returned to Otis' courtroom and pleaded guilty to the two indictments.

In an unusual move, Otis asked him why he had thrown away his life. "I don't know what it is," T. J. tried to explain his horse-betting fever, "but it has been with me all my life."

Prosecutor Milligan described T. J. as "a broken old man," yet Judge Otis said he felt the power of the boss' presence. Tears rolled down Pendergast's cheeks as he heard the judge describe him as "a very human man, kind to his family, generous with his friends." Otis had other unjudgely remarks about the guilty party before him. "I can understand the feeling that has been expressed for him here by his friends," he said. "I believe if I had known him, I, too, might have been one of his friends. I think he is a man of the character that makes friends."

Judge Otis sentenced him to fifteen months in Leavenworth, fined him $10,000, and agreed to a payment of $434,000 by T. J. to settle his back income taxes, a figure Treasury officials said later should have been at least a half million dollars more. O'Malley got a year and a day and a fine of $5,000. The U.S. Marshal replied when asked if O'Malley would go to the same prison as Pendergast, "They went down together. Maybe they'll go up together." The St. Louis *Post-Dispatch* in commenting on T. J.'s sentence complained that he "merited a far heavier sentence."

The fall of T. J. was a signal for action against many of his associates. A few days after T. J. was first indicted, Henry McElroy resigned as city manager and went home to his old square house. "I'm as cool as a cucumber, but I'm saying nothing, not a thing," he told reporters who visited him. Yet they saw he was pale as a result of a heart attack and was confined to a wheelchair with his daughter Mary serving as his nurse.

Shortly after he quit city hall, audits by Federal and city accountants got under way, and the findings regarding his country bookkeeping were revealing. In a decade, he had extracted over $10 million in kickbacks from city employees, handed out much of the contracts under the $32 million Ten-Year Plan without going through competitive bidding, diverted an $11 million fund to repay water bonds to purposes of his own choosing, gave Pryor and Boyle $2 million for machinery rentals and $356,000 to look for water leaks, handed over garbage collection contracts to a disguised Pendergast firm, and kept 3,000 nonworking ward-heeler Goats on the city payroll. An educated "guesstimate" was that the city was on the edge of bankruptcy with a $19 million shortage in accounts and claims.

First legal action against McElroy was an order that he appear before a Federal grand jury on tax evasion charges. But on September 15, 1939, while the jury was assembling, word came that he had suffered a fatal heart attack. Not long afterward, his daughter Mary killed herself.

The tightening net around T. J.'s other associates caught contractor John Pryor who got two years for tax evasion, as did Matthew Murray, the Missouri head of WPA and Kansas City director of public works. Police Director Otto Higgins, who failed to report protection money he collected from vice operators, also got two years, and his conviction helped Governor Stark win approval of a bill to return control over Kansas City's police to the governor. Big Charley Carollo was hit with an eight-year term for tax evasion, and Charles Gargotta of the old Lazia gang was a three-year Federal guest.

Tom Pendergast's son Tom, Jr., and nephew Jim drove him to Leavenworth, Kansas, on May 29, 1939, and once inside the big gate he was renamed No. 55,259. He seemed stoical about his fate until he was shown a picture of himself in prison garb. His reaction was to suffer an almost fatal heart attack. But he recovered and was assigned to take down medical histories of the convicts.

T. J.'s fellow inmates expressed anger over his sentence when he first arrived at Leavenworth. "The bigger the crook, the lighter the punishment," went their refrain. But he was treated with general awe after acquaintanceship because of his strong personality, and there was sympathy because of his heart attack and the tube in his side. A newspaper story printed on January 6, 1940, gave outsiders a picture of T. J. in the big house. It read in part, "The first inmate to arise each morning is T. J. Pendergast. He is dressed, washed and standing in his doorway before 5 o'clock. At that hour sounds the clump of the newspaper distributor's stride down the corridor. When the paper drops in front of the former boss' tiny room, he reaches out, takes it up and returns to his bed. At 6:00 there comes the clang of the morning bell. Throughout the prison, the voices of 3,000 men hum. In a few moments the cell doors clang open, the men march down the hallways and into the dining room. He remains in his room, his breakfast going to him on a tray." Regarding his work, "When the physician is examining an inmate, he dictates his findings to Pendergast. The boss sets them down in his firm, clear, rather rotund handwriting. That afternoon or night he transfers them to the case ledger." A rumor throughout the prison was "that Pendergast amused himself by betting fabulously imaginary sums on the horses. . . . But he refuses even to discuss the outcome of a race."

For his good behavior, T. J.'s fifteen-month sentence was cut to a year and a day, and he was released from prison on May 30, 1940. But he had little joy, for his private and political life was a shambles. His wife had left him while he was in Leavenworth, and he had the lonely three-story Ward Parkway mansion to rattle around in by himself. As for other aspects of his life, part of his original sentence was a prohibition from engaging in gambling and politics for five years. One specific provision barred him from going to 1908 Main Street.

When his troubles began, T. J. had designated his nephew, Jim Pendergast, as his five-year successor, but trained as he was, Jim could not stave off the evil times that descended on the Goats. In the April, 1940, city elections, the nonpartisan Citizens Reform Organization (CR) ticket of businessmen and women's clubs easily wrested control from the Pendergast machine, electing John P. Gage, a cattleman, as mayor and seven CR men to the eight-seat city council. Like a haunting ghost from the past, hoary Jim Reed played an aggressive role for the nonpartisan CR ticket, denouncing T. J. and machine politics with all the fury of an ingrate. There was widespread enthusiasm for the Gage regime in Kansas City except from union and Negro quarters, for the new police chief acted as though police brutality was the soundest method for dealing with disgruntled labor and blacks.

In the midst of the Goat shambles, Harry Truman had to run for re-election in 1940. Roosevelt wanted Stark to replace him and offered Truman a seat on the eleven-member Interstate Commerce Commission. But Truman angrily rejected the Roosevelt plan to get him out of the way.

When Stark announced himself a candidate for the Senate in the Democratic primary scheduled in August, 1940, Truman wrote him "a blistering letter and called him everything in the goddam book," said Vic Messall, his secretary, to this author. Yet it was only with reluctance that Truman paid his filing fee for the contest, for he knew he was going to be called a member of the "Pendergast thieves." Furthermore, newspapers gave him no chance against Stark, who possessed the state's patronage machine, ample campaign funds, and, of course, presidential backing. But Truman had learned from T. J. that a divided opposition was a candidate's good fortune, and he grew more optimistic when U.S. Attorney Maurice Milligan also filed because the prosecutor could only cut into the Stark total.

T. J. spent the primary campaign period riding between his house and the Ready-Mixed Concrete office, grumbling most of the time that he could not put his forty years of political experience behind underdog Harry Truman. He managed a few surreptitious talks with his nephew Jim about the campaign, Tom Evans, Goat drugstore tycoon, told me, "but he couldn't do more because the probation officer might get wind of it."

Jim Pendergast put the state's hardcore 100,000 Goat votes behind Truman, and a labor union daily flooded the 114 counties with its endorsement of the bespectacled Senator. But from the small crowds he drew and the relentless newspaper attacks on him as "Tom Pendergast's stooge," he seemed to be an even more convincing loser as the campaign wound up.

However, when the votes were counted on August 6, a shock spread throughout Missouri; and T. J. had his first good laugh in a long time. Truman, the sure loser, had won by 8,000 votes over second-place Stark. The margin of his startling victory had been provided by Robert B. Hannegan, a thirty-seven-year-old St. Louis sub-boss, who had been pledged to Stark but threw his key votes to Truman in a last-minute switch. Hannegan's move gave Truman an 8,411-vote lead over Stark in St. Louis—and the election.

T. J. also took a great deal of satisfaction from the extraordinary events of 1944 when Bob Hannegan, who had been brought to Washington by Truman and rewarded with patronage plums, became chairman of the Democratic National Committee. In 1943, T. J. had petitioned FDR for a release from Judge Otis' five-year prohibition against his resumption of political activity, but Roosevelt had refused to grant him the necessary pardon. Nevertheless, there were many who believed T. J. violated his parole in 1944 by playing a behind-the-scenes role with National Committee Chairman Hannegan, Chicago's mayor and boss Ed Kelly, and Jersey City's Mayor Frank Hague to boost Truman into the nomination for Vice President in Roosevelt's fourth-term bid.

Truman corroborated this in a speech back home in Missouri that summer: "I'm a Jackson County Democrat, and I'm proud of it," he said. "That's the way I got to be a county judge, a Senator, and a candidate for Vice President."

Once the five-year prohibition would end in May, 1945, Tom Pendergast was looking forward to becoming an open boss again. The Goats were beginning to stir, even though Gage was re-elected to a third term as mayor in 1944. In the county, T. J.'s machine gained several offices in the election, and Tom's choice won the Democratic nomination for governor. However, in an interview in October, 1944, T. J. was careful to avoid any show of political eagerness. "It's too late to get back into politics, to start the day's work at 5 or 6 o'clock in the morning, to see my friends from morning until night. No, I am too old for that.

"All I want to do is go ahead with my business here, to provide for my family and to take care of any poor friends as I did in the past. I've had a good life. I got into trouble, but I am not blaming anybody but myself.

"I've done a lot for Kansas City—for the poor of Kansas City. I've done more for them than all the big shots and bankers, all of them put together.

"And I've never broken my word. Put this down: I've never broken my word to any living human being I gave it to. That is the key to success in politics or anything else."

T. J. did not go to Harry Truman's inauguration as Vice President on January 20, 1945, because he would have violated his parole. Then only six days later, just before he was going to bed on January 26, he had another heart attack and died. The Vice President came in an army bomber to attend the funeral. "I'm as sorry as I can be," said Truman. "He was always my friend, and I have always been his."

So the ex-boss died. Had he lived a mere three months longer, he would have seen one of his lowly Goats become President of the United States.

Acknowledgments and Bibliography

I wish to express my indebtedness for his cooperative labors to James Neyland, editor with The Macmillan Company. I also owe a special debt to the Library of Congress in Washington, D.C.

Because a complete listing of the materials I examined would be useful chiefly to a small group of academicians, I have restricted the bibliography below to a selected list. For the record, I have gone through dozens of newspapers for the decades covered, harvested the period's magazines, gleaned legislative investigations and legal suits, and talked to some individuals with first-hand involvement in the affairs described in this book on American bosses.

Some of my sources were:

GENERAL

Adams, S. H., *Incredible Era: The Life and Times of Warren Gamalie Harding*, Boston, 1939

Allen, Robert S., ed., *Our Fair City*, New York, 1947

———, *Our Sovereign State*, New York, 1949

American Guide Series, Writers' Program, Works Progress Administration (WPA)

Baker, Ray Stannard, *Woodrow Wilson, Life and Letters*, 8 vols., New York, 1927–1939

Cox, James M., *Journey Through My Years*, New York, 1946

Farley, James A., *Behind the Ballots*, New York, 1938

Flynn, Edward J., *You're the Boss*, New York, 1947

Frost, Stanley, *The Challenge of the Klan*, Indianapolis, 1924
Gunther, John, *Inside USA*, New York, 1947
Handlin, Oscar, *Al Smith and His America*, Boston, 1958
Hofstadter, Richard, *The Age of Reform*, New York, 1953
Hoover, Herbert, *The Memoirs of Herbert Hoover: The Cabinet and the Presidency, 1920–1932*, New York, 1952
Irey, Elmer L., and William J. Slocum, *The Tax Dodgers*, New York, 1948
Key, V. O., *Southern Politics in State and Nation*, New York, 1949
Link, Arthur S., *Woodrow Wilson and the Progressive Era*, New York, 1954
Lippmann, Walter, *Public Opinion*, New York, 1922
Luthin, Reinhard H., *American Demagogues*, Boston, 1954
Michie, Allan A., and Frank Ryhlick, *Dixie Demagogues*, New York, 1939
Orth, Samuel P., *The Boss and the Machine*, New Haven, 1919
Peterson, Lorin, *The Day of the Mugwump*, New York, 1961
Pringle, Henry F., *Alfred E. Smith*, New York, 1927
Salter, J. T., *Boss Rule*, New York, 1935
——, *The American Politicians*, Chapel Hill, 1938
Schlesinger, Arthur M., Jr., *The Age of Roosevelt; Crisis of the Old Order, 1919–1933*, New York, 1957
Steffens, Lincoln, *The Shame of the Cities*, New York, 1904
Swing, Raymond Gram, *Forerunners of American Fascism*, New York, 1935
Van Devander, Charles, *The Big Bosses*, New York, 1944
Wallis, James H., *The Politicians*, New York, 1935
Zink, Harold, *City Bosses in the U.S.*, Durham, N.C., 1930

ONE. FRANK HAGUE: *I Am the Law*

Bloodgood, Fred L., *The Quiet Hour*, Trenton, 1940
Blum, John M., *Joe Tumulty and the Wilson Era*, Boston, 1950
Case Committee Report, *New Jersey Senate Journal*, 1929
Cunningham, John T., *America's Main Road*, New York, 1966
Edge, Walter E., *A Jerseyman's Journal*, Princeton, 1947
Hague v. Committee for Industrial Organization (CIO), Transcript of Testimony, U.S. Federal District Court, 1938
Kerney, James, *The Political Education of Woodrow Wilson*, New York, 1926
Link, Arthur, *Woodrow Wilson: Road to the White House*, Princeton, 1947
McKean, Dayton D., *Pressures on the Legislature of New Jersey*, New York, 1938
—— *The Boss: The Hague Machine in Action*, Boston, 1940

Noble, Ransom E., Jr., *New Jersey Progressivism before Wilson*, Princeton, 1946

Rapport, George C., *The Statesman and the Boss*, New York, 1961

Report of the Committee on Civil Rights of the Junior Bar Conference of the American Bar Association, 1938

Sackett, William E., *Modern Party Battles of Trenton*, 2 vols., New York, 1931

Salter, J. T., ed., *Public Men In and Out of Office*, Chapel Hill, 1946

Tumulty, Joseph P., *Woodrow Wilson As I Knew Him*, New York, 1921

TWO. ED CRUMP: *Plan Your Work and Work Your Plan*

Allan, Leslie H., *Bryan and Darrow at Dayton*, New York, 1967

Anderson, Jack, and Frederick Blumenthal, *The Kefauver Story*, New York, 1956

Capers, Gerald, *The Biography of a River Town; Memphis, Its Heroic Age*, Chapel Hill, 1935

Cash, Wilbur J., *The Mind of the South*, New York, 1941

Folmsbee, S. J., *Tennessee, A Short History*, Knoxville, 1969

Goodman, William, *Inherited Domain*, Knoxville, 1954

Hutchens, Fred, *What Happened in Memphis*, Kingsport, Tenn., 1965

Lee, George W., *Beale Street: Where the Blues Began*, New York, 1934

Mason, Lucy R., *To Win These Rights*, New York, 1952

McFerrin, John B., *Caldwell and Company*, Chapel Hill, 1939

Miller, William D., *Memphis During the Progressive Era*, Memphis, 1957

——, *Mr. Crump of Memphis*, Baton Rouge, 1964

Perry, Jennings, *Democracy Begins at Home: The Tennessee Fight on the Poll Tax*, New York, 1944

Shields, McIlwaine, *Memphis Down in Dixie*, New York, 1948

Tennessee Senators, Kingsport, Tenn., 1942

Young, J. P., *Standard History of Memphis, Tennessee*, Knoxville, 1912

THREE. JAMES MICHAEL CURLEY: *The Joyous Plague of Boston*

Amory, Cleveland, *The Proper Bostonians*, New York, 1947

Blodgett, Geoffrey, *The Gentle Reformers*, Cambridge, Mass., 1966

Coolidge, Calvin, *Have Faith in Massachusetts*, Boston, 1919

——, *Autobiography*, New York, 1929

Curley, James M., *I'd Do It Again: A Record of All My Uproarious Years*, Englewood Cliffs, N.J., 1957

Cutler, John H., *Honey Fitz: Three Steps to the White House*, Indianapolis, 1962

370 ACKNOWLEDGMENTS AND BIBLIOGRAPHY

Dinneen, Joseph F., *Ward Eight*, New York, 1936
——, *The Purple Shamrock: James Michael Curley*, New York, 1949
Donnelly, Edward L., ed., *That Man Curley*, Boston, 1947
Ely, Joseph, *The American Dream*, Boston, 1944
Garraty, John A., *Henry Cabot Lodge*, New York, 1953
Hennessy, M. E., *Four Decades of Massachusetts Politics, 1890–1935*, Norwood, Mass., 1935
Hill, Edwin C., *The American Scene*, New York, 1933
Herlihy, Elisabeth M., ed., *Fifty Years of Boston*, Boston, 1932
Huthmacher, J. J., *Massachusetts People and Politics, 1919–1933*, Cambridge, Mass., 1919
Wayman, Dorothy G., *David I. Walsh: Citizen Patriot*, Milwaukee, 1952
——, *Cardinal O'Connell of Boston*, New York, 1954
White, William Allen, *A Puritan in Babylon*, New York, 1938

FOUR. HUEY LONG: *A Storm for My Bride*

Beals, Carleton, *The Story of Huey P. Long*, Philadelphia, 1935
Davis, Edwin, *The Pelican State*, Baton Rouge, 1959
Davis, Forrest, *Huey Long*, New York, 1935
Harriss, Thomas O., *The Kingfish*, New Orleans, 1938
Kane, Harnett T., *Louisiana Hayride*, New York, 1941
Long, Huey P., *Every Man A King*, New Orleans, 1933
Sindler, Allan P., *Huey Long's Louisiana*, Baltimore, 1956
Smith, Webster, *The Kingfish*, New York, 1933
Williams, T., *Huey Long*, New York, 1969

FIVE. GENE TALMADGE: *Wild Man in Red Galluses*

Arnall, Ellis G., *The Shore Dimly Seen*, Philadelphia, 1946
Brooks, Robert P., *The Agrarian Revolution in Georgia, 1865–1912*, New York, 1912
Cooper, Walter G., *The Story of Georgia*, New York, 1938
Coulter, E., *Georgia, A Short History*, Chapel Hill, 1947
Gosnell, Cutler B., *Government and Politics in Georgia*, New York, 1936
Henson, Allen Lumpkin, *Red Galluses, A Story of Georgia Politics*, Boston, 1945
Saye, A. B., *Constitutional History of Georgia*, Athens, Ga., 1948
Steed, Hal, *Georgia: Unfinished State*, New York, 1942
Woodward, C. Vann, *Tom Watson, Agrarian Rebel*, New York, 1938

SIX. TOM PENDERGAST: *Missouri's Compromiser*

Beach, Marjorie, *The Mayor's Wife*, New York, 1953

Brown, A. T., *The Politics of Reform*, Kansas City, Mo., 1958

Daniels, Jonathan, *The Man of Independence*, Philadelphia, 1950

Dorsett, L. W., *The Pendergast Machine*, New York, 1968

Garwood, Darrell, *Crossroads of America*, New York, 1948

Haskell, Henry C., and Richard B. Fowler, *City of the Future*, Kansas
    City, Mo., 1950

Lowe, Frank, Jr., *A Warrior Lawyer*, New York, 1942

Mayerberg, Samuel, *Chronicle of an American Crusader*, New York, 1944

Meriwether, Lee, *Jim Reed*, Webster Grove, Mo., 1948

Miller, W. H., *The History of Kansas City*, 1880

Milligan, Maurice, *Missouri Waltz*, New York, 1948

Missouri Crime Survey, New York, 1926

Political History of Jackson County, Kansas City, Mo., 1902

Political History of Kansas City, 1902

Powell, Gene, *Tom's Boy Harry*, Jefferson City, Mo., 1948

Reddig, William M., *Tom's Town*, Philadelphia, 1947

Steinberg, Alfred, *Man from Missouri: The Life and Times of Harry S.
    Truman*, New York, 1962

Index